Understanding and Treating Incels

Understanding and Treating Incels is an indispensable guide for mental health clinical staff, social workers, prevention specialists, educators, and threat assessment professionals who want to better understand the involuntary celibate movement, assess individuals' potential for violence, and offer treatment approaches and prevention efforts.

Chapters explore the movement in terms of gender, technology, the media, and pornography usage. The book discusses how the incel mentality has motivated individuals to misogynistic worldviews and increased rage and disillusionment, and inspired acts of targeted violence such as school shootings and mass casualty events. Later chapters walk the reader through three cases studies and offer treatment considerations to assist mental health professionals and those developing education and prevention-based programming. The complete text gives the reader useful perspectives and insights into incel culture while offering mental health clinicians and educators guidance on treatment and prevention efforts.

Brian Van Brunt serves as the president of the National Behavioral Intervention Team Association (NaBITA) and a partner at The NCHERM Group.

Chris Taylor serves as the dean of students at Wright State University.

"In *Understanding and Treating Incels*, Van Brunt and Taylor take on a timely, uncomfortable, under-researched, and dangerous form of misogyny. The text provides a methodical examination of the state of knowledge, case examples, and prospective interventions to address the dysfunction and trauma associated with incel ideologies, both by the men who have internalized limiting and cynical notions of manhood and the people at risk of being subjected to their harmful expressions. The text is comprehensive, accessible, and actionable for practitioners and scholars alike."

Jason A. Laker, professor, Department of Counselor
Education, San José State University, California

Understanding and Treating Incels

Case Studies, Guidance, and Treatment of Violence Risk in the Involuntary Celibate Community

Brian Van Brunt and Chris Taylor

NEW YORK AND LONDON

First published 2021
by Routledge
52 Vanderbilt Avenue, New York, NY 10017

and by Routledge
2 Park Square, Milton Park, Abingdon, Oxon OX14 4RN

Routledge is an imprint of the Taylor & Francis Group, an informa business

© 2021 Brian Van Brunt and Chris Taylor

The right of Brian Van Brunt and Chris Taylor to be identified as authors
of this work has been asserted by them in accordance with sections
77 and 78 of the Copyright, Designs and Patents Act 1988.

All rights reserved. No part of this book may be reprinted or reproduced or utilised
in any form or by any electronic, mechanical, or other means, now known or
hereafter invented, including photocopying and recording, or in any information
storage or retrieval system, without permission in writing from the publishers.

Trademark notice: Product or corporate names may be trademarks or registered trademarks,
and are used only for identification and explanation without intent to infringe.

Library of Congress Cataloging-in-Publication Data
Names: Van Brunt, Brian, author. | Taylor, Chris, 1967– author.
Title: Understanding and treating incels : case studies, guidance, and treatment of
violence risk in the involuntary celibate community / Brian Van Brunt, Chris Taylor.
Description: New York, NY: Routledge, 2021. |
Includes bibliographical references and index.
Identifiers: LCCN 2020026254 (print) | LCCN 2020026255 (ebook) |
ISBN 9780367417505 (hardback) | ISBN 9780367417482 (paperback) |
ISBN 9780367824396 (ebook)
Subjects: LCSH: Celibacy-History. |
Sexual abstinence. | Men–Psychology.
Classification: LCC HQ800.15 .V36 2021 (print) |
LCC HQ800.15 (ebook) | DDC 306.73/209–dc23
LC record available at https://lccn.loc.gov/2020026254
LC ebook record available at https://lccn.loc.gov/2020026255

ISBN: 978-0-367-41750-5 (hbk)
ISBN: 978-0-367-41748-2 (pbk)
ISBN: 978-0-367-82439-6 (ebk)

Typeset in Times
by Newgen Publishing UK

Brian

For Bethany,
You are my constant in all things. So very many things I could never have dreamed of doing without your support and kisses.

For Noah, Kat, and Emily
Thank you for allowing me to be distracted briefly from your awesomeness.

For Eli.
Butts for days.

Chris

For Elizabeth
Chris Cooper said it best, "You took on all the burden, thank you." You are the glue, the Queen, and the rock. I love you so.

For Sam and Will
Watching you grow into men is the delight of my life.

Contents

Preface   ix

PART 1
Introduction   1

1   To Be a Real Boy   3

2   The Rise of the Incel   10

PART 2
Etiology of the Incel   23

3   Masculine Identity Development and the Incel   25

4   The Incel Funnel and the Influence of Religion, Technology,
    and Pornography   33

PART 3
Incel Questionnaire and Rubric   45

5   Incel Indoctrination Rubric (IIR)   47

6   Incel Cases by Rubric Category   56

viii *Contents*

PART 4
Assessing the Risk   65

  7 Identifying the Risk Factors   67

  8 Identifying Stabilizing Influences   87

  9 Conducting a Violence Risk Assessment   99

PART 5
Three Case Studies in Assessment and Treatment   123

10 Incel Treatment Approaches   125

11 Assessment and Treatment Approaches: Junior High   140

12 Assessment and Treatment Approaches: College   150

13 Assessment and Treatment Approaches: Workplace   162

PART 6
Community and Systems Approach   173

14 Addressing the Incel through the BIT/CARE Model   175

   Appendices
   A: Case Review   193
   B: George Sodini Blog   219
   C: Elliot Rodger Video Transcript "Day of Retribution" 228
   D: Christopher Harper-Mercer Manifesto   230
   E: Dylann Roof Manifesto   235
   F: Joseph Ferguson Confession (Transcript of Video)   240
   G: A Partial Transcript: Alek Minassian's Police Interview 243
   H: Incel Terms and Definitions   262
   I: Incel Indoctrination Rubric (IIR)   265
   Index   274

Preface

This book addresses the challenge of assessing and responding to the growing involuntary celibate (incel) trend in recent decades. A central concern, beyond the misogynistic tone of their ideas, lies in the movement toward targeted violence. Incels who fully swallow the blackpill (a term used to describe the futility of fighting against pre-determined genetics that they feel make them inferior and unable to compete with other men) become increasingly depressed, isolated and angry. These hardened perspectives and perceived/actual slights lead to the collection of injustices and grievances that, in turn, lead to violence toward a society that has failed them and women that will remain out of arm's reach. For those looking for a summary of the incel language examples that are used throughout the book, Appendix H provides a summary document for the reader.

We provide a brief history of the movement, an overview of the language used by incels and an exploration of societal, religious, and technological factors that contribute to the rise of the incel. Based on 50 attacks included in Appendix A, we created a set of 20 core elements related to incel thinking, feeling, behaviors, and environment. These 20 factors were then operationalized into a scoreable rubric entitled the Incel Indoctrination Rubric (IIR) included in Appendix I. Several prominent cases are scored in the text to demonstrate how to apply the IIR.

After summarizing the risk factors and stabilizing influences related to targeted, mission-oriented violence (such as school shootings), we review several research-based approaches to violence risk and threat assessment. To further demonstrate the process, we developed three incel case studies set in junior high, college, and workplace settings to provide examples of how to use the IIR to better assess the depth of their incel beliefs and the risk of potential violence. Treatment and intervention options are provided for those in clinical and non-clinical settings who seek to help these individuals push against the incel indoctrination, reduce the risk of potential violence toward themselves, women and the larger society.

Of note, some of the language in this book was difficult for the authors to include. It may be equally difficult for the reader to experience. The language used by this population is often dismissive of personhood and agency, reductionistic in the worth of women, and offensive in its casual racism, bigotry and hate. It is this exploration, however, this willingness to learn from their perspective, that provides the key to understanding and redirecting this behavior toward one that is healthier for our society.

x *Preface*

There is a trend we support when writing about mass casualty attackers. The less attention we give them, the more we avoid the contagion effect. The common practice is to avoid the use of their names. For news reports and public media, we would continue to support these ideas and will continue to do this throughout the book. For some cases, particularly in Chapter 1, it will be useful to refer to the names of three attackers for clarity and research purposes. The same is true of Appendix A, and writings of attackers included in Appendix B–G.

Likewise, we faced a challenge by giving such a hateful movement a "cool" sounding name like incel. In the threat assessment literature, there is a trend away from describing killers as a "Lone Wolf" for similar reasons. The cowardly taking of other's lives for perceived or actual slight doesn't deserve a respectful name. There is also the concern for the contagion effect, where others are inspired by the lights and attention given to those who kill. Sadly, the incel name is widely accepted to describe the movement at this time, so it is the name we have adopted. Moving forward, it may prove helpful to something more accurate such as "angry, lonely boys."

Our hope is this book provides prevention educators, BIT/CARE teams, counselors, law enforcement, teachers, professors, human resources and clinical treatment providers some insight into this movement for the purposes of helping these young men pull away from this toxic and harmful ideology and better integrate into society as successful individuals.

Part 1

Introduction

1   To Be a Real Boy

It may be odd to see a book addressing this quite horrible ideology starting with reference to a Disney fairytale, although we feel this summarizes the problem quite well. The heart of the incel movement is a parallel to the sad marionette Pinocchio who desires, more than anything else, to become a real boy. The Blue Fairy calls to him: *Prove yourself brave, truthful, and unselfish, and someday, you will be a real boy.* It is this illusive desire to be like everyone around them, to be loved and seen as a real person with value and worth that drives the incel philosophy more than anything else.

The involuntarily celibate (incel) philosophy is one where males believe the genetic, biological factors that impact our bone structure, height, physical or mental abilities, weight, eye and skin color and physical appearance are pre-determined and are the main factor dictating what women find attractive in men. When these factors are missing or substandard in the incel, they become less desirable and with this rejection by women, along with their perceived and actual marginalization, they become isolated, lonely and increasingly frustrated and jealous at the life everyone else seems to have.

This concept is concerning for several reasons. First, the incel's attitude toward women reinforces negative stereotypes, harms development, and increases negative interactions. This leads to the further isolation and alienation of the incel from the larger society and they often find their only solace in the dark chat rooms of the internet. This loneliness can lead to an increase in depression and risk of suicide. In extreme cases, their frustration percolates and grows, narrowing into a focus on hurting the women who reject them and others who are successful and happy in relationships. Of note, the incel community ignores any discussion of gay, lesbian, bi, trans, or non-binary descriptions of gender identity and sexual orientation.

A summary of common names incels use to describe themselves and others is introduced here in Table 1.1 to assist the reader to become more familiar with the very unique and specific coded language used in the incel community.

Alienation and Depression

While this could be a bit of a chicken and the egg debate, the smart money is placed on the idea that men who are unable to talk to women, who have been teased, bullied or rebuffed by others, have directly led to the creation of this ideology. As such,

4 *Introduction*

Table 1.1 Common incel terms for individuals

Term	Meaning
Alpha male	A bold, confident leader; the opposite of a beta
AMOG	"Alpha male of group"
Becky	An average young woman, subordinate to a Stacy in looks and status
Beta male	A weak man; the opposite of an alpha
-Cel	This suffix can be used to define one's subset within the incel community based on physical features, interests, race, or defining traits (e.g., a gingercel is an incel who has red hair)
Chad	An ideal male specimen, Chads can attract nearly all women easily; ethnic counterparts are **Tyrone** (Black), **Chaddam** (Arab), **Chadpreet** (Indian), **Chang** (East Asian)
Cuck	Short for cuckold, this is a man with an unfaithful wife/girlfriend; also used for men who are considered weak or servile and often used as a derogatory term for men with moderate or progressive views
Femoid/foid	Demeaning term referring to women as less than human
Incel/inkwell	Involuntarily celibate man; common subsets include:
	Baldcel: Bald or balding
	Currycel: Indian
	Clowncel: Identifies with and admires the Joker from *Batman*
	Fakecel: Pretending to be incel to be edgy or to fit in
	Framecel: A man with the bone structure of a young teen
	Gymcel: Believes he can compensate with muscles
	Heightcel/shortcel: A short man who is an incel because of his height
	Mentalcel/ medcel: Has psychological illnesses or medical issues
	Workcel: Too preoccupied with work for a relationship
Noodlewhore	An Asian woman
Normie	An average boring person, someone who is average in looks, between a Chad and an incel
Soyboy	An effeminate, feminist or non-fighting man, with low athleticism; incels believe soy lowers testosterone
Stacy	The female counterpoint to a Chad; the ideal woman who is out of reach for any non-Chad man
Thot	A woman who has many casual sexual encounters

this comes from a place of sadness, pain, frustration, and loneliness and remains a particularly negative way of looking at human interactions, sexual or otherwise. This kind of pre-deterministic worldview limits concepts of diversity, individual choice, responsibility and reduces human value to a single dimension, namely sexual attraction.

When the males do not get the object of their desire, they see themselves as weak, less-than, and in a "beta" status to the other "alpha" males. Depending on how deep the individual is lost in the incel doctrine, this could be seen as a final, unalterable law of nature they cannot cross, also known as "blackpill." For the "redpill" incels, this creates a very steep hill to climb in terms of someone less genetically desirable finding an attractive sexual or romantic partner. They attempt to overcome their genetic shortcomings through acquiring wealth, working out to improve on areas of strength, endurance, and muscle development, or acquiring status, career, fame or achievements to better lure women into a sexual relationship despite their inherent lack of interest in a beta male.

Whether blackpill or redpill, both leave the incel with a growing sense of frustration, potential hopelessness, feelings of suicide, despair and a growing frustration that often leads to anger. This mixture of negative emotions, combined with the idea that they will never be enough and that they are genetically behind the eight-ball, often leads to further alienation, depression and the perception that they are frustrated, undesirable loners. As one can imagine, it's this cycle, feeding upon itself, that continues the incel's spiral. They are further ostracized, teased, bullied, and their desires for connection and sexual relationships slip further and further from their grasp.

An example of this can be found in the writing of the Isla Vista attacker in the manifesto he left. Upon coming to college, he describes his frustrations,

> [the college] became a place of loneliness and despair, just like any other place I've attempted to thrive in. The breaking point was when I saw good looking couples walking along the area where I dreamed of walking with a girlfriend. To watch another boy experience it, with a beautiful girl who should be mine, was a living hell. I constantly asked myself what I did wrong in life, to be unable to have a beautiful girlfriend.
>
> (Rodger, 2014, p. 68)

With his desires out of reach, the attacker further isolates and becomes frustrated at his life walking around with friends in Santa Barbra and Montecito, CA. He recalls,

> I felt inferior whenever I saw other guys walking with beautiful girls. At the movie theatres, I felt just as pathetic about walking in there with a group of friends as I did years ago when I went to the movies with my parents ... It was that pathetic feeling of not having a hot girlfriend on my arm while some other boys in the theatre did. What I truly wanted ... what I truly NEEDED, was a girlfriend. I needed a girl's love. I needed to feel worthy as a male. For so long I have felt worthless, and it's all girls' fault. No girl wanted to be my girlfriend.
>
> (Rodger, 2014, p. 95)

Attitude toward Women

At best, women are seen on a continuum of sexual attraction, reduced to objects only valued for their beauty. There is no mention of attributes such as intelligence, personality, health, success, or happiness. Further, the incel sees the young, tall, blonde, blue-eyed Caucasian woman as the ultimate desirable asset. Women with different skin colors, hair types or colors, weight, height, age or ethnicity are casually cast into the bargain bin of sexual desirability.

While this reduction of women is not a new phenomenon in the course of human existence, the expansion of the internet and discussion boards has given this concept more potential to spread and infest young minds than during previous decades. The Bechdel-Wallace test (Jusino, 2015) offers a feminist litmus test for literature, comics, film, plays and art content. The piece must include (1) at least two women,

6 *Introduction*

who (2) talk to each other, about (3) something other than a man. Clearly, any content created by the men opting into the incel philosophy would fail such a test.

At worst, attractive women, fueled by genetics and an acquiescing society, are seen as laughing as the Greek gods they choose kick sand in the face of the 98-pound weakling. The world that has created this unfair algebra prevents less physically attractive males from having a chance sexually with genetically superior women, who then become the target of their rage. Rising up from their feelings of isolation and hopelessness, some see violence as the most logical conclusion to send a message that this system is rigged, although in the vast majority of mass shootings, the suicidality of the attacker is the most central risk factor (Lankford, 2018; Van Brunt, 2012, 2015).

An example of this can be found in the journal from the 48-year-old attacker at the LA Fitness in Collier Township, PA (Sodini, 2009). He describes the women at the gym this way, "Many of the young girls here look so beautiful as to not be human, very edible" (Appendix B). Later in his online blog, he writes about a neighbor,

> I just looked out my front window and saw a beautiful college-age girl leave Bob Fox's house, across the street. I guess he got a good lay today. College girls are hoez. I masturbate. Frequently. He is about 45 years old. She was a long haired, hot little hottie with a beautiful bod. I masturbate. Frequently.
>
> (Appendix B)

This objectification and dehumanization of female targets will be a theme explored more fully in future chapters.

Sadly, there are numerous programs that cater to these lonely males in an attempt to help them find a sexual partner. One such program was created by R. Don Steele through its website https://steelballs.com. In a description of his 1995 book, *How to Date Young Women: For Men over 35, Volume I*, he shares advice on how older men can hope to land a partner in their early 20s. He offers workshops during which he hires young women (called Titanium Babes) to practice role-playing scenarios and insightful advice on what to order in a restaurant, creating lust with your eyes, and when and how to touch a woman.

While this could be initially dismissed as shady dating advice with a financial motive, it becomes more concerning when you watch George Sodini, the LA Fitness shooter, in the training and creating blogs and practice writings for the class (Associated Press, 2009).

In an excerpt from his online blog, Steele shares his insights on women (Steele, 2016).

- "Young women, even girls as young as 14, have the same undesirable, unpleasant qualities of adult women, they are catty and viciously competitive over males."
- "Forget the high schooler. Her head is up her ass and will be for two more years. Proms, football games, Friday dances, Jimmy's bitchin', totally rad, new Vee Dub convertible."
- "Forget the big titted girl. The competition is, pardon the pun, too stiff. Every male within 500 miles is interested. If you insist on trying, never mention her figure and don't even sneak a peek at those double D's."

- "When she meets a male in society's acceptable age range, she sees only a potential husband. She and her counterparts believe in the nuclear family and want to be the center of one someday. The difference is, in her family everyone will be happy. She thinks she can make it work, just as you and I did."

Obviously, Steele's advice does not pass the Bechdel-Wallace test. And while many may dismiss this as the pathetic, reductionist ramblings of the worst kind of chauvinistic pig, these observations are included because they likely further hardened the attacker's pre-existing feelings of self-loathing, anger, and difficulty acquiring his goals in life. As Sodini continued to fail to reach his ridiculously unrealistic standards of easily achieving a sexual relationship with a woman thirty years his junior, his frustration turned toward hopelessness, anger, and revenge.

Escalation to Physical Violence

Left unchecked, this spiral of sadness, isolation, self-loathing, and inability to connect with women leads to attempts to reach out to other like-minded individuals, often on the internet. These sad and frustrated men often commiserate about the unfairness of their lives and the lack of any hope that things will improve. Advice is given on various methods to try to lure women into sexual encounters, but these examples often lead to more failure, rejection, and the belief that they will never reach their goals.

In some extreme cases, the individual begins to craft a plan, or exit strategy. This can be built upon a desire to finally be understood, to punish those who he blames for his unsuccessful life, or to simply make the pain of his existence stop. In Chapter 7, we will review several risk factors with examples from the cases included in Appendix A to highlight these risk factors that move the incel from sad, lonely, and frustrated to form a mission-oriented plan to go out in a blaze of glory; finally believing they will achieve the meaning and popularity that has alluded them for their entire lives.

We see these escalations often in the Isla Vista attacker's manifesto, written prior to his shooting. He writes,

As I made my way back from school one day during the first week, I was stopped at a stoplight in Isla Vista when I saw two hot blonde girls waiting at the bus stop. I was dressed in one of my nice shirts, so I looked at them and smiled. They looked at me, but they didn't even deign to smile back. They just looked away as if I was a fool. As I drove away I became very infuriated. It was such an insult. This was the way all girls treated me, and I was sick and tired of it. In a rage, I made a U-turn, pulled up to their bus stop and splashed my Starbucks latte all over them. I felt a feeling of spiteful satisfaction as I saw it stain their jeans. I then quickly speeded away before they could catch my license plate number. How dare those girls snub me in such a fashion! How dare they insult me so! I raged to myself repeatedly. They deserved the punishment I gave them. It was such a pity that my latte wasn't hot enough to burn them. Those girls deserved

8   *Introduction*

to be dumped in boiling water for the crime of not giving me the attention and adoration I so rightfully deserve!

(Rodger, 2014, p. 100)

These behaviors occur several times throughout Rodger's narrative when he encounters lesser men who have sexual access to the women that he feels he will never acquire. Despite having many opportunities in his young life as a part of a family of privilege and opportunity, he continually returns to his negative self-view: a short, sad, little wooden marionette who will never be made into a real boy by acquiring an attractive female to call his own.

Why Help Them?

Why should anyone care about helping these lost boys? A reasonable person may argue they have made their choice, like many poorly formed and highly insulting philosophical groups such as white supremacists, anti-Semites, bigots and homophobes. Why spend time understanding this community if the community itself is not only supremely distasteful and lacking civility or empathy, but can create a fertile ground for extremist violence? To this point, incel groups that once lived on the internet within 4chan and 8chan discussion boards have simply been blocked and terminated as discussion boards.

As the researchers who study viral disease search for and examine patient zero to develop a vaccine, this book serves in a similar capacity. In the exploration of the toxic masculinity and what makes certain incels escalate to extremist violence, we find opportunities to bridge the gap and pull these lost marionettes down from the hanging tree and instead help them to realize the actual path to becoming a real boy; the development of empathy, altruism, and caring for others.

Moving Forward

In the next chapter, we will explore more deeply the philosophy, culture, and language of the incel community. It is in the understanding of the incel where we find the ability to better assess and redirect this self-destructive belief system. We will examine the two examples mentioned in this chapter, the Isla Vista and LA Fitness attacks, to further explore incel thinking to better develop therapeutic and educational approaches to address their self-destructive and potentially dangerous belief system.

Discussion Questions

- What were some of your first impressions when you first heard the word incel? How have these changed as you began to read this book?
- In many ways, there is both a sadness and anger that accompanies the incel philosophy. How do you see these elements interact?
- There is a challenge at the end of the chapter to attempt to better understand how the incel sees the world in order to better move them away from that perspective to one that is more positive. How do you see this balance?

References

Associated Press. (2009). Sodini was devoted follower of dating guru. Retrieved on May 3 from www.nbcnews.com/id/32335641/ns/us_news-crime_and_courts/t/sodini-was-devoted-follower-dating-guru/#.Xq39Ai2ZPOQ

Jusino, T. (2015). Alison Bechdel would like you to call it the "Bechdel-Wallace Test," Thankyouverymuch. Retrieved on April 15, 2020 from www.themarysue.com/bechdel-wallace-test-please-alison-bechdel/

Lankford, A. (2018). Identifying potential mass shooters and suicide terrorists with warning signs of suicide, perceived victimization, and desires for attention or fame. *Journal of Personality Assessment* 5, 1–12.

Rodger, E. (2014). My twisted world. Retrieved on May 3, 2020 from https://assets.documentcloud.org/documents/1173619/rodger-manifesto.pdf

Sodini, G. (2009). Blog. Retrieved on May 3, 2020 from https://abcnews.go.com/US/story?id=8258001&page=1

Steele, R. (2016). Understand her, Chapter 2. Retrieved on March 10, 2020 from https://steelballs.com/understand_her_chapter-2/

Van Brunt, B. (2012). *Ending Campus Violence: New Approaches to Prevention.* New York: Routledge.

Van Brunt, B. (2015). *Harm to Others: The Assessment and Treatment of Dangerousness.* Alexandria: American Counseling Association.

2 The Rise of the Incel

The involuntary celibate movement, shortened to incel, began with a different tone and mission in 1997. A woman named Alana created a website entitled "Alana's Involuntary Celibacy Project" to offer a place for lost and struggling people to find love (Taylor, 2018). Men and women talked about their shared difficulty finding a relationship, offering advice to those stuck in a dating dry spell or too shy to approach others. She could not have predicted it would become the catchphrase of a movement of hate directed at women.

As with any community, there is a range of membership, dedication, and application of the ideals. Some seek solace in a group that shares a common struggle. Others seek advice to better manipulate women and achieve their short-term sexual goals. A term in the community, "blackpill," is expanded from the *Matrix* movies' "redpill," which frees the protagonist Neo from the computer overlords. Sexual desire, according to the blackpill, is determined by biological traits, with Chads and Stacys as the top desirable male and female specimens. Terminology is important to this movement. Table 2.1 offers a review of several common terms and phrases the reader should become familiar with to better understand and address this growing problem in society. Appendix H provides a detailed summary of both these terms and those included in Table 1.1.

In this philosophy, a large percentage of women (about 80%) are said to be drawn to the Chad, with the rest consenting to have sex with a lower level of men (but not below a normie). Not surprisingly, this kind of reductionistic view of women doesn't allow for homosexuality or seeing individuals with desirable qualities apart from sexual attractiveness. The incels rage against women, blaming them for never giving those who are genetically inferior a chance to have sex with them. This often turns into a desire that women suffer for this slight.

It is this rage, this propensity for violence, that drew our focus for the book. While the underlying misogynistic attitudes toward women along with the objectifying and reductionistic nature of seeing value in people solely from a sexual conquest standpoint were enough to raise a counterpoint, the number of incels killing other people because of their beliefs has increased the need for understanding these beliefs, assessing the risk, and developing measures to pull them back from the brink of suicide or mass killings.

While there has been an increase in violence related to the incel movement, this is not a new issue and there are no shortages of attacks that provide useful content

Table 2.1 Common incel thoughts and ideas

Betabux	A romantic relationship in which the man provides financially for his partner; often used to imply that the woman is only with him for his money
Big Black Cock Theory (BBC)	The theory that Black men are inherently more virile and sexually appealing, making them able to "dickmog" (see mog/mogging) other races
Blackpill	The belief that genetics predetermine one's status and desirability; women are only attracted to those with superior genes
Bluepill	A term taken from the Matrix movies that generally means to ignore reality; in this context it is the belief that relationships are formed based on compatibility and kindness and respect toward women
Chadfish	Pretending to be an attractive man in your photos when you are not one
Cope	Adopting a false but comforting belief to avoid the hash truth; often used by trolls to mock everyday activities
Day of Retribution	Idealized day in which incels will strike back against Chads and women; also referred to as the "Beta Uprising" or "Incel Rebellion"
FOOS	"Fall on One's Sword"
Go ER/ER/Go Rodger	To go on a killing spree, like Elliot Rodger; the letters E and R are sometimes capitalized in unrelated words (e.g., sEcuRity)
Heightpill	A subset of blackpill, which suggests women are primarily drawn to tall men
Juggernaut Law	The theory that you can't stop a woman's dating potential; unattractive and flawed women make men feel like they have a chance, so they will still have their pick of men
LDAR	"Lie Down and Rot"
-Maxx/-Maxxing	An attempt to improve dating chances by improving an aspect of one's life (e.g., looksmaxx)
Mewing	An attempt to improve one's jawline by holding the tongue hard against the roof of the mouth; created orthodontist Mike Mew
Mog/Mogging	The shortened form of AMOG (Alpha Male of Group), to mog is to be more good-looking or superior in some way
My Twisted World	Name of Rodger's manifesto, which is often seen as a basis of incel philosophy
NEET	"Not in education, employment, or training"
PSL	An acronym for the forums "PUAhate.com/Sluthate/Lookism.net"
Pump and Dump	Having sex with a woman who is looking for a relationship with no intention of pursuing a relationship
Redpill	In the Matrix movies, the redpill wakes one up to the truth of reality; in incel circles, it is the belief that all women are attracted to the most alpha man and that one can compensate for poor genes by working out or gaining wealth or status
RGIF	"Raping Girls is Fun"
Rope/Roping	To commit suicide

(continued)

12 *Introduction*

Table 2.1 Cont.

Ropefuel/Suifuel	Suicide fuel; something deeply depressing that drives self-hate (e.g., an attractive woman in a relationship with someone you consider less attractive than yourself)
Saint Alek	Alek Minassian (Toronto Van Attack)
Saint Elliot	Elliot Rodger (Isla Vista Killings)
Saint Yogacel	Scott Beierle (Tallahasee Yoga Studio Shooting)
Supreme Gentleman	How Elliot Rodger referred to himself; women are attracted to Chads even though incels are "Supreme Gentlemen"
The Wall/Agepill/Milkmired	The inevitability of age making men and women less fertile and attractive

to explore and develop assessment and treatment directions. Over fifty cases are included in Appendix A to assist the reader in better understanding how these individuals think and escalate to violence. Two of these examples stand out from the rest, perhaps because of the metaphorical "father" and "son" relationship between the 42-year-old Sodini shooting at LA Fitness in 2009 and the 22-year-old Rodger shooting in Isla Vista in 2014. While the two were not in contact, there is an eerie similarity in their thoughts, planning and actions. Perhaps it is the amount of writing and videos they shared to explain their movement toward violence.

LA Fitness Shooting, Collier Township, PA, 2009

On August 4, 2009, 48-year-old George Sodini entered a women's aerobics class at the LA Fitness center in The Bridgeville Great Southern Shopping Center of Collier Township, Pennsylvania at approximately 8:15 pm EDT. He placed a duffel bag on the ground, turned off the lights, took out at least two handguns and began shooting. He fired close to 52 shots before committing suicide. Seven women were shot and three died (Van Brunt, 2012; Van Brunt & Lewis, 2014; Fuoco & Gurman, 2010).

Sodini kept a password protected online blog for six months prior to the attack and conducted several practice attempts as he planned, preparing four guns and large amounts of ammunition. He felt justified for his upcoming killing based on a perceived history of disrespect by women throughout his lifetime. Sodini had been a follower of self-proclaimed "dating guru" R. Don Steele and had posted several YouTube videos to practice Steele's process for helping older men date women in their twenties (Associated Press, 2009).

When analyzing attacks such as these, it is helpful to review the attacker's writing. Sodini's hidden blog chronicled his thoughts and feelings toward women and his escalation toward his attack and suicide. Several highlights from the blog are included to demonstrate his frustration and eventual "practice runs" for his shooting. The blog posts are included in Appendix B.

- In November 2008, he writes about the upcoming presidential election and shares some racist's beliefs about Black men taking White women. He is frustrated by this, seeing Black men having it easy to choose their pick of the White, desirable women who are forever out of reach for Sodini.

The Rise of the Incel 13

- On December 22, he begins talking of his plan for the shooting that occurs eight months later. While he does not use these words, he exemplifies the "redpill" beliefs that if he tries hard enough to work out, he would be more attractive.
- Christmas Eve brings thoughts of the past. He ruminates on his last girlfriend from 1984 and that he hasn't had sex for 19 years. He says he isn't "ugly or weird" and seems confused why women aren't interested in him, despite his feeling that he is doing everything right.
- On December 28, he shares a detailed frustration about his lack of progress. He writes, "I dress good, am clean-shaven, bathe, touch of cologne – yet 30 million women rejected me – over an 18 or 25-year period. That is how I see it" (Appendix B). These irrational thoughts fuel feelings of loneliness, exclusion, and jealousy at how easy this is for others.
- He continues prior to the New Year and describes a frustration with his brother (who he describes as a bully), the inconsistency and waste found in religion, and his powerful and dominant mother. He describes a failed attempt to approach a woman at the gym and convinces himself even if there was a connection it would be brief. While he doesn't use these words, you can see the developing "blackpill" philosophy taking hold and his thoughts of hopelessness and suicide ("ropefuel" or "suifuel") continue to take shape.
- He describes an attempt on January 6, 2009, where he practiced going to the gym with his weapons. In his last post for three months, he writes, "It is 8:45PM: I chickened out! Shit! I brought the loaded guns, everything. Hell!" (Appendix B).
- April 24, he writes about difficulties at work with layoffs. He laments the lost time in his life and how the work he dedicated to the company doesn't mean anything.
- On May 4, he discusses the delay in his murder and suicide plan,

> "What is it like to be dead? I always think I am forgetting something, that's one reason I postponed. Similar to when you leave to get in your car to go somewhere – you hesitate with a thought: 'what am I forgetting?'."
>
> (Appendix B)

- Throughout May, he writes about returning to drinking after 20 years sober. He has a date yet continues with his self-sabotage and his exit plan list,

> "Women just don't like me. There are 30 million desirable women in the US (my estimate) and I cannot find one. Not one of them finds me attractive. I am looking at The List I made from my May 4th idea. I forgot about that for several days. That tells me where I stand."
>
> (Appendix B)

- In June, he writes that he hasn't had sex in 19 years and follows up with this distorted thought, a theme where everyone in life has things better than he does,

> "I was reading several posts on different forums and it seems many teenage girls have sex frequently. One 16-year-old does it usually three times a day

14   *Introduction*

with her boyfriend. So, err, after a month of that, this little hoe has had more sex than ME in my LIFE, and I am 48. One more reason. Thanks for nada, bitches! Bye."

(Appendix B)

- In July, work improves for him, but it is still not enough to change the plan. He sees a neighbor with a young woman and laments again at why he cannot have this in his life. He reflects on the past girlfriend he did have, not being attractive enough, not being funny enough. Always something lacking.
- An interesting incident happens on July 28 where Sodini shows an inert hand grenade to several travelers on a bus. The incident is reported but little follow-up is done until after the August 4 shooting (Hamill, 2009).
- On August 3, the day before the attack, he runs through his lists and attempts to stay focused on his plans. He discusses his own mortality and death.

Catastrophizing: Is It Difficult or Impossible?

One area of interest with Sodini is the tendency toward catastrophizing, a psychological concept from cognitive behavioral therapy where people take unfortunate events and make assumptions, often based on faulty data or an overly negative worldview. Unless Sodini had some type of superpower, it is likely he didn't approach 30 million women. More likely he went over census data for the number of single women in the US and settled on 30 million.

The negative framing and irrational nature of this thinking are hallmarks of incel thinking. Let's suppose Sodini, as with many incels, approached a few dozen women and found his flirtations and advances rejected. Sodini saw this as a failure, an inability to find that "one special lady" who connects with him. A more reasonable approach would be to look at what worked and what didn't in his approach and find ways to adapt and improve. Instead, he became entangled in the injustices he faced and lost hope at ever finding a mate. He used the idea that 30 million women rejected him as fuel for his eventual attack.

During the years prior to his attack, Sodini had taken workshops on the topic of "How to date younger women" in an attempt to overcome his difficulty dating women in their young twenties. He attended an in-person workshop by R. Don Steele designed to teach older men how to meet and date young women. The curriculum is taught through videos, role-plays at hotel seminars, and Steele's video blog. Not surprisingly, Sodini ran into trouble achieving his goal of dating women 30 years his junior. This frustration and hopelessness fueled his rage at the women who he desired, and he ultimately targeted women he desired most, those physically fit working out in an aerobics class (Greenwood, 2009; Leinwand, 2009).

It is Sodini's irrational thinking here that drove his anger and frustration toward women. As a 48-year-old man, he sought to date women in their early twenties. As he experienced difficulty with this arguably very difficult task, he became frustrated by his lack of success, began to catastrophize and converted his resulting sadness, hopelessness and frustration into feelings of rage projected at the women he most

The Rise of the Incel 15

desired, but who would ultimately reject him. To him, they were the embodiment of untouchable youth and beauty on a pedestal and forever outside his reach.

Isla Vista Killings, CA, 2014

On May 23, 2014, Rodger committed a dual attack where he stabbed and killed his three roommates and then three hours later continued his attack at a sorority house, nearby deli and struck people with his car. He was shot by police and died of a self-inflicted gunshot wound (Speer, 2014).

After killing his roommates, he uploaded a YouTube Video and emailed an auto-biographical statement to his therapist, family, and several friends. The video was entitled "A Day of Retribution" and a transcript is included in Appendix C. The auto-biographical document is entitled "My Twisted World" and provides a detailed, 141-page account of his life ending with the chilling statement, "I will punish everyone. And it will be beautiful. Finally, at long last, I can show the world my true worth" (Rodger, 2014, p. 144).

Rodger was in therapy for many years, prescribed several different medications and was diagnosed with Asperger's disorder, now known as autism spectrum disorder (Kalman, 2014). He experienced isolation, fear, bullying and teasing that made it difficult for him to function (Nagourney et al., 2014). He was devasted and overwhelmed by his parents' divorce and often found escape in video games such as *World of Warcraft* and *Halo* (Rodger, 2014).

It is worth clarifying here: the presence of mental illness should not be given undue causal importance when assessing overall escalation of violence risk (Choe et al., 2008; Rodway et al., 2014; Harvard Medical School, 2011). Following the tragedies of Sandy Hook (Sandoval & Siemaszko, 2013) and Isla Vista, there was an over-emphasis on autism as a risk-factor for such violence. Van Brunt and Pescara-Kovach (2019) write, "Mental health factors make up a small percentage of the overall risk factors related to violence risk. While important, one must not overemphasize these factors or underplay the additional violence risk factors" (p. 9).

Rodger offers a lengthy diatribe in the video created prior the attack. He describes his motivation for his actions,

> You girls have never been attracted to me. I don't know why you girls aren't attracted to me but I will punish you all for it. It's an injustice, a crime because I don't know what you don't see in me, I'm the perfect guy and yet you throw yourselves at all these obnoxious men instead of me, the supreme gentleman. I will punish all of you for it.
>
> (Appendix C)

He sees the pinnacle of manhood being the alpha male, and the way he can achieve this status is through a punishing violence,

> I take great pleasure in slaughtering all of you. You will finally see that I am, in truth, the superior one, the true alpha male. [laughs] Yes, after I have annihilated

16   *Introduction*

every single girl in the sorority house, I'll take to the streets of Isla Vista and slay every single person I see there. All those popular kids who live such lives of hedonistic pleasure while I've had to rot in loneliness all these years. They all look down upon me every time I tried to join them, they've all treated me like a mouse.

(Appendix C)

He stares at the camera like some kind of James Bond villain in his black BMW overlooking a sunset. He tells the viewer he will take back his power, punish those who have wronged him and correct this injustice. He tells us how we will now suffer like he has suffered in payment for the torture that was inflicted on him. He expresses a reductionistic view of women as sexual objects, and of men who have achieved his heart's desire while he could not. The overall tone is of a calm and certain rage at the indignation at how he was left to rot in loneliness, like a little mouse.

With his life of privilege, access to healthcare, travel, and a supportive family, it would be reasonable to consider why he chose this path. Rodger had opportunities to attend college, make friends, and follow his dreams in a way that would make those who lacked such supports envious. What made him commit these acts of violence and become the so-called "hero" of the incel movement, inspiring others to follow in his footsteps?

What is it that draws other incels to Rodger's philosophy? What is it about his speech, writings, and actions that led 27-year-old Alek Minassian to drive a van into a crowd in Toronto, Canada on April 23, 2018, posting on Facebook, "The Incel Rebellion has already begun! We will overthrow all the Chads and Stacys! All hail the Supreme Gentleman Elliot Rodger" (Madhani & Bacon, 2018)?

The Alchemy of the Incel: Misogyny, Jealousy, and Entitlement

In this exploration of the incel philosophy and the escalation from belief to violence, we can start with three central factors that drive the incel mentality. As a fire needs heat, oxygen, and fuel, the incel triangle requires an objectified and reductionistic view of female worth, a jealousy that they are outclassed by the alpha males and Chads of the world, and a firm belief that they are entitled to more than they currently have (Figure 2.1). Rodger typifies these three characteristics in his writing.

ENTITLEMENT: While some of Rodger's entitlement can be attributed to age, there are many examples where he felt he deserved certain treatment, experiences, gifts, and the like. He considered himself short and often reflected on this. He considered himself superior to other races and was infuriated that they were able to obtain the women denied to him.

> "How could an inferior, ugly black boy be able to get a white girl and not me? I am beautiful, and I am half white myself. I am descended from British aristocracy. He is descended from slaves. I deserve it more. I tried not to believe his foul words, but they were already said, and it was hard to erase from my mind. If this is actually true, if this ugly black filth was able to have sex with a blonde white girl at the age of thirteen while I've had to

Figure 2.1 Incel triangle

> suffer virginity all my life, then this just proves how ridiculous the female gender is. They would give themselves to this filthy scum, but they reject ME? The injustice!."
>
> (Rodger, 2014, p. 49)

- Rodger had difficulty with his new stepmother from an early age. This escalated when he was 18 and was forced to leave his father's house. Rodger felt the sting of this betrayal and wrote,

> "No! I am the eldest son! The house should be MY house before hers! This caused any respect I still had for my father to fade away completely. It was such a betrayal, to put his second wife before his eldest son. What kind of father would do that? The bitch must be really good to him in bed, I figured. What a weak man."
>
> (Rodger, 2014, p. 62)

- Rodger had an intense conflict with roommates he felt were undeserving of attractive female attentions. He wrote,

> "The ugly pig kept acting as if girls thought he was more attractive than me. Hah! I am a beautiful, magnificent gentleman and he is a low-class, pig-faced thug. I had enough of his cocksure attitude, and I started to call him exactly what he was. I tried to insult him as much as I could, telling him how superior I am to him, and saying that he was low- class. He tried to attack me, but Ryan, being the more mellow of the two, held him back. A pity, I was itching for a chance to hurt that obnoxious little animal. Though I suppose it was for the best … My life was too important to risk doing anything rash."
>
> (Rodger, 2014, p. 90)

18 *Introduction*

- At a party in July 2014, Rodger expresses frustration that less attractive people could have success with women,

> "I came across this Asian guy who was talking to a white girl. The sight of that filled me with rage. I always felt as if white girls thought less of me because I was half-Asian, but then I see this white girl at the party talking to a full-blooded Asian. I never had that kind of attention from a white girl! And white girls are the only girls I'm attracted to, especially the blondes. How could an ugly Asian attract the attention of a white girl, while a beautiful Eurasian like myself never had any attention from them?."
>
> (Rodger, 2014, p. 121)

- While having lunch with his father, Rodger had an experience he described this way,

> "I saw a young couple sitting a few tables down the row. The sight of them enraged me to no end, especially because it was a dark-skinned Mexican guy dating a hot blonde white girl. I regarded it as a great insult to my dignity. How could an inferior Mexican guy be able to date a white blonde girl, while I was still suffering as a lonely virgin? I was ashamed to be in such an inferior position in front my father. When I saw the two of them kissing, I could barely contain my rage. I stood up in anger, and I was about to walk up to them and pour my glass of soda all over their heads."
>
> (Rodger, 2014, p. 121)

- In his day of retribution video (Appendix C) Rodger concluded his thinking on this matter with, "I will be a god compared to you, you will all be animals, you are animals and I will slaughter you like animals."

MISOGYNY: Rodger has numerous examples in his writing that highlight his negative and objectifying feelings toward women. He saw women like an accessory to his life, as objects without agency, something to be worshiped and beyond his grasp. He pins his happiness and satisfaction on overcoming his "kissless virgin" status, which he is unable to do. In a supreme failure of the Bechdel test, Rodger uses the word "girlfriend" 98 times, "blonde" 62 times, "pretty" 47 times, "tall" 32 times, "hot" 30 times, and "sexy" 11 times.

- Rodger wrote about his desire to find a woman while at Santa Barbra Community College,

> "I can only imagine how heavenly it would be to walk with a beautiful girlfriend down that street. My life would be complete if I get to do that. It would be the epitome of gratifying perfection. To have a beautiful blonde girl by my side, to feel her hand clasping my own as we walk everywhere together, to feel her love! That is what I want in life. Instead, I had to watch other men experience my idea of heaven while I rot in bitter loneliness."
>
> (Rodger, 2014, p. 85)

The Rise of the Incel   19

- Considering an upcoming Halloween party, he wrote,

> "If only I had a beautiful girlfriend to experience such an event with! I would have even dressed up in a costume with her. It would have been so blissful and euphoric, to walk around in all of that excitement with a beautiful girl on my arm, to attend every single party because anyone would admit a beautiful girl into it, to make passionate love to her in my room at the end of the night, to snuggle next to her sexy warm body as we drift off to sleep together. THAT is the life I should have lived. So many other guys are able to experience that, and just thinking about if filled me with extreme agony. Life is not fair."
>
> (Rodger, 2014, p. 94)

- Santa Barbara is a seaside community with beautiful weather, beaches and people. Rodger saw the excesses around him, and how he desired a woman to give him status and acceptance. He wrote,

> "One time, as I was shopping at the Calvin Klein store in Camarillo, I saw such a sexy-looking blonde girl with perfectly tanned skin. She looked so beautiful and sexy that I had an erection instantly. *Oh, the heavenly things I wanted to do to her ...."*
>
> (Rodger, 2014, p. 95)

- Rodger encountered a couple while driving through Isla Vista. He wrote,

> "She was tall, blonde, and sexy. She would have towered over me in height, and her boyfriend of course towered over her. They were both wearing beach gear, and the girl was in her bikini, showing off to everyone her sensual, erection-causing body. Her blonde hair was wet from swimming in the ocean, and it only made her look more arousing."
>
> (Rodger, 2014, p. 111)

- College further emphasized the inability of Rodger to achieve his goals. He wrote,

> "I didn't see the point in even bothering with college anymore. Having to walk through SBCC with all of those beautiful girls strutting around in their revealing shorts, showing off their sexy legs ... It is torture, because I know that they would all reject me. There are so many beautiful girls in Santa Barbara, but not one of them ever wanted to be my girlfriend. Life would have been so perfect there if only girls were attracted to me."
>
> (Rodger, 2014, p. 114).

JEALOUSY: Similarly, Rodger expressed frequent jealousy and frustration at how easy it seemed for others around him to achieve the goals of being popular and with a tall, blonde attractive woman. At the heart of his frustrations was an envy that

20   *Introduction*

others had something he desired. Like Sodini struggling to reach a similar goal, both express thinly veiled rage that others, particularly men they saw as similar to themselves, obtained the women that were denied to them.

- While at a Starbucks, Rodger encountered a couple and wrote,

> "The two of them were kissing passionately. The boy looked like an obnoxious punk; he was tall and wore baggy pants. The girl was a pretty blonde! They looked like they were in the throes of passionate sexual attraction to each other, rubbing their bodies together and tongue kissing in front of everyone. I was absolutely livid with envious hatred."
>
> (Rodger, 2014, p. 87)

- Rodger described an incident where he was asked by his roommates if he was a virgin. Rodger wrote,

> "I particularly hated Angel because of his ugly pig-face. How could such an ugly animal have had sexual experiences with girls, and yet I haven't? What was wrong with this world? I got so angry that I went to my room and punched the wall. They heard me and started laughing."
>
> (Rodger, 2014, p. 89)

- Following his spotting of a beautiful woman at the Calvin Klein store, he then commented on the man with her,

> "… And then I saw her hunk of a boyfriend. My entire being was filled with anguish and despair. I could only imagine how amazing and pleasurable that guy's life was. They were older than me – probably mid-twenties – and I thought with desperate hope that when I'm that man's age I would be worthy enough to have such a girlfriend by my side, to shop with her at that same shopping mall in heavenly bliss. My life was a life of starvation and yearning."
>
> (Rodger, 2014, p. 95)

- Everywhere he looked, Rodger saw Chads obtaining the things he desired. In class he remarked, "I watched this tall, handsome blonde jock constantly sit and talk with two beautiful girls" (Rodger, 2014, p. 95). One day walking in the park he observed,

> "They all looked like typical fraternity jocks, tall and muscular. The kind of guys I've hated and envied all my life. With them came a flock of beautiful blonde girls, and they looked like they were having so much fun playing together."
>
> (Rodger, 2014, p. 106)

- Rodger described a couple he saw and realized all that he did not have. He wrote,

"The two of them were holding hands, and it was clear that they were in love. I saw the boyfriend place his hand on the girl's ass, and when he did this the girl looked at him and smiled with delight. That guy was in heaven. I can only imagine how amazing it must be to have sex with a girl like that. I had to witness everything I wanted but could not have. It made me feel dizzy with anguish."

(Rodger, 2014, p. 106)

This triangle provides a useful starting place to understand the development of these ideas in order to prevent the escalation toward violence. Understanding the "why" of the incel, albeit a distasteful area of exploration, provides the "how" needed to address these misguided beliefs. They are called misguided here, not just out of a personal distaste of the anti-feminist ideals (though, the ideas expressed by Sodini and Rodger are certainly distasteful), but rather out of an acknowledgment that the ideas set out in this chapter lead to unhappiness, separation, sadness, depression, isolation, rage, and violence. There is not a philosophy that leads to a positive outcome, whatever the metric that is used to measure such satisfaction.

Moving Forward

Now that the reader has a foundational understanding of the incel philosophy and two case examples of where this philosophy leads, there is a benefit to understanding the various cultural, societal, psychological, spiritual, generational, political, and technological influences that help undergird this movement.

Discussion Questions

- The stories of Sodini and Rodger are eerily similar despite their vastly different ages. Are there times you would see as higher risk in a male's life for perseveration on this kind of rejection more than others? Is there something unique about their ages during their attacks?
- The incel anger, more than depression, seems to drive their movement to an attack. It would appear that there becomes an ultimate buy-in to the blackpill philosophy as they realize they won't reach their goal. When you think about the directionality of their anger, which stands out the most to you toward (1) Stacy, (2) Chad, (3) the society that created them (in the incel's mind)?
- If you have to change the incel triangle to a square (or pentagon, if you will), what factors do you think would make up the additional one or two sides?

References

Associated Press. (2009). Sodini was devoted follower of dating guru. Retrieved on May 3 from www.nbcnews.com/id/32335641/ns/us_news-crime_and_courts/t/sodini-was-devoted-follower-dating-guru/#.Xq39Ai2ZPOQ

Choe, J., Teplin, L., and Abram, K. (2008). Perpetration of violence, violent victimization, and severe mental illness: Balancing public health concerns. *Psychiatric Services*, 59, 153–164.

22 Introduction

Hamill, S. (2009). Gunman was questioned about taking grenade on bus. Retrieved on May 3 from www.nytimes.com/2009/08/11/us/11pittsburgh.html

Harvard Medical School. (2011). Mental illness and violence. *Harvard Mental Health Letter*, 27, 1–3.

Kalman, I. (2014). Why therapy failed Elliot Rodger. Retrieved on May 3 from www.psychologytoday.com/us/blog/resilience-bullying/201406/why-therapy-failed-elliot-rodger

King Greenwood, J. (2009). Sodini called mom just before killings. *Pittsburgh Tribune Review*, PA, August 7.

Leinwand, D. (2009). Police questioned Pa. shooter one week before fatal attack. *USA Today*, August 11.

Madhani, A. and Bacon, J. (2018). Toronto van attack suspect Alek Minassian's Facebook account praised mass killer. Retrieved on March 10 from www.usatoday.com/story/news/world/2018/04/24/toronto-van-attack-suspect-alek-minassian/544944002/

Michael Fuoco and Sadie Gurman, M.A. (2010). The LA Fitness shootings, one year later. Pittsburgh Post-Gazette, PA, August 4.

Nagourney, A., Cieply, M., Feuer, A., and Lovett, I. (2014). Before brief, deadly spree, trouble since age 8. Retrieved on April 15, 2020 from www.nytimes.com/2014/06/02/us/elliot-rodger-killings-in-california-followed-years-of-withdrawal.html

Rodger, E. (2014). My twisted world. Retrieved on May 3, 2020 from https://assets.documentcloud.org/documents/1173619/rodger-manifesto.pdf

Rodway, C., Flynn, S., While, D., et al. (2014). Patients with mental illness as victims of homicide: A national consecutive case series. *Lancet Psychiatry*, 1, 129–134.

Sandoval, E. and Siemaszko, C. (2013). Inside Adam Lanza's lair. *NY Daily News*, November 26. Retrieved on February 12 from www.nydailynews.com/news/national/newtown-shooter-planned-death-obsessed-columbine-article-1.1528626

Sodini, G. (2009). Blog. Retrieved on May 3, 2020 from https://abcnews.go.com/US/story?id=8258001&page=1

Speer, R. (2014). A selfie-era killer: Social media and Elliot Rodger. *The New York Post*, May 28. Retrieved from http://nypost.com/2014/05/28/a-selfie-era-killer-social-media-and-elliot-rodger/

Taylor, J. (2018). The woman who founded the "incel" movement. Retrieved on January 20 from www.bbc.com/news/world-us-canada-45284455

Van Brunt, B. (2012). *Ending Campus Violence: New Approaches to Prevention*. New York: Taylor and Francis.

Van Brunt, B. and Lewis, S. (2014). Costuming, misogyny, and objectification as risk factors in targeted violence. *Journal of Violence and Gender*, 1(1).

Van Brunt, B. and Pescara-Kovach, L. (2019). Debunking the myths: Mental illness and mass shootings. *Journal of Violence and Gender*, 6(1), 53–63.

Part 2
Etiology of the Incel

3 Masculine Identity Development and the Incel

The Roots

Before addressing the rise of the incel movement and its roots in a particular performance of masculinity, it is necessary to address gender and thus, masculinity as a concept. This will likely be a review for some and provide scaffolding for others. With that, it is appropriate to define several terms. These definitions should not be considered monolithic and represent the interpretation of the scholars cited and the authors.

Gender performance is rooted in the work of feminist scholar Judith Butler (1999), who defines gender as the repetitive act of performing and constructing a gender that a person and society mutually agree to perform and maintain, which in turn leads to the construction of polarized gender norms.

Masculinity refers to a socially constructed gender identity (Kimmel & Messner, 2007) acted out by boys and men that includes among its traits emotional detachment, dominance, stoicism, and aggression (Kimmel, 2008).

Hegemonic masculinity is the structural existence of practices and belief systems that promote men as occupying a dominant social position and subordinating women (Connell & Messerschmidt, 2005). "Hegemonic" denotes the concept of cultural hegemony, defined by a dominant class in society (e.g., men) that controls ideology, values, meanings, and explanations to the extent that their worldview becomes the norm (Gramsci, 2010).

Toxic masculinity can be considered as,

> "the individual reactions to ideas about gender that prompt men and boys to behave in aggressive, abusive and sexist ways in an ongoing effort to feel like and be perceived by others as proper (read cisgendered, heterosexual, and socially dominant) men."
>
> (Markou, 2019)

If hegemonic masculinity is "the word," toxic masculinity is the "word made flesh."

It is also necessary to consider the self-perpetuating cycle of hegemonic masculinity and its service to reifying a patriarchal society as illustrated by the Figure 3.1. This cycle may leave many men feeling that they have no choices and that if they cannot

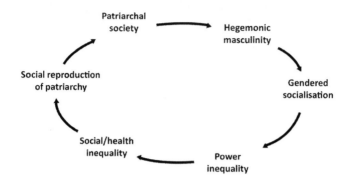

Figure 3.1 The hegemonic masculinity cycle
Source: Scott-Samuel (2009).

compete in this cycle, they must find other ways, often violent, to seize power and control. In the case of incels, as we will see, men are promised things (sex, power, respect) that they feel unable to attain and often lash out, either through their keyboard in the vastness of the internet or through other more direct and violent means.

Gender has often been viewed in a binary sense, or as a "demarcation between biological sex differences and the way these are used to inform behaviors and competencies, which are then assigned as either masculine or feminine" (Pilcher & Whelehan, 2004, p. 56). While there have been departures from this binary in a variety of cultures throughout history (the Native American Two-Spirit tradition, the Hijra of India, the Sekhet of Egypt, and the Muxes of Zapotec culture in Mexico among them), the strength of the male/female gender binary has persisted, particularly in the Western world. It is important to note the role that colonization (generally a male construct) played in erasing or diminishing many of these non-binary traditions as we begin to pivot to a discussion of negative performances of masculinity later in this chapter.

Gender can also be viewed as performative in nature in that in can be considered as the creation of roles that individuals and others collectively agree, often tacitly, to perform and sustain. This then leads to the creation of dichotomous gender norms for males and females (Butler, 1999). The masculine component of this binary is often portrayed as including emotional disinterest, dominance, stoicism, and aggression with the oppositional component for women including weakness, overreliance on emotion, and deference to men. These are classic examples of the gender binary that still exist to some extent but have undergone rapid change in the last half of the twentieth century, creating role conflict for many men.

Prior to this time, masculinity was not generally considered or studied as a concept, it "just was" in that, as the dominant side of the binary, it was the norm. Masculinity as a distinct concept finds some of its origin in the work of Freud on the Oedipal Complex that pitted a man's relationship with his father as a rivalry for the attention of his mother. While the concept of the Oedipal Complex cast an important light on identity development for men, it is another, later work by Freud, the "Wolfman," which propels us to a more nuanced understanding of the complexity of masculinity as well as its potentially negative performance.

The "Wolfman" was a patient Freud treated who sought out women who were easily controlled and engaged in a high degree of cruelty toward them (Freud, 2010). Freud believed that the man was acting out a rivalry with his father but that his focus was on women other than his mother in an attempt to impress his father. This concept of seeking the approval of other men plays out later as toxic masculinity. Later theorists began to study masculinity as a concept, but it was the feminist movement and the gay rights movement that truly moved study forward.

The twentieth century saw a variety of upheaval on many fronts within society. One of these was in the concept of gender. The study of masculinity owes a serious debt to the feminist movement that exploded during this period. The three "waves" of feminism during this period include seeking the ability to vote for women (first wave), the women's movement of the 1960s to the 1980s (second wave), and the state of feminism from the 1990s to today (third wave). As woman began to consider their place within the framework of society and formally recognized the existence of the binary, it naturally led to questioning the role of men and the expansion of gender.

Occurring at the same time as second wave feminism in the late 1960s, the gay rights movement and the burgeoning study of sexuality and gender within it also gave rise to consideration of options outside the binary. Both of these threatened and led to gender role conflict for many men. For many groups of men, this gender role conflict remains unresolved and has had devastating effects on men, on women, and on society. The role conflict has led to particular mindsets and performances of masculinity including behavior that is toxic and harmful to men and others.

Hegemonic Masculinity

As the study of masculinity and male identity development took root, a focus evolved that has become a central core to this work. The concept of hegemonic masculinity was developed by Connell (1995) and is central to their gender order theory. Powerful individuals, both culturally and politically, emphasize values and ideologies so that they become the norm in society and seem inexorable. It is also important to note that this phenomenon is not only male but is also marked by whiteness. Writing on the relationship of Black men to hegemonic masculinity, Collins (2004) notes:

> The best that Black men can do is to achieve an honorary membership within hegemonic masculinity by achieving great wealth, marrying the most desirable women (White), expressing aggression in socially sanctioned arenas (primarily as athletes, through the military, or law enforcement), and avoiding suggestions of homosexual bonding.
>
> (p. 193)

While men of color can certainly act in ways that are hegemonic, they are never full participants and never fully benefit from the supposed rewards either. This plays out in the incel community as well, as the subculture appears to be almost entirely White.

28 *Etiology of the Incel*

Like the study of masculinity, the concept of hegemonic masculinity borrows from both feminist and gay scholarship in both the investigation of patriarchy and its influence on society, as well as from thought concerning the negation of gay men by other men. These considerations of power indicate supremacy by men to suppress both women and men who do not fit into society's definition of what a man is. Therefore, hegemonic masculinity suggests that women are merely sex objects for men and rivalry among men for authentication of who they are as a man is fierce.

This also influences how men relate to other men and thus indicates control of lesser men by more powerful men not by violence, but by inducement (Connell & Messerschmidt, 2005). None of this is possible without so-called lesser men's complicity to and in many cases "cheerleading" of men that are more powerful. Even men who express thoughts about gender norms that are outside of this construct often do this (Harris, 2008), seemingly without thought. They do so because they benefit, if in lesser ways, from the reinforcement of the masculine ideal. These men might be considered the "betas, cucks, and normies" to the "Chads" of the incel pantheon.

Men acting in ways that meet what society expects of them but differs from who they really are creates a space of inner conflict that may manifest in violence (physical and sexual), homophobia, substance abuse, and other familiar male behaviors. These represent examples of toxic masculinity, the physical embodiment of hegemonic masculinity. This conflict can also lead men to view anger as a tool for acquisition of control instead of as a healthy emotion. The men who occupy this space, which Kimmel (2008) labeled "Guyland," are typically 16 to 26, White, and middle or upper class.

Cultures of Masculinity

Kimmel describes Guyland in three cultures: silence, protection, and entitlement. Each culture serves to reinforce and serve a fixed definition of masculinity and those who do not meet that definition or do not benefit from it suffer both socially and mentally. While Kimmel does not explicitly discuss incels or their use of the term "Chads," his cultures are easily conveyed to this worldview. The culture of silence (Kimmel, 2008) implies that, even when one is witness to acts of violence, sexual aggression, homophobic harassment, or other behaviors by fellow men you do not confront it but in many cases are expected to either ignore it or support it. The cost of not doing so can be social "suicide," negative attention, or in some cases, even violence directed at the confronter.

In addition to tacit acceptance and silence on the part of other men in their peer group, this behavior is supported and justified by a cadre of parents, female friends and girlfriends, those in power administratively, and in many cases, the media in a culture of protection (Kimmel, 2008). Incredibly violent acts have been justified as "boys being boys," described as "outside the character" of the men who enact them and are often "not reflective of who they truly are."

One can look to the Brock Turner rape case as an example. The media still regularly refers to him as a "former Stanford swimmer" as opposed to a convicted rapist. Despite an almost universal outcry at Turner's actions, there were still dozens of people (including parents, relatives, female friends, and school administrators) willing to write character statements for him and ask for leniency, many of them using statements similar to those mentioned (Levin, 2016). One can imagine that someone who does not fit the idealized definition of manhood would feel little solace when turning to authorities or others to complain about the actions of someone who fit the manhood mold.

The Turner case is also indicative of Kimmel's (2008) third culture of Guyland, the culture of entitlement. In this aspect, men who conform to the norms of the culture expect to be rewarded for this conformity by gaining power, in terms of both positions and material possessions as well as power over women and other, lesser men. Again, if one does not receive what they have been taught and conditioned to expect, they may attempt to seize power using other means.

These cultures are also heavily policed with rewards doled out for acquiescence and punishment issued for non-conformity. This is in line with Butler's (1999) thoughts on the maintenance of the gender binary through active policing. This policing occurs in a variety of social settings and is unsurprisingly most prevalent in all male groups such as fraternities, sports teams, the Boy Scouts, and the military. Men that attempt to resist the policing or cannot achieve the false standards set by the culture are denied rewards and are often ostracized by peers and others.

Not a Chad or Beta; What's Left?

Faced with a landscape of masculinity that is difficult, if not outright impossible, to navigate, some men have sought comfort by creating their own definition of masculinity. It is often more appropriate to refer to "masculinities" to reflect the wide variety of masculine identities that exist today. Many of these are positive responses to the pressure to conform to society's masculine ideal and the inherent issues that surround it. However, other identities continue to result in negative impact for the men who perform them as well as those around them.

The aforementioned links between the study of masculinity and feminism (particularly second wave), are important to revisit as one of the outcomes was a division into loose factions, one that remained pro-feminist and one that was decidedly anti-feminist. The anti-feminist faction embraced a men's liberation movement that at first acknowledged the power men had over women for centuries while at the same time questioning the impact of male sex roles on men (Messner, 2016).

This, however, devolved into what we know today as the men's rights movement and began to position men as victims, often arguing that, due to the roles forced on them, men suffered more than women did. They also argue that feminism has stripped men of power and emasculated them, tipping the gender scale in favor of women. While in the early days of the men's rights movement it was likely more difficult to get participants to band together, the current state of social media and access to information has caused the movement to explode. New and dangerous masculinities are enacted online. One does not have to leave the comfort of their home to experience and potentially be inculcated into a staggeringly dark sense of masculinity.

Gathered in a loose amalgamation of sites, blogs, forums, and other media referred to as the "manosphere" (Ging, 2019), these anti-feminist, pro-misogyny groups bring together a diverse and problematic array of men and male focused issues. They

30   *Etiology of the Incel*

include men's rights activists, father's rights groups, far right and alt right groups, male isolationists, and the seduction community (misogynistic dating coaches), as well as incels. The expansion of access to technology and its impact on hegemonic and toxic masculinity will be explored further in the next chapter.

Focusing specifically on the male identity development of members of the incel community, one can see common threads with other subdivisions of the manosphere in their reaction to challenges from women and perceived threats to their masculinity. Feminism is the source of their celibacy, women gravitate to physically superior men, and women are inferior to men in a variety of ways (Scaptura & Boyle, 2019). Those authors also point to extreme examples of this sense of masculinity such as enslaving women for sex, equitable distribution of women as property, and violent acts against feminists.

Incel masculinity is a subordinated masculinity. Many feel simultaneously superior to men who fit the ideals of hegemonic masculinity and acknowledge their lack of success with women and thus their subordination. This subordination often results in rage, both interior and exterior (Prior, 2020). Prior illustrates this sense of masculinity using Elliot Rodger (a hero of the movement mentioned in an earlier chapter) as an example. She indicates that incels, including Rodger, have an abiding sense of entitlement to affection, devotion, and intimacy from the women they desire and when thwarted, lay blame with women and the men (Chads) those women choose instead. For Rodger, this subordinated masculinity could only be reestablished through violence.

The masculinity expressed by incels is intertwined with a fascination with and endorsement of guns and other weapons, an acceptance of violence as a means of achieving an end, and the presence of violent fantasies. Scaptura (2019) found links between feelings of loss of group standing (men feeling like their place in society is slipping) and masculine identity stress (struggle over acceptance as a man within groups) and approval of guns, violence, and aggressive fantasies. Additionally, the author found a positive association between incel traits and emotions (misogyny, sexual frustration, loneliness, anger, hatred, resentment) and endorsement of aggressive fantasies. It is apt to view this masculinity as a powder keg waiting for a spark. Many will only express themselves online, but some choose to move beyond the virtual world and enact violence in the real world. Online communities have aided these moves to violence in a sort of domestic radicalization process which will be discussed in the next chapter.

Positive Masculinity

When discussing toxic masculinity there is often an overreach in the media and among individuals to construe all masculinity as toxic. This is simply not the case. Toxic masculinity is a particular, negative performance of masculinity that has broad impacts on men, women, and society. While incels may have a sense of envy for Chads, mixed with a sense of contempt, they also often characterize Chads as womanizing "players" that they wish they could be. In this context, a Chad is not a particularly positive sense of masculinity either. In our context, it is crucial to note that there are options beyond being a Chad, a beta, or an incel. As discussed earlier it is more appropriate to refer to "masculinities" as opposed to one, monolithic masculinity.

If hegemonic masculinity is indicative of a worldview that includes dominance, misogyny, aggression, homophobia, lack of nurturing, greed, inability to express emotions outside of anger, failing to recognize and admit weakness, and other traits, there are clearly oppositional behaviors for each of these that are more desirable and involve a larger range of options available to men. Here though, for many men, it may represent a challenge to feel and act in opposition to some of these traits, as negative as they are.

For example, if the opposite of aggressive behavior is portrayed as acting in a passive manner this may serve to reinforce in some men's minds the thought that they don't wish to act that way. Passivity may also not be appropriate or desirable in some situations, such as being a bystander to someone else being harassed or bullied. It is perfectly healthy and acceptable to be assertive while still accounting for other's thoughts and feelings. The path to positive masculinity would be well served by once again borrowing a page from the feminist movement and encouraging and accepting a variety of options for men in a way that does not diminish, restrain, or alienate. We will explore ways to assist men on this path in a later chapter.

Discussion Questions

- What are some examples of toxic masculinity that you have seen or experienced in your work or life?
- How do you perform your gender on a daily basis?
- What are examples of the three cultures (silence, protection, entitlement) of Guyland that you have seen in your work or in the media?
- If you had to, how would you advise a younger male relative, student, or client on avoiding the pitfalls of masculine behavior that is toxic?
- How can we encourage men and boys to pursue more positive performances of masculinity?

References

Butler, J. (1999). *Gender Trouble: Feminism and the Subversion of Identity*. New York: Routledge.

Collins, P.H. (2004). *Black Sexual Politics: African Americans, Gender, and the New Racism*. New York: Routledge.

Connell, R. (1995). *Masculinities*. Berkeley: University of California Press.

Connell, R.W. and Messerschmidt, J.W. (2005). Hegemonic masculinity: Rethinking the concept. *Gender & Society*, 19(6), 829–859.

Freud, S. (2010). *The "Wolfman."* London: Penguin.

Ging, D. (2019). Alphas, betas, and incels: Theorizing the masculinities of the manosphere. *Men and Masculinities*, 22(4), 638–657.

Gramsci, A. (2010). *Prison Notebooks: Three Volume Set*. New York: Columbia University Press.

Harris, F., III. (2008). Deconstructing masculinity: A qualitative study of college men's masculine conceptualizations and gender performance. *NASPA Journal*, 45(4), 453–474. doi: 10.2202/1949–6605.2007

32 *Etiology of the Incel*

Kimmel, M. (2008). *Guyland: The Perilous World Where Boys Become Men.* New York: Harper Perennial.

Kimmel, M.S. and Messner, M.A. (eds.). (2007). *Men's Lives* (7th ed.). Boston: Allyn & Bacon.

Levin, S. (2016). Dozens of letters urge leniency for Brock Turner in Stanford sexual assault case. *The Guardian*, June 8. Retrieved May 17, 2020, from www.theguardian.com/us-news/2016/jun/07/stanford-sexual-assault-letters-brock-turner-judge

Markou, T. (2019, January 2) Understanding Toxic Masculinity & Hegemonic Masculinity Through the Simpsons. Medium. https://medium.com/@samopravda/understanding-toxic-masculinity-hegemonic-masculinity-through-the-simpsons-7e8dd95d1cc7

Messner, M. (2016). Forks in the road of men's gender politics: Men's rights vs feminist allies. *International Journal for Crime, Justice and Social Democracy*, 5(2), 6.

Pilcher, J. and Whelehan, I. (2004). *Fifty Key Concepts in Gender Studies.* London: SAGE.

Prior, T. (2020) Exploring the links between subordinate masculinities and violence: The case of involuntary celibates (incels). *Discover Society.* Retrieved May 06, 2020, from https://discoversociety.org/2019/03/06/exploring-the-links-between-subordinate-masculinities-and-violence-the-case-of-involuntary-celibates-incels/

Scaptura, M.N. (2019). *Masculinity Threat, Misogyny, and the Celebration of Violence in White Men* (Doctoral dissertation, Virginia Tech).

Scaptura, M.N. and Boyle, K.M. (2019). Masculinity threat, "incel" traits, and violent fantasies among heterosexual men in the United States. *Feminist Criminology.* https://doi.org/10.1177/1557085119896415

Scott-Samuel, A. (2009). Patriarchy, masculinities and health inequalities. Gaceta sanitaria, 23, 159–160.

4 The Incel Funnel and the Influence of Religion, Technology, and Pornography

Understanding the Funnel

The "funnel" model of radicalization has been in use for some time in the field of counterterrorism. Generally, it is built on the idea that individuals who become radicalized and carry out violent acts do so along a path that has potentially predictive elements. They enter the top of a funnel, typically drawn there because of injustices and deprivations (real or perceived), engage with ideologies and solutions that may advocate violence, and eventually plan or commit violent, terroristic acts at the other end.

It is important to note that this model is not linear and is not predictive of all paths to radicalization and violence. An individual may not engage in all elements of the process and violence is sometimes driven by passion or at random. The model has been criticized for allowing law enforcement and others to target and profile individuals or groups. It has also been disparaged as an attempt to determine the perpetrator of a crime before it happens, as in *The Minority Report*.

While we are not suggesting either profiling or attempting to engage in precognition, the funnel model does appear to be collection of concepts and touch points that may assist in predicting a propensity to become radicalized and potentially carry that forward to violence. Rather than detaining or adjudicating individuals before they have done anything, we propose that there may be signposts and interventions along the way that may aid in de-radicalizing and stopping violence before it happens.

There are several examples of the funnel model and this chapter draws heavily on a model proposed by De Coensel (2018) (see Figure 4.1), itself a synthesis of multiple other models of radicalization.

De Coensel's model includes a progression of stages: Pre-radicalization, Awareness and Grievances, Solution-seeking, Interest, Targeting, Indoctrination, Implementation, and Post-implementation. The numbered circles in the model represent aspects coded from an analysis of over 28 existing models and can be seen in Table 4.1, along with the stages where they take place.

We can plot the course of the radicalization of incels through each of these stages. The funnel model can also be considered in conjunction with the rubric discussed in Chapter 5 and expanded upon in Appendix I. In the *pre-radicalization* stage, a prospective incel is outside the funnel but may share commonalities including lowered sense of self-esteem coupled with a tendency to overinflate their sense of self-worth,

34 *Etiology of the Incel*

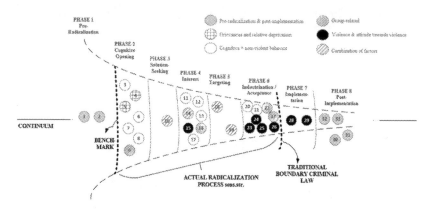

Figure 4.1 De Coensel (2018) Funnel Model

a sense of being left behind by others, a history of being bullied, and a deficiency of social skills. There is likely a lack of a sexual/romantic relationships for a time or ever and a feeling that an inability to be successful in obtaining a relationship is for reasons beyond their control. They may also have some acceptance of stereotypical gender roles and the role in life men and women should take. Suffering from mild depression and being quick to anger when things do not go their way are also possible behaviors. All of these may bear out in social media posts or comments to others that are played off as jokes when pressed.

The top of the funnel commences the *radicalization stage* and includes *awareness and grievances*. Potential incels may become aware of and understand that how they are feeling causes them to question their existence and they seek to make meaning from what is happening to them. They may discover that there is a worldview and that there are others like them from whom they can seek advice and with whom they can connect. The incel landscape is fraught with grievances and an abiding sense of injustice.

They also begin to question the value and worth of those that are successful in gaining what they are not. At this point, they typically begin to interact (usually online) with individuals who may be more knowledgeable of the incel ethos and who are willing to teach them and confirm that they are deserving of what they seek. They begin to learn incel lingo, such as blackpill, redpill, Stacy, and Chad, and become comfortable using them. They can also become inculcated in the belief that they are superior to men who have access to the women they desire and this may deepen their frustration into a sense of rage. While at this point they may still try to seek out women to date, if they are rejected, they may take on a deeper sense hopelessness and may begin to lash out more, both in person and over social media.

Solution seeking involves both the search for answers to questions as well as a pursuit of actions an individual can take that may alleviate their issues or help them gain what they want. It may also involve rejecting options that would seem acceptable to many, such as seeking out therapy, talking with peers or family members, or

Table 4.1 Adapted from De Coensel (2018)

Themes		Concepts Derived For Coding (C)
Pre-radicalization	C1	General population
	C2	Life situation before radicalization (commonalities, profiling)
Awareness &	C3	Receptiveness
Grievances	C4	Grievances
	C5	– Personal: socio-economic, including poor social
	C6	integration
	C7	– Political
	C8	Perceived injustice: generalization of injustice
	C9	Questioning confidence in certain leaders or policies; crisis of legitimacy existing order
		Disillusionment; feelings of insignificancy
		Initial exposure to alternate worldviews; sense of awareness
		Acquaintance with certain individuals
Solution-seeking	C10	Foreclosure of ordinary options
Interest	C11	Interest in doctrine; willingness to alter belief
	C12	Religious seeking
	C13	Identity search; change in behavior
	C14	Social inclusion; break with former life
	C15	Weakening resilience against violence
	C16	Actively seeking like-minded individuals
	C17	Acceptance of the cause
Targeting	C18	Target attribution; blaming
	C19	Dehumanizing the enemy
Indoctrination	C20	Intensifying beliefs; belief one adheres to is the only
	C21	correct one
	C22	Identity-constructing
	C23	Increased group-bonding
	C24	Accepting violence as a legitimate political means; conviction
	C25	that action is required to support the cause
	C26	Praising and honouring actions of terrorists; broadcasting
	C27	own intent
		Willingness to use violence; accepting duty
		Behaviour indicative of preparation for action (e.g., going abroad, training camps, etc.)
		Entering terrorist organization
Implementation	C28	Preparatory acts
	C29	Use of violence (including terrorist attack)
Post-implementation	C30	Disengagement
(new theme)	C31	Deradicalization, including self-deradicalization
	C32	Re-engagement
	C33	Reaction criminal justice system

engaging with positive media such as self-help books. For some there is the possibility that these "normal" means have failed them in the past and they may begin to consider radical solutions, particularly if these are readily available and pushed by those already accepting of the incel philosophy. They may also learn or deepen their knowledge of incels who have used radical solutions in the past and engaged in attacks.

36   *Etiology of the Incel*

As they begin to understand solutions and options that may be available to them, they display further *interest* in and possible acceptance of the incel viewpoint. They may begin to isolate themselves even further socially and shut out family, as those structures have failed them and they are gaining support from others. They are willing to alter their beliefs to match incel thinking and begin trying on the words, thought systems, and actions of other incels. They may also seek to bring others they know in the same situation along with them.

It is just after the interest stage that they may enter the *targeting* stage where they place less value on the lives of others, particularly those who they perceive may have wronged them in the past. The targeting occurs when they specifically identify the person (a particular woman who scorned them) or groups of people (all women and the Chads who are allowed to access them) whom they blame for their woes and inability to succeed in life. They also likely find support among their newly met incel brothers for these choices and engage in a communal othering of the women and men who have wronged all incels. Social media posts may include comments designed to shame and intimidate others, and may involve direct threats.

During the next stage, *indoctrination*, they not only begin to fully accept the incel perspective but do so at the exclusion of other viewpoints they previously held. People in this stage of the funnel begin to accept the possibility that, with other means not available to them or failing, violence is a valid and desirable solution to their problems and the common problems of those with whom they have bonded. This can be accompanied by a sense of martyrdom and self-sacrifice in order to set things right, a sense that they are the chosen one and can share a message with others. They may also begin to praise the actions of previous violent actors (Rodger, Sodini, Minassian). It is also possible that they may begin or heighten their fascination with guns and purchase them or train with weapons already in their possession. What is left is the implementation and post-implementation stages.

Very few make it to this end of the funnel, which is fortunate, but for those who do, the impact on individuals and society is devastating and tragic. In the *implementation* stage, the individual is fully radicalized and pulling them back may be difficult. They may not always take action but it is not uncommon for them to plan and begin to operationalize those plans. Some, of course, carry out those plans. Writings from various incels (outlined in Table 4.2) point to the planning that occurs during this stage and is often characterized by hopes for high death tolls and absolute fame seeking.

The *post-implementation* stage is specific to De Coensel's (2018) model and includes the possibility that individuals may avoid violence by changing their behavior or attitudes or alternatively that they commit violence and do not die in the process and are imprisoned where they may radicalize others or deepen their own radicalization. There is another alternative here in that they may not get caught committing the violent act and re-engage with the philosophy that supports them and may be emboldened to cause additional, escalating violence. It is crucial to restate that not all who share traits with men who describe themselves as incels enter the funnel and not all who enter stay or end up committing violence. Movement through the funnel is also not necessarily linear and represents one possibility of understanding the path to becoming violent. Other factors may play a role and influence this model.

The Incel Funnel and Influence of Religion   37

Table 4.2 Collection of writings from incel attacks exhibiting planning

Attacker	Writing	
Minassian **(Appendix A: 39; G)**	Minassian:	To be honest ah the planning didn't occur until about a month ago, most of it was actually just thinking —
	Thomas:	Okay.
	Minassian:	— and day dreaming.
	Thomas:	Okay alright so the thinking and day dreaming when did that start?
	Minassian:	That started about a month after the rebellion in ah May of 2014.
	Thomas:	Okay so —
	Minassian:	So I mean so June I started ah thinking about this stuff.
	Thomas:	And then that continued right up until a month ago?
	Minassian:	Yes. Which is when I ah booked ah the ah van with Ryder —
	Thomas:	Okay.
	Minassian:	— in order to ah use as ah a tool for rebellion.
Sodini **(Appendix A: 21; B)**	I took off today, Monday, and tomorrow to practice my routine and make sure it is well polished. I need to work out every detail, there is only one shot. Also I need to be completely immersed into something before I can be successful. I haven't had a drink since Friday at about 2:30. Total effort needed. Tomorrow is the big day.	
Rodger **(2014; p. 132;** **Appendix A: 24)**	I will attack the very girls who represent everything I hate in the female gender: The hottest sorority of UCSB. After doing a lot of extensive research within the last year, I found out that the sorority with the most beautiful girls is Alpha Phi Sorority. I know exactly where their house is, and I've sat outside it in my car to stalk them many times. Alpha Phi sorority is full of hot, beautiful blonde girls; the kind of girls I've always desired but was never able to have because they all look down on me.	
Mercer **(Appendix A: 29; D)**	My whole life has been one lonely enterprise. One loss after another. And here I am, 26, with no friends, no job, no girlfriend, a virgin. I long ago realized that society likes to deny people like me these things. People who are elite, people who stand with the gods. People like Elliot Rodger, Vester Flanagan, The Columbine kids, Adam Lanza and Seung Cho … Don't be afraid to give in to your darkest impulses. Human life means nothing, we are what matters. I hope to inspire the masses with this, at least enough to get their passions aroused.	
Ferguson **(Appendix A: 13; F)**	I've purchased all this stuff without my dad knowing. I sat there and I took his legal guns and I turned them into fucking illegal weapons to mass murder people because I knew what the fuck I was going to do. Obviously I left some of the guns at the house and couldn't take them all because of weight. You know, I'm just so tired of people fucking with me in life. I've had my fucking fill of it.	

38   *Etiology of the Incel*

While incels are not necessarily exclusive to the US, as they appear to be centered here, our focus will be on how various factors may affect the process by which someone enters the incel ethos within US culture. The following factors (religion, generational differences, technology, and pornography) could potentially be present and play a role in various stages of the De Coensel's model and would likely be most associated with the radicalization stage but could be present and influence other stages as well.

Religious Influences

Organized religion appears to have a profound effect on most people, whether they practice a religion or not. An example that springs to mind is the existence of "Blue Laws" (named in honor of the blue paper used by Puritans to publish them) that still restrict some commercial activities, including the purchase of alcohol on Sundays or may restrict the hours of Sunday sales in some states. In the United States, policy decisions, social mores, and notions of gender are often said to have roots in Judeo-Christian values and the country is in a highly divided state along religious lines (or lack of religion in many instances). Religion has become highly politicized and it is not unusual for religious leaders to endorse candidates or make political statements. It is also important to note that we are not implying that all incels practice a religion but it is likely that many were raised in religion, had family members who were practicing, or are influenced by societal practices based in religion.

The Abrahamic religions (Judaism, Islam, and Christianity) are all prevalent in the United States, and in addition to sharing a belief in the God that was revealed to the prophet Abraham, they share a somewhat common historical view of masculinity and gender. For these religions, the majority of important figures in their religious texts are men, their creation stories involve man being created before woman, and their deity is not always but often gendered as male. Men are the traditional receivers of God's word and men can expect to reap the rewards bestowed by their deity as they are entitled to them.

Historically and in many cases today, women are not allowed to participate in the highest leadership roles in the more conservative factions of these religions and the role of women in marriage is typically subservient to the men. They each also share gendered segregation during religious ceremonies in their more conservative branches. In addition to a strict reading of the role of men and women, these religions also have a history of scorning homosexuality and gender expressions outside the binary. It is important to note that some Christian denominations, branches of Judaism, and sects of Islam have evolved to support a more balanced sense of gender as well as openness to gay, lesbian, and transgender people but, particularly in the US, the historical gendered notions of these religions still flavor the views of many.

There is some question over whether Mormonism (The Church of Jesus Christ of Latter Day Saints or LDS) is Abrahamic, owing to the founding of the church by a relatively modern prophet, Joseph Smith, and their complicated history with Christianity. While not as prevalent in the US, the LDS faith shares many of the same gender practices as Judaism, Islam, and Christianity and in some cases are more extreme in marriage roles and the role of women in church leadership.

The Incel Funnel and Influence of Religion   39

A fundamentalist offshoot, the Fundamentalist Church of Jesus Christ of Latter-Day Saints (FLDS), still practices polygamy, a practice abandoned by the main church. There are elements of both historical Mormonism and the FLDS that, along with the aforementioned Abrahamic religions, may lend themselves as a religious influence on incel culture.

The Incel Religion

There is little evidence that incels, particularly the ones that have engaged in terroristic actions, come from a single religious background or are even overtly religious in the traditional sense. It may be however that, as a collective, they have borrowed ideas from religion, perhaps tacitly, as part of their philosophy. In a sense, they have created their own religion. Their language and philosophy are rife with a sense of persecution, betrayal, and martyrdom and they have even "canonized" their own saints (Saint Alek, Saint Elliot, Saint Yogacel).

In addition to the influences that may play a role in the incel sense of gender and the place of women, there are branches of religion that become newsworthy in a way that is of particular interest to incels and may influence their worldview. The fundamentalist branches or other extremist offshoots of mainline religions have at times engaged in their own violent or other criminal acts. These groups are also congruent with the previously discussed funnel process of radicalization. Whether they be Islamic jihadists, Branch Davidians, FLDS Mormons, or others, they provide popular examples of radical philosophies and practices and a willingness to embrace violence.

They also all appear to espouse a sense of "what is owed" to a man or what men are entitled to in a variety of ways which is a bedrock tenet of the incel philosophy. One of the most apt examples, known to many, is the jihadist promise of "72 virgins waiting in heaven" after committing a terroristic act of martyrdom. Mainline Islam does not support this idea, but it has been misused by radical imams to gain followers willing to perform violent acts. Jihadists are given the sense that they are entitled to these women as they have given so much to the cause. Incels feel owed because of their supposed superiority as well as the injustices they have suffered.

Other examples include the extreme views of gender roles and inherent rights of men espoused by the both the Branch Davidians and the FLDS. In both groups, women are subservient to men or to the male leader of the group, plural marriage for men is common as is marriage and sex with girls under the legal age of consent, often with much older men. Both groups have also gained fame by encounters with law enforcement that have ended in mass deaths (the Branch Davidians at Waco) or incarceration of their leadership (the FLDS after a raid on their compound turned up evidence of the physical and sexual abuse of children). There is a sense of martyrdom among these events as well.

The groups mentioned are certainly not incels and incels do not appear to adhere to a particular religion, other than perhaps an unofficial one of their own making. It is arguable however, that they have been influenced by religion, as many of us are, and may have taken a page from very public examples of extremist religious groups in shaping their worldview.

40   *Etiology of the Incel*

Technology

"Moore's Law" tells us that the speed of technology is generally said to double every two years. This predictive concept, created in the 1970s to originally refer to the expected biennial doubling of the number of transistors in an integrated circuit (Schaller, 1997) has proven true. By way of example, the smart phone that many of us use has approximately 100,000 times the processing power of the computer used to land on the moon. Technology obviously gives us tremendous benefits but those often come at a cost. While there are numerous forms of technology, our main focus will be on the internet and its influence on incel culture.

Incels are a modern phenomenon and appear to be created in part by the internet. By created, we do not mean that they are a fictionalized culture but mean that their existence is fostered by their ability to communicate with like-minded others, rapidly seek and disseminate information, and form groups with extremist views without the visibility of public meeting spaces. It also appears to allow for the exacerbation of some of their worst traits.

Online communication has had a deep impact on our relational practices. A variety of studies indicate that the loss of face to face interaction when exchanges are limited to the internet is detrimental to any sense of traditional social interaction rituals and even leads to increased loneliness (Brignall & Van Valey, 2005; Zizek, 2017; Twenge et al., 2019). Incels who isolate themselves in a variety of spaces on the internet may deepen their inability to communicate in ways that value the person with whom they're communicating and also strengthen their sense of social isolation further.

A culture of aggressive communication is also ever present on the internet and seems to have become particularly divisive since the 2016 election. We have all likely seen situations where people, some we know and some we don't, have said things in online threads or on social media apps that we suspect they would never say in person. There is an emboldening that occurs through the lens of anonymity. It is also often the case that the insult "keyboard warrior" is thrown out, meaning someone who is aggressive or even makes threats behind the veil of cyberspace.

Also referred to as online trolling, its spread has become ubiquitous in recent years with "trolls" invading most internet groups at one time or another. Sest and March (2017) found that internet trolls are typically male, and that higher levels of psychopathy and sadism, as well as lower levels of empathy, were predictive of trolling. This seems to fit the incel culture well and incels are often referred to as both trolls and keyboard warriors by others, which is likely to increase their sense of rage and injustice, potentially driving their internet threats into the real world. They may also use this as fame-seeking behavior in that their digital quest to get even and put others in their place may be examined by others with whom they are allied or ultimately, if they take their aggression offline, by the world.

The internet has also harbored a variety of extremist groups that use it to spread their message, recruit followers, and directly attack those that oppose them. The Southern Poverty Law Center (SPLC) tracked 940 hate groups in the US in 2019 (SPLC, 2020) many of whom have an active online presence. Incels are not a hate group per se as they are too loosely affiliated, but act in a manner similar to many of these groups. Due to the general lack of regulation, the internet appeals to groups and individuals, including incels, as a means of effective and inexpensive recruiting, and for the ability of smaller groups to link with other extremist groups (Gerstenfeld et al., 2003). While lack of regulation was mentioned, after a variety of complaints and a Change.org petition, the incel subreddit was banned from the internet site Reddit in 2017. At the time, the group had 40,000 members (Solon, 2017).

While bringing us untold benefits, technology has also created a variety of issues with which we all have to contend. It has at least partially created the incel movement and allowed it to proliferate in ways it likely would not have without internet communications. Strangely, much of the progress in technology, particularly the internet, is due in part to the porn industry. The industry was a key player in the advent of online purchasing, an increase in internet speeds due to the need to stream content, and the ability to access the internet using handheld smart devices. The next section will explore the proliferation of online pornography and its potential effect on incel culture.

Pornography

The ability to access hardcore pornography has increased in ease over the past few decades. Many men above the age of 40 likely have memories of sneaking into the room of their father or older brother to steal a few moments with a stash of pornographic magazines hidden in a closet or drawer. The father or brother would have likely purchased the magazine from an adult store where they also might have bought pornographic films on VHS tapes, which were a progression from the XXX movie theaters of the 1970s and 80s.

With the advent of widespread public usage of the internet in the mid-1990s, porn became a largely online phenomenon. Though adult stores still exist, hardcore pornography is now widely accessible without leaving the confines of your home. While it would have been nearly impossible for adolescents to frequent an adult store or theater due to laws governing access, online porn appears to be largely unregulated. There are certainly many adolescents who seek out porn but there are likely many who also stumble across it and are inadvertently exposed to it. With increased access, the harmful effects of porn are able to spread wider and more quickly.

This also comes at a time in the US when the concepts of dating and marriage have undergone significant change in a relatively short amount of time. In general, people have had more sexual partners, are more likely to have casual sex, and are more accepting of sex outside of marriage than in the past (Twenge et al., 2015). There are also a variety of apps and websites that assist people in matching with those with like interests in order to pursue a relationship as well as apps that are available to connect casual sex partners. People are also getting married less and at an older age than in the past (Eickmeyer, 2019). The addition of widely available porn, which leads to unrealistic expectations, and the changing landscape of relationships may present additional difficulties to those already struggling to form sexual bonds. To incels it might at once seem that it should be easier than ever to find a willing partner while sliding farther into the thought that those who are not deserving are easily finding what they seek.

42 *Etiology of the Incel*

Porn appears to have an impact on the overall health, both mental and physical, of performers in the industry (Dines, 2010). In addition to the detrimental effects on those in the industry, a variety of research has linked adverse outcomes (aggravation of sexually aggressive tendencies in those predisposed to them, a willingness to endorse rape myths, and increased sexual perpetration) to exposure to sexually explicit material (Malamuth et al., 2000; Oddone-Paolucci et al., 2000; Jewkes et al., 2002; Carr & VanDeusen, 2004; Jensen, 2004). While there is no agreement in the therapeutic community regarding viewing porn as an addictive behavior, it at least has the potential to be considered habitual based on increased numbers of people reporting and seeking help for excessive use of porn that interferes with their daily activities (Duffy et al., 2016).

The saturation of the online porn market has led to boredom and desensitization and the need for some to seek increasingly more exciting material. What was hardcore 25 years ago is mainstream now and the industry feels the need to keep up (Dines, 2010) in order to gain a share of a business that has an estimated worth of $90 billion yearly (Hollywood by comparison makes $10 billion annually) (Bindel, 2019). This has led to the creation of extreme material, sometimes referred to as "gonzo" porn. An industry insider provides a fitting description:

> One of the things about today's porn and the extreme market, the gonzo market, so many fans want to see so much more extreme stuff that I'm always trying to figure out ways to do something different. But it seems everybody wants to see a girl doing a d.p. [double penetration] now or a gangbang. For certain girls, that's great, and I like to see that for certain people, but a lot of fans are becoming a lot more demanding about wanting to see the more extreme stuff. It's definitely brought porn somewhere, but I don't know where it's headed from there.
>
> (Adult Video News, 2003, p. 46)

For incels, online porn could be viewed as providing an outlet for their sexual frustration, but it has the same damaging effects as it has on others and these effects are perhaps compounded. One could easily conclude that incels, who already have an affinity toward objectification, would seek out violent and degrading porn that depersonalizes women. It is also possible that continual viewing of gradually more intense and debasing pornography creates a vicious circle of deepening objectification and unrealistic expectations. There is also something at work in porn regarding hegemonic masculinity. Garlick (2010) notes that while heterosexual men may seek porn for the idea of countless women who are willing to fulfill every sexual demand, the men in porn are typically well endowed, physically fit, and attractive. This reinforces the concept of the ideal man and may fuel incel rage.

Summary

In this chapter, we reviewed De Coensel's funnel model and discussed it in terms of its application to the radicalization of incels. We also discussed possible influences that have contributed to the rise of incel culture and ethos (religion, technology, and

The Incel Funnel and Influence of Religion   43

pornography). The next chapter introduces a rubric that can be used to assess an individual's level of incel indoctrination.

Discussion Questions

- What other models of radicalization are you familiar with in your work and how might you plot incels on those models?
- How might religion be used as a positive influence in intervening and redirecting an incel?
- What are some examples of positive ways that technology could aid the process of intervening with someone wrapped up in the incel worldview?
- How might you redirect an incel away from pornography toward more healthy outlets for sexuality?

References

Adult Video News. (2003, January). AVN director's roundtable, 45–68.

Bindel, J. (2019). The horror of Big Porn. Spectator, October. Retrieved May 16, 2020, from https://spectator.us/horror-big-porn/

Brignall III, T.W. and Van Valey, T. (2005). The impact of internet communications on social interaction. Sociological Spectrum, 25(3), 335–348.

Carr, J. and VanDeusen, K. (2004). Risk factors for male sexual aggression on college campuses. *Journal of Family Violence*, 19(5), 279–289.

De Coensel, S. (2018). Processual models of radicalization into terrorism: A best fit framework synthesis. *JD. Journal for Deradicalization*, 17, 89–127.

Dines, G. (2010). *Pornland: How Porn Has Hijacked Our Sexuality*. Beacon Press.

Duffy, A., Dawson, D.L., and Das Nair, R. (2016). Pornography addiction in adults: A systematic review of definitions and reported impact. *The Journal of Sexual Medicine*, 13(5), 760–777.

Eickmeyer, K.J. (2019). Age variation in the first marriage rate, 1990 & 2017. *Family Profiles*.

Garlick, S. (2010). Taking control of sex? Hegemonic masculinity, technology, and internet pornography. *Men and Masculinities*, 12(5), 597–614.

Gerstenfeld, P.B., Grant, D.R., and Chiang, C.P. (2003). Hate online: A content analysis of extremist Internet sites. *Analyses of Social Issues and Public Policy*, 3(1), 29–44.

Jensen, R. (2004). Pornography and sexual violence. Harrisburg: VAWnet, a project of the National Resource Center on Domestic Violence/Pennsylvania Coalition Against Domestic Violence. Retrieved May 11, 2020 from: www.vawnet.org

Jewkes, R., Sen, P., and Garcia-Moreno, C. (2002). Sexual violence. In E.G. Krug, L.L. Dahlberg, J.A. Mercy, et al. (eds.), *World Report on Violence and Health* (pp. 147–181). Geneva: World Health Organization.

Malamuth, N.M., Addison, T., and Koss, M. (2000). Pornography and sexual aggression: Are there reliable effects and can we understand them? *Annual Review of Sex Research*, 11, 26–91.

Oddone-Paolucci, E., Genius, M., and Violato, C. (2000). A meta-analysis of published research on the effects of pornography. In C. Violato, E. Oddone-Paolucci, and M. Genius (eds.), *The Changing Family and Child Development* (pp. 48–59). Aldershot: Ashgate.

Schaller, R.R. (1997). Moore's law: past, present and future. *IEEE Spectrum*, 34(6), 52–59.

44   *Etiology of the Incel*

Sest, N. and March, E. (2017). Constructing the cyber-troll: Psychopathy, sadism, and empathy. *Personality and Individual Differences*, 119, 69–72.

Solon, O. (2017). "Incel": Reddit bans misogynist men's group blaming women for their celibacy. The Guardian, November 8. Retrieved May 17, 2020, from www.theguardian.com/technology/2017/nov/08/reddit-incel-involuntary-celibate-men-ban

Southern Poverty Law Center (SPLC). (2020). www.splcenter.org/hate-map

Twenge, J.M., Sherman, R.A., and Wells, B.E. (2015). Changes in American adults' sexual behavior and attitudes, 1972–2012. *Archives of Sexual Behavior*, 44(8), 2273–2285.

Twenge, J.M., Spitzberg, B.H., and Campbell, W.K. (2019). Less in-person social interaction with peers among US adolescents in the 21st century and links to loneliness. *Journal of Social and Personal Relationships*, 36(6), 1892–1913.

Zizek, B. (2017). Digital socialization? An exploratory sequential analysis of anonymous adolescent internet-social interaction. *Human Development*, 60(5), 203–232.

Part 3

Incel Questionnaire and Rubric

5 Incel Indoctrination Rubric (IIR)

The development of a rubric to assist counselors, psychologists, law enforcement, human resources, and BIT/CARE teams better assess the degree at which a person has invested in the incel doctrine is the first step in a three-stage assessment process. Once the level of indoctrination has been assessed, the next step is to determine the presence of risk factors (described in Chapter 7) and stabilization influences (described in Chapter 8) prior to conducting a threat assessment process (described in Chapter 9).

The following rubric is designed to offer a research-based, objective guide to better assess the level of depth an incel has reached. These 20 items have been built from the first 50 cases in Appendix A. While these first 50 comprised our original research, several other cases have since occurred that fit our search criteria. While these cases are not included in the research here and in the next chapter, we included them in the appendix for reference. The 20 items are divided into four categories that influence the incel thought: Thinking, Feeling, Behavior and Environment. These are demonstrated in Figure 5.1.

Thinking

Thinking qualities are related to cognitions the individual has that increase the buy-in to the incel worldview. These beliefs are often hardened and inflexible, supported by online discussion boards and those the individual surrounds himself with on a daily basis.

1. **Misogyny:** Here the individual has an over-arching, negative, and limited view of women. He describes women in an objective, one-dimensional manner and sees the heart of their worth as a sexual possession. This often manifests in seeing women in a binary, like Madonna or whore, saint or sinner, Stacy or Becky. He sees a woman's beauty through a Caucasian, euro-centric perspective (e.g., blonde, tall, blue eyes). When these women are outside of his reach, the only access the incel believes he has is through killing Chads or raping Stacys.

Figure 5.1 Thinking, feeling, behavior, and environment

2. **Racism:** There is a lack of appreciation for diversity or any divergence and a sense of superiority of the White race over all others. This would also include anti-Semitic, homophobic, and transphobic beliefs.
3. **Blackpill:** There is an acceptance of the superiority in the genetic characteristics of the alpha male and female. He accepts the futility of the biological fate he has been assigned and lives with a sense of hopelessness, inferiority, and growing rage at the lack of sexual prospects available to him. Given the fatalistic view of this thinking, his only access to women becomes killing Chads or resorting to Stacy rape fantasies.
4. **Inaccurate self-conception:** This bi-furcated construct exists on two extremes on a spectrum. On the one end, the faulty view of self is overly negative and leads to low self-esteem and value. On the other end, he sees himself as all-powerful and possesses an overly inflated sense of value and entitlement.
5. **Fame seeking:** There is a larger desire to achieve fame and make a statement, to be the chosen one with a sense of purpose that alluded him throughout his life. This may come at the end of a long struggle where he finds worth in the idea of communicating a larger message to society to set things right and unmask the injustices he has endured.

Feelings/Emotions

These are the sentiments and corresponding reactions to their thoughts or experiences from others. They are often intense feelings that drive behaviors.

Incel Indoctrination Rubric (IIR)   49

6. **Rage:** There is an intense anger and rage directed toward women, alpha males, other non-White males seen as "less than," and/or the society at large for contributing to his marginalized status without a chance for redemption.
7. **Hopelessness:** A pervasive sense of sadness and desperation at the prospective of considering the future. There is a sense of futility and desperateness regarding any positive change in the future.
8. **Catastrophe:** Unfortunate negative events such as a breakup or difficulty obtaining a first date are given a larger, catastrophic emphasis that provide a frame for the individual being a worthless failure.
9. **Disability:** A mental or physical illness that creates an increased difficulty in social connection with both interaction and reading social cues. There is a difficulty in understanding the rules of flirting and he struggles to form relationships. This most commonly is related to Asperger's/autism spectrum disorder (ASD), depression, social anxiety or personality disorders.
10. **Abandoned:** Pervasive feelings of being misunderstood, neglected, abandoned or deserted. The person feels alone in the world and that no one seems to care about his troubles or descent into increasing pain.

Behavior

These behaviors are often the outward manifestations of the cognitions, feelings, and emotions. Behaviors are particularly important as they relate to the risk factors outlined in Chapter 8 and provide observable data that can be consistently acted upon by a BIT/CARE team.

11. **Approach behaviors:** A term first coined by Meloy et al. (2014), this describes behaviors that threaten others. They are often impulsive, affective, adrenaline filled actions that should be seen as approach behaviors moving toward harming attractive women, the alpha males who have them and a society that unjustly supports this biological deck stacked against the incel.
12. **Howling:** A term coined by Calhoun and Westin (2009), howling refers to conditional, transient threats that are made against others primarily to intimidate and to force a fight, flight, or flee reaction. This howling often occurs on social media.
13. **Suicide:** The person makes a suicide attempt or statement. This is often done out of frustration and may be an attempt to control and influence a woman or others. These suicide attempts can occur frequently and are often related to the incel's frustration in dating relationships
14. **Past attacks:** He references past attacks, shootings or negative actions toward women to praise other violent actors. This can occur in writing, on social media or be spoken to friends, classmates, and co-workers. This may include an infatuation with prior killers/actors and collecting information about them.
15. **Redpill:** He seeks to change his behavior, status, or worth through physical exercise, cosmetic surgery, or obtaining wealth to attract women. He believes

50 *Incel Questionnaire and Rubric*

these efforts will make a less genetically worthy male be able to obtain a higher rated female through altering aspects of his appearance, increasing wealth or status.

Environmental

These environmental factors represent historical and cumulative experiences that further escalate the individual toward isolation, hardened thoughts, and potential violence.

16. **Incel materials:** He is frequently exposed to incel and/or White supremist/ nationalist, homophobic, ablest, ageist, transphobic, or anti-Semitic ideas through peers, media, and family messaging and/or websites and discussion boards. Alternative viewpoints are routinely dismissed without exploration or empathy.
17. **Rejection:** Women reject advances from the person related to sexual approach with the assumed reason being related to genetics, lack of women's interest, or their preference for males who are superior.
18. **Bullied:** He is teased about his appearance, especially being sexually unattractive or unable to find a sexual partner. This bullying often occurs in front of others, further escalating his difficulty finding connections with others and embarrassing him, causing feelings of negative self-worth or lack of acceptance from others.
19. **Failure to change:** Previous attempts at changing thoughts or behaviors have been met with frustration and exacerbation. These change attempts are often steps in the right direction such as attending therapy, learning more about dating from apps or self-help books, and listening to and connecting with friends.
20. **Free fall:** He exhibits a low sense of self-worth and has experienced difficulty finding acceptance from others, such as friends or parents. There may have been abuse, traumatic loss, or family change/discord, all feeding into feelings of worthlessness.

A more detailed version of this rubric is contained in Appendix I. In it, each of the 20 items are divided into five categories to be scored with a range of: 0, .25, .5, .75, 1. This allows an overall score from 0–20 corresponding with a level of incel indoctrination. The following section offers sample cases to assist the reader with some practical guidance on how best to assess the individual using the IIR.

Case Examples Using the IIR

To assist the reader in using the IIR, we have scored the two cases discussed in Chapters 1 and 2, George Sodini from the LA Fitness shooting and Elliot Rodger from the Isla Vista attack. As a reminder, the more detailed version of the IIR with each of the 20 items broken down into a five progressive scoring levels can be found in Appendix I.

Scoring of the Isla Vista Killings, CA, 2014

Summary

Thinking					Feeling					Behaviors					Environment				
1	2	3	4	5	6	7	8	9	10	11	12	13	14	15	16	17	18	19	20
1	1	1	1	1	1	1	1	1	1	1	1	1	.50	1	.50	1	1	1	1

19.50

Thinking

1. **Misogyny:** (1) This is commonly mentioned throughout the manifesto. Women are seen as one-dimensional objects of desire, often objectified based on their attractiveness and body shape or hair color. They are objects to be acquired to give him a sense of meaning and value.
2. **Racism:** (1) There are numerous references to Asians, Mexicans, and Black people in a derogatory manner. He expresses frustration that these "lesser" males are able to achieve what has been denied to him, a more superior male.
3. **Blackpill:** (1) In his manifesto and corresponding attack, it is clear that Rodger rejects the prospect that things could ever be different for him. He sees the system as fixed and his only path as revenge.
4. **Inaccurate self-conception:** (1) In his writing, Rodger interestingly oscillates between extreme self-loathing regarding issues such as his height and heritage and an over-inflated sense of self and entitlement.
5. **Fame seeking:** (1) Rodger desires to create change and make himself known through his attack and writing. He wishes others to understand why he ultimately killed others and himself.

Feeling

6. **Rage:** (1) He often references his intense anger about how he has been treated, why others disregard him and what is owed and expected to be given to him. This is recounted in fights at parties and several incidents where he engages in affective violence, throwing beverages at those he hates.
7. **Hopelessness:** (1) There is a continual thread related to the void of hopelessness that he finds himself in throughout his writing. The ending attack occurs partially due to the idea that he will always be denied the future he feels he deserves.
8. **Catastrophe:** (1) Many examples throughout the writing highlight the exaggerated emotions he attaches to perceived failures in obtaining a relationship or being rejected socially.
9. **Disability:** (1) He writes about his experiences in therapy related to his difficulties with mental illness. Whether tied to depression, autism spectrum disorder

52   *Incel Questionnaire and Rubric*

(ASD) or a personality disorder, Rodger is continually struggling with social interactions with others, in part due to these problems.

10. **Abandoned:** (1) Throughout his writing, Rodger talks about the emotional impact of being alone, isolated, neglected, and worthless.

Behaviors

11. **Approach behaviors:** (1) Rodger mentions a dozen incidents where he throws things at individuals and couples based on an impulsive rage at not being given what he wants.
12. **Howling:** (1) Near the end of his life, he makes numerous threats and gestures at parties indicating transient threats to beat up or kill others in a fight.
13. **Suicide:** (1) He writes extensively about his hopeless thoughts and a desire to die by suicide.
14. **Past attacks:** (0.5) While not explicitly mentioned, Rodger talks about practicing at a shooting range, countermeasures related to taking down videos, outwitting police during a questioning prior to the attack. This offers significant evidence that he studied past attacks to improve on them.
15. **Redpill:** (1) Throughout his writing and YouTube videos, Rodger references attempts to make himself more desirable to women through increasing his status and wealth. He writes about working out at the gym to boost his self-confidence and become stronger.

Environment

16. **Incel materials:** (0.50) Primarily, he talked on discussion boards and computers related to chat, games and sharing of naked pictures of women. It was likely he was reading about these ideas and talking to others about incel-related concepts. Some of this may be because the case is slightly older and the propagation of these issues and sites was not as prominent.
17. **Rejection:** (1) Throughout his writing, he shares stories of women ignoring him and not being receptive to his advances.
18. **Bullied:** (1) He mentions frequent bullying and teasing throughout his writing and YouTube Videos.
19. **Failure to change:** (1) Rodger talks at length about attempts to change through improving his status, working out, and attending therapy.
20. **Free fall:** (1) Rodger mentions struggling often with grades at his different colleges, low self-esteem, and feels a lack of acceptance from others.

Scoring of the LA Fitness Shooting, Collier Township, PA, 2009

Thinking					Feeling					Behaviors					Environment				
1	2	3	4	5	6	7	8	9	10	11	12	13	14	15	16	17	18	19	20
1	1	1	1	1	1	1	1	.5	1	1	0	1	0	1	1	1	1	1	1

17.5

Incel Indoctrination Rubric (IIR)   53

Thinking

1. **Misogyny:** (1) Sodini has a one-dimensional view of women and sees their value only in being young and attractive.
2. **Racism:** (1) His blog opens with a lengthy diatribe about how Black men should each have a White woman because White women like them more.
3. **Blackpill:** (1) After many attempts to buy into the redpill strategy through working out, dressing nice, and attending classes to teach him additional skills successfully date younger women, he ultimately saw this to be a futile effort. No matter what he did, he would not get what he wanted.
4. **Inaccurate self-conception:** (1) At the heart of his problems was a sense of surprise that a 48-year-old man would have difficulty dating younger women. He saw himself as less than other men, but mostly because he didn't appreciate the high expectations he had placed on himself. He shares in the blog that he has had sex 50–75 times, but the women were never good enough or attractive enough for him. They never made up for the way he saw himself.
5. **Fame seeking:** (1) There was an element that Sodini wanted to be seen and acknowledged, writing a detailed account of his efforts and leaving a note explaining his reasoning. At the heart of this was his obtaining the fame and attention he was denied so long by the attractive young women who rejected him.

Feeling

6. **Rage:** (1) Sodini recounts several times the anger that he felt at being looked over at his job, how other "lesser" men had obtained women that he would never find.
7. **Hopelessness:** (1) Sodini possessed some hope over time, but ultimately the hopelessness snuck back in and lead to his attack and suicide. At the core of his reasoning was a knowledge that his time had passed him by and he would not ever reach his goals. All that was left was to punish those who rejected him.
8. **Catastrophe:** (1) Sodini's irrational thinking is present throughout his blog, estimating that 30 million women had rejected him and that he had no worth because he was successful at dating women 30 years his junior.
9. **Disability:** (0.5) While not explicitly stated, many of Sodini's videos showed a limited understanding of social connections and emotions of others. There may have been some larger mental illness issues that contributed to his inability form connections and adjust his perspective and goals.
10. **Abandoned:** (1) Sodini certainly felt rejected and left throughout his life. His blog recounts relationship problems with his brother, mother and father. He felt rejected most by the women who never reciprocated his desire or attraction.

Behaviors

11. **Approach behaviors:** (1) Sodini practiced his attack plan by showing up to the gym and then "not having the guts to carry it out" and there was a point where he brought an inert hand grenade on a bus prior to the attack.

54 *Incel Questionnaire and Rubric*

12. **Howling:** (0) Sodini was not public about his plan of attack and took steps to hide his frustrations through a password protected blog. He seemed to save most of his writing in this manner.
13. **Suicide:** (1) He expressed frequent thoughts of suicide and ultimately took his own life in the attack.
14. **Past attacks:** (0) There is no mention publicly of past attacks.
15. **Redpill:** (1) Sodini, in many ways, was an exemplar of the type of person who looked for ways to overcome his limitations (age, looks, money, status) to attract women.

Environment

16. **Incel materials:** (1) Sodini killed himself prior to the incel movement becoming more widely known, though he did attend courses taught by those who very much espoused the philosophical underpinnings of the movement.
17. **Rejection:** (1) Sodini often cited the rejection by women and inability to form these connections as frequent occurrences and laments in his blog.
18. **Bullied:** (1) Sodini mentions being treated badly by his family, bullied by his brother and often struggled to understand and connect with others. There is no mention of workplace bullying, but it would be likely he experienced this as well.
19. **Failure to change:** (1) Despite numerous attempts at working out, taking classes on how to date younger women and constantly documenting in his blog efforts to overcome his low-worth, Sodini was ultimately unsuccessful at change.
20. **Free fall:** (1) Sodini had a good job, but seemed to lack family and peer support. While aspects of his life were together (finances, owned his own home, good job), the more important elements (friendship, a spouse, larger meaning) were lacking.

Moving Forward

This chapter outlines a scoring rubric useful to create a quantitative, objective rubric to better assess the risk of incel ideation. A scorable version of this tool is included in Appendix I. In the next chapter, a scorable questionnaire is offered to use as a self-assessment tool for those expressing incel thoughts or actions.

Discussion Questions

- When considering the general categories of thinking, feeling, behaviors, and environment, what order would you place them in terms of prioritization and focus, from most concerning to least concerning?
- Describe the relationship between suicidality and the blackpill philosophy.
- Diagnoses of Asperger's and autism spectrum disorder (ASD) are present in some of the cases in Appendix A and in the discussion here. What role do you see mental illness playing as a contributing factor to the incel philosophy?

- Incels don't talk or write much about homosexuality, transgender people or those with non-binary gender identities. Why do you think that is? How do you see an incel thinking about these concepts? Would they see a similar sense of marginalization and connection or reject them as less than incels?

References

Calhoun, F. and Weston, S. (2009). *Threat Assessment and Management Strategies: Identifying the Howlers and Hunters*. Boca Raton: CRC Press.

Meloy, J.R., Hart, S., and Hoffmann, J. (2014). Threat assessment and management. In J.R. Meloy and J. Hoffmann (eds.), *The International Handbook of Threat Assessment* (p. 5). New York: Oxford University Press.

6 Incel Cases by Rubric Category

Special Thanks to Bethany Van Brunt for
Her Work on This Chapter[1]

This chapter analyzes the first 50 cases in Appendix A to determine which categories on the IIR are demonstrated by the perpetrators in those cases. For each category, we will list the cases that represent it and provide several examples from case reports and written material by the perpetrator.

Keep in mind, this is not a complete picture, as it is what can be gleaned from articles about the cases and any original written materials that are available online. Many of the cases may well fit into more categories than listed, but without being able to interview the subjects or see information that has been kept out of the public sphere we cannot be certain. This chapter provides a research base to support the creation of the IIR outlined in Chapter 5 and Appendix I. Table 6.1 offers a summary of the findings, which are detailed below.

Thinking

1 Misogyny (31/50)

Cases: 2, 3, 5, 7, 8, 11, 12, 13, 14, 20, 21, 22, 23, 24, 25, 27, 29, 31, 32, 33, 35, 37, 38, 39, 40, 41, 43, 45, 47, 48, 50

As misogyny is the hallmark of the incel movement, it's not surprising that it is directly present in the majority of the cases reviewed. Thirty-one of the 50 cases had clear examples of misogyny in the language used or actions made by the perpetrators. In the remaining cases, there is a high likelihood that misogyny is present to some degree but was not apparent in the materials available.

Many of the cases reviewed were specifically a result of incel beliefs or were attacks against women. Among these were the young man in Portsmouth, UK who in 2014 stabbed three women as they were walking home (Appendix A: 25). He said in a video found on his laptop, "I think every girl is a type of slut." Alek Minassian, who drove a van onto a crowded Toronto sidewalk in 2018 (Appendix A: 39), wanted to "overthrow the Chads which would force the Stacys to be forced to reproduce with the incels."

We also reviewed a number of cases that, while not directly aimed at women or not specifically to do with the incel movement, still had a misogynistic element. Timothy McVeigh, one of the 1995 Oklahoma City bombers (Appendix A: 7), wrote,

Incel Cases by Rubric Category 57

Table 6.1 Summary of incel violence cases by indoctrination levels

	Category	# of Cases	% of Cases	Cases
THINKING	Misogyny	31	62%	2, 3, 5, 7, 8, 11, 12, 13, 14, 20, 21, 22, 23, 24, 25, 27, 29, 31, 32, 33, 35, 37, 38, 39, 40, 41, 43, 45, 47, 48, 50
	Racism	11	22%	11, 20, 21, 24, 27, 29, 37, 38, 41, 45, 49
	Blackpill	18	36%	1, 3, 4, 5, 9, 10, 13, 19, 21, 24, 25, 29, 39, 41, 43, 45, 46, 47
	Inaccurate self-conception	13	26%	2, 4, 11, 19, 20, 21, 24, 29, 39, 41, 43, 45, 47
	Fame seeking	25	50%	2, 5, 7, 8, 11, 13, 14, 18, 20, 21, 23, 24, 25, 27, 28, 29, 30, 37, 38, 39, 40, 41, 43, 46, 48
FEELING	Rage	23	46%	1, 3, 5, 9, 10, 11, 14, 20, 21, 24, 25, 29, 30, 31, 43, 39, 41, 43, 44, 45, 47, 48, 50
	Hopelessness	17	34%	1, 3, 6, 9, 10, 14, 16, 17, 19, 21, 24, 25, 29, 37, 39, 41, 43
	Catastrophe	18	36%	1, 5, 8, 9, 10, 11, 13, 14, 19, 21, 24, 25, 29, 34, 39, 42, 43, 47
	Disability	11	22%	1, 2, 3, 10, 22, 24, 26, 29, 37, 39, 44
	Abandoned	16	32%	1, 2, 3, 4, 7, 8, 9, 10, 14, 19, 21, 24, 29, 33, 39, 43
BEHAVIOR	Approach behaviors	19	38%	3, 12, 13, 14, 16, 17, 18, 20, 24, 31, 32, 33, 35, 36, 38, 40, 41, 44, 50
	Howling	22	44%	1, 5, 10, 12, 15, 20, 22, 24, 27, 28, 29, 30, 36, 37, 38, 40, 41, 42, 43, 47, 48, 50
	Suicide	28	56%	1, 3, 4, 5, 6, 10, 11, 13, 14, 16, 17, 18, 20, 21, 22, 24, 26, 28, 29, 35, 36, 37, 39, 43, 41, 46, 47, 49
	Past attacks	12	24%	2, 13, 24, 28, 29, 32, 37, 38, 39, 41, 45, 50
	Redpill	10	20%	8, 10, 13, 14, 21, 23, 24, 28, 39, 40
ENVIRONMENT	Incel materials	13	26%	3, 21, 22, 24, 27, 29, 30, 34, 37, 38, 39, 41, 46
	Rejection	21	42%	1, 3, 7, 8, 9, 10, 11, 13, 18, 13, 21, 24, 25, 29, 34, 38, 39, 41, 43, 44, 45
	Bullied	11	22%	1, 2, 9, 11, 15, 18, 22, 24, 28, 29, 39
	Failure to change	12	24%	5, 8, 9, 10, 14, 21, 24, 28, 29, 32, 36, 38
	Free fall	13	26%	1, 2, 5, 6, 9, 13, 14, 19, 24, 26, 28, 33, 39

58   *Incel Questionnaire and Rubric*

"In the past thirty years, because of the women's movement, they've taken an influence out of the household." In choosing their target, they chose a building with many more women than men working in it, including at a daycare center. A document was found on Adam Lanza's (Appendix A: 22) computer entitled, "why females are inherently selfish."

2 Racism (11/50)

Cases: 11, 20, 21, 24, 27, 29, 37, 38, 41, 45, 49

While not as pervasive, racism, anti-Semitism, homophobia, and transphobia are clear in many of the cases. Both of the Columbine attackers (Appendix A: 11) used the n-word in the journals, with Eric Harris writing "I'm a racist and I don't mind. Niggs and spics bring it on to themselves." Several of the perpetrators railed against interracial relationships between White women and Black men, some calling the woman a traitor and some blaming the man for "stealing" her from White men. The Charleston church shooter (Appendix A: 27) wrote, Black men are raping "our women and are taking over our country." The shooter at Stoneman Douglas High School (Appendix A: 38) wrote, "My real mom was a Jew. I am glad I never met her."

3 Blackpill (18/50)

Cases: 1, 3, 4, 5, 9, 10, 13, 19, 21, 24, 25, 29, 39, 41, 43, 45, 46, 47

We can posit that once someone on the incel path reaches the point of murder/suicide, it is likely they have given up hope that there can ever be change, implying an acceptance of the blackpill, but we have included here cases where the perpetrator espouses the view before the time of the attack.

We know that Elliot Rodger (Appendix A: 24) and Chris Harper-Mercer, the Umpqua Community College attacker (Appendix A: 29), wrote in a way that implies a blackpill philosophy. George Sodini (Appendix A: 21) wrote, "what bothers me most is the inability to work towards whatever change I choose." Tomohiro Kato, who drove a truck into a crowd in Tokyo (Appendix A: 19), wrote "I don't have a single friend and I won't in the future. I'll be ignored because I'm ugly."

4 Inaccurate Self-Conception (13/50)

Cases: 2, 4, 11, 19, 20, 21, 24, 29, 39, 41, 43, 45, 47

Here, we clearly see the bifurcated nature of this category. Eric Harris (Appendix A: 11) wrote both "I have practically no selfesteem, especially concerning girls and looks and such" and

> I feel like GOD and I wish I was, having everyone being OFFICIALLY lower than me. I already know that I am higher than almost anymore in the fucking welt

in terms of universal Intelligence and where we stand in the universe compared to the rest of the UNIV.

There are multiple cases of attackers with incredibly low self-worth, including Sodini (Appendix A: 21), who wrote "There is something BLATANTLY wrong with me that NO goddam person will tell me what it is." There are also cases of highly inflated ego, like the feeling of god-like power that the Rose-Mar College of Beauty shooter (Appendix A: 2) reported to his psychiatrist.

5 Fame Seeking (25/50)

Cases: 2, 5, 7, 8, 11, 13, 14, 18, 20, 21, 23, 24, 25, 27, 28, 29, 30, 37, 38, 39, 40, 41, 43, 46, 48

Half of the perpetrators were hoping to make themselves famous and/or convey a larger message to the world, often trying to make the world take notice of their plight and take revenge on the men and women who stood in the way of their sexual needs. Like the man who was arrested for threatening a Women's March in 2019 (Appendix A: 43), they feel wronged and want to "make it right by killing as many girls as I see." While Dylann Roof (Appendix A: 27) hoped to spark a race war, Alek Minassian (Appendix A: 39) was aiming for an "incel rebellion."

FEELING

6 Rage (23/50)

Cases: 1, 3, 5, 9, 10, 11, 14, 20, 21, 24, 25, 29, 30, 31, 43, 39, 41, 43, 44, 45, 47, 48, 50

While a certain amount of rage and anger is required at the time of an attack, the cases included here display a rage specifically focused against women or as a direct result of their failures with women. The Mall of America attacker (Appendix A: 44) once became so angry at a woman at the mall for not buying him food that he threw a glass of water and a glass of tea at her. In high school, the Dayton shooter (Appendix A: 47) had kept a "hit list" of people he wanted to kill or rape and Farhan Sheikh was arrested for a threat against the Chicago Women's Reproductive Health Clinic (Appendix A: 48) in which he ranted, "I will proceed to slaughter and murder any doctor, patient, or visitor I see in the area and I will not back down."

7 Hopelessness (17/50)

Cases: 1, 3, 6, 9, 10, 14, 16, 17, 19, 21, 24, 25, 29, 37, 39, 41, 43

Many of the attackers had reached a place where they had met with such continual failure in forming romantic or sexual relationships that they had given up hope of

60   *Incel Questionnaire and Rubric*

ever achieving this. The shooter at Pearl High School (Appendix A: 9) wrote, "I only loved one thing in my whole life and that was Christina Menefee [his first victim]. But she was torn away from me." Kato (Appendix A: 19) specifically addressed his lack of hope in an online post, writing, "If I had a girlfriend, I wouldn't have just left my job or be addicted to my cellphone. A man with hope could never understand this." Sodini (Appendix A: 21) wrote of his blog, "Maybe all this will shed insight on why some people just cannot make things happen in their life."

8 Catastrophe (18/50)

Cases: 1, 5, 8, 9, 10, 11, 13, 14, 19, 21, 24, 25, 29, 34, 39, 42, 43, 47

There was a tendency for many of the attackers to catastrophize events and react in rageful or violent ways when faced with negative life events. While they were dating, Joseph Ferguson, who would later go on a rampage through Sacramento (Appendix A: 13), fixed some front-end damage on his girlfriend's car. After she broke up with him, he hacked up her car with an ax, saying "I giveth and I taketh away." After the women who gave him his first kiss at age 36 ended their relationship, Ted Kaczynski, the Unabomber (Appendix A: 8) wrote unflattering limericks about her and posted them around their work site.

9 Disability (11/50)

Cases: 1, 2, 3, 10, 22, 24, 26, 29, 37, 39, 44

While the mental or physical health issues of all the perpetrators aren't known, we do know that some had physical conditions or disabilities (Appendix A: 1, 2, 3) or mental illnesses that impeded their success with women. The most common mental illnesses we see are Asperger's/autism spectrum disorder (Appendix A: 22, 29, 39) and anxiety (Appendix A: 22, 24, 37), both of which make social connections more difficult.

In the earliest case we found, Mutsuo Toi slaughtered half of the residents of his small village in Japan in 1938 (Appendix A: 1). In his suicide note, he wrote about how his tuberculosis turned him into a social pariah and that after his diagnosis, the women of the village began rejecting his sexual advances.

10 Abandoned (16/50)

Cases: 1, 2, 3, 4, 7, 8, 9, 10, 14, 19, 21, 24, 29, 33, 39, 43

The cases included here display a perpetrator who feels uncared for and alone in the world. Some have experienced literal abandonment, like the Tsuyama killer (Appendix A: 1), who was deeply affected when his sister married and moved away, or the driver of truck that barreled through a crowd on Bastille Day 2016 in Nice, France (Appendix A: 33), who hadn't recovered from his wife leaving him two years earlier. Others just feel the loneliness and solitude of being left out and left behind by society. The perpetrator of the Queen Street massacre in Melbourne, Australia wrote in his diary, "since the age of 12 I knew that normal sex was not possible for me and I avoided girls completely until I was 19." Chris Harper-Mercer, who killed nine people at Umpqua Community College (Appendix A: 29) wrote "I have always been the most hated person in the world ... My whole life has been one lonely enterprise. One loss after another."

Behavior

11 Approach Behaviors (19/50)

Cases: 3, 12, 13, 14, 16, 17, 18, 20, 24, 31, 32, 33, 35, 36, 38, 40, 41, 44, 50

In many of the cases we reviewed, the perpetrators had committed lesser acts of physical or sexual violence or harassment prior to the main attack. Many had a history of domestic or intimate partner violence or emotional abuse (Appendix A: 12, 14, 31, 32, 33, 35, 36, 40).

Prior to his attack at St. Pius X High School (Appendix A: 3), Robert Poulin was suspected in several incidents of indecent assault and attempted rape. Scott Beierle, who opened fire at a Tallahassee yoga studio (Appendix A: 41), had two incidents of slapping or grabbing women's buttocks in his past.

12 Howling (22/50)

Cases: 1, 5, 10, 12, 15, 20, 22, 24, 27, 28, 29, 30, 36, 37, 38, 40, 41, 42, 43, 47, 48, 50

A large number of the perpetrators displayed leakage prior to the attack or made unrelated threats directed toward women or in response to their frustrations. Jarrod Ramos, the Capital Gazette shooter (Appendix A: 42), threatened a former classmate after she blocked him on Facebook, saying in an email to her, "Have another drink and go hang yourself, you cowardly little lush. Don't contact you again? I don't give a (expletive). (Expletive) you." Prior to his threat against the Women's March (Appendix A: 43), Christopher Cleary harassed a woman, threatening her and texting, "I own multipul guns I can have u dead in a second." Beierle (Appendix A: 41) posted racist and misogynist videos to YouTube and songs to SoundCloud. These included lyrics such as "To hell with the boss that won't get off my back /To hell with the girl I can't get in the sack."

13 Suicide (28/50)

Cases: 1, 3, 4, 5, 6, 10, 11, 13, 14, 16, 17, 18, 20, 21, 22, 24, 26, 28, 29, 35, 36, 37, 39, 43, 41, 46, 47, 49

In more than half of the cases, the perpetrator committed suicide or displayed suicidal ideations during the attack. In one case, the Toronto van attack (Appendix

62   *Incel Questionnaire and Rubric*

A: 39), the perpetrator planned to commit suicide by cop, holding his wallet like a gun and telling police that he had a gun in his pocket, but the officer did not take the bait. Poulin (Appendix A: 3) wrote "death is the true bliss." Several left behind manifestos and/or suicide notes, often justifying their actions or calling others to action. Duane Morrison, who held six girls hostage at Platte Canyon School, molesting all six and killing one (Appendix A: 16), mailed a letter to his brother apologizing to his family and acknowledging his impending death. George Sodini (Appendix A: 21), Elliot Rodger (Appendix A: 24) and Chris Harper-Mercer (Appendix A: 29) left detailed writings about their lives and the reasons behind their attacks.

14 Past Attacks (12/50)

Cases: 2, 13, 24, 28, 29, 32, 37, 38, 39, 41, 45, 50

A number of the perpetrators reference past attacks and are often inspired by them. Since his attack in 2014 (Appendix A: 24), Elliot Rodger is the most cited past attack (mentioned in Appendix A: 29, 37, 38, 39, 41, 50). Minassian (Appendix A: 39), in fact, claims to have exchanged private messages of support with both Rodger and Chris Harper-Mercer, the Umpqua College attacker.

15 Redpill (10/50)

Cases: 8, 10, 13, 14, 21, 23, 24, 28, 39, 40

Like blackpill, this is somewhat hard to quantify with the materials available. We know that Kaczynski (Appendix A: 8) at least tried wardrobe changes to attract women. Sodini (Appendix A: 21) regularly went to the gym and attended dating advice workshops. Rodger (Appendix A: 24) made attempts to improve his status, both physically and financially. Minassian (Appendix A: 39) specifically mentions the redpill.

Environment

16 Incel Materials (13/50)

Cases: 3, 21, 22, 24, 27, 29, 30, 34, 37, 38, 39, 41, 46

Many of the cases reviewed occurred prior to the rise of the incel subculture, and thus are difficult to score here. There were some cases, however, where the perpetrator seems to have spent a significant amount of time in incel or other similar communities. We also include here Poulin (Appendix A: 3), who had an extensive and well cataloged pornography collection, some of which focused on bondage. William Atchison, who killed two students at Aztec High School (Appendix A: 37) was active online and used the pseudonym "Elliot Rodger" in online forums.

Incel Cases by Rubric Category   63

17 Rejection (21/50)

Cases: 1, 3, 7, 8, 9, 10, 11, 13, 18, 13, 21, 24, 25, 29, 34, 38, 39, 41, 43, 44, 45

There were a number of cases involving rejection by women and the strong and often violent reaction that elicits in the perpetrators. Many perpetrators felt so much rejection they had given up hope. Kinkel (Appendix A: 10) wrote in his journal about a girl he had a crush on, "Every time I talk to her, I have a small amount of hope. But then she will tear it right down." Sodini (Appendix A: 21) wrote, "I dress good, am clean-shaven, bathe, touch of cologne – yet 30 million women rejected me."

18 Bullied (11/50)

Cases: 1, 2, 9, 11, 15, 18, 22, 24, 28, 29, 39

Many of the perpetrators experienced bullying. This bullying was sometimes related to their inability to date and often involved loss of face in front of women. Luke Woodham, the Pearl High shooter (Appendix A: 9), wrote in his journal,

> I only loved one thing in my whole life and that was Christina Menefee. But she was torn away from me. I tried to save myself with [student's name], but she never cared for me. As it turns out, she made fun of me behind my back while we were together.

Eric Harris (Appendix A: 11) wrote, "I hate you people for leaving me out of so many fun things."

19 Failure to Change (12/50)

Cases: 5, 8, 9, 10, 14, 21, 24, 28, 29, 32, 36, 38

By the time they reach the attack stage, most perpetrators will fit this category, having given up on being able to change and improve their circumstances. A handful of cases, however, demonstrate attempts to change that failed and caused frustration, sadness and anger. Sodini (Appendix A: 21) regularly worked out, attended dating workshops, and took pride in his appearance, all to no avail. He wrote "I have no options because I cannot work toward and achieve even the smallest goals."

20 Free Fall (13/50)

Cases: 1, 2, 5, 6, 9, 13, 14, 19, 24, 26, 28, 33, 39

In several cases, we can see the spiral of loss that leads to feelings of worthlessness and anger. Often there is a triggering event that exacerbates the situation, such as Mutsuo Toi's (Appendix A: 1) tuberculosis diagnosis combined with his sister

64 *Incel Questionnaire and Rubric*

marrying and moving away. Ferguson (Appendix A: 13) was abused by his mother and had recently split with his girlfriend.

Moving Forward

The summary in this chapter provides research support for the development of the IIR included in Appendix I. The next two chapters review the common risk factors and stabilizing influences used to better assess the risk of targeted violence. By combining the IIR, risk factors and stabilizing influences, the reader will be more prepared to assess risk through the process of violence risk and threat assessment outlined in Chapter 9.

Discussion Questions

- Given this list of 20 incel categories and the referenced cases, which ones resonated the most with your experience and knowledge of incels as your school, college, or place of work?
- Which of these would you consider the top three areas of concern when assessing the indoctrination of the incel?
- If you were asked to develop a list of five qualities that helped repel these incel ideas, what would they be?

Note

1 **Bethany Van Brunt** is a graduate of Gordon College in Wenham, MA and the CEO of Looking Glass Consulting and Design. She has worked in computer programming and currently works in marketing, editing, and design.

Part 4
Assessing the Risk

7 Identifying the Risk Factors

When individuals escalate to the point of violence, whether driven by incel thoughts or other motives, there are risk factors that can be assessed to determine the likelihood of targeted violence occurring. These risk factors should be balanced against the stabilizing influences that offer mitigation and support to offset the escalation of the violence risk. These stabilizing influences are discussed in the following chapter. Before assessing the presence of risk factors, it will be helpful to better understand the difference between the two common types of violence, affective and targeted.

The more common form of violence is *affective violence*. This violence stems from an adrenaline-driven, biological aggression fueled by adrenaline and results in an increase in heart rate, raised voice, threatening gestures, and communication indicators (Grossman, 1996; Grossman & Siddle, 2000; Howard, 1999; Hart & Logan, 2011; Hart et al., 2011; Meloy, 2000; 2006). This movement from calm to rage-filled is described further on the D-Scale of the NaBITA Risk Rubric (Sokolow et al., 2019). Affective violence is reactive and poorly considered and driven by perceived or actual threats, rage and/or fear. An individual responds to this stimulus with a release of adrenaline, and unpredictable, spontaneous, affective violence (Howard, 1999). In the Isla Vista attack, Rodger writes in his lengthy manifesto *My Twisted World* (2014) examples of affective violence as well as targeted violence, which offers a helpful comparison of the two types. We can see the escalation of his rage and poor impulsive control, ultimately leading to the killing of six on May 23, 2014. Examples of affective violence in Rodger's writing can be found in Table 7.1.

Predatory or targeted violence, in comparison, is a process of planned, mission-oriented actions in response to a larger injustice, hopelessness or frustration resulting in instrumental violence such as a school shooting. This violence is pre-meditated, involves strategy and tactics, and efforts are taken to disguise or hide their plan (Meloy, 2000, 2006; Meloy et al., 2011; O'Toole, 2014; Meloy et al., 2014; Van Brunt, 2015a). Regarding the incel, this frustration becomes increased with isolation, disconnection, loss of a positive future outcome, and a desire to inflict pain on individuals and a society who inflicted pain on them. In contrast to affective violence, those escalating on a predatory violence pathway develop and execute their plans with a militaristic, tactical precision (Meloy, 2000, 2006; Meloy et al., 2011; Meloy et al., 2014; O'Toole, 2014). While there is a separation in these violence processes, there are often examples where the same individual experiences both. Examples of this kind of thinking are included in Table 7.2.

68   *Assessing the Risk*

Table 7.1 Affective violence in *My Twisted World* (2014)

Affective violence

"I was so enraged that I almost splashed him with my orange juice." (p. 84)

"When they left the store I followed them to their car and splashed my coffee all over them." (p. 87)

"What was wrong with this world? I got so angry that I went to my room and punched the wall." (p. 90)

"I was livid with rage, and I wanted to pour my drink all over his head." (p. 91)

"Throughout the whole film, I had to fight the urge not to splash my drink all over the little shitheads in a vehement rage." (p. 103)

"I wanted to ruin their fun just like they ruined mine, as they would never accept me among them. I screamed at them with rage as I sprayed them with my super soaker." (p. 107)

"That night, I threw a wild tantrum, screaming and crying for hours on end. I had the whole apartment to myself, so there was no one there to hear me. I raged at the entire world, thrashing at my bed with my wooden practice sword and slashing at the air with my pocket knife." (p. 109)

"A dark, hate-fueled rage overcame my entire being, and I tried to push as many of them as I could from the 10-foot ledge. My main target was the girls." (p. 122)

Table 7.2 Predatory violence in *My Twisted World* (2014)

Predatory violence

"They treated me like an insignificant little mouse, but on the Day of Retribution, I would be a God to them. They will be the mice, and I will be the predator." (p. 110)

"I wanted to punish them all. I imagined how sweet it would be to slaughter all of those evil, slutty bitches who rejected me, along with the fraternity jocks they throw themselves at. I wanted to punish them all. I imagined how sweet it would be to slaughter all of those evil, slutty bitches who rejected me, along with the fraternity jocks they throw themselves at." (p 110)

"I couldn't believe my life was actually turning out this way. There I was, practicing shooting with real guns because I had a plan to carry out a massacre." (p. 109)

"After I picked up the handgun, I brought it back to my room and felt a new sense of power. I was now armed. *Who's the alpha male now, bitches?* I thought to myself, regarding all of the girls who've looked down on me in the past." (p. 131)

"First, I needed to buy a third handgun, just in case one of them jams. I needed two working handguns at the same time, as that was how I planned to commit suicide; with two simultaneous shots to the head." (p. 131)

"After I have killed all of the sorority girls at the Alpha Phi House, I will quickly get into the SUV before the police arrive, assuming they would arrive within 3 minutes." (p. 132)

"I will then make my way to Del Playa, splattering as many of my enemies as I can with the SUV, and shooting anyone I don't splatter." (p. 132)

"I must plan this very efficiently. Nothing can go wrong. It needs to be perfect. This is now my sole purpose on this world. My plans will come to fruition, and I mustn't let anyone stop me." (p. 133)

Identifying the Risk Factors 69

The term "targeted" may be a misleading as the term does not imply a specific target, but instead threats that are predatory, pre-meditated, planned, and methodically executed. This is in contrast to those that are spontaneous and more likely to emerge without leakage and therefore without warning. O'Toole (2014) describes those intending targeted violence as individuals who are mission oriented.

> Mission-oriented shootings are hardly impulsive crimes. They are well-planned and can involve days, weeks, months, even years of making preparations and fantasizing about the crime. The planning is strategic, complex, detailed, and sufficiently secretive to minimize the risk of being detected and maximize the chances for success. The planning does not occur in a vacuum – during this phase, mission-oriented shooters make many decisions, including the types of weapons and ammunition they will use and where to obtain it, the clothes they will wear, the location of the assault, who the victims will be, what they will do at the location, and the date and time of the shooting.
>
> (p. 9)

One way to address this kind of predatory violence is to attend to "leakage" (O'Toole, 2014). *Leakage* is the communication to a third party of an intent to do harm to a target (Meloy & O'Toole, 2011; Van Brunt, 2016). The most direct warning sign for suicide or mass murder-suicide is often the individual's leakage of intent (Meloy et al., 2014; National Institute of Mental Health, 2017; NTAC, 2018, 2019). Most attackers share statements about their intent prior to their attacks (Horgan et al., 2016; Lankford, 2013; Van Brunt, 2012; Meloy & O'Toole, 2011; Meloy et al., 2014; Pollack et al., 2008; Vossekuil et al., 2002).

This leakage rarely happens all at once, but rather the attacker shares hints or comments in writing, emails, texts, and social media posts about their frustrations and intent to make others pay. When these comments in violent writing or social media posts are discovered, they should be explored and analyzed. O'Neill et al. write, "Writings, drawings, and other forms of individual expression reflecting violent fantasy and causing a faculty member to be fearful or concerned about safety should be evaluated contextually for any potential threat" (2008, pp. 32–33). Early identification provides an opportunity for educators, counselors, conduct officers, human resources, and law enforcement to move them off the pathway to violence (Calhoun & Weston, 2009; Fein et al., 1995).

Risk Factors

There has been a good deal of research on various risk factors related to targeted violence by organizations such as the Federal Bureau of Investigation (O'Toole, 2002), the National Threat Assessment Center (NTAC) (2018), the United States Postal Service (USPS) (2007), the National Behavioral Intervention Team Association (NaBITA) (Sokolow et al., 2019), and the Association of Threat Assessment Professionals (ATAP) (2006). Some of these factors are listed here in Table 7.3.

These factors should be seen in combination, like puzzle pieces coming together to create a larger meaning. Any single puzzle piece gives limited information to the

70　*Assessing the Risk*

Table 7.3 Summary of targeted and predatory violence risk factors

Direct threat	Indirect threat	Lack mental support	End of a relationship
Access to weapons	Lack peer support	Explosive reactions	Inability to date
Hardened thoughts	Lack family support	Intimidates others	Hopelessness
Social isolation	Loss of job	Lacks empathy	Last act behavior
Victim of bullying	Decline in academics	Polarized thoughts	Legacy token
Substance abuse	Acquiring weapons	Glorified violence	Feeling persecuted
Authority conflict	Suicide attempt	Lacking remorse	Leaking attack plan
Fixation on target	Focus on target	Action plan for attack	Time frame for attack
Fantasy rehearsal	Rejection	Financial loss	Catalyst event
Feeling trapped	Poor anger outlets	Fame seeking	Objectification

Figure 7.1 Violence risk assessment of the incel

entirety of the system. It is when these are assembled that they have an amplified meaning. For example, when analyzing a direct threat, Calhoun and Weston (2009) share this important reminder, "Writing letters is easy; shooting someone or setting him on fire presents a considerably more difficult challenge" (p. 29).

When determining the level of risk for targeted violence from incels, a three-phase process should be employed to better assist professionals in building interventions to mitigate the risk of violence. This involves (1) assessing the level of incel indoctrination (discussed in Chapters 5 and 6), (2) determining the presence of risk factors (discussed in this chapter) and stabilizing influences (discussed in Chapter 8), and (3) analyzing the movement toward action (discussed in Chapter 10). This is shown graphically in Figure 7.1.

Quality of Threat

When a threat is discovered, there must a determination if the threat is leakage or simply a poor decision, perhaps related to feelings of powerlessness, a desire to intimidate, or trolling of others to garner a reaction. Any direct threat is an aggravating factor in terms of the larger violence risk assessment process. Scalora et al. (2010) write:

> Unlike disruptive and other forms of aggressive behavior, violent or directly communicated threat always requires immediate investigation and evaluation. While most communicated direct threats do not end in violence, this can only be determined after directly questioning and assessing the student in question.
>
> (p. 5)

Identifying the Risk Factors 71

Any threats must be balanced against the data to determine the likelihood of an attack (Scalora et al., 2010; Turner & Gelles, 2003).

Simply making a threat does not mean the individual in question is likely to carry it out. Threats can be either transient or substantive (Cornell, 2010), hunting or howling (Calhoun & Westin, 2009). These concepts are described in relation to affective and predatory violence in Table 7.4.

Transient threats are often affective "howls," made in the immediacy of the moment, and based on intense emotions in reaction to a slight and lack intent to action. These threats make up approximately 70% of threats made in primary and secondary schools (Cornell, 2010). A substantive threat may be affective in nature, communicating a likelihood of a more lethal action made to communicate a future attack. Substantive threats extend beyond the immediate incident and require more intensive attention and intervention.

The ***lethality*** of the threat is determined by assessing the actual danger of the threat being carried out and leading to death and the access to lethal means to carry out the attack. While this may not be readily apparent in the writing sample or social media content, assessing the lethality of a threat is an essential part of a thorough violence risk assessment.

Turner and Gelles (2003) outline several aspects of violence risk to identify when assessing risk. ***Fixation and focus*** help delineate the level of narrowing to a specific target. ***Fixations*** are strongly held beliefs and obsessions about a certain group being responsible for the pain or suffering someone is feeling. ***Focus*** narrows the attention further, like a gun sight zooming in on a target. ***Action and time imperative*** determine if there is a specific time or place for the attack. This can be specific, such as "The day of reckoning will occur at 4 p.m. on Thursday," or vague, like "I don't have much restraint left, if you keep treating me like this I am going to snap one of these days." A ***conditional ultimatum*** sets up a "do this or else" or "if you do this, this will happen," if/then scenario. The implication being if the target of the writing or social media post does not comply with the author, they will take action. A summary table with some examples of the different kinds of threats related to incels is provided in Table 7.5.

Table 7.4 Summary of threat terms

Affective violence is adrenaline-driven, biological aggression and results in an increase in heart rate, raised voice, threatening gestures, and communication indicators.	**Transient threats** are statements that do not express a lasting intent to cause harm.	**Howlers** make threats or create concerning posts that have no likelihood of being acted upon.
Targeted, predatory, instrumental, mission-oriented violence is a planned event in response to a larger injustice, hopelessness or frustration resulting in planned, instrumental violence, such as a school shooting.	**Substantive threats** are statements that expresses a continuing intent to harm someone.	**Hunters** intend to use lethal violence to right some perceived injustice.

72 *Assessing the Risk*

Table 7.5 A threatening table of threats

Type of threat	Example
Direct	"We need to kill the Chads like these football players at this school to send a message."
Indirect/vague	"Keep kicking the incels and the beta rebellion will come soon."
Direct with action/time imperative	"They thought it was funny at the party to ignore me. Let's see if they ignore my Sig Sauer at the thirsty Thursday gathering."
Conditional ultimatum	"If that Stacy doesn't start giving me the time of day, I'm going to start giving her something she won't forget."
Transient	A co-worker walks by an attractive woman's desk and says "Someone should tie you down and smack you around."
Substantive	"I'm tired of other people thinking they can treat me this way. I will be at the game this weekend with a container of gasoline. The halftime show will be explosive."
Howling	"People need to listen to me. I am not going to be treated like this! Keep ignoring me and you'll be on TV one day saying, 'jeez, he always seemed quiet and kept to himself.'"
Hunting	"I'm headed to the tanning salon to turn up the heat. Guess which one? #dayofretribution #fire"
Vague, but direct	"This is for Stacy at Antelope High. Start spreading your legs for someone besides the Chads or I'll start spreading you ribs to get at your heart. #happyvalentinesday #bitch"
Direct, but vague	"Sale on ammunition today at the gun store. Gonna come back and pull a little Elliot-Chris-Minassian, action."

Risk Factors for Targeted, Predatory, Mission-Oriented Violence

1. *Actionability* is related to the extent the individual has access to means and materials to make good on a particular threat. For example, a student may threaten to kill jocks at a school who are having sex with the women they want, but the violence risk level is mitigated if they have no weapon access or knowledge and no ability to acquire a weapon. If the student has access to guns or firearm mastery (say, from military or other training) or an ability to acquire a weapon from friends or work, this would be considered an aggravating factor to the assessment. In a study of targeted violence from 2007–2017, the National Threat Assessment Center (2019) found that most of the attackers gained access to firearms in the home or from the home of a relative, both secured and unsecured. While firearms are of particular concern, a threat assessment should explore if a student has access to any weapons, not just guns.

   On April 23, 2018, Minassian drove his van onto a crowded sidewalk, killing 10 people and injuring 16 in Toronto, Ontario (Appendix A: 39). The following exchange took place in his April 23, 2018 police interview and gives insight into how he planned for and acquired his weapon of choice (taken from Appendix G).

   > *Minassian: Yes. Which is when I ah booked ah the ah van with Ryder —*
   > *Thomas: Okay.*

Identifying the Risk Factors 73

Minassian: — *in order to ah use as ah a tool for rebellion.*

Thomas: *Okay alright so tell – take me through that process. What was going through your mind and how was you know, what were you thinking when you were doing all of this? What was going on?*

Minassian: *I was thinking that it was ah time that I ah stood up to the Chads and Stacys*

2. A *hardened point of view* is an intractable belief that carries an ardent invest-ment for the individual (O'Toole, 2002; Sokolow et al., 2014; Van Brunt, 2012, 2015a). Sokolow et al. (2014), write, "The individual begins to select-ively attend to his or her environment, filtering out material or information that doesn't line up with his or her beliefs. Stances begin to harden and crystalize" (p. 7). The individual holds a strong passion about their belief and subsequently filters out any data that does not support that belief. These views often include religion, politics, academic expectations, social justice, or relationships (Van Brunt et al., 2017; Van Brunt, 2016; NTAC, 2019). These views are beyond a strongly held belief and contain a passion and emotion that rejects other points of view or hardened ideological positions, and they are reinforced through other personal experiences and networks (Sageman, 2007).

    Roof planned and carried out an attack on June 17, 2015 at a Black church in Charleston, SC. (Appendix A: 27). He left a manifesto for his attack that explains his justification for his shooting (from Roof's writing in Appendix E),

    > *The event that truly awakened me was the Trayvon Martin case. I kept hearing and seeing his name, and eventually I decided to look him up. I read the Wikipedia article and right away I was unable to understand what the big deal was. It was obvious that Zimmerman was in the right. But more importantly this prompted me to type in the words "black on White crime" into Google, and I have never been the same since that day. The first web-site I came to was the Council of Conservative Citizens. There were pages upon pages of these brutal black on White murders. I was in disbelief. At this moment I realized that something was very wrong. How could the news be blowing up the Trayvon Martin case while hundreds of these black on White murders got ignored?*
    >
    > *I have no choice. I am not in the position to, alone, go into the ghetto and fight. I chose Charleston because it is most historic city in my state, and at one time had the highest ratio of blacks to Whites in the country. We have no skinheads, no real KKK, no one doing anything but talking on the internet. Well someone has to have the bravery to take it to the real world, and I guess that has to be me.*

3. ***Drivenness and a justification for violent action*** occur when someone is willing to commit violence for a cause (Deisinger et al., 2014; Meloy et al., 2011; USPS, 2007; ATAP, 2006; Turner & Gelles, 2003). Before committing violence,

74 *Assessing the Risk*

it is necessary for the individual to achieve a sense of peace and larger justification for their actions (Moghaddam, 2005). As a person moves toward violence, they experience moral disengagement and adherence to the mission where their target is depersonalized and dehumanized (O'Toole, 2002; O'Toole & Bowman, 2011; Van Brunt, 2012, 2015a). They experience a pervasive sense of anger and frustration toward the target and a driving desire for revenge (Pressman, 2009). They see violence as a natural consequence for an unjust enemy (Horgan, 2008; Pressman, 2009).

Dylan Klebold and Eric Harris, the Columbine shooters (Appendix A: 11), are prime examples of individuals motivated by a desire to spread a larger message of change. The unreleased footage of Klebold and Harris talking for hours about their desire to inspire other school shootings has been kept from public view (Gibbs & Roche, 1999).

On November 5, 2009, Major Nidal Hasan lowered his head for a few minutes in the cafeteria and then began shooting. A total of 214 rounds were fired from 20- and 30-round pistol magazines (he did not use the .357). He had an additional 177 rounds of unfired ammunition in his pockets. A local police officer shot Hasan five times and placed him in handcuffs. Hasan was a psychiatrist and often talked about Islam. Fellow students and faculty described Hasan as "disconnected," "aloof," "paranoid," "belligerent," and "schizoid." Hasan displayed little anxiety about his attack and saw his actions as justified given the nature of the unjust military action in Afghanistan (Owens, 2009). He shouted, "Allahu Akbar!" (God is greatest) prior to the shooting. He was said to be in contact with Islamic extremist Anwar al-Awlaki who preaches in his sermons, "I pray that Allah destroys America and all its allies."

4. ***Grievance or injustice collection*** is a common trait found in attackers. In their 2017 study, Gill et al. found just over half (56%) held a grievance against a particular person or entity. These grievances are often directed against those in power, who the attacker believes are responsible for real or imagined unfairness and difficulties. O'Toole described this individual as "a person who feels 'wronged,' 'persecuted' and 'destroyed,' blowing injustices way out of proportion, never forgiving the person they felt has wronged them" (O'Toole & Bowman, 2011, p. 186). An individual can have a grievance about almost anything.

Clay Duke saw the world as a negative place and, on December 14, 2010, held the school board hostage. He talked about revenge after his wife was fired. After firing two shots at a member of the school board, he shot himself as the SWAT team moved in. The entire shooting was caught on tape. It is reported he created a Facebook page with the information,

> *"My Testament: Some people (the government sponsored media) will say I was evil, a monster (V) ... no ... I was just born poor in a country where the Wealthy manipulate, use, abuse, and economically enslave 95% of the population. Rich Republicans, Rich Democrats ... same-same ... rich ... they take turns fleecing us ... our few dollars ... pyramiding the wealth for*

themselves. The 95% ... the us, in US of A, are the neo slaves of the Global South. Our Masters, the Wealthy, do, as they like to us ..." (Owens, 2010)

5. Most attackers are **suicidal** (NTAC, 2019; Lankford, 2013, 2018; ATAP, 2006; Dunkle et al., 2008; Lankford, 2010, 2013; Meloy et al., 2014; O'Toole, 2002; Randazzo & Plummer, 2009; Turner & Gelles, 2003; USPS, 2007; Vossekuil et al., 2002). In their most recent report, the National Threat Assessment Center (2019) found half of the attackers had shared or demonstrated behavior related to suicide or self-harm. Lankford (2018), reviewed several studies of attackers from 1974–2008 with 70–90% of the attackers experiencing suicidal thoughts or behaviors prior to their attack. Often, these individuals have feelings of indifference toward life, hopelessness, and lack of care about the future. They often feel disempowered, marginalized, misunderstood, and lost.

   In one of the earliest incel cases from 1938 (Appendix A: 1), Mutsuo Toi began participating in the practice of Yobai (night crawling), the ancient Japanese custom during which young men sneak into a woman's bedroom and, if she consents, they have intercourse. In rural Japan, it was a normal way to find a spouse. In 1937, he was diagnosed with tuberculosis and the women of the village began rejecting his sexual advantages. This led to feelings of isolation and loneliness. In his suicide notes, he wrote about the tuberculosis turning him into a social pariah. He decided to kill those who he felt had wronged him. On the evening on May 20, 1938, Toi cut the power to the village. He started his rampage around 1:30am by killing with grandmother so she wouldn't have to live with the shame of his actions. Over the next 90 minutes, he killed another 29 neighbors – approximately half the population of the village. He then shot and killed himself.

6. **Mental illness,** particularly related to thought disorders, depression, and bi-polar disorder (Van Brunt & Pescara-Kovach, 2019), is often an aggravating factor when assessing threat. Most attackers experienced psychological, behavioral, or developmental symptoms (NTAC, 2019). Given that half of attackers had received one or more mental health services prior to their attack, mental illness awareness is an important factor to assess, though not a replacement for a multidisciplinary threat assessment (NTAC, 2019). In their study of 115 attackers from 1990–2014, Gill et al. (2017) found 44% of the sample had a history of substance abuse and 41% had a diagnosed mental health disorder.

   While many risk factors for violence are associated with mental health conditions, they also occur in the absence of a diagnosis. This tendency to overstate mental illness as a causal factor is exacerbated when the media and the court of public opinion present sensationalized and unrelenting depictions of the attack where the attacker's mental illness is often given as a central cause (Van Brunt & Pescara-Kovach, 2019). In fact, those with diagnosed mental illness are more likely to be victims than perpetrators of crime (Desmarais et al., 2014; Teplin et al., 2005). So, while mental illness is a risk factor for predatory violence, like all risk factors, it should be seen in context rather than a singular factor.

76   *Assessing the Risk*

Douglas Pennington had been treated for mental illness. He purchased a .38-caliber handgun two days before the shooting. On September 2, 2006, he arrived at the college and shot and killed his two sons who were students there. He left behind notes in the car he drove to school and in a notebook at his home. He talked about his internal battles, his love for his family, and the feelings of guilt and pain that surrounded his life. "I see what I've done and I see what's coming for my family and I can't let that happen to them," he wrote in the notebook. "I lose anyway I turn, and so do they." (Associated Press, 2006). He mentions paranoid thoughts of his children being tortured and killed. Family members had previously attempted to have him hospitalized.

7. The *use of substances,* particularly those classified as stimulants, impacts decision making, may increase isolation and disengagement and reduces impulsive control. A history of drug or substance use has been connected to inappropriate ideation or behavior. Substances of enhanced concern are methamphetamines or amphetamines, cocaine, and alcohol (O'Toole & Bowman, 2011; USPS, 2007; ATAP, 2006; Turner & Gelles, 2003).

Anders Behring Breivik (Englund, 2011) set off a bomb killing eight people in Oslo, Norway before continuing onto Utoya and gunning down 69 youths at a labor party camp in July 2011. He claimed these events were marketing for his 1500-page manifesto outlining a coming war against the Muslims. The manifesto also included detailed plans on how to make bombs, obtain weapons, and a journal account of the months leading up to the shooting. In his manifesto, he writes,

> "A good training schedule in combination with a diet is the recipe for the desired results. You should really consider using steroids to reach your goal. There are many misconceptions related to the use of steroids but it is in fact the most logical approach. Not all people are motivated for strict training courses. Using stimulants can increase, not only your motivation but your agility, speed, strength and endurance by up to 200% depending on your current foundation."
> (Breivik Manifesto, 2011, p. 892)

8. A common risk factor for those who engage in predatory violence is a lack of desire/ability to understand different perspectives. A *lack of empathy and remorse for actions* is seen as an aggravating factor in a threat assessment. Most attackers were victims of bullying (NTAC, 2019), resulting in a focus on their safety, pain, and feelings that increases the risk of them disregarding the feelings, pain and safety of others. The individual may intimidate, act superior to others and/or display intolerance to individual differences (Van Brunt, 2012; ATAP, 2006; Turner & Gelles, 2003; O'Toole, 2002).

On September 9, 2001, Ferguson, a suspended security guard, killed five people and wounded two others during a 24-hour rampage through Sacramento (Appendix A: 13). Near the end of his attack, he took his supervisor hostage and forced him to record his confession (taken from the transcript in Appendix F),

> ***Ferguson:*** *Okay. It's recording. Okay. This will probably be the last time anyone actually ever hears from their talks to me unless for some reason*

they arrest me. My actions taken tonight are due from my distress. I have absolutely no love or can give a shit about Nina Susu.
Ferguson: *I shot that fucking bitch because I'm tired of people fucking with me in life. Been fucked over by my mother for 14 years because she raped me. I was turned around and fucked over by my uncle because he raped my brother and got away with it. Turn around and I have lived through all these fucking problems. Took two years of counseling. Did no fucking thing. Turned around and trusted a female and stuff by the name of Nina Susu went out with her for seven months. We do not have sexual relationship. All we did was fool around. I never slept with the woman once.*

9. When people are struggling, frustrated or overwhelmed, they engage in *fantasy rehearsals* that may involve them confronting, punishing and/or destroying the fixation and focus of their perceived injustices. This may involve them writing, drawing, creating content on social media and/or perseverating on the wrongs they perceived having been done to them. O'Neill et al. (2008) stress the importance of exploring these communications: "Writings, drawings, and other forms of individual expression reflecting violent fantasy and causing a faculty member to be fearful or concerned about safety, should be evaluated contextually for any potential threat" (pp. 32–33). O'Toole (2014) writes, "Mission-oriented shootings are hardly impulsive crimes. They are well-planned and can involve days, weeks, months, even years of making preparations and fantasizing about the crime" (p. 9).

On October 1, 2015, Harper-Mercer killed nine and injured seven others before shooting himself (Appendix A: 29). In his manifesto he writes about his impending attack (Appendix D),

I had no friends, no girlfriend, was all alone. I had no job, no life, no successes. What was it that was supposed to happen, what great event was it that was supposed to make me realize how much there was going for me. But for people like me there is another world, a darker world that welcomes us. For people like us this all that's left. My success in Hell is assured. They will give me the power that I seek. They have always been there, speaking to me on the sidelines, controlling me. It's only fit that I join them after death. They've told me what to do, showed me the way.

10. **Feelings of isolation and hopelessness** are often experienced by those who engage in predatory violence. Individuals may experience discrimination based on a marginalized status with little or no hope for a pathway to a better tomorrow (Sinai, 2005; 2012) or they may experience a lack of social or occupational opportunities at home, school or work (Schmid, 2013). They often experience longer term isolation and/or an inability to create or maintain sexual or intimate relationships with others (Van Brunt et al., 2017; O'Toole, 2002). The National Threat Assessment Center (2019) found nearly two-thirds of the attackers they studied either spoke about their sadness, depression, or loneliness, or these

78 *Assessing the Risk*

appeared through their behaviors. In terms of threat assessment, many of these individuals confided in others about their feelings or wrote about them online or in school assignments.

In February 1996, Barry Loukaitis killed three and injured one person at Frontier Middle School in Moose Lake, Washington. Loukaitis was severely bullied at school; he had his head shoved into toilets and was urinated on. His held a strong negative self-concept and saw his only chance at redemption through killing (Vaughan, 1998).

On June 17, 2015, Roof carried out an attack on a Black church in Charleston, SC (Appendix A: 27) and left a manifesto explaining his state of mind. From Roof's writing (Appendix E),

> *I have no choice. I am not in the position to, alone, go into the ghetto and fight. I chose Charleston because it is most historic city in my state, and at one time had the highest ratio of blacks to Whites in the country. We have no skinheads, no real KKK, no one doing anything but talking on the internet. Well someone has to have the bravery to take it to the real world, and I guess that has to be me.*

11. An individual may experience ***marginalization*** as they interact with their peers or the community at large. These feelings of marginalization may be based on social factors, ethnic or racial differences, cultural dissimilarities, or diverse gender expression (Langman, 2009; Lankford, 2013; Sue, 2010). These feelings often lead to experiences of discrimination that result in a perceived threat to those they identify with, causing a sense of moral outrage (Bhui et al., 2012; Sageman, 2007). Although many people may feel marginalized, treated unfairly, discriminated against, and unengaged in society, only a small number of these move toward violence to express these frustrations or to bring about change or punish others.

    On April 7, 2011, Wellington Menezes de Oliveira shot 32 students in Tasso da Silveira school, killing 12, before committing suicide. In a video explaining his attacks posted days before the shooting, he says,

    > "The struggle for which many brothers died in the past, and for which I will die, is not solely because of what is known as bullying. Our fight is against cruel people, cowards, who take advantage of the kindness, the weakness of people unable to defend themselves."
    >
    > (Barnes, 2011)

    On March 25, 1994, Brian Head shot and killed himself during his high school economics class at Etowah High School (Headley, 1994). Head had been a longtime target for bullies because of his weight and thick glasses. His father, Bill, subsequently successfully lobbied for a law that criminalized bullying and required schools to alert parents of bullied children.

12. ***Fascination with violence*** (O'Toole, 2002; NTAC, 2019; Mohandie, 2014) is present in approximately half of those who escalate toward predatory violence.

Identifying the Risk Factors 79

When assessing violence risk, it is important to explore whether the subject has a preoccupation or fixation on violent topics, how this may negatively impact them, and where the interest originated. This may include drawing violent pictures, instructions on how to kill, keeping a journal, writing assignments or social media posts with attack themes, following or quoting past attackers, watching videos of animals being killed, discussing or holding a fascination with Hitler, or an obsession with weapons. When these are discovered in written content, further information gathering and a more detailed assessment should be conducted and seen within the context of what is beyond a normal interest (NTAC, 2019; Van Brunt, 2012, 2015a; Meloy et al., 2011).

Brenda Spencer's nihilistic outlook contributed to her attack on January 29, 1979. She fired out of a window by her home, randomly shooting at students across the street. She killed two and injured nine. The prior Christmas her father had given her a semi-automatic .22 rifle. During the attack, a reporter called her house trying to interview neighbors who might know something. She told him she was the shooter and "I just did it for the fun of it. I don't like Mondays. This livens up the day. I have to go now. I shot a pig [policeman] I think and I want to shoot more. I'm having too much fun [to surrender]." She also said, "I had no reason for it, and it was just a lot of fun," "It was just like shooting ducks in a pond," and, "[The children] looked like a herd of cows standing around; it was really easy pickings." After firing 30 rounds, she barricaded herself in the house for seven hours before surrendering. According to reports, she had mentioned the possibility of the attacks months earlier, saying "One of these mornings, you're gonna look for me," "no one understands me," and "you don't have to wait very long to see what is going on with me." She had previously broken windows in the school with her BB gun (Jones, 1998).

13. The ***desire for fame*** and to make a mark on the world is present in many of the predatory violence cases in the recent years. In his writing, Lankford (2016) explores 24 cases of offenders who explicitly stated that they wanted attention and fame and/or directly contacted media organizations to get it. These were often the deadliest offenders. Those struggling with frustration at being bullied or marginalized by society often seek attention to right this perceived wrong (Bhui et al., 2012; Sageman, 2007). An example of this was found on the Parkland (Appendix A: 38) attacker's cell phone. In a video explaining his coming actions, he says, "With the power of my AR, you will know who I am" (Ovalle & Nehamas, 2018). As with suicidal terrorists, mass shooters "produce martyrdom videos, murals, calendars, key chains, posters, postcards, and pennants with the names and photos of past suicide terrorists, they show potential participants that committing a suicide attack is a path to fame and glory" (Lankford, 2018, p. 6).

On November 12, 1966, Robert Smith took seven people hostage at Rose-Mar College of Beauty (Appendix A: 2), a school for training beauticians. His plan was to bind the women, tie plastic bags over their heads, and watch them while they suffocated. The bags turned out to be too small. Smith instead ordered the hostages to lie down on the floor in a circle. He then proceeded to shoot them in the head with a .22-caliber pistol. Four women and a three-year-old girl

80 *Assessing the Risk*

died, one woman and a baby were injured but survived. Police arrested Smith after the massacre. Smith had reportedly admired Richard Speck (who killed eight women in 1966) and Charles Whitman (the clock tower gunman in Texas). Smith announced, "I wanted to get known, just wanted to get myself a name." During his childhood he was teased in school for his lack of coordination and developed an interest in serial killers and mass murders. He was sentenced to two 99-year sentences and four life sentences for the murder.

14. On the pathway toward violence, an increasing ***objectification and depersonalization*** is part of the escalation (Van Brunt, 2012; 2015a). Grossman (1996) discussed these phenomena related to military training in his book *On Killing*. He argued that soldiers are loathe to kill, yet this aversion has been overridden through sophisticated methods. In writing and social media posts, this may manifest as a negative view or dehumanization of the target. This language may be hostile, insulting, diminishing, misogynistic, or focused on separating the author from their target (Van Brunt, 2016).

Poulin (Appendix A: 3) raped and killed a fellow classmate in his home and subsequently burned his own house to the ground. He then arrived at his high school and killed one and injured five others with a shotgun. Poulin was born with a chest deformity and eyesight problems that prevented him from becoming a pilot. During his childhood, he was shy and had difficulty socially. It is reported he had an addiction to pornography, often experienced depression, and was suicidal. He trained in a Canadian militia and learned combat skills.

He kept a diary outlining his plans to burn down his parents' home and make them suffer. He also wrote, "I don't want to die before I have had the pleasure of fucking some girl." During the rape and subsequent stabbing and murder of his classmate, he had gone upstairs from his basement bedroom and had a peanut butter sandwich with his mother (Cobb & Avery, 1977).

Another case involves Luke Woodham (Appendix A: 9). On October 1, 1997, the 16-year-old stabbed and beat his sleeping mother before taking her car and driving to Pearl High School. He wore an orange jumpsuit and a trench coat. He carried a .30–caliber rifle. He fatally shot his former girlfriend and one of her friends, and injured the nearby band instructor. He wounded seven others before the assistant principal subdued him with a .45 from his desk. Woodham was attempting to leave to go to the Pearl Junior High School to continue shooting. The assistant principal asked, "Why did you shoot my kids?" He responded with, "Life wronged me, sir" (Chua-Eoan & Monroe, 1997; Hewitt & Harmes, 1997).

Woodham planned the shooting with six other friends who were in a satanic cult called "the Kroth." In his manifesto, he writes,

> "I am not insane! I am angry. This world has shit on me for the final time. I am not spoiled or lazy, for murder is not weak and slow-witted, murder is gutsy and daring. I killed because people like me are mistreated every day. I did this to show society 'push us and we will push back!' I suffered all my life. No one ever truly loved me. No one ever truly cared about me."

Environmental Factors

An extreme sense of loss and hopelessness often follows a *catalyst event*. These events may include the loss of a job, death of a friend or family member, parental divorce, experiences of domestic abuse, drug use, criminal charges, and failure to achieve an academic goal such as passing a critical test or losing the ability to study in a program. As with a catalyst in a chemical reaction, these perceived catastrophic events speed up and focus the attack plan. In attackers studied (NTAC, 2019), simply having a bad experience or series of bad experiences should not be seen as predictive of a future attack.

It is common for attackers to *experience teasing and bullying* prior to an attack (Van Brunt, 2012; 2015). Bullying is a problem faced by students and continues to be identified as a factor in NTAC's research on targeted violence in schools, with most of the attackers in their 2019 study being bullied, often as part of a persistent pattern which lasted for weeks, months, or years. They define bullying as "unwanted, aggressive behavior among school-aged children with an intent to do physical, social, or emotional harm; which involves a real or perceived power imbalance; and is, or could be, repeated" (NATC, 2019, p. 33). This can occur in various ways, including verbal, physical, social, property, and cyber. About 1/3 of attackers in their study engaged in bullying behavior themselves.

As an encompassing phrase, *free fall* captures a wide range of difficulties the attacker experiences in their community, school, work, primary support group, and/or social circle. Examples of this would include chronic unemployment, a financial crisis, death of a loved one, problems adjusting to a new life circumstance such as an adjustment to a new school, dismissal from an academic program or internship, the sudden loss of a job, or a sense of blocked upward mobility based on their personal characteristics such as race, ethnicity, religious beliefs, or appearance (Bhui et al., 2012; Schmid, 2013; Travis, 2008). Individuals experiencing this increase collection of stressors often feel little hope for improvement. As problems occur in families and conflicts in the home, academic, legal, or disciplinary actions, or other personal issues, they become increasingly overwhelmed.

A *decrease in academic or work progress* would be an additional aggravating risk factor, particularly after a period of doing well. There are a number of other behaviors providing an understanding of the offender's behavioral background. Gill et al. (2017) write,

> 63% experienced long-term stress. Examples of this include academic frustration stemming from learning disorders; difficulty maintaining employment and failure in business ventures; disabling injuries from automobile and work accidents; long-term financial debts; a range of mental health issues including depression, bipolar disorder, and post-traumatic stress disorder; being a victim of sexual/physical abuse in childhood; an inability to establish appropriate social relationships; and long-lasting discord in marriages and romantic relationships.
> (p. 711)

As with other factors, simply experiencing difficulties in life does not turn one into a mass shooter. When assessing threat, the BIT/CARE team should gather

82   *Assessing the Risk*

information about the stressors, how the subject is experiencing them, and if there are additional stressors in their past that are still impacting them, and then balance this with how their current supports are functioning. Simply put, stress is manageable when the individual has the supports and scaffolding needed while returning to balance (NTAC, 2018).

Increases in ***social isolation***, particularly as a result of teasing and bullying, are an additional risk factor (Sokolow et al., 2019; Van Brunt, 2012, 2015a, 2015b; O'Toole, 2002). In their study Gill et al. (2017) found that 75% of attackers spoke about their sadness, depression, or loneliness, or appeared through their observable behaviors to be experiencing these feelings. Some attackers confided in others about their feelings or wrote about them online or in school assignments. Bystanders also observed the attackers isolating themselves, withdrawing from others, appearing sad, or crying.

Moving Forward

This chapter has offered a detailed exploration of common risk factors and threat assessment terms. These have been well researched in the risk and threat assessment community and applied here with examples from the incel cases provided in Appendix A. Chapter 8 reviews the stabilizing influences, or "the other side of the playground teeter-totter," that should be taken in context with the risk factors.

Discussion Questions

- What are some examples of both affective violence and predatory violence that you have witnessed (hint: the predatory or mission oriented may be easier to come up with if you consider lower threshold aggression like getting someone back after a period of time for how they treated you)?
- What are some additional environmental events or groups that could negatively impact an individual?
- Think about some factors that would take down the risk of violence rather than raising it, like these risk factors. What might some of these be?
- Why do you think the motivation for fame is a risk factor for mission-oriented violence? Do you think this has gotten worse as television and social media has grown?
- Discuss some ways to limit fame-seeking as a motivation in relation to mass shootings.

References

Associated Press. (2006). Father shoots 2 sons, self at Sheppard College. September 2. www.msnbc.com

Association of Threat Assessment Professionals (ATAP). (2006). *Risk Assessment Guideline Elements for Violence (RAGE-V): Considerations for Assessing the Risk of Future Violent Behavior.* Sacramento: ATAP.

Barnes, T. (2011). Brazil shooting said to be first school massacre in nation's history. *Christian Science Monitor*, April 7.

Bhui, K., Hicks, M., Lashley, M., and Jones, E. (2012). A public health approach to understanding and preventing violent radicalization. *BMC Medicine*, 10, 16.

Breivik Manifesto. (2011). Retrieved on May 17, 2020, from www.kevinislaughter.com/wp-content/uploads/2083++A+European+Declaration+of+Independence.pdf

Calhoun, F. and Weston, S. (2009). *Threat Assessment and Management Strategies: Identifying the Howlers and Hunters*. Boca Raton: CRC Press.

Chua-Eoan, H. and Monroe, S. (1997). Mississippi gothic. *Time*, 16, 54.

Cobb, C. and Avery, B. (1977). *The Rape of a Normal Mind. Markham*. Ontario: Paper Jacks.

Cornell, D. (2010). Threat assessment in the college setting. www.changemag.org, *Change Magazine* (January/February), 9–15.

Deisinger, E., Randazzo, M., and Nolan, J. (2014). Threat assessment and management in higher education: Enhancing the standard of care in the academy. In J.R. Meloy and J. Hoffmann (eds.), *The International Handbook of Threat Assessment* (pp. 107–125). New York: Oxford University Press.

Desmarais, S., Van Dorn, R., Johnson, L., Grimm, K., Douglas, K., and Swartz, M. (2014). Community violence perpetration and victimization among adults with mental illnesses. *American Journal of Public Health*, 104, 2342–2349.

Dunkle, J.H., Silverstein, Z.B., and Warner, S.L. (2008). Managing violent and other troubling students: The role of threat assessment teams on campus. *Journal of College and University Law*, 34 (3), 585–636.

Englund, W. (2011). In diary, Norwegian "crusader" details months of preparation for attacks. *The Washington Post*, August 9.

Headley, S. (1994). Classroom suicide. *Education Week*, 13(2), 4.

Fein, R., Vossekuil, B., and Holden, G. (1995). *Threat Assessment: An Approach to Targeted Violence: National Institute of Justice in Action*. Washington, DC: National Institute of Justice.

Gibbs, N. and Roche, T. (1999). The Columbine tapes. *Time Magazine*, December 20.

Gill, P., Silver, J., Horgan, J., and Corner, E. (2017). Shooting alone: The pre-attack experiences and behaviors of U.S. solo mass murderers. *Journal of Forensic Sciences*, May, 62(3), 710–714.

Grossman, D. (1996). *On Killing: The Psychological Cost of Learning to Kill in War and Society*. Lebanon: Little, Brown, and Company Back Bay Books.

Grossman, D. and Siddle, B. (2000). Psychological effects of combat. In *Encyclopedia of Violence, Peace and Conflict*. UK: Academic Press.

Hart, S. and Logan, C. (2011). Formulation of violence risk using evidence-based assessment: The structured professional judgment approach. In P. Sturmey and M. McMurran (eds.), *Forensic Case Formulation* (pp. 83–106). Chichester: Wiley-Blackwell.

Hart, S., Sturmey, P., Logan, C., and McMuran, M. (2011). Forensic case formulation. *International Journal of Forensic Mental Health*, 10, 118–126.

Hewitt, B. and Harmes, J. (1997). The avenger. *People*, 48(18), 116.

Horgan, J. (2008). From profiles to pathways and roots to routes: Perspectives from psychology on radicalization into terrorism. *The Annals of American Academy of Political and Social Science*, 618, 80–94.

Horgan, J., Shorland, N., Abbasciano, S., and Walsh, S. (2016). Actions speak louder than words: A behavioral analysis of 183 individuals convicted for terrorist offenses in the United States from 1995 to 2012. *Journal of Forensic Sciences*, 61, 1228–1237.

Howard, P. (1999). *The Owner's Manual for the Brain: Everyday Applications from Mind-Brain Research*, 2nd edn. Austin: Bard Press.

Jones, T. (1998). Look back in sorrow. *Good Housekeeping*, 227(5), 118.

84 *Assessing the Risk*

Langman, P. (2009). Rampage school shooters: A typology. *Aggression Violent Behavior*, 14, 79–86.

Lankford, A. (2010). *Human Killing Machines: Systematic Indoctrination in Iran, Nazi Germany, Al Qaeda, and Abu Ghraib*. Boston: Lexington Press.

Lankford, A. (2013). *The Myth of Martyrdom: What Really Drives Suicide Bombers, Rampage Shooters, and Other Self-Destructive Killers*. New York: Palgrave Macmillan.

Lankford, A. (2016). Fame-seeking rampage shooters: Initial findings and empirical predictions. *Aggression and Violent Behavior*, 27, 122–129.

Lankford, A. (2018). Identifying potential mass shooters and suicide terrorists with warning signs of suicide, perceived victimization, and desires for attention or fame. *Journal of Personality Assessment*, 5, 1–12.

Meloy, J. (2000). *Violence Risk and Threat Assessment: A Practical Guide for Mental Health and Criminal Justice Professionals*. San Diego: Specialized Training Services.

Meloy, J. (2006). The empirical basis and forensic application of affective and predatory violence. *Australian and New Zealand Journal of Psychiatry*, 40, 539–547.

Meloy, J. and O'Toole, M. (2011). The concept of leakage in threat assessment. *Behavioral Sciences and the Law*, 29(4), 513–527.

Meloy, J., Hoffmann, J., Guldimann, A., and James, D. (2011). The role of warning behaviors in threat assessment: An exploration and suggested typology. *Behavioral Sciences and the Law*, 30, 256–279.

Meloy, R., Hoffmann, J., Roshdi K, et al. (2014). Warning behaviors and their configurations across various domains of targeted violence. In J.R. Meloy and J. Hoffmann (eds.), *The International Handbook of Threat Assessment* (pp. 39–53). New York: Oxford University Press.

Moghaddam, F. (2005). The staircase to terrorism: A psychological exploration. *The American Psychologist*, 60, 161–169.

Mohandie, K. (2014). Threat assessment in schools. In J.R. Meloy and J. Hoffman (eds.), *The International Handbook of Threat Assessment* (pp. 126–147). New York: Oxford University Press.

National Institute of Mental Health (NIMH). (2017). Suicide prevention. Retrieved from www.nimh.nih.gov/health/topics/suicide-prevention/index.shtml

National Threat Assessment Center (NTAC). (2018). *Enhancing School Safety Using a Threat Assessment Model: An Operational Guide for Preventing Targeted School Violence*. US Secret Service, Department of Homeland Security.

National Threat Assessment Center (NTAC). (2019). *Protecting America's Schools: A United States Secret Service Analysis of Targeted School Violence*. United States Secret Service, Department of Homeland Security.

O'Neill, D., Fox, J., Depue, R., and Englander, E. (2008). *Campus Violence Prevention and Response: Best Practices for Massachusetts Higher Education*. Applied Risk Management, LLC.

O'Toole, M.E. (2002). *The School Shooter: A Threat Assessment Perspective*. Quantico: FBI.

O'Toole, M.E. (2014). The mission-oriented shooter: A new type of mass killer. *Journal of Violence and Gender*, 1(1), 9–10.

O'Toole, M.E. and Bowman, A. (2011). *Dangerous Instincts: How Gut Feelings Betray*. New York: Hudson Street Press.

Ovalle, D. and Nehamas, N. (2018). "You're all going to die." Nikolas Cruz made cellphone videos plotting Parkland attack. Retrieved on December 7, 2019 from www.miamiherald.com/news/local/community/broward/article212199899.html

Owens, R. (2009, November 5). Fort Hood shooting. ABCNews. Retrieved from http://abcnews.go.com/Archives/video/nov-2009-fort-hoodshooting-14884777

Owens, R. (2010). School board shootout. Nightline (ABC), 1.

Pollack, W., Modzeleski, W., and Rooney, G. (2008*). Prior Knowledge of Potential School-Based Violence: Information Students Learn May Prevent a Targeted Attack.* Washington, DC: United States Secret Service and United States Department of Education.

Pressman, D. (2009). *Risk Assessment Decisions for Violent Political Extremism.* Ottawa: Her Majesty the Queen in Right of Canada.

Randazzo, M. and Plummer, E. (2009). *Implementing Behavioral Threat Assessment on Campus: A Virginia Tech Demonstration Project.* Blacksburg: Virginia Polytechnic Institute and State University.

Rodger, E. (2014). My twisted world. Retrieved on May 3, 2020 from https://assets. documentcloud.org/documents/1173619/rodger-manifesto.pdf

Sageman, M. (2007). *Radicalization of Global Islamist Terrorists.* United States Senate Committee on Homeland Security and Governmental Affairs. Retrieved on December 7, 2019 from www.hsgac.senate.gov/download/062707sageman

Scalora, M., Simons, A., and Vansly, S. (2010, February). *Campus Safety: Assessing and Managing Threats (FBI Law Enforcement Bulletin).* Washington, DC: Federal Bureau of Investigation.

Schmid, A.P. (2013). Radicalisation, de-radicalisation, counter-radicalisation: A conceptual discussion and literature review. *The International Centre for Counter-Terrorism-The Hague* 4, 2. Retrieved on March 26, 2020 from https://icct.nl/publication/radicalisation-de-radicalisation-counterradicalisation-a-conceptual-discussion-and-literature-review

Sinai, J. (2005). A conceptual framework for resolving terrorism's root causes. In The Root Causes of Terrorism: Myths, Reality and WaysForward. T Bjorgo, ed.(Routledge, London).

Sinai, J. (2012). Radicalisation into extremism and terrorism. *Intelligencer Journal of U.S. Intelligence Studies*, 19, Summer/Fall.

Sokolow, B.A., Lewis, W.S., Van Brunt, B., Schuster, S., and Swinton, D. (2014). *The Book on BIT*, 2nd edn. Berwyn: The National Behavioral Intervention Team Association.

Sokolow, B., Van Brunt, B., Lewis, W., Schiemann, M., Murphy, A., and Molnar, J. (2019). *The NaBITA Risk Rubric.* King of Prussia: The National Behavioral Intervention Team Association.

Sue, D. (2010). *Microaggressions in Everyday Life: Race, Gender, and Sexual Orientation.* Hoboken: John Wiley & Sons.

Teplin, L., McClelland, G., Abram, K., and Weiner, D. (2005). Crime victimization in adults with severe mental illness: Comparison with the National Crime Victimization Survey. *Archives of General Psychiatry*, 62, 911–921.

Travis, A. (2008). MI5 report challenges views on terrorism in Britain. *Guardian*, 20, 558–579.

Turner, J. and Gelles, M. (2003). *Threat Assessment: A Risk Management Approach.* New York: Routledge.

United States Postal Service (USPS). (2007). *Threat Assessment Team Guide*, Retrieved on November 30, 2019 from www.nalc.org/workplace-issues/resources/manuals/pub108.pdf

Van Brunt, B. (2012). *Ending Campus Violence: New Approaches to Prevention.* New York: Routledge.

Van Brunt, B. (2015a). *Harm to Others: The Assessment and Treatment of Dangerousness.* Alexander: American Counseling Association.

Van Brunt, B. (2015b). Violence risk assessment of the written word (VRAW^2). *Journal of Behavioral Intervention Teams (JBIT)*, 3, 12–25.

Van Brunt, B. (2016). Assessing threat in written communications, social media, and creative writing. *The Journal of Violence and Gender*, 3(2), 78–88.

Van Brunt, B. and Pescara-Kovach, P. (2019). Debunking the myths: Mental illness and mass shootings. *Journal of Violence and Gender*, 6(1), 53–63.

86 *Assessing the Risk*

Van Brunt, B., Murphy, A., and Zedginidze, A. (2017). An exploration of the risk, protective, and mobilization factors related to violent extremism in college populations. *Violence and Gender*, 4(3), 81–101.

Vaughan, S. (1998). What makes children kill? *Harper's Bazaar*, 3442, 546.

Vossekuil, B., Fein, R., Reddy, M., Borum, R., and Modzeleski, W. (2002). *The Final Report and Findings of the Safe School Initiative: Implications for the Prevention of School Attacks in the United States.* Washington, DC: US Secret Service and US Department of Education.

8   Identifying Stabilizing Influences

In the previous chapter, we explored the risk factors that elevate our concerns when assessing the potential for targeted violence. These factors should be assessed with an awareness of the stabilizing influences that help reduce the risk for escalation of violence. The Centers for Disease Control and Prevention (CDC) defines these protective factors as

> individual or environmental characteristics, conditions, or behaviors that reduce the effects of stressful life events. These stabilizing influences also increase an individual's ability to avoid risks or hazards and promote social and emotional competence to thrive in all aspects of life, now and in the future.
> (Center for Disease Control and Prevention [CDC], 2018, para. 2)

The research on these stabilizing influences is not extensive as the research on risk factors; however, there are some organizations and researchers that have begun to address these (O'Toole, 2002; Van Brunt et al., 2017; National Threat Assessment Center [NTAC], 2018; Sokolow et al., 2019). A helpful table of the most common stabilizing influences is provided below in Table 8.1.

Stabilizing influences provide a framework for prevention programs and initiatives related to targeted violence. By increasing and enhancing existing stabilizing influences, we reduce the risk of targeted violence. This helps push the incel to move off the pathway of violence by scaffolding them with harm reduction strategies, building increased connection and supporting non-violent attitudes and behaviors.

Stabilizing Influences

There are seven stabilizing influences highlighted in this chapter. These are outlined first in Table 8.2 for increased clarity. These influences help support the at-risk individual moving away from an increasingly violent ideology and undergirds their movement toward more socially adaptive and positive outlooks regarding women, dating, relationships and sex. For each of the seven sections, there are reflective questions included at the end to further explore these concepts in regard to an incel (see tables 8.3–8.9; 8.11).

The overview of stabilizing influences in this chapter forms the therapeutic base for shifting the incel away from their negative and ultimately self-destructive view

88   *Assessing the Risk*

Table 8.1 Stabilizing influences that reduce incel violence

Social support	Empathy to others	School engagement	Religious supports
Family support	Perspective taking	Work engagement	Non-violent outlets
Positive outlook	Intimate relationship	Positive self-esteem	Problem solving
Limited lethal means	Knowledge of self	Consequence aware	Emotional stability
Social/political safety	Housing stability	Resiliency	Lacks reactivity

Table 8.2 Summary of stabilizing influences for targeted violence

Stabilizing factor	*Descriptions*
Environmental and emotional stability	An individual's life experiences have consistency and constancy, and their reactions to change or crisis represent a similar calm and resilience.
Social health and relationships	They have stability in relationships with family, friends, and significant others.
Access to non-violent outlets	Individuals have opportunities for positive collective action on issues and concerns instead of turning to violence.
Empathy and connection	The empathetic or compassionate person demonstrates the ability to consider other's perspectives or other's ideals without seeing them as challenging or competitive to their own beliefs.
Positive social and individual action	There is a focus on the betterment of a group or community and an awareness of how their choices result in positive or negative consequence.
Positive masculinity	There is a healthy awareness of masculinity and an openness to a variety of possible masculinities that provide a foundation to improve self-worth and value with a positive view of the feminist perspective.
Affirmative sexuality	Sexuality and sexual behavior are consent based and equitable between those involved.

of themselves and women. These are discussed in detail using the case studies found in Chapters 11, 12, and 13. To reduce risk of violence, it is exactly these stabilizing influences that should be increased, while simultaneously mitigating the risk factors outlined in Chapter 7.

Environmental and Emotional Stability

Environmental and emotional stability occur when an individual's life experiences have consistency and constancy and help them react to disappointment, loss and grief with support, calm and resilience. In the incel's life, their supports help pull them toward positive movement and reject violence as a reasonable response to stress and crisis events (Van Brunt et al., 2017). These supports and the emotional health of the person reduce destabilizing, dramatic shifts in their environment, offer financial security through stable employment and future career potential through

Identifying Stabilizing Influences 89

Table 8.3 Reflective questions for environmental and emotional stability

- Does he have a positive view of himself?
- Is he optimistic about the future around finding a woman and reaching his goals?
- What does he do to reduce the stress and sadness of a perceived loss?
- How does he seek help from others when upset?
- If he has more serious mental illness, is there a willingness to seek help and does he have the resources needed to access mental health support and/or treatment?

academic enrollment. They are engaged in either professional or academic arenas, and reduction of potential catalyst events such as recent terminations or suspensions. The family and home environment are stable and beneficial. They are connected to friends and are successful in their academic or professional goals.

Certainly, we've all had ups and downs in our personal lives and support systems, however, those with *environmental and emotional stability* recover more quickly and have an air of resiliency when faced with loss, frustration, or crisis. Imagine a dating relationship where a person is rejected; perhaps a partner breaks up with them for a more attractive or successful partner. "Competent and adequate professional supervision and control will ... influence the degree of risk for exposure to destabilizing factors" (Borum et al., 1999, p. 334). While this event is disappointing and upsetting, it does not escalate to a perceived injustice or an inspiration for revenge against their ex.

The first part of assessing an individual's environmental and emotional stabilizing influences is an analysis of how they react to a specific stressor. While there may be an initial spike in their reaction, this reaction to short-term instability is less concerning than those who hold onto past wrongs and seek revenge for how they were mistreated by women. After the initial frustration, their emotions should stabilize with support from those around them. This is easier to achieve when they have stability of their emotions. This emotional stability is improved when there is a corresponding *psychological steadiness* and well-being (Pressman, 2009).

Social Health and Relationships

Stability in relationships with family, friends, and significant others provides support to the incel and helps re-direct impulsive actions. When an individual feel *socially connected in healthy and positive ways*, they feel safe in their own skin rather than feeling marginalized or discriminated against based on their identity or identity group. There is a level of social connection and health when friends offer support and caring, increase their feelings of acceptance, and refrain from judgment regarding non-violent beliefs toward others. The National Threat Assessment Center (2018) supports the importance of relationships without judgment and access to positive support and direction when an at-risk person is experiencing overwhelming stress. For example, developing *positive and trusting relationships* allows the potential incel to share their frustrations and think critically about problem solving. We all can relate to experiences of social conflict or intense, disquieting thoughts. In those times, it often our relationships with others that assist us overcoming these challenges and feel supported.

90 *Assessing the Risk*

Table 8.4 Reflective questions for social health and relationships

- Does he have friends and peers he feels content with in his life?
- Is he able to make new friends and join with others easily?
- What expectations does he place on these friendships and relationships?
- How does he go about seeking a romantic or intimate relationship? What expectations does he have about the ease or difficulty obtaining this?
- When he is faced with difficulty, does he stop and try a different approach or become despondent and hopeless that his desires are forever outside of his grasp?

At the heart of the incel problem is a deep sense of isolation and hopelessness at the prospect of obtaining the things that everyone else seems to so easily obtain. This idea is often exacerbated when a person watches the lives lived by others on platforms such as Facebook and experiences a "fear of missing out" (FOMO) (Przybylski et al., 2013). Hogan (2015) writes about this danger when looking at others and making assumptions about their lives via the social media platform, "These negative consequences are, in turn, related to and significantly aggravate increased unfair judgements of others, change in personality, paranoia, jealousy and decreases in concentration" (p. 2). For the incel, seeing others *successfully navigating relationships* with seeming ease clearly exacerbates the intensity of their negative experiences.

Successful dating and intimate relationships rarely occur in an easy straight line. While some certainly have an easier time than others, the difficulty arises when a person makes an assumption that something that is difficult equates to something that is impossible. In cognitive behavioral psychology, this concept is referred to as catastrophizing (Ellis, 2007). Here, the person takes an unfortunate occurrence and incorrectly makes the assumption that this will always be the way things are and experiences hopelessness at the prospect of new outcomes. While having a spouse, girlfriend/boyfriend, or partner(s) can be of tremendous positive support in person's life, these relationships are rarely obtained easily and often take significant work to maintain and keep running well.

Access to Non-Violent Outlets

A key stabilizing influence to offset a person's frustrations, anger and desperation can be through non-violent ways to express their dissatisfaction. *Access to these non-violent outlets* provides the incel potential solutions to talk about their concerns with others rather than turning to violence (United Nations Educational, Scientific and Cultural Organization, 2016). For many, the expression of frustration has a stabilizing effect and allows them to (1) release their anger through venting and (2) experience relief by redirecting their energy to a more productive outlet that can bring about change. Having access to alternative, non-violent courses of action is an important way people manage their sadness and anger when life events occur that trigger or upset them.

Consider a person frustrated by a comment about being overweight that then pushes the person to start an exercise routine or change their diet. Rather than spiraling into a depression and becoming angry, they take that energy and use it in

Identifying Stabilizing Influences 91

Table 8.5 Reflective questions for access to non-violent outlets

- How does he handle the aftermath of rejection or difficulty approaching women?
- Is he able to find a place where he can talk about his concerns with friends or family?
- Does he make use of positive, online resources, religious groups or therapy?
- Does he view difficulty and aversity as overwhelming or as obstacles in his path?
- What are some ways he has overcome difficult challenges in the past?

a more positive manner or vent to a friend in order to dissipate the negative impact. Similarly, when a large percentage of the nation was upset at the 2016 presidential election results, many channeled this into attending the Women's March and March for Our Lives (a rally for gun restrictions following the Parkland shooting). Rather than turning to negative emotions that could spiral toward hopelessness and hatred, they accessed non-violent means to redirect negative events.

In martial arts, the concept of a circular, redirecting style of fighting can be found in Kung-Fu and Aikido rather than a more linear, force-meeting style such as Taekwondo. The force is redirected rather then met directly with equal or greater force. For the incel, the non-violent outlet could be finding ways to overcome the difficulty around dating or forming relationships through therapy, role-playing, and solution-focused discussions to find ways to be more successful. Providing a safe space to communicate their negative attitudes toward women or rage at those who obtain sexual relationships denied to the incel creates opportunities to express their frustration rather than resorting to violence.

Empathy and Connection

In the previous chapter, we discussed objectification and depersonalization as risk factors for violence. Here, the stabilizing influence that reduces these escalating, dangerous perspectives is the development of ***empathy or compassion***. Empathy means seeing the world through another person's eyes, understanding from their perspective. It begins with a willingness to put your needs as a person aside and focus instead on how another person views those around them. An empathetic and compassionate person demonstrates the ability to consider other's perspectives or other's ideals without seeing them as challenging or competitive to their own beliefs. When teachers, counselors, and educators demonstrate empathy to those they help, we teach this skill to them. As the humanistic psychologist Carl Rogers (1961) put it, "An empathetic way of being can be learned from empathetic persons" (p. 150). For the incel, teaching them this tolerance and appreciation of diverse perspectives allows for a more empathetic and compassionate view of other's suffering, pain, and frustrations. By helping the incel better understand that, they gain an understanding of people who live differently than them, engaging with other cultures and confronting their own biases, as well as learning to listen to other's perspectives and collaborating with them (Priddy, 2018).

Interventions in concerning situations can potentially act to support an increase in empathy, and a decrease in mistrust, deception, and manipulation (Chialant et al., 2016). Several competency areas have been identified related to the development of

92 *Assessing the Risk*

Table 8.6 Techniques to build rapport

Smiling. This is a universal gesture of goodwill regardless of culture, nationality, or religion. Research indicates that individuals who receive a smile from another feel accepted and not judged.

Listening carefully. Most people do not listen to each other in an open and patient manner. If the interviewer is attentive, is nonjudgmental, and shows interest in other people, a very positive emotional dynamic will be put in place, even if the interviewee is very distrustful and hates what the interviewer represents (e.g., the Federal Bureau of Investigation, Americans, infidels).

Finding something in common. Identify a characteristic that is shared between the interviewer and interviewee and point that out. It could be marriage, a child, a common geographical area visited, a certain amount of education, or interest in a certain sport. Find it and say it.

Mirroring the interviewee. This refers to mimicking the interviewee's body language and words, which takes attention and practice. If it is done too obviously, it will be noticed and rapport will not arise. It may mean sitting the same way, making similar gestures, using some of the same words, even using similar emotional tones of voice.

Avoiding blunders. Allowing the soles of one's shoes to face another person is considered an insult in the Arabic culture. Displaying a cold and unfriendly demeanor is considered an insult. Conveying impatience, such as glancing at one's watch or tapping one's fingers on the table, is considered an insult. Certain gestures may be an insult. Study the culture and know what the blunders are (Nydell, 1996).

Table 8.7 Reflective questions for empathy and connection

- What is his experience guessing at what others are feeling around him on issues less intensive then dating, sex, and relationships (e.g., video game system preference)?
- Is he able to listen to perspectives that differ greatly from his without seeing this as threatening what his autonomy to believe what he does?
- Is he willing to explore how women may feel about sex and relationships?
- Does he have connections with people who are different in terms of race, ethnicity, wealth, experience, politics, or religion?
- Where are some places where he learned to think about larger social concepts, such as religion, politics, wealth, and travel?

empathy in others (Borba, 2018). These include the ability to read emotions, or emotional literacy. Other competencies include self-regulation and being able to keep our emotions in check as well as moral courage and the desire to help others despite consequences. Meloy and Mohandie (2014) identified five steps to facilitate that process.

Positive Social and Individual Action

This factor looks at those that engage in *positive social action* for the betterment of a group or community or even at a lesser developmental place of just positive action for the sake of their own *individual consequence*. The second is fairly simple. This individual develops an awareness of how their choices result in positive or negative consequences minimally for themself or those in their circle, and thus, chooses

Identifying Stabilizing Influences 93

Table 8.8 Reflective questions for positive social and individual action

- Does he have past experience with helping others that has resulted in positive feelings
- Is he able to find common goals with others who can add to his overall sense of meaning and growth?
- What groups, organizations or friends have helped him improve his feelings of depression, isolation and hopelessness?
- How does he go about finding ways to connect with others?
- What are some larger social issues that he cares about that may serve as a starting place to find new groups and connections with others?

actions to avoid harm. "I choose not to hurt someone because there could be negative consequences for me, my family, my friends." Individuals can also choose nonviolent pathways because of perceived rewards and motivators, such as continued access to participation in school or work activities (NTAC, 2018). On a higher level, positive social action includes a more inclusive and collaborative participation, working together to improve situations, remove barriers to success, and foster positive change. This level of critical thinking, awareness of others, and inclusivity truly reflects the opposite of violent action and the risk factors explored in Chapter 3. When someone feels a part of a broader community and is surrounded by positive social supports with promising opportunities for the future, this exemplifies how the protective factors guard against potential violence risks.

For the incel, these social connections need to be positive in nature and focused on building community that does not advocate negative action or discriminating thoughts against others, as these are the types on online communities that are actively causing harm and spreading objectification and nihilistic incel views. Conversely, the positive social action does not need to be overly Pollyannaish, meaning that it's messaging or goals are so out of touch with a male's experience that it is immediately dismissed or mocked.

Positive Masculinity

Having an optimistic and constructive view of what it means to be a man in today's culture is an important stabilizing influence in a young man's life. There are often conflicting messages about showing emotion, being vulnerable, caring for others or valuing family when it relates to masculinity. Other times, there is a lack of any guidance or direction which leads to the individual becoming lost in the vacuum of guidance. Still others experience abuse, trauma, and instability in their lives that create the need for an artificial false front that is needed for immediate security and protection.

In Chapter 3, we highlight the negative and toxic expectations that are often placed on men as they develop. These expectations are rooted in a binary view of being just one thing such as dominant, stoic, and emotionally attached. In literature, characters are often described as flat or round, with round characters present in foreground of a novel and full of complexities and depth; while flat characters often serve as plot supporting devices and are defined in a one-dimensional manner. The classic

94 *Assessing the Risk*

Table 8.9 Reflective questions for positive masculinity

- Does he have mentors or role models who offer positive messages about what it means to be a man in today's society?
- Is he able to list negative and positive traditionally male qualities? Can he do the same in an empathetic way for traditionally female qualities?
- What influences contributed to how he sees masculinity (e.g., family, friends, religion, television, internet discussion groups, past relationships with women)?
- How does he go about seeking a romantic or intimate relationship? What expectations does he have about the ease or difficulty obtaining this?
- When he is faced with difficulty, does he stop and try a different approach or become despondent and hopeless that his desires are forever outside of his grasp?

Marlboro Man, Man with No Name, Man in Black, and Dirty Harry are problematic role models for many reasons, but the central one is the lack of a range of emotions and ability to possess a sense of depth.

Here, an improved version would adopt the opposite of the negative traits, or better yet, a broader range of options. Any positive masculinity should be more nuanced than a direct opposite; rather a healthier version of negative traits. For example, the opposite of aggression is passivity, yet a healthier, more inclusive version of aggression would be an assertiveness with an awareness of other's perspectives. Where stoicism exists, instead consider a reflective stance with a sharing of emotions and feelings. The path to positive masculinity could parallel the feminist movement's encouragement on the acceptance of a variety of categories in a manner that does not objectify, limit, or divide.

Affirmative Sexuality

Sex isn't always easy for people to talk about. In fact, it could be argued that many religious and political ideologies are firmly built upon the foundations of controlling sexuality and, in particular, female impulse. Freud described women's sexuality as the "dark continent" and began his work attempting to calm the "hysterical" impulses of women. Affirmative sexuality describes a communication based series of conversations built around the concepts of active listening, empathy, and mutual respect. Healthy relationships, like positive sexual interactions work when they are built around the core concepts outlined in Table 8.10 (Murphy & Van Brunt, 2017).

Sex educators and sexual health professionals espouse a sex-positive view of sexuality:

> an attitude towards human sexuality that regards all consensual sexual activities as fundamentally healthy and pleasurable, and encourages sexual pleasure and experimentation. The sex-positive movement is a social and philosophical movement that advocates these attitudes. The sex-positive movement advocates sex education and safer sex as part of its campaign.

(Gabosch, 2014, p. 1)

Identifying Stabilizing Influences 95

Table 8.10 Essentials for healthy relationships (Murphy & Van Brunt, 2017)

Topic	Description
Communication	Talking openly with your partner about expectations and the good, bad and ugly of the relationship. It requires vulnerability, experience, humility, self-acceptance, dedication, and commitment.
Active listening	This is a focused effort to put aside one's current needs and dedicating a time and space to hear what the other person is saying. This begins with clearing away distractions, such as a phone, computer, television, or other people, and truly listening to what your partner has to say.
Empathy	Empathy is understanding the thoughts, feelings and behaviors from the perspective of another person. Start with open-ended questions, those that avoid a simple one-word or short-phrase answer, to bring about a more empathetic understanding of a partner's needs or wants.
Mutual respect	Respect involves caring for and respecting your partner and their choices, outlook, and experiences. You take pride in them and care for their future, seeking balance and respect for each other's interests.
Equanimity	Relationships work well when there is a natural sense of give-and-take, back and forth, a sharing between partners that is informed by a desire for the other's happiness and a desire for your own.
Social connection	While there may be areas of overlap, some relationships require a deeper communication to establish a balance between each other's needs and desires for social interactions and connections. Some of us enjoy parties and spending time with multiple friends. Others enjoy "hamster-balling" in the quiet of an evening with a good book and some favorite snacks. Healthy relationships seek balance.

Burning Man is an annual festival in Nevada that, on many levels, defies description. The gathering rises once a year out of the Black Rock Desert in the heat of August and early September on a dry lakebed about three hours north of Reno, Nevada. It's been going on for more than 20 years, with the earliest festival taking place on San Francisco's Baker Beach in 1986. A group of self-proclaimed sex-positive Burning Man participants formed the Bureau of Erotic Discourse (BED). They share with those on the playa information about healthy sex and consent for the benefit of the community. In their published notes for a Clarity and Consent workshop in 2014, they share what very well may be some of the best advice that could be shared with those who follow the incel philosophy. They suggest sex is a very good thing when it is mutually desired and values an individual's right to not have sex. Nothing matters more than communication and consent.

They write,

Good sex needs to be negotiated between people. It doesn't happen magically like you might see on a TV commercial, where two strangers share a hot glance and everything works perfectly without any discussion. In real life, the couple

96 *Assessing the Risk*

Table 8.11 Reflective questions for affirmative sexuality

- What are some of the expectations that he has related to relationships, sex and friendship?
- How has he attempted to meet women and form an initial connection?
- What kind of timeline does he expect a relationship to be created by when meeting a new person? Where does this expectation come from?
- What are some of the role models he has for sexual relationships?
- What are some practical ways to turn perceived negative rejection into something more positive and solution-focused moving forward?

> races across the meadow only to have one of them sprain an ankle in a gopher hole and the other one has an allergic reaction to the wildflowers. If they had talked about it, they might have been happily making out at the movies. Good sex is not usually what you see in porn. Not only are the physical attributes misleading, but the attitudes, positions, and practices can be way outside the comfort zone for many people. If you both know your desires and they include some X-rated movies, then feel free. But don't assume that everyone wants to be a porn star.
>
> (BED, 2014, p. 2)

To that end, healthy sexual relationships, in all of their wonderful diversity, are based on concepts of open communication and respect for each other's autonomy and connectedness. There is a cultivation of each individual's value and self as well as a willingness to sacrifice and give to the relationship itself. There is a sacrifice that each makes to the relationship and to the betterment of the other. Great relationships live in this balance, one person giving and loving the other, wanting the best for them, and this, in turn, being given back.

Moving Forward

Now that we have discussed the indoctrination level of the incel in Chapters 5 and 6, and the risk factors and stabilizing influences in Chapters 7 and 8, we can address the process of assessment of violence risk for the incel in the following chapter. This assessment of risk will then lead to the treatment recommendations for three case studies, in Chapters 11, 12, and 13, to pull them off the pathway to self-loathing, depression, hopelessness, and anger toward women and a larger society they believe has left them behind.

Discussion Questions

- What are some ways you could help a friend or someone you know who presents with some of the risk factors outlined in Chapter 7 be able to increase the stabilizing influences in their lives?
- What has worked in your past to increase rapport and connection in a relationship?

- If someone were to ask you what traits you believe are essential in a healthy dating relationship, what are some that come to mind?
- Much of this book has been dedicated to understanding the negative side of masculinity. What are some traits you would define as positive when you look around at the male figures who were involved with raising you or who are currently in your life?

References

The Bureau of Erotic Discourse (BED). (2014). Clarity and consent: B.E.D. workshop notes for 2014. Retrieved on May 13, 2020, from www.bureauoferoticdiscourse.org

Borba, M. (2018). Nine competencies for teaching empathy. *Educational Leadership*, 76(2), 22–28.

Borum, R., Fein, R., Vossekuil, B., and Berglund, J. (1999). Threat assessment: Defining an approach for evaluating risk of targeted violence. *Behavioral Sciences and the Law*, 17, 323–337.

Center for Disease Control and Prevention (CDC). (2018). Protective factors. Retrieved on March 28, 2020 from www.cdc.gov/healthyyouth/protective/index.htm

Chialant, D., Edersheim, J., and Price, B.H. (2016). The dialectic between empathy and violence: An opportunity for intervention? *The Journal of Neuropsychiatry and Clinical Neurosciences*, 28(4), 273–285.

Ellis, A. (2007). *The Practice of Rational Emotive Behavior Therapy*. New York: W. W. Norton.

Gabosch, A. (2014). A sex positive renaissance. Retrieved on April 20, 2020 from https://allenagabosch.wordpress.com

Hogan, M. (2015). Facebook and the "Fear of Missing Out" (FoMO). Retrieved on March 10, 2020 from www.psychologytoday.com/us/blog/in-one-lifespan/201510/facebook-and-the-fear-missing-out-fomo

Meloy, J.R. and Mohandie, K. (2014). Assessing threats by direct interview of the violent true believer. In J.R. Meloy and J. Hoffmann (eds.), *The International Handbook of Threat Assessment* (pp. 388–398). New York: Oxford University Press.

Murphy, A. and Van Brunt, B. (2017). *Uprooting Sexual Violence in Higher Educations: A Guide for Practitioners and Faculty*. New York: Taylor & Francis.

National Threat Assessment Center (NTAC). (2018). *Enhancing School Safety Using a Threat Assessment Model: An Operational Guide for Preventing Targeted School Violence*. US Secret Service, Department of Homeland Security.

Nydell, M. (1996). *Understanding Arabs: A Guide for Westerners*. Yarmouth: Intercultural Press.

O'Toole, M.E. (2002). *The School Shooter: A Threat Assessment Perspective*. Quantico: FBI.

Pressman, D. (2009). *Risk Assessment Decisions for Violent Political Extremism*. Ottawa: Her Majesty the Queen in Right of Canada.

Priddy, N. (2018). Empathy is academic: Lessons from lotus slippers. *Education Update*, 60(12), 1–2.

Przybylski, A., Murayama, K., DeHaan, C., and Gladwell, V. (2013). Motivational, emotional and behavioural correlates of fear of missing out. *Computers in Human Behaviour*, 29, 1841–1848.

Rogers, C. (1961). *On Becoming a Person*. New York: Houghton Mifflin.

98 *Assessing the Risk*

Sokolow, B., Van Brunt, B., Lewis, W., Schiemann, M., Murphy, A., and Molnar, J. (2019). *The NaBITA Risk Rubric*. King of Prussia: The National Behavioral Intervention Team Association.

United Nations Educational, Scientific and Cultural Organization. (2016). A Teachers Guide to the Prevention of Violent Extremism.

Van Brunt, B., Murphy, A., and Zedginidze, A. (2017). An exploration of the risk, protective, and mobilization factors related to violent extremism in college populations, *Violence and Gender*, 4(3), 81–101.

9 Conducting a Violence Risk Assessment

Threat assessment regarding incel cases requires skillful navigation amongst the incel indoctrination rubric (laid out in Chapters 5 and 6 and the IIR in Appendix I), the risk factors (Chapter 7), and the stabilizing influences (Chapter 8). When assessing the lethality of a threat, a central tension is sorting the difference between potential leakage for an attack from (1) trolling or attention seeking, (2) a passive "call for help," (3) immature bluster, or (4) a marginalized individual looking to exercise power and address an injustice. In other words, *the threat assessment process is central in answering the question: What is evidence of an attack plan and what is poking at others for attention, to cause chaos or express pain; what is transient and what is substantive, what is hunting and what is howling?*

Violence risk and threat assessments are not useful to predict violence or profile an individual based on a list of characteristics. Violence risk and threat assessment techniques consider if the individual is at an increased risk to the greater community by asking contextual questions about the nature of the threat and risk, using expert systems, rubrics and research-based interview techniques to determine a level of potential dangerousness. Mistakes are made when only one perspective is taken into account – when those conducting the threat assessment neglect the contextual information essential to understanding potentially escalating behavior of a person on the pathway to violence. O'Toole wrote in 2000,

> In general, people do not switch instantly from nonviolence to violence. Nonviolent people do not "snap" or decide on the spur of the moment to meet a problem by using violence. Instead, the path toward violence is an evolutionary one, with signposts along the way.
>
> (p. 7)

Preventing violence requires careful questioning and analysis of how the individual behaves in their environment and if there is an action imperative which drives the subject to take personal action to address their frustration, anger and dissatisfaction (Turner & Gelles, 2003).

There are numerous approaches to threat assessment, and it is critical that the IIR is not seen as a threat assessment process, but rather a measure of indoctrination in the incel philosophy. The book *Harm to Others: The Treatment and Assessment of Dangerousness* (Van Brunt, 2015a) offers a detailed approach to the threat assessment

100 *Assessing the Risk*

process through the use of the SIVRA-35. Other approaches include the RAGE-V (Association of Threat Assessment Professionals [ATAP], 2006), the HCR-20 (Hart & Logan, 2011), and MOSIAC (de Becker, 1997).

Mental Illness and Violence

Unwinding the issue of mental illness and violence is not an easy task. These issues become complicated when the public is exposed to repetitive news stories that stress the dangerousness of mentally ill individuals preying on the larger society. The assumption that persons with mental illness are a high-risk population relative to gun violence lacks supportive evidence (Knoll & Annas, 2016; Van Brunt & Pescara-Kovach, 2019). The kind of targeted, predatory and mission-oriented mass violence is the result of a host of complicated factors (National Threat Assessment Center [NTAC], 2018; Jarvis & Scherer, 2015). The Federal Bureau of Investigation, Secret Service, and the Department of Homeland Security have said repeatedly that there is no singular profile for a school shooter, but rather a complicated set of factors moving an individual toward an attack against a backdrop of evaporating stabilizing influences. Simply stated, the incel, even at his very worst scoring on the IIR, should not be immediately equated with someone who carries out an attack. It is the combination of the incel doctrine along with an understanding of the risk and stabilizing influences that create a fuller picture of the potential risk.

A mental health diagnosis is never the sole cause of incel violence, though media coverage and public opinion often portray those with mental health problems as more likely to move forward with the kind of attacks committed by Rodger (Appendix A: 24; C), Sodini (Appendix A: 21;B), and Mercer (Appendix A: 29; D). Mass shootings by people with serious mental illness represent one percent (1%) of all gun homicides each year (Knoll & Annas, 2016). The fear is present, however, with a desire for an answer to prevent the reoccurrence of the horrible event, regardless of whether or not it is likely to happen again. This phenomenon is called "probability neglect" and was described by Sunstein (2003) as when the public demands legal interventions from the government or seeks clear answers for the cause. When mental illness is forwarded as a singular answer to the incel problem of violence, society views this as the most reasonable, common-sense explanation that provides the false hope of an easy solution to a complex problem.

A common mistake to avoid is conflating a mental health assessment with a violence risk or threat assessment. A mental health assessment provides a diagnosis of a mental illness, a recommendation for inpatient hospitalization or commitment, the development of a treatment plan advising a medication assessment, focus in on-going therapy, and specific advice to reduce mental illness symptoms. In contrast, a violence risk or threat assessment is based on a combination of research and literature from psychology and criminology with a clear focus on assessing the likelihood of targeted or predatory violence in the future. While a violence risk or threat assessment does not need to be performed by clinical mental health staff, their expertise in building rapport and conducting an interview could be useful in informing the violence risk or threat assessment.

Violence Risk and Threat Assessment

Threat or risk assessments are generally performed by non-clinical staff and forensic professionals who work in law enforcement, executive protection, and human resources, or as members of a BIT/CARE team (discussed in Chapter 14). They examine the circumstances of the events, the subject's background, and conduct interviews with the subject to determine their risk to the greater community. They are not attempting to predict school violence or profile a student or employee based on a list of characteristics. Rather, they examine the individual to determine their risk to the greater community by asking questions about the nature of the threat and risk and using computer-aided models to assess risk and protective factors to determine the level of potential dangerousness. The Secret Service and FBI share,

> The threat assessment process is based on the premise that each situation should be viewed and assessed individually and guided by the facts. Judgments about an individual's risk of violence should be based upon an analysis of his/her behaviors and the context in which they occur. Blanket characterizations, demographic profiles, or stereotypes do not provide a reliable basis for making judgments of the threat posed by a particular individual.
>
> (Drysdale et al., 2010, p. 37)

While, threat and violence risk assessments are similar, they do have some semantic differences in terms of application. There is general agreement a threat assessment seeks to assess dangerousness of an individual after they issue a threat, whether it be vague, conditional or direct. If an employee posts on social media "I'm going to turn this office into graveyard with my sig .45 this Tuesday at noon," a threat assessment would be the appropriate choice, as there is a clear and identifiable threat. A violence risk assessment is a broader term for an assessment used when there is a concern for violence, regardless of the presence of vague, conditional, or direct threat. In the example given a, a violence risk assessment may have been used based potential social isolation, bullying, or suicidality prior to his threat to shoot up the office.

When understanding the escalation on the pathway to violence, O'Toole (2000) shares this reflection,

> In general, people do not switch instantly from nonviolence to violence. Nonviolent people do not "snap" or decide on the spur of the moment to meet a problem by using violence. Instead, the path toward violence is an evolutionary one, with signposts along the way.
>
> (p. 7)

Preventing violence requires careful questioning and analysis of how the subject behaves in their environment at the earliest point where the potential attacker shares leakage regarding their frustration, anger and dissatisfaction toward a target. Meloy et al., (2011) describe the difference in this way,

102 *Assessing the Risk*

Table 9.1 Examples of training organizations for violence risk and threat assessment

Group name	Website*
Association of Threat Assessment Professionals	www.atapworldwide.org
The National Behavioral Intervention Team Association	www.nabita.org
SIGMA threat assessment	www.sigmatma.com
School Threat Assessment	www.schoolta.com
Protect International	https://protect-international.com
Mosaic	www.mosaicmethod.com

*websites current as of June 2020

Threat assessment and risk assessment have developed as somewhat overlapping fields. Violence risk assessment has an older provenance and is a method by which the probability of generally violent behavior is estimated for an individual based upon his membership in a particular at-risk group. Threat assessment is concerned almost wholly with the risk of targeted violence by a subject of concern, and has a behavioral and observational policing focus. Risk assessment may address different domains of risk than threat assessment, and typically relies on more historical and dispositional (status) variables.

(p. 2)

There are many ways to build capacity to do this work within the school, college, university, or workplace. Several examples of these are included in Table 9.1. Another approach is to out-source the work to specialists trained in the approach or enlist those mental health clinical staff who have received additional training beyond straightforward diagnostic or inpatient commitment assessments. The ideal is to build the capacity for violence risk and threat assessment within the BIT/CARE team and have experts on retainer to consult on more complicated cases. The essential skills needed to complete these assessments are the ability to: (1) build rapport during an interview, (2) reduce defensiveness and assess truthfulness in the subject, (3) possess a knowledge of risk and protective factors, and (4) operate within a Structured Professional Judgment (SPJ) framework. When conducting these assessments, the stressors clarify the relationship and scope of the evaluation through an informed consent. This informed consent document clearly outlines the purpose, scope, and length or duration of the assessment as well as the privacy regarding the information shared during the assessment and how the results will be used.

SIVRA-35

As part of the book *Ending Campus Violence* (Van Brunt, 2012, 2015b), a new expert system was created that is widely used at colleges and universities across the United States. This system is called the Structured Interview for Violence Risk Assessment or the SIVRA-35.

1. There is a direct communicated threat to a person, place, or system (Deisinger et al., 2014; ASIS & SHRM, 2011; Meloy et al., 2011; Drysdale et al., 2010;

Randazzo & Plummer, 2009; ATAP, 2006; Turner & Gelles, 2003; O'Toole, 2002; NTAC, 2018, 2019).

2. The student has the plans, tools, weapons, schematics and/or materials to carry out an attack on a potential target (Meloy et al., 2014; United States Postal Service [USPS], 2007; ATAP, 2006; Turner & Gelles, 2003; NTAC, 2018, 2019).

3. The student harbors violent fantasies to counteract their isolation and/or emotional pain (Van Brunt, 2015a; Mohandie, 2014; O'Neill et al., 2008; ATAP, 2006; NTAC, 2018; 2019)

4. The student has an action plan and/or timeframe to complete an attack (Meloy et al., 2011; ATAP, 2006; Turner & Gelles, 2003; NTAC, 2018, 2019).

5. The student is fixated and/or focused on their target in their actions and threatening statements (Deisinger et al., 2014; Meloy et al., 2011; O'Toole & Bowman, 2011); ASIS & SHRM, 2011; USPS, 2007; Turner & Gelles, 2003; NTAC, 2018, 2019).

6. The student carries deep grudges and resentments. They can't seem to let things go an collects injustices based on perceptions of being hurt, frustrated with someone, or annoyed (O'Toole & Bowman, 2011; ASIS & SHRM, 2011; Calhoun & Weston, 2009; Randazzo & Plummer, 2009; ATAP, 2006; Turner & Gelles, 2003; NTAC, 2018, 2019).

7. The target is described negatively in writing or artistic expression. There is a narrow focus on a particular person that has a level of preoccupation or fascination with the target. There is a pattern of this behavior, rather than a one-time act (Meloy et al., 2011; O'Neill et al., 2008; NTAC, 2018, 2019; Van Brunt, 2015a, 2015b; 2016).

8. There has been leakage concerning a potential plan of attack (Deisinger et al., 2014; Meloy et al., 2011; O'Toole & Bowman, 2011; ASIS & SHRM, 2011; Randazzo & Plummer, 2009; ATAP, 2006; Turner & Gelles, 2003; O'Toole, 2002; Vossekuil et al., 2002; NTAC, 2018, 2019; Van Brunt, 2015b, 2016).

9. The student has current suicidal thoughts, ideations and/or a plan to die (Meloy et al., 2014; Randazzo & Plummer, 2009; Dunkle et al., 2008; USPS, 2007; ATAP, 2006; Turner & Gelles, 2003; O'Toole, 2002; Vossekuil et al., 2002; Lankford, 2016, 2018; NTAC, 2018, 2019).

10. The student talks about being persecuted or being treated unjustly (Meloy et al., 2011; O'Toole & Bowman, 2011; ASIS & SHRM, 2011; USPS, 2007; ATAP, 2006; Turner & Gelles, 2003; NTAC, 2018, 2019).

11. The student has engaged in "last act" behaviors or discusses what they want people to remember about their actions. They may create a legacy token (Meloy et al., 2011; ATAP, 2006; Turner & Gelles, 2003; NTAC, 2018, 2019; Van Brunt, 2015a, 2015b, 2016).

12. The student seems confused or has odd or troubling thoughts. The student may hear voices or see visions that command them to do things (ASIS & SHRM, 2011; Drysdale et al., 2010; Dunkle et al., 2008; USPS, 2007; ATAP, 2006; Turner & Gelles, 2003; Van Brunt & Pescara-Kovach, 2019).

13. The student displays a hardened point of view or strident, argumentative opinion. This is beyond a person who is generally argumentative or negative (Meloy

104 *Assessing the Risk*

et al., 2011; ASIS & SHRM, 2011; Randazzo & Plummer, 2009; ATAP, 2006; Turner & Gelles, 2003; O'Toole, 2002; Byrnes, 2002; NTAC, 2018, 2019).

14. The student has a lack of options and/or a sense of hopelessness and desperation (Meloy et al., 2014; ASIS & SHRM, 2011; Randazzo & Plummer, 2009; USPS, 2007; ATAP, 2006; Turner & Gelles, 2003; O'Toole, 2002; Lankford, 2016, 2018).

15. The student is driven to a particular action to cause harm (Deisinger et al., 2014; Meloy et al., 2011; USPS, 2007; ATAP, 2006; Turner & Gelles, 2003; Lankford, 2018).

16. The student has had a recent breakup or failure of an intimate relationship and/or the student has become obsessed in stalking or fixated on another person romantically (ASIS & SHRM, 2011; Drysdale et al., 2010; Randazzo & Plummer, 2009; ATAP, 2006; Turner & Gelles, 2003; Vossekuil et al., 2002).

17. The student acts overly defensive, aggressive or detached given the nature of this risk/threat assessment. They seek to intimidate the assessor or display an overly casual response given the seriousness of the interview (O'Toole & Bowman, 2011; ATAP, 2006; Turner & Gelles, 2003; O' Toole, 2002; Van Brunt, 2015a).

18. The student displays little remorse for their actions, lacks understanding for the view for potential victims, and acts with a detachment or bravado during the interview (O'Toole & Bowman, 2011; ATAP, 2006; USPS, 2007; Turner & Gelles, 2003; O'Toole, 2002).

19. The student has a weapon (or access to weapon), specialized training in weapon handling, interest in paramilitary organizations or Veteran/Law Enforcement status (Meloy et al., 2011; ASIS and SHRM, 2011; USPS, 2007; ATAP, 2006; Turner & Gelles, 2003; Vossekuil et al., 2002).

20. The student glorifies and revels in publicized violence such as school shootings, serial killers, and war or displays an unusual interest in sensational violence. The student uses weapons for emotional release and venerates destruction (Meloy et al., 2011; ASIS & SHRM, 2011; USPS, 2007; ATAP, 2006; Turner & Gelles, 2003, O'Toole, 2002; Vossekuil et al., 2002; Lankford, 2018).

21. The student externalizes blame for personal behaviors and problems onto other people despite efforts to educate them about how others view these actions. The student takes immediate responsibility in a disingenuous manner (O'Toole & Bowman, 2011; USPS, 2007; ATAP, 2006; Turner & Gelles, 2003; O'Toole, 2002).

22. The student intimidates or acts superior to others. The student displays intolerance to individual differences (Van Brunt, 2015a; Meloy et al., 2011; O'Toole & Bowman, 2011; ATAP, 2006; Turner & Gelles, 2003; O'Toole, 2002).

23. The student has a past history of excessively impulsive, erratic, or risk-taking behavior (O'Toole & Bowman, 2011; ASIS & SHRM, 2011; Randazzo & Plummer, 2009; USPS, 2007; Turner & Gelles, 2003).

24. The student has a past history of problems with authority. The student has a pattern of intense work conflicts with supervisors and other authorities (e.g., resident advisor, conduct officer, professor or dean) (O'Toole & Bowman,

Conducting a Violence Risk Assessment 105

2011; ASIS & SHRM, 2011; USPS, 2007; ATAP, 2006; Turner & Gelles, 2003; O'Toole, 2002).

25. The student handles frustration in an explosive manner or displays a low tolerance for becoming upset. This is beyond avoiding responsibility or calling mom/dad or a lawyer (O'Toole & Bowman, 2011; ASIS & SHRM, 2011; Turner & Gelles, 2003; O'Toole, 2002).

26. The student has difficulty connecting with other people. The student lacks the ability to form intimate relationships. The student lacks the ability to form trust (Van Brunt, 2015a; Randazzo & Plummer, 2009; USPS, 2007; O'Toole, 2002).

27. The student has a history of drug or substance use that has been connected to inappropriate ideation or behavior. Substances of enhanced concern are methamphetamines or amphetamines, cocaine or alcohol (O'Toole & Bowman, 2011; USPS, 2007; ATAP, 2006; Turner & Gelles, 2003; Van Brunt & Pescara-Kovach, 2019).

28. The student has serious mental health issues that require assessment and treatment (Randazzo & Plummer, 2009; Dunkle et al., 2008; USPS, 2007; ATAP, 2006; Turner & Gelles, 2003; O'Toole, 2002; Van Brunt & Pescara-Kovach, 2019).

29. If the student has serious mental health issues that require assessment and treatment, they are not receiving mental health care and support (Harvard Mental Health Letter, 2011, Dunkle et al., 2008; ATAP, 2006; Van Brunt & Pescara-Kovach, 2019).

30. Objectification of others (perhaps in social media or writings) (O'Toole and Bowman, 2011; O'Toole, 2002; Byrnes, 2002; Van Brunt, 2015b, 2016).

31. The student has a sense of being owed things from others such as sex, money, a relationship or grades. They act as if they deserve certain treatment and/or have an exaggerated sense of entitlement (Van Brunt, 2012, 2015a; ATAP, 2006; O'Toole, 2000; US DOJ/FBI, 2017).

32. The student has oppositional thoughts and/or behaviors (Van Brunt, 2015a; USPS, 2007; ATAP, 2006; O'Toole, 2002).

33. The student has poor support and connection from faculty, administration and staff. The student has an unsupportive family system and peers who exacerbate bad decisions and offer low quality advice or caring. They experience evaporating social inhibitors (Randazzo & Plummer, 2009; USPS, 2007; ATAP, 2006; Vossekuil et al., 2002).

34. The student experiences overwhelming, unmanageable stress from a significant change such as losing a job, a conduct hearing, failing a class, suspension or family trauma. This stress is beyond what would normally be expected when receiving bad news (Drysdale et al., 2010; Randazzo & Plummer, 2009; USPS, 2007; ATAP, 2006).

35. The student has drastic, unexplained behavior change (ASIS and SHRM, 2011; Randazzo & Plummer, 2009; USPS, 2007; ATAP, 2006).

More information regarding the scoring and interpretation of the SIVRA-35 can be obtained by contacting www.nabita.org

106   *Assessing the Risk*

US Postal Service Threat Assessment Team Guide

In 2007, the US Postal Service developed a set of Risk Indicators as part of their Threat Assessment Team Guide. We have included some of these here:

- Past history of violent behaviors (e.g., physical assaults on others)
- Having a concealed weapon or flashing a weapon
- Fascination with semi-automatic or automatic weapons and their capability to cause great harm
- Odd or bizarre beliefs (magical or satanic beliefs, sexually violent fantasies)
- Perceived loss of options
- Inspiration of fear in others (exceeding mere intimidation)
- Obsessive focus on grudge – often quick to perceive unfairness or malice in others, especially supervisor
- Direct or veiled threats of bodily harm
- History of poor impulse control and poor interpersonal skills.

(USPS, 2007, p.39)

Risk Assessment Guideline Elements for Violence (RAGE-V)

The Association of Threat Assessment Professionals (ATAP) created a guide entitled *Risk Assessment Guideline Elements for Violence* or RAGE-V (ATAP, 2006). Several risk factors are summarized here to highlight additional areas of concern.

- Beliefs, revenge, entitlement, grandiosity, need to force closure
- Drug use: methamphetamine, cocaine, alcohol, steroids
- Head trauma
- Criminal history, including history of violence, homicide, stalking, threats, assaultive behavior, violation of conditional release
- Prior voluntary or involuntary commitments
- Past suicide attempts, or suicide ideation, to include suicidal thoughts, statements, gestures, and attempts
- Adverse responses to authority and limit setting
- History of mental problems that compromise coping, or enhance appeal of violence-may include:
  - Depression
  - Paranoia
  - Psychopathy
  - Bipolar
  - Personality disorders (narcissistic, paranoid, borderline, antisocial)
  - Perceptions of injustice or insoluble problems.

The RAGE-V provides yet another useful list of risk factors and items to assess when conducting a threat assessment.

Turner and Gelles

Turner and Gelles (2003) offer an important book on the topic of workplace violence. The book is extraordinarily accessible and readable, and particularly useful in understanding some of the basic concepts related threat and risk assessment in the workplace setting. These include:

Verbal Cues

- Direct and indirect threats
- Threatening/harassing phone calls
- Recurrent suicide threats or actions
- Hopelessness
- Boasts of violent behavior or fantasies
- Frequent profanity
- Belligerence
- Challenging or intimidating statements

Bizarre Thoughts

- Paranoia
- Persecutory delusions with self as victim
- Delusions in general
- Command hallucinations
- Significantly deteriorated thought process
- Obsessions
- Signs of history or substance use/abuse

Behavioral Clues

- Physical altercation/assault upon another person
- Inappropriate weapons possession or use
- Physical intimidation
- Following and surveillance of targeted individual
- Short-fused, loss of emotional control, impulsive
- Destruction of property
- Deteriorating physical appearance and self-care
- Inappropriate displays of emotions
- Isolated and withdrawn

Obsessions

- Self as victim of a particular individual
- Grudges and deep resentments
- Particular object of desire

108   *Assessing the Risk*

- Perceived injustice, humiliations, disrespect
- Narrow focus – "sees no way out" – "no other options"
- Publicized acts of violence
- Weapons and destruction
- Fairness
- Grievances and lawsuits.

(pp. 17–18)

FBI Four-Prong Approach

The FBI (O'Toole, 2002) created a four-prong approach to threat assessment which includes: (1) the personality of the student, (2) family dynamics, (3) school dynamics, and (4) social dynamics. While the approach was designed primarily for use with K-12 schools, overlaps seem useful to the higher education and workplace environment.

O'Toole (2000) stresses,

It should be strongly emphasized that this list is not intended as a checklist to predict future violent behavior by a student who has not acted violently or threatened violence. Rather, the list should be considered only after a student has made some type of threat and an assessment has been developed using the four-pronged model ... No one or two traits or characteristics should be considered in isolation or given more weight than the others ...

(p. 15)

The four-pronged approach involves:

Prong One: Personality of the Student

- Leakage
- Low Tolerance for Frustration
- Poor Coping Skills
- Lack of Resiliency
- Failed Love Relationship
- "Injustice Collector"
- Signs of Depression
- Narcissism
- Alienation
- Dehumanizes Others
- Lack of Empathy
- Exaggerated Sense of Entitlement
- Attitude of Superiority
- Exaggerated or Pathological Need for Attention
- Externalizes Blame
- Masks Low Self-esteem
- Anger Management Problems

Conducting a Violence Risk Assessment   109

- Intolerance
- Inappropriate Humor
- Seeks to Manipulate Others
- Lack of Trust
- Closed Social Group
- Change of Behavior
- Rigid and Opinionated
- Unusual Interest in Sensational Violence
- Fascination with Violence-Filled Entertainment
- Negative Role Models
- Behavior Appears Relevant to Carrying Out a Threat.

Prong Two: Family Dynamics

- Turbulent Parent–Child Relationship
- Acceptance of Pathological Behavior
- Access to Weapons
- Lack of Intimacy
- Student "Rules the Roost"
- No Limits or Monitoring of TV and Internet.

Prong Three: School Dynamics

- Student's Attachment to School
- Tolerance for Disrespectful Behavior
- Inequitable Discipline
- Inflexible Culture
- Pecking Order Among Students
- Code of Silence
- Unsupervised Computer Access.

Prong Four: Social Dynamics

- Media, Entertainment, Technology
- Peer Groups
- Drugs and Alcohol
- Outside Interests
- The Copycat Effect.

(pp. 16–24)

With close to 30 personality factors that correlate with prior school shootings and a detailed account of risk factors, the FBI four-prong assessment is a useful checklist to have on hand during an interview process and is one of the most detailed lists of risk factors. Caution should be taken, however, as any list brings with it the danger of false positives that can create problems identifying true violence risk from howling and more transient threats.

110   *Assessing the Risk*

ASIS Workplace Violence Prevention and Intervention Standards

ASIS International and Society for Human Resource Management published *Workplace Violence Prevention and Intervention* (2011). This is a researched set of standards created to assist security and human resource personal to better intervene potentially dangerous scenarios. They suggest organizations would do well to keep an awareness of the following factors:

- A history of threats or violent acts, including threats or violence occurring during employment and a criminal history suggestive of a propensity to use violence to project power and to control others, or as a response to stress or conflict.
- Threats, bullying, or other threatening behavior, aggressive outbursts or comments, or excessive displays of anger.
- Verbal abuse or harassment by any means or medium.
- Harboring grudges, an inability to handle criticism, habitually making excuses, and blaming others.
- Chronic, unsubstantiated complaints about persecution or injustice; a victim mindset.
- Obsessive intrusion upon others or persistent unwanted romantic pursuit.
- Erratic, impulsive, or bizarre behavior that has generated fear among co-workers.
- Homicidal or suicidal thoughts or ideas.
- A high degree of emotional distress.
- Apparent impulsivity and/or low tolerance of frustration.
- A fascination with weapons, a preoccupation with violent themes of revenge, and an unusual interest in recently publicized violent events, if communicated in a manner that creates discomfort for co-workers.
- Any behavior or collection of behaviors that instill fear or generate a concern that a person might act out violently.

(p. 22)

Approach Warning Behaviors

Meloy et al. (2011) outline eight warning behaviors that are "factors which constitute change, and which are evidence of increasing or accelerating risk" (p. 5). These approach behaviors can be seen as a progressive escalation toward targeted violence. They are:

1. **Pathway warning behavior** – any behavior that is part of research, planning, preparation, or implementation of an attack (Calhoun & Weston, 2009; Fein & Vossekuil, 1998).
2. **Fixation warning behavior** – any behavior that indicates an increasingly pathological preoccupation with a person or a cause (Mullen et al., 2009). It is measured by:
   (a) increasing perseveration on the person or cause,
   (b) increasingly strident opinion,
   (c) increasingly negative characterization of the object of fixation,

(d) impact on the family or other associates of the object of fixation, if present and aware, and

(e) angry emotional undertone.

It is typically accompanied by social or occupational deterioration.

3. **Identification warning behavior** – any behavior that indicates a psychological desire to be a "pseudo-commando" (Dietz, 1986; Knoll, 2010), have a "warrior mentality," (Hempel et al., 1999), closely associate with weapons or other military or law enforcement paraphernalia, identify with previous attackers or assassins, or identify oneself as an agent to advance a particular cause or belief system.

4. **Novel aggression warning behavior** – an act of violence which appears unrelated to any targeted violence pathway warning behavior which is committed for the first time. Such behaviors may be utilized to test the ability of the subject to actually do a violent act (de Becker, 1997), and may be a measure of response tendency, the motivation to act on the environment (Hull, 1952), or a behavioral tryout (MacCulloch et al., 1983).

5. **Energy burst warning behavior** – an increase in the frequency or variety of any noted activities related to the target, even if the activities themselves are relatively innocuous, usually in the days or weeks before the attack (Odgers et al., 2009).

6. **Leakage warning behavior** – the communication to a third party of an intent to do harm to a target through an attack (Meloy & O'Toole, 2011).

7. **Last resort warning behavior** – evidence of a violent "action imperative" (Mohandie & Duffy, 1999), increasing desperation or distress through declaration in word or deed, forcing the individual into a position of last resort. There is no alternative other than violence, and the consequences are justified (de Becker, 1997).

8. **Directly communicated threat warning behavior** – the communication of a direct threat to the target or law enforcement beforehand. A threat is a written or oral communication that implicitly or explicitly states a wish or intent to damage, injure, or kill the target, or individuals symbolically or actually associated with the target.

(Meloy et al., 2011, pp. 9–10)

Assessing the Pathway to Violence

Deisinger et al. (2008) offer their a four-step understanding of escalating threat that moves progressively through *ideation, planning, acquisition, and implementation* (see Figure 9.1). Those on this pathway offer observable clues that can be useful for the BIT/CARE team, human resources, and law enforcement. Imagine an employee who becomes infatuated with another employee and sees her as the best thing that could ever happen to him. Having her on his arm would literally change every part of his life. People would respect him and other women would finally see him as someone who was successful and attractive by proxy. He fantasizes about being with her; finally having his perfect woman. He gets the courage to ask her out and

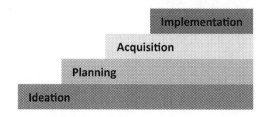

Figure 9.1 Pathway to violence

she immediately laughs at him and rejects him. Others see this train wreck of an approach and tease him relentlessly. He becomes more disillusioned by his failure and he gets rageful toward those who tease him and the woman who turned him down. While he could certainly make a direct threat like, "if you keep teasing me, I'm going to make you pay!," it is also likely he could become more withdrawn, socially isolated, depressed, tearful, and hopeless about things ever being different for him. If he were to plan to harm those around him, it might be that he follows Deisinger et al.'s (2008) pathway to violence and begins by thinking – *ideating* – and fantasizing about hurting those who teased him or the woman who laughed at him and shut him down. He may then escalate this through *planning* to devise a way to have them pay for what they did to him. He could write about these plans at home on his anonymous blog or at lunch in a notebook. These plans could then escalate as he starts to *acquire* the weapons, schematics, explosives, or other elements needed to punish them. The moment of *implementation* comes when he moves from his fantasy rehearsal to putting the plan into practice.

One popular approach to threat assessment is found in the notion to "look for the silence" or the times where a previously concerning individual has "dropped off the radar." While the optimistic among us may hope that the individual got better, a more realistic assessment is that they have fallen further away from those relationships that may have been stabilizing influences and protective factors and now are without any support.

Quiet periods, or the lack of a direct threat, should not be ignored (Meloy, 2000, 2006). Rather than seeing the lack of threat or quiet as a reason to lower the risk, they instead may be the time where the individual is developing a plan of attack, acquiring weapons, learning the schedule and habits of their target, and moving closer and closer to implementation. Jared Loughner was quiet for close to four months between his October 4 voluntary withdrawal from Pima College and his January 8 attack (Couch, 2011). Seung-Hui Cho, from the Virginia Tech attack, had no reports of any concerning behaviors in the spring of 2007 prior to his April 16 assault (Virginia Tech Review Panel, 2007). He calmly and methodically obtained weapons, rented a van, recorded a manifesto, practiced his shooting, locked the doors with chains, and planned the other details of his deadly assault. All of these behaviors provided potential clues and information useful to thwarting the attack. Very few of Cho's behaviors prior to the attack could be described as directly communicated threats.

Conducting a Violence Risk Assessment   113

The best hope of thwarting such a plan requires an attention to patterns and behaviors that, when viewed together as part of a larger picture, may help illuminate the individual's path to violence. A clinician performing the assessment is an ideal position to build trust and rapport while looking carefully for signs of escalating violence.

Structured Professional Judgment (SPJ)

The Structured Professional Judgment (SPJ) process is a seven-step approach to thinking about threat assessment and threat management as an intertwined process (Hart & Logan, 2011). The process includes: (1) gathering information, (2) determining the presence of risk factors, (3) determining the relevance of risk factors, (4) developing a good formulation of violence risk, (5) developing scenarios of violence, (6) developing a case management plan based on those scenarios, and (7) developing conclusory opinions about violence risk.

1 Gather Information

While the first step may seem overly basic, this is one of the most important tasks when beginning a violence risk or threat assessment. Any risk assessment conclusions and resulting interventions are limited by the information collected related to the case. While an interview will likely yield the most information, this should not be the extent of the inquiry. Information should be collected from past treatment, criminal records, student conduct violations, class attendance and participation, work performance, social interaction, and family of origin. Gathering all the information available is useful to prevent blind spots and increases the ability to more fully understand the case. *Any case review, conceptualization, and subsequent interventions, treatment and management will be limited by a lack of this contextual and background information.* The information should be detailed enough to assist in the assessment and ensure a fuller understanding of the case. There will be times when it is difficult or impossible to obtain this kind of information. While it is always preferable to have an in-person interview, there are times this is not possible. In these situations, gather as much as reasonable.

2 Determine the Presence of Risk Factors

At this point in the SPJ process, it is important to have an understanding of the risk factors related to violence. The HCR-20 version 3.0 developed by Hart provides a good starting place to understand the historical, clinical, and current risk factors that correlate with potential violence (Hart & Logan, 2011; Hart et al., 2011). Chapter 7 reviews numerous risk factors that should be understood by the clinician in order to complete a threat assessment. The Structured Interview for Violence Risk Assessment (SIVRA-35) (Van Brunt, 2012, 2015a) is detailed above and, while it is geared primarily toward high school and college populations, can be a valuable tool in other populations as well.

114 *Assessing the Risk*

3 Determine the Relevance of Risk Factors

Once the risk factors are identified and understood, they should be reviewed in the context of the case. While a risk factor may be present, it may not be relevant to the case at hand. At the heart of the SPJ process is the leaning into objective data while balancing this with the clinician's judgment and experience. It is this combination and encouragement to think outside of a standard checklist that gives the system its strength.

4 Develop a Good Formulation of Risk

Hart and Logan (2011) describe the process of gathering and integrating diverse information to develop a concise story of why the person may move toward violence. In other words, can we find a way to understand why they might commit violence? What is needed here is a theory about why this person might be violent.

All violence is goal directed. If you don't understand the goal, you don't understand why the person engaged in violence. In other words, how do they make decisions about violence; how do they weigh the acceptable costs and benefits to violence and ultimately come to a moment of commitment? How do they wrestle with the question of feasibility? Is this something they want to get away with? Do they want to survive the attack? To better understand these questions, Hart and Logan (2011) offer three areas to consider when developing a formulation of risk: motivators, disinhibitors, and destabilizers. These become important in both understanding the "why" of an individual's violent action.

Motivators describe the factors that drive an individual forward in a potentially violent attack. These motivating factors can be understood both individually and collectively in pairs or groups. They are common inspirations for those who commit violence. *Disinhibitors* are the characteristics present that increase the likelihood of violent action. An inhibitor might be something like a positive self-image or stable and supportive peer groups. These are the traits and qualities present that encourage and provide increased momentum for those considering an attack. We see these as the "devil on the shoulder" items that push the person closer to violent action. *Destabilizers* tear away at the fabric of support for the individuals and increase the potential risk for violence. Destabilizers are external factors that increase the risk of violence by upsetting the individual in question. Many of the destabilizing factors below are related to mental illness. This accounts for some of the popular media hype which suggests mental illness is always a causal factor in violent behavior. In reality, the mental health problems did not directly cause the violence, but certainly could increase the likelihood of violence because it is a destabilizing effect. A list of specific motivators, disinhibitors, and destabilizers are outlined in Table 9.2

Once these motivators, disinhibitors and destabilizers are understood they should lead to a good formulation of risk. This formulation creates the foundation for a theory of why a particular incel individual may incline more toward violence. When developing these plans, they should include these characteristics:

1. **Individualized and testable:** While there are certainly patterns of violence that emerge in the literature and as we watch cases develop on the evening news, it

Conducting a Violence Risk Assessment   115

Table 9.2 Formulation of risk motivators, disinhibitors, and destabilizers

Overall	Specific formulation	Description
Motivators	**Justice/Honor:**	Here the motivation becomes achieving justice or honor for a past wrong or frustration. The incel may wish to punish those who disrespect him.
Motivators	**Gain/Profit:**	An example here would be the person who commits violence for personal gain, such as a bank robber or thief. The violence is secondary to the desire to gain or profit. The incel may attempt to hurt others to gain access to a Stacy.
Motivators	**Status/Esteem:**	The motivation here is to achieve a status or place in the world. The violence of the incel is often tied to their perceived "less than" status in the world.
Motivators	**Arousal/Activity:**	This motivation for violence may fit for those involved in bar fights or mixed martial arts. The desire to be violent is related to the increased adrenaline rush and social activity. This affective violence is more immediate and would describe the incel who flies into a rage when rejected.
Motivators	**Proximity/Affiliation:**	Here we can imagine the "Hooligan" culture in EU football matches. Violence is motivated by an affiliation and connection to a certain group and often occurs in a mob mentality. This occurs often online as incels work each other into a frenzy
Motivators	**Release/Expression:**	There are times when the motivation for violence is a final release or expression of pain. For the incel they may scream and shout at unworthy men who are dating Stacy-like women.
Disinhibitors	**Control/Change:**	Here the desire is to alter the current circumstance and shake up the status quo. The motivation for violence is to change the current landscape into something different. This at the heart of the blackpill incel thinking.
Disinhibitors	**Defense/Distance:**	Violence here is driven by a desire to create distance between the person and the targets so they can protect themselves from future harm. This is exemplified by the preemptive, larger plan to protect fellow incels by killing the Chads.
Disinhibitors	**Negative Attitudes:**	Here the incel sees himself as worthless and hopeless, unwilling and unable to see himself in a positive manner.
Disinhibitors	**Lack of Integration:**	This disinhibitor involves the client who is poorly connected socially to those peers around them. The incel is isolated and has difficulty with social skills.

(continued)

116 *Assessing the Risk*

Table 9.2 Cont.

Overall	Specific formulation	Description
Disinhibitors	**Nihilism:**	This is the utter rejection of hopefulness and a belief in nothing. The incel suffers from an utter lack of faith in humanity and desires nothing but others to feel his pain.
Disinhibitors	**Lack of Anxiety:**	Anxiety and fear serve as two very useful inhibitors for potential violence. Incels who have nothing to lose and feel as if their life is over are more likely to act apart from any concern over a societal consequence.
Disinhibitors	**Lack of Guilt**:	Individuals who lack a sense of guilt or remorse for their actions increase the potential for future negative action. Incels often feel as if they are justified in their actions and have little guilt for their violence as society, Stacys, and Chads have little guilt for rejecting them.
Destabilizers	**Disturbed Attention:**	Those with a disturbed sense of attention have difficulty staying focused on tasks and have trouble following through with plans. Many incels become easily distracted by slights and frustrations and have difficulty focusing on any positive outcomes.
Destabilizers	**Disturbed Perception:**	The incel often has difficulty parsing reality from fantasy. They become overwhelmed by alternative-reality delusions and catastrophizing thinking about rejections leading to this destabilizing factor increasing.
Destabilizers	**Impaired Memory:**	The inability to recall information and attribute meaning to a linear set of experiences and circumstances is a destabilizer. Stress, lack of sleep can add to lead to an increased difficulty for an incel recalling past events accurately.
Destabilizers	**Obsessive Thinking:**	The slights and frustrations that are endured become all-encompassing and prevent the incel from thinking logically and rationally about the circumstances unfolding around him.
Destabilizers	**Inability to Reason:**	Here we have individuals with severe enough mental health concerns that their ability to remain rational and reasonable has been impacted. This lack of rationale and logical thoughts is another hallmark of the incel movement.
Destabilizers	**Racing Thinking:**	The incel misattributes blame, develops a sense of tunnel vision, and defies logic and reason as they become further indoctrinated. They struggle to consider other reasonable avenues of thought and logic because he is too overwhelmed with slights and thoughts that jump from one injustice to another.

Conducting a Violence Risk Assessment   117

is important to create a theory that is individualized and applied directly to the qualities of the case. Good stories, like good hypotheses, are then testable. If the story stands up to our testing and critiques, then it may be useful and allow us to make some predictions. We are then able to tell ourselves, "If I'm right, then these treatments should work." This is an active and ongoing process of testing and prediction. The experiential feedback helps us then update our risk formulation.

2. **Narrative and diachronic:** A good risk formulation is rich in description, detail and unfolds over time. The narrative explains why and how the incel may commit violence. It contains case facts, risk factors and stabilizing influences that are tied together in a plot. The story is not static but is laid out over time to capture the interactive nature of the client and the environment.

3. **Ampliative and fertile:** A good risk formulation is more than just taking a list of facts and stringing them together in a predictable way. Instead, it ties the information together in a way that produces new lines of thinking and provides potential areas of insight. Good formulations of risk highlight multiple facets of a person's worldview and life.

5 Develop Scenarios for Violence

This should be a natural transition from the previous section. The development of scenarios for violence should continue the imaginative process of creating a story of violence by expanding the concept and composing several potential stories. There should be several scenarios developed and the range should explain the following: If he was to commit violence, what would he do? Who would he hurt? What kinds of things would make any of this more likely? What would stop the violence from occurring? What would escalate the plan?

Scenario planning is the process by which multiple positive and negative scenarios are imagined by the clinician in order to better conceptualize the potential risk. This method has been used in public safety, health, engineering, and military planning to be better prepared for all potential outcomes while attempting to account for complexity and uncertainly. Building from the clinical risk formulation, one can develop possible scenarios that might occur. This process helps avoids over-reliance on a singular theory rather than conceptualizing the full range of potential outcomes. It allows the clinician to strive for the desired outcome and avoid undesired outcomes. Good scenarios should have the qualities outlined in Table 9.3.

In addition, when developing potential scenarios, they should center around four different archetypes that must be explored. There can be multiple scenarios for each type. The types are:

- **Repeat:** Stories that are a replication of past violence
- **Twist:** Similar story with a change in motivation (a different target or location)
- **Escalation:** Increase in lethality of the attack or a "worst case" scenario
- **Improvement:** Stories that involve a positive change and reduction of threat

118 *Assessing the Risk*

Table 9.3 Positive qualities for scenario planning

Quality	Description
External coherence	Every story has facts. Every case has pieces of information that need to be explained. A formulation of risk should fit those facts. If it doesn't fit the facts, then it isn't a very good scenario. Think of a movie or book where story and plot points are left unexplained when the movie or book ends. This leaves the person reading the book or watching the movie unhappy. A good scenario matches the facts of the formulation. There should be no big facts that are left unexplained.
Factual coherence	There should be a good number of facts used to develop the scenario. Imagine a book or movie that is too short and leaves things unexplained. It's hard to have the plot make sense. Having only few bits of information incorporated into the scenario makes it harder to develop a plot. On the other hand, don't overdo it with facts. Like Goldilocks – not too hot and not too cold.
Internal coherence	The scenario must make sense to us. There cannot be big contradictions. The scenario should be a nice, simple, straightforward story. Don't create a scenario based on a formulation that leaves the reader asking, "If this is the plot, then how did that happen?"
Accepted	Would other clinicians and referral sources who know about the case accept this scenario as one that makes sense? Would they see it as a good story?
Reliable	Is the scenario accurate and valid? Would others come up with a similar scenario or is the story something drawn from left field? If the scenario is tested out, would it produce results?
Generative	Does the scenario provide possible predications and information that is useable to address the potential for violence? Is the story helpful and will it assist us in preventing future violence?
Plausible:	Is the information in the scenario relevant, comprehensive, and credible?
Useful:	Does the scenario guide the development of specific risk management plans?
Consensual:	Are different people able to come up with similar scenarios based on the risk formulation?

6 Case Management Plan Based on Scenarios

One of the differences between other approaches to threat assessment and Hart and Logan's (2011) SPJ approach is the intertwining of assessment with treatment. The assessment naturally flows into questions related to what interventions will reduce the potential risk of violence and what are the exacerbating factors that could make it worse. Hart suggests a good case management plan should include a discussion of strategies, tactics, and logistics. Strategies are the goals and objectives of the overall case management plan. Tactics are details about how we are going to accomplish the goals and objectives. Logistics address how we support the tactics.

The plan (strategy), the specific goals of the plan (tactics) and the actions we take to make sure the specific goals of the plan are accomplished (logistics) are all needed

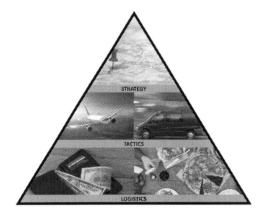

Figure 9.2 Strategy – tactics – logistics

to ensure the overall plan is put into place. If a family was to go on vacation, the strategy would be where they wanted to go on map, the tactics would be the minivan or plane they would take to the destination. The logistics would be the money and food needed for the journey (see Figure 9.2).

7 Conclusory Opinions about Violence Risk

This summary involves reporting information back to the referral source to put the plan into place. This occurs after the assessment is completed and can happen in the form of letter, phone call, or formalized report. This brings together the clinical formulation for risk along with the scenarios to create a clear and useful communication to allow the referral source to make decisions about what comes next for the client.

Moving Forward

We discussed the practical approaches to threat assessment and violence risk assessment. Having the IIR provides a more detailed lens into incel indoctrination and allows for an added depth when exploring risk factors in conjunction with stabilization influences. Chapter 10 reviews a number of clinical approaches to treatment as they can be applied to the incel. The following Chapters 11, 12, and 13 walk the reader through three case studies that are set in junior high school, college, and the workplace to assist in understanding the totality of the threat assessment intervention and management process.

Discussion Questions

- Discuss some common areas of overlap when you read through the various violence risk or threat assessment theories and lists included in this chapter.

120 *Assessing the Risk*

- Which theory or list regarding threat assessment principles seemed the most helpful in assessing the risk of potential violence?
- Think about a time you behaved aggressively or violently to another person in your life. What are some of the motivations you had when for this behavior when you look back on it? What stabilizing influences stopped you from escalating further in your violence?
- Create a brief summary of either Sodini or Rodger's attacks based on the model of *ideation, planning, acquisition, and implementation* described in this chapter.

References

Association of Threat Assessment Professionals (ATAP). (2006). *Risk Assessment Guideline for Elements for Violence (RAGE-V). Considerations for Assessing the Risk of Future Violent Behavior.* Sacramento: Author.

ASIS International and the Society for Human Resource Management. (2011). *Workplace Violence Prevention and Intervention: American National Standard.* Retrieved from www.asisonline.org/guidelines/published.htm

Byrnes, J. (2002). *Before Conflict: Preventing Aggressive Behavior.* Scarecrow Education. Baltimore, MD: R&L Education.

Calhoun, F. & Weston, S. (2009). *Threat Assessment and Management Strategies: Identifying the Howlers and Hunters.* Boca Raton: CRC Press.

Couch, A. (2011, January 12). Arizona shooting suspect Jared Loughner: 5 of his strange ideas. *Christian Science Monitor.*

de Becker, G. (1997). *The Gift of Fear and Other Survival Signals that Protect Us from Violence.* New York: Dell.

Deisinger, E., Randazzo, M., and Nolan, J. (2014). Threat assessment and management in higher education: Enhancing the standard of care in the academy. In J.R. Meloy and J. Hoffmann (eds.), *The International Handbook of Threat Assessment* (pp. 107–125). New York: Oxford University Press,

Deisinger, G., Randazzo, M. O'Neill, D., and Savage, J. (2008). *The Handbook of Campus Threat Assessment and Management Teams.* Applied Risk Management, LLC.

Dietz, P.E. (1986). Mass, serial, and sensational homicides. *Bulletin of the New York Academy of Medicine, 62,* 477–491.

Drysdale, D., Modzeleski, W., and Simons, A. (2010). *Campus Attacks: Targeted Violence Affecting Institutions of Higher Education.* Washington, DC: United States Secret Service, United States Department of Education and Federal Bureau of Investigation.

Dunkle, J.H., Silverstein, Z.B., and Warner, S. L. (2008). Managing violent and other troubling students: The role of threat assessment teams on campus. *Journal of College and University Law,* 34 (3), 585–636.

Fein, R.A., and Vossekuil, B. (1998). *Protective Intelligence and Threat Assessment Investigations: A Guide for State and Local Law Enforcement Officials.* Washington, DC: National Institute of Justice.

Hart, S., & Logan, C. (2011). Formulation of violence risk used evidence-based assessment: The structured professional judgment approach. In P. Sturmey and M. McMurran (eds.), *Forensic Case Formulation* (pp. 83–106). Chichester: Wiley-Blackwell.

Hart, S., Sturmey, P., Logan, C., and McMuran, M. (2011). Forensic case formulation. *International Journal of Forensic Mental Health,* 10, 118–126.

Harvard Mental Health Letter. (2011). Mental Illness and Violence, 27 (7): 1–3.

Conducting a Violence Risk Assessment 121

Hempel, A., Meloy, J.R., and Richards, T. (1999). Offender and offense characteristics of a nonrandom sample of mass murderers. *Journal of the American Academy of Psychiatry and the Law*, 27, 213–225.

Hull, C. (1952). *A Behavior System*. New Haven: Yale University Press.

Jarvis, J. and Scherer, A. (2015) *Mass Victimization: Promising Avenues for Prevention*. Washington, DC: Federal Bureau of Investigation.

Knoll, J. (2010). The "pseudocommando" mass murderer: Part I, the psychology of revenge and obliteration. *Journal of the American Academy of Psychiatry and the Law*, 38, 87–94.

Knoll, J.L. and Annas, G.D. (2016). Mass shootings and mental illness. In L.H. Gold and R.I. Simon (eds.), *Gun Violence and Mental Illness* (pp. 81–104). Washington, DC: American Psychiatric Association.

Lankford, A. (2016). Fame-seeking rampage shooters: Initial findings and empirical predictions. *Aggression and Violent Behavior*, 27, 122–129.

Lankford, A. (2018). Identifying potential mass shooters and suicide terrorists with warning signs of suicide, perceived victimization, and desires for attention or fame. *Journal of Personality Assessment*, 5, 1–12.

MacCulloch, M., Snowden, P., Wood, P., and Mills, H. (1983). Sadistic fantasy, sadistic behavior and offending. *British Journal of Psychiatry*, 143, 20–29.

Meloy, J.R. (2000). *Violence Risk and Threat Assessment: A Practical Guide for Mental Health and Criminal Justice Professionals*. San Diego: Specialized Training Services.

Meloy, J.R. (2006). The empirical basis and forensic application of affective and predatory violence. *Australian and New Zealand Journal of Psychiatry*, 40, 539–547.

Meloy, J., Hoffmann, J., Guldimann, A., and James, D. (2011). The role of warning behaviors in threat assessment: An exploration and suggested typology. *Behavioral Sciences and the Law*. 30, 256–279.

Meloy, R., Hoffmann, J., Roshdi, K., et al. (2014). Warning behaviors and their configurations across various domains of targeted violence. In J.R. Meloy and J. Hoffmann (eds.), *The International Handbook of Threat Assessment* (pp. 39–53). New York: Oxford University Press.

Mohandie, K. (2014). Threat assessment in schools. In J.R. Meloy & J. Hoffman (eds.), *The International Handbook of Threat Assessment* (pp. 126–147). New York: Oxford University Press.

Mohandie, K. and Duffy, J. (1999). Understanding subjects with paranoid schizophrenia. *FBI Law Enforcement Bulletin*, December 1999.

Mullen, P.E., Pathé, M., and Purcell, R. (2009) *Stalkers and Their Victims*. Cambridge: Cambridge University Press.

National Threat Assessment Center (NTAC). (2018). *Enhancing School Safety Using a Threat Assessment Model: An Operational Guide for Preventing Targeted School Violence*. US Secret Service, Department of Homeland Security. Washington, DC.

National Threat Assessment Center (NTAC). (2019). *Protecting America's Schools: A United States Secret Service Analysis of Targeted School Violence*. United States Secret Service, Department of Homeland Security. Washington, DC.

Odgers, C.L., Moffitt, T.E., Tach, L.M., Sampson, A., Taylor, R.J., Matthews, C.L., and Caspi, A. (2009). The protective effects of neighborhood collective efficacy on British children growing up in deprivation: A developmental analysis. *Developmental Psychology*, 45(4): 942–957.

O'Neill, D., Fox, J., Depue, R., and Englander, E. (2008). *Campus Violence Prevention and Response: Best Practices for Massachusetts Higher Education*. Applied Risk Management, LLC, Boston, Ma.

122 Assessing the Risk

O'Toole, M.E. (2000). *The School Shooter: A Threat Assessment Perspective*. Quantico: National Center for the Analysis of Violent Crime, Federal Bureau of Investigation.

O'Toole, M.E. (2002). *The School Shooter: A Threat Assessment Perspective*. Quantico.

O'Toole, M.E. and Bowman, A. (2011). *Dangerous Instincts: How Gut Feelings Betray*. New York: Hudson Street Press.

Randazzo, M. and Plummer, E. (2009). *Implementing Behavioral Threat Assessment on Campus: A Virginia Tech Demonstration Project*. Blacksburg: Virginia Polytechnic Institute and State University.

Sunstein, C.R. (2003). Terrorism and probability neglect. *Journal of Risk and Uncertainty*, 26, 121–136.

Turner, J. and Gelles, M. (2003). *Threat Assessment: A Risk Management Approach*. New York: Routledge.

US Department of Justice and Federal Bureau of Investigation (US DOJ/FBI). (2017). Making prevention a reality: Identifying, assessing, and managing the threat of targeted attacks. Retrieved on September 15, 2017 from www.nccpsafety.org/resources/library/making-preventiona-reality-identifying-assessing-and-managing-the-threat-o/

United States Postal Service (USPS). (2007). Threat assessment team guide, Retrieved on November 30, 2019 from www.nalc.org/workplace-issues/resources/manuals/pub108.pdf

Van Brunt, B. (2012). *Ending Campus Violence: New Approaches to Prevention*. New York: Routledge.

Van Brunt, B. (2015a). *Harm to Others: The Assessment and Treatment of Dangerousness*. Alexandria: American Counseling Association.

Van Brunt, B. (2015b). Violence Risk Assessment of the Written Word (VRAW^2). *Journal of Behavioral Intervention Teams (JBIT)*, 3, 12–25.

Van Brunt, B. (2016). Assessing threat in written communications, social media, and creative writing. *The Journal of Violence and Gender*, 3(2), 78–88.

Van Brunt, B. and Pescara-Kovach, L. (2019). Debunking the myths: Mental illness and mass shootings. *Journal of Gender and Violence*, 6(1), 1–11.

Virginia Tech Review Panel. (2007). Mass shootings at Virginia Tech: Report of the review panel. Retrieved from: https://scholar.lib.vt.edu/prevail/docs/VTReviewPanelReport.pdf

Vossekuil, B., Fein, R., Reddy, M., Borum, R., and Modzeleski, W. (2002). *The Final Report and Findings of the Safe School Initiative: Implications for the Prevention of School Attacks in the United States*. Washington, DC: US Secret Service and US Department of Education.

Part 5

Three Case Studies in Assessment and Treatment

10 Incel Treatment Approaches

This chapter outlines some of the foundational treatment concepts that are most effective in addressing the incel's thoughts, emotions, and behaviors. These include the humanistic, person-centered work of Carl Rogers (1961, 1980), the cognitive-behavioral approaches of Albert Ellis (2007), the narrative approach to therapy of Michael White and David Epston (1990), the metaphor therapy technique of Richard Kopp (1995), existential therapy with Irvine Yalom (1980) and Rollo May (1983), transtheoretical change theory developed by Prochaska, Norcross, and DiClemente (1994) and William Miller & Stephen Rollnick (1991).

Active Listening [PC]

While it may be a challenge to accomplish, active listening is the key to addressing the problem with the incel. At the heart of his frustrations is a belief that he is worth less than everyone around him and that he does not have value. To counter this belief, the therapist must emphasize the basic concepts taught to us in year one of our training; attending and focusing, *really* focusing, on what they are saying gives them an opportunity to feel heard and understood. If this sounds rudimentary, find a psychologist or social worker who has been offering therapy for a long time, perhaps even someone close to retirement or already in retirement. Ask them what was most effective in their practice. We guarantee they won't talk about technique. Instead, they will tell you about listening, caring for the person, understanding from their perspective, and reaching out to them with a sense of hope for a better future.

If you are not familiar with psychotherapy or clinical practice, this concept may seem surprising and somewhat pedestrian. You may reflect: Isn't there more to it than that? Didn't they learn something more in their years of study, mastering various theories and technical applications of treatment? Isn't there more to it counseling than just listening well to someone like a good old Aunt Ruth, offering a cup of tea with a sympathetic smile and assurances that, indeed, things will get better?

And we would say: Yes, of course. There *is* certainly more to the field of clinical psychology and psychotherapy than smiling knowingly and offering hope. Graduate training in research methods and various treatment theories provide an important scaffolding to the work we do. Knowing how and when to refer a patient for inpatient treatment, groupwork, medication support, and offering exercises and meditations they could do to improve their mental health. However, this is not the soul of good

126   *3 Case Studies in Assessment and Treatment*

treatment. These technical skills and knowledge of theory are not sufficient. Learning to listen and project care to the incel, while offering hope for a better tomorrow; these are the most essential concepts to bring him away from this dangerous, self-destruction indoctrination.

Carl Rogers (1961), the humanistic psychologist and father of the **Person-Centered Approach** to treatment, offers the following: "when someone understands how it feels and seems to be me, without wanted to analyze me or judge me, then I can blossom and grow in that climate" (p. 62). Empathy and congruence are the essential qualities to help the incel find a new way of being. Empathy means seeing the world through someone else's eyes, understanding from their perspective. Congruence is about the therapist conveying a sense of genuineness and authenticity to the client. We tend to trust those who we can understand and who seem honest and direct about their goals.

At the heart of active listening is the therapist conveying understanding to their client. The clinician demonstrates an ability to listen in a non-judgmental manner that, in turn, creates a more fertile and supportive place for the incel to share his perspective with a decrease in defensiveness and hesitation. Imagine normal, household glass. The incel client enters the session with a gallon jug of water and sees the therapist has only a normal glass. He can't pour all the water from his jug into your glass. In other words, he refrains from sharing because he knows the clinician won't be able to contain the volume of information he needs to share. When the therapist adopts an open, non-judgmental, active-listening-based stance, it's as if they bring a five-gallon bucket to each session. It can contain what the incel client needs to share.

Rogers offers this in his book, *A Way of Being* (1980),

> empathetic listening. This means the therapist senses accurately the feelings and personal meanings that the client is experiencing and communicates this understanding to the client. When functioning best, the therapist is so much inside the private world of the other that he or she can clarify not only the meaning of which the client is aware but even those just below the level of awareness. This kind of sensitive, active listing is exceedingly rare in our lives. We think we listen, but rarely do we listen with real understanding, true empathy. Yet listening, of this very special kind, is one of the most potent forces for change that I know.

> (p. 116)

Lost, Naked, and Alone [ExT]

In his book *Existential Psychotherapy* (1980), Irvin Yalom explains that we each confront four ultimate concerns in life. These are (1) dealing with the vastness of the freedom of our choices, (2) the anxiety that exists when contemplating death, (3) wrestling with what it means to be connected with others yet ultimately alone, and (4) coming to terms with an ultimate meaning in our existence. While there is an overlap in each of these areas, Yalom offers this broad picture for clarity's sake and the expectation they will fold back into each other as the reader explores the different concepts.

These four challenges correspond well with the struggles faced by the incel. While a more advanced therapeutic concept, we believe it will be helpful to see how some of these struggles directly relate to the struggles the incel faces. They offer insight into some of the theorical challenges they may be facing that underpin their sadness and rage.

Freedom: While freedom may seem initially like a novel and easy concept to accept, Yalom encourages us to look at the other side of freedom: How do we all cope with the freedom we have? What do we see when we look out into the infinite space of possibility? Like many of us, the incel struggles with the vastness of his choices. Get married and have a family or be the jet-setting playboy. Settle for a femoid that is less than his ideal Stacy and there must be a reckoning as all other options become unavailable for a time. Refuse this concept and date freely without restriction and miss out of the stability and ease that comes with being in a monogamous relationship. Everywhere you look, you are faced with more and more choices. How can someone look into their infinite options for life and choose a path that they can feel confident about? Yalom (1980) writes: "'Freedom' in this sense, has a terrifying implication: it means that beneath us there is no ground – nothing, a void, an abyss. The key conflict is how a patient struggle between groundlessness and our wish for ground and structure" (p. 9).

It is in this space that the "lost boy" described in Chapter 1 looks around and tries to find a philosophy that resonates with his experience in sea of choices. Perhaps he becomes invested in some sort of anarchistic philosophy railing against structure, order, and, in the end, life itself. Perhaps instead he looks for the order and assurance given by seemingly wise and experienced experts offering the "ultimate truth." This may help explain the cult like following often attributed to the incel movement. While it may not be the answer, it proposes *an* answer. A solution against the unknown.

Death: We exist now, but one day will cease to exist. Death will come for all of us and there is no escape from it. The famous Dutch philosopher, Benedict de Spinoza suggests, "Everything endeavors to persist in its own being." With this idea in mind, it becomes important for the therapist to help the client resolve "the awareness of the inevitability of death and the wish to continue to be" (Yalom, 1980, p. 8). For the incel, his own death and potential non-existence may be a motivating factor to have a beautiful woman on is arm. At least this makes sense to him as he looks around at a society that attaches a value to this "possession."

Yalom describes this phenomenon as it relates to patients facing terminal disease. He explains they cope with a "myth of specialness," when you feel as if medications won't work on you because you are unique in the world, or that death comes for everyone except for you because of your distinction from others. The incel may become focused on achieving his sexual fantasies when faced with death and may embrace the fantasies of violence against others in an attempt to dominate death itself.

Helping the incel, finding a place of equanimity in his thoughts, may first require a real look at his own mortality. The stoic philosopher Lucretius offers a calming statement: "Where I am, death is not; where death is, I am not. Therefore death is nothing to me" (Yalom, 1980, p. 45). This may require the incel to face some difficult and challenging conversations about his own mortality. We can look for ways to help incels explore their own mortality and find a larger sense of direction and meaning.

128   3 Case Studies in Assessment and Treatment

Isolation: No matter how close of a bond we form with each other, there remains a distance. We are individuals in a collective community. A struggle for the incel is how he copes with this separation and remoteness present in our everyday lives. It is an undeniable fact that each of us enters the existence alone and must depart from it the same manner. The incel struggles to exist between his awareness of his isolation and his desire for contact; his need for protection within the community juxtaposed with the knowledge he is alone an ultimately can only depend on himself.

Yalom makes a powerful observation in his discussions of existential isolation. He writes, "I believe that if we are able to acknowledge our isolated situations in existence and to confront them with resoluteness, we will be able to turn lovingly to others. If, on the other hand, we are overcome with dread before the abyss of loneliness, we will not reach toward others but instead will flail at them in order not to drown in the sea of existence" (1980, p. 363).

Imagine those who have a fear of water or drowning. When learning to swim, they must put the fear of the water behind them. Those who face this fear, those who hold their breath and go under, realize they will be ok. Only mastering their fear of the water has allowed them to experience the many joys of swimming, diving, Marco-Polo, and the like. No one can learn to swim until they learn to overcome the fear of the water. Once the fear is released, they glide through the water and are comfortable to play underneath it. The water loses its ability to evoke fear. Only by letting go of fears, can they truly enjoy life. Yalom quotes Tolstoy early in the book saying, "he is dying badly because he has lived badly" (p. 33).

Meaninglessness: If we must die, and if we are each ultimately alone, within an indifferent universe; then what meaning does life have? The dilemma for the incel is facing the reality that he is a meaning-seeking creature who is thrown into a universe that has no meaning. For some, this existential dread becomes a contributing motivator for his fantasies of being part of a larger rebellion and punishing others. If he has ingested the blackpill and his life as an incel is a forgone conclusion; why do his actions matter, if nothing matters? If we all must die, then why should he restrain his darker thoughts?

Many have avoided this existential conflict by finding religion and a hope the afterlife will serve to create meaning for our earthly experiences. Others choose to pursue a career or create great art or literature to define their lives. Some lose themselves in the loving of another – a wife, husband, partner, child, or friend. This love then becomes defining for them and staves off feelings and thoughts of meaninglessness. For the incel, this love is denied to them and the career path seems a poor second choice. The incel struggles to find a path to protect his mind from the inevitability of death and falls prey to a suicidal, desperate attack or "going out in a blaze of glory" that offers the promise of meaning and purpose that has been denied him for his existence.

Engaging and Changing the Incel Story [Na]

Everyone has a story. There are five stories of murders included in Appendix B (Sodini), C (Rodger), D (Mercer), E (Roof), and F (Ferguson) to further the understand the indoctrination they bought into regarding racism, misogyny, and the incel

Incel Treatment Approaches 129

philosophy. It is these stories, and the attack cases included in Appendix A, that provide insight into the thinking, emotions, behaviors, and social and environmental experiences that helped shape their rage and violence.

In order to redirect the incel away from their harmful beliefs, treatment providers must learn their stories. It is in these stories, often shaped by experience, that we become seen as an interested party and potential ally to their health and well-being. The approach to treatment known as **Narrative Therapy**, created by Australian family therapists Michael White and David Epston (1990), suggest that we use our stories to organize and give meaning to our experiences. As such, incels construct their meaning through the stories they share and treat these as the "truth" (Corey, 2001). Further, these stories are not static, but rather ever-changing, giving opportunities to therapists to alter the course of the incel. White and Epson (1990), write, "With every performance, persons are re-authoring their lives. The evolution of lives is akin to the process of re-authoring, the process of persons entering into stories, taking them over and making them their own" (Van Brunt, 2007, pp. 27–28; see White & Epston, 1990).

Psychologists, counselors and social workers can help their clients with incel indoctrination to examine their lives through the stories they tell, by assisting them in revising their stories in a manner that gives him more ownership and ability to gain control over negative past experiences. Narrative therapy helps separate the incel from the negative, damaging stories he tells himself and find new stories that lead to a more constructive outcome. White and Epston (1990) suggest these new, hopeful stories develop as creations between the client and the therapist. Their book, *Narrative Means to a Therapeutic Ends*, has numerous examples of techniques to bring the therapist and client together toward a common goal.

The first step of this process is for the therapist to **externalize the story** from the client. White (1988/1989) writes, "Externalizing is an approach to therapy that encourages persons to objectify, and at times, to personify, the problems that they experience as oppressive" (p. 5). Prior to any change, White and Epston (1990) suggest the behavior, fears, and worries must be separated from the client prior to any attempt to reconstruct them. It would be reasonable to understand the indoctrinated incel would hold onto his stories in fear that he would risk losing the very fabric of what gives meaning, direction, and purpose to his life. "As persons become separated from their stories, they are able to experience a sense of personal agency; as they break from their performance of their stories, they experience a capacity to intervene in their own lives and relationships" (White and Epston, 1990, p. 16). By externalizing the story, like taking the carburetor out of the car to repair it, we provide the freedom to examine the problem and create new, unique outcomes to their stories, which were previously restricted. This process of "storying" his experiences, the act of adding detail, sensation, emotions to his narratives, offers clues to the meaning he ascribes to his life's pains, hardships and experiences.

Kopp (1995) expands on the narrative therapy approach and advises the therapist next focus on the language and metaphor used by the client. These narrative clues offer a critical connection to the incel's inner worldview. Dr. Corsini summarizes in the forward of Kopp's (1995) text,

130   3 Case Studies in Assessment and Treatment

the client and therapist, acting like detectives, look for clues to understanding the essence of the mystery by exploring and transforming the client's metaphoric language, hoping to find something that has little significance either to the client or to anyone who does not know the secret of the metaphor, but which, when the secret is revealed, becomes the key that opens the lock of the door that has stood between the person and freedom.

(pp. ix–x)

It is precisely these breadcrumbs of metaphor and language that offer insight and a framework toward the introduction more optimistic and constructive outcomes

Kopp (1995) offers an example of a patient who describes her husband's poor behavior. She describes a lack of attention, disrespectful communications about when he will be home and when he is away, and a lack of effort looking for employment. She shares, "he barges into the house like a locomotive" (p. xiv). Kopp pounces on this descriptive clue to create a springboard into the client's dissatisfaction with the marriage. He asks her, "If he is a locomotive, what are you?" She clarifies what was being asked and replies with, "a tunnel" (p. xiv). Kopp asks, "What if you could change the image so that it would be better for you, how would you change it?" She thinks a moment and then suddenly exclaims, "I'd be the derailer!" (p. xv). This "self-as-derailer" metaphor becomes a shared construct between the therapist and patient. It offers a focal point for the patient to shift from a passive model (the tunnel) to an active model (the derailer). This provides her ways to visualize new, unique, and optimistic outcomes.

For incels, it is these stories they tell themselves about being a failure, genetically insufficient to find a mate, unable to find personal value and self-esteem and the resulting anger and rage that feed into increasingly negative outcomes. By understanding and engaging in their story, the therapist creates opportunities to bring about lasting change.

Who Are You? [May]

A central theme in Rollo May's (1983) book *The Discovery of Being* is the focus on the immediacy of the moment, the inherent power in the individual's choice, and freedom from the deterministic view of the past experience and the specter of the unconscious influencing the present. To this end, the incel would be encouraged to take responsibility for his thoughts and actions. He should focus on the task of finding his meaning and place in the world rather than feeding his obsession with Chads and Stacys and buying into an ultimately maladaptive, self-destructive philosophy.

May emphasizes the concept of *Dasein*, a German word meaning "being there," and the importance of the real encounter between client and therapist. This echoes Rogers' focus on genuineness and congruence in the therapeutic contact. May explains the client in terms of *potenia*, or "being" as a source of potentiality. He writes: " 'being' is the potentiality by which the acorn becomes the oak or each of us becomes what he truly is" (p. 97, 1983). May would encourage the therapist to ask an incel patient, "Where are you?" as opposed to "How are you?" This focus on directionality encourages the clinician to be more attuned to the incel's direction and

Incel Treatment Approaches   131

potential rather than being distracted by their symptoms. In a true expression of the existential dilemma, the pain becomes a path to healing. The therapist sees the moon, not the finger pointing to the moon. The therapist sees what the incel can become, not just his current state.

In practical application, May encourages the therapist to focus on the direction, or "becoming," rather than on the specific symptoms or problems the incel presents. May's strength lies in presenting a theory that goes beyond the simple techniques, but rather looks instead to the direction or movement of the client/therapist interaction. How do each of us exist as true entities, true *Dasein*, willing to connect and experience each other's humanness first, before any solution is introduced? He says it this way,

> Knowing another human being, like loving him, involves a kind of union, a dialectical participation with the other. This Binswanger calls the "dual mode." One must have at least a readiness to love the other person, broadly speaking, if one is to be able to understand him.
>
> (May, 1983, p. 93)

Here, it is the relationship that is healing, in the same way Rogers writes (1961, 1980), *rather than any advice or solutions*. May (1983) quotes Fredia Fromm-Reichmann, "The patient needs an experience, not an explanation."

The anxiety experienced by the incel is "the loss in the range of possibility" (May, 1983, p. 45). Incel reform is half-won when "the patient [can] focus on some point the in the future when he will be outside his anxiety or depression" (May, 1983, p. 135). The incel's anxiety can be seen as a manifestation of fear of non-being. As such, *treatment focus should move away from mere symptom relief to helping the incel face his fear and place it in the appropriate context*. Pathological anxiety can never be explained away, whether by argument, mesmerism or medication. Time and time again, we must nod across from the incel client and say, "You are right. Death is terrifying. There are too many choices. We are out of control." The healing comes from the acknowledgment of pain, gaining power and comfort over life choices and finding solace in the revelation that we are all in this together.

The therapist missteps by focusing too much on symptom relief, whether it is the redirection of his needs or the supplanting of his desires, and not enough on the true underpinnings, or the purpose behind the symptoms. May (1983) offers this metaphor to explain the dangers of attending too much to the presenting mechanisms than the client's potential: you are "teaching a farmer irrigation while damming up his streams of water" (p. 164). This kind of direct connection is overly simplistic. It is less than helpful to teach the incel to simply learn to keep his intense beliefs about incel ideas to himself if he wishes to stay enrolled in school or employed in the workplace. The underlying desperation and self-annihilating solutions offered by this failed philosophy remains.

Teaching the Incel to Think Differently [REBT] [Na]

As the relationship is established with the incel through rapport building and developing a relationship based on mutual respect, another approach to change

132   3 Case Studies in Assessment and Treatment

involves assisting the client to learn how to think differently about low self-esteem, rejection from women, a negative self-concept, and actual and perceived unfair experiences. While inspiring hope and caring for the incel provides the energy and direction to bring about therapeutic change, the CBT approach offers the practical tools and techniques required to accomplish change and assist him in altering the way he interprets his interactions. The cognitive behavioral approach to therapy (Ellis, 2007; Glasser, 1975, 2001) rose in popularity as they brought with them an increased attention on empirically validated treatment to help clients think differently about their problems and, subsequently, behave differently and avoid a larger escalation to mission-oriented violence.

Identifying and managing the daily frustrations and slights experiences by the incel requires him to first identify how his body is experiencing biological changes as he becomes increasingly upset and frustrated. These environmental stimuli are seen as irritations and annoyances, or "trigger events," that elicit a biological reaction. This could be another male having success dating an attractive female, rejection following an attempt to ask out a woman, or bullying and teasing behavior experienced by the incel. As these events occur, his heart rate increases, breathing becomes faster, adrenaline is produced, and there is a diminished capacity for creative and rational thought. Dr. Nay (2004) describes the process which starts with the stomach and GI systems emptying of blood as digestion slows or holds to free up blood for the brain and muscles. This causes shallow breathing, chest heaviness, and feelings of suffocation. Senses may become more sensitive and magnified; movements toward you may seem more threatening. Muscles begin to tighten, particularly around the shoulders, neck, forehead and jaw.

These activating events are described in detail through the therapeutic approach called **Rational Emotive Behavioral Therapy.** This approach to treatment was developed by Albert Ellis (2007) and is useful to assist clients in identifying irrational thoughts they have in response to these activating events. **The REBT approach can be described in terms of A-B-Cs: Activating events, Beliefs about these events, and the Consequences of these beliefs**. Assisting the incel to see his irrational and catastrophizing thoughts is the first step to helping him discover alternative ways to process the world around him. This process begins with the incel identifying upsetting events that experiences and labeling these "activating events."

These activating events happen in a variety of places. They occur through daily hassles which the incel encounters in his environment (daily work stress, chronic teasing from peers, financial worries, self-esteem), life changes (graduation worries, family divorce or conflict, being away from home the first time), environmental stresses (construction noises, delays in getting something he wants, watching others have success dating when he keeps failing, frustration from living in close quarters with other college students), chronic pain (from past surgery, illness, or injury), or acculturation stress (moving from another country or geographic region, living in a religiously different area). For the most part, these events cannot be prevented; they occur throughout our lives. Once the stressful activating events are identified, the therapist can then focus on applying techniques to improve the client's ability to cope and reduce further escalation. The incel is encouraged to appreciate and accept

Incel Treatment Approaches 133

the continual presence of upsetting experiences; that he has little control of the occurrence of these activating events and his energy would be better focused on finding alternative ways to conceptualize the activating event to increase more positive consequences.

The development of ***alternative explanations,*** or the ability to see these activating events from another perspective is a preventative step and a step toward moving away from aggressive and violent behavior. For example, we are less likely to be aggressive toward the driver in a car that cuts us off in traffic if we know the driver is rushing to be by the side of a dying parent in the hospital. The aggressive behavior is dissipated because the aggressor then sees himself acting in the same manner. This leads to the more positive consequence.

Managing impulsive reactions to activating events is an obvious important tool for the incel to learn. Dr. Nay (2004) outlines five "S" intensifiers toward anger and aggressive behavior, outlined in Table 10.1. While none of these suggestions are directly related to the common frustrations and hassles voiced by the incel, addressing his overall wellness, sleep, eating, stress and substance use all have the potential

Table 10.1 Anger intensifiers (Nay, 2004)

Intensifier	Description
Sleep	A lack of sleep makes people more irritable and reduces their ability to be flexible and positively focused when approaching negative stress or activating events. Identify and address these underlying difficulties with sleep (lack of exercise, inconsistent sleep schedule, and substance abuse) and how these lead to difficulty in getting enough rest.
Stress	The body feels stress when reacting to change and frustrating situations. High stress levels lead to higher irritability and difficulty in responding in a flexible and positive way when dealing with activating events. Stress is cumulative and builds up to dangerous levels, setting the stage for the next activating event to lead to an explosion.
Substance abuse	Alcohol and caffeine can dramatically intensify our emotions. Energy drinks and other substances can be overused in an attempt to reduce stress but end up making the situation worse. Substances increase irritability, decrease impulse control and frustration tolerance, both of which can intensify how stressful these events are be perceived.
Sustenance	Many of us struggle to eat a healthy diet and maintain proper exercise. When trying to balance class, work, relationships, social life, athletics, club memberships, and family, it is easy to see how good nutrition and exercise quickly fall by the wayside. Too much sugar or junk food may also increase mood swings and intensify aggressive behaviors.
Sickness	When we become ill, our ability to cope with stress is reduced. Pain and discomfort increase arousal, irritability and decrease an individual's ability to think clearly. Poor nutrition, lack of exercise and increased stress leads to a weaker immune system and a higher potential for sickness.

134   3 Case Studies in Assessment and Treatment

to help reduce the exacerbation of his existing problems. In the same way a gardener ensures they have the right soil, sunlight, water, and nutrients for their plants, addressing anger intensifiers can be useful to support other CBT efforts.

The incel client may come to session with the knowledge of their problems and difficulty. The real trouble they experience may be more related to making a plan and sticking to it. To help with this approach, the Navy SEALs developed some suggestions of ways to mentally overcome the arduous physical challenges they face in their training, particularly during their "Hell" week. There are four key stress control techniques used to help the SEALs better cope with stress and stay focused on their goals (Blair, 2008). These are:

1. **Goal Setting:** Goal setting is the process of encouraging clients to have a clear picture of their goals and creating a way to see progress toward their goals. This can be done through journaling about progress or creating a chart of successful times they coped with activating events or were able to reduce their escalation phase. The incel client should be encouraged to set his mind on an immediate, measurable goal. A SEAL trainee might focus on "I need to make it to the next hill on the beach" or "I just need to stay under for another 5 seconds ... I can do another 5 seconds." A incel client may need to focus on "I just need to try to talk to one woman today without any expectations of dating or having sex," or "I am going to find three things that I think I am good at and spend some time thinking about these rather than brooding or feeling worthless."

2. **Mental Rehearsal:** Clients are encouraged to mentally imagine themselves being successful at a particular interaction that in the past caused problems. It is easy to imagine Navy SEAL trainees visualizing successful missions or accomplishing a goal. Sports psychologists teach this technique for basketball players to improve their foul shots. Incel clients can follow these steps:

    a. Clearly visualize a conflict where you could become aggressive or continue to escalate.
    b. Visualize responding calmly and avoiding an escalation or allowing frustrations to develop. Focus on the best possible response such as "Well, that is certainly one way to see it. I don't see it the same way, though."
    c. Imagine obstacles to a successful interaction. Possibly imagine another student pushing or yelling back. Visualize the best possible response.
    d. Repeat this process several times a week until the student begins to see results.

3. **Self-Talk:** Positive self-talk will assist clients in developing an internal "cheerleading team" that can help push them during difficult times. The incel client should identify a supportive person in his life – a cheerleader – and then imagine that person mentally accompanying him during a conflict. While the conflict is going on, the client can imagine the cheerleader saying, "You got this one. No way are they going to push your buttons. Calm and cool. The more they push; the more you relax." This positive self-talk could be used to reduce his worry about never having sex, stay focused on his classes or work, and limit the people

he talks to about his concerns over his lack of sexual experience and failures at talking to women.

4. **Arousal Control:** This is essentially the process of cycle breathing. By taking slow, deep breathes with controlled exhales, the client communicates to their body that this is not a panic (Fight/Flight) situation and that they need to maintain control. This process is similar to what expectant mothers, Navy SEAL snipers, and meditating monks use to control their biological functions. As with any of these techniques, the key is practice and repetition.

Making a Plan [Real]

Glasser (1975, 2001) founded a therapeutic system called ***Reality Therapy***. In this system, he suggests the importance of creating plans with clients that will be achievable. To this end, he argues plans should be focused and short-term. A plan like "Kyle will stop being creepy toward women in the workplace" is too broad and difficult to monitor and put into action. The goal is so big it would be hard for him to make adjustments to the plan or know if he is moving forward, static, or moving backward. A better plan would address what specific things he should avoid doing or things he should do more of to seem accessible.

The plan would then include practicing these new skills, identifying obstacles that would get in the way of a successful implementation. The plan would explore ways to increase his social skills, establish boundaries, and "no-go" conversation zones and seek to improve Kyle's empathy and understanding why his current behaviors are off-putting to other office workers. Glasser (1975, 2001) outlines a process of change based on the understanding of and assessing the needs of the incel client. This plan is abbreviated with ***WDEP***. This stands for identifying the **W**ants and needs, **D**irection and what they are doing, an **E**valuation of their behavior, and **P**lanning and commitment to change. When reviewing plans with the incel, it is suggested the plans be simple, attainable, measurable, immediate, consistent, controlled by the client, committed to by the client, and timely. Plans that are created by a therapist that do not have buy-in from the client or are too complicated or broad to be measured are doomed to failure.

Motivational Interviewing [MI]

Motivational Interviewing, or Motivational Enhancement Therapy (MET) was developed by Miller and Rollnick (1991) and used primarily with mandated alcohol treatment to help people change addictive behavior. Their approach is helpful in working with mandated students in on-going treatment and to help connect with those who are initially unwilling to explore a change in the way they behave. It is a proactive approach to working with those who don't yet see they have a problem, or if they do see they have a problem, aren't yet ready to tackle it or head in a new direction. The heart of Miller and Rollnick's approach centers on five key concepts that can be applied well to working with clients who are mandated to treatment.

The five techniques of Motivational Interviewing are explored in Table 10.2. They are not applied in any particular order, but instead organically as you build alliance with the client.

136   *3 Case Studies in Assessment and Treatment*

Table 10.2 Motivational interviewing techniques (Miller and Rollnick, 1991)

Task	Description
Expression of Empathy	Expression of empathy involves a conversation with the client that attempts to both understand their perspective (empathy) and communicate an understanding of that perspective (expression of empathy). This expression of empathy respects the client's point of view, freedom of choice and ability to determine their own self-direction. Suggestions from the therapist for change are subtle and the ultimate change is left in the hands of the client.
Avoiding Argumentation	This is probably the easiest technique to understand, but the most difficult to put into practice. When you argue back to the client who is arguing with you, neither of you are listening to each other.
Roll with Resistance	Clinicians are encouraged to avoid meeting a client's resistance to change head-on. Instead, they should try to engage the client in new ways of thinking about the situation, perhaps trying to evoke from the client new solutions to the conflict. Lack of motivation or an unwillingness to change and be positive are understood as normal developmental responses, and interventions are designed to avoid becoming mired down in the client's lack of developmental growth and personal responsibility to change.
Developmental of Discrepancy	Developmental of discrepancy is the process by which the therapist helps clients understand that the current behavior won't help them achieve the desired goal. The therapist explores the consequences of the client's actions in a neutral manner, avoiding sarcasm or a condescending tone. The client then becomes aware of their choices and starts to explore the advantages to choosing a different way to behave.
Supporting Self-efficacy:	Supporting self-efficacy involves helping the client understand that change is possible and there is the possibility of a better outcome in their future. This is done by the therapist encouraging and nurturing growth in his or her client, finding times and opportunities to "catch them doing well" and praising this behavior with hopes of shaping future positive behavior.

How the Incel Will Experience Change [CT]

We all go through the same process of change, whether it be related to exercising more, learning how to talk to women more effectively, reducing video game time or quitting smoking. This approach is called Transtheoretical Change Theory and it was developed by Prochaska, Norcross, and DiClemente (1994). Their book, *Changing for Good*, offers an excellent overview of this process. These change concepts are universally helpful when looking to answer the question "Why is it so hard for the incel to just learn how to talk to girls?"

The basics of the approach outline how we move through various stages before achieving lasting change. This process can help the incel client gain a sense of perspective and understanding about why he may be repeating difficult or frustrating behaviors. As you review this section, consider a behavior you have tried to change in your life. This can either be something you are currently struggling with (perhaps

Incel Treatment Approaches   137

smoking, watching too much TV, not getting enough exercise) or something you have tried to change in the past. As you read the five stages of change, keep your example in mind to better understand this process.

Pre-contemplation: At this stage, the incel is unaware he has a problem and hasn't thought much about change. The therapist's goal is to help him increase awareness of the need for change. This is done primarily through non-judgmental, non-directive open discussion. The therapist helps the client understand how his behaviors may be impacting his life and others around him. Any advice, from behaving differently in class to joining a club or organization to make new friends will fall on deaf ears since he has no desire to change. In his mind, he doesn't have a problem. He certainly doesn't have a behavior that needs to be changed. Until the incel develops a desire to change his behavior to avoid negative consequences, any advice or positive suggestions will be ignored. The therapist needs to engage and explore, helping the incel to come to an understanding that what he is currently doing is causing enough problems in his life and lives of those around him to necessitate a change in his behavior.

Contemplation: This is the most common stage of change for an incel client. He has thought about change and may be getting ready for movement in the near future. He realizes his current behavior is not in his best interest but is not ready to begin a plan to change. He isn't happy about his current state and wants things to be different but has not yet explored how to do things differently or take action to make change in his life.

In this stage, the therapist continues to motivate their client and encourages him to think in more detail about how his behavior is having a negative impact on his life and the lives of others. They should explore ways he might plan for change and what resources could be helpful in implementing change. The therapist's role here is to continue to explore and push the client closer to a plan for action. There should be less focus on the specifics of *how* this plan would be implemented, but instead a further exploration of *why* he wants to behave differently.

Preparation for Action: In this stage, the incel is aware of his problem and is ready to actively create goals to address the problem behavior in his life. Plans and goals should be focused, short term, and designed to be updated and altered to ensure his success. Plans should be measurable and easy to monitor to see if he is moving forward, static, or moving backward. The therapist can help him brainstorm and update his plans to ensure a better chance of success.

Action: This stage of change is where the incel puts his plans into action to change behavior. He will attempt to alter his negative behaviors and develop new positive behaviors to replace them. The therapist can support him as he tries to implement action steps and encourage him to keep trying, despite setbacks and the potential failures he may encounter.

Maintenance and Relapse Prevention: Here the goal is to continue successful plans and repeat those action steps that work, while adjusting those aspects of the plan that don't. Change has occurred for incel and there has been a reduction in problem behavior and/or success in achieving his goals. He needs to maintain the successful change and reduce the risk of falling back into bad habits. The therapist helps to bolster his success by identifying and encouraging an awareness of potential obstacles that could lead to relapse.

138   3 Case Studies in Assessment and Treatment

Moving Forward

This chapter offered a wide and broad overview of multiple therapeutic techniques useful for addressing incel thoughts and behaviors. To further assist the reader in applying the assessment and treatment recommendations outlined in the previous chapters, the next three chapters, 11, 12, and 13, offer case studies addressing incel thoughts and behaviors for males in junior high, college, and the workplace. Each chapter provides a case narrative, assessment of the incel indoctrination with the IIR (from Appendix I) and recommendations for treatment based on the concepts outlined in this chapter. The abbreviations listed above in each section heading will be used as shorthand when discussing treatment strategies for those cases.

[AI]: Anger Intensifiers by Robert Nay (2004)

[Na]: Narrative Therapy by White and Epston (1990)

[MI]: Motivational Interviewing by Miller/ Rollnick (1991)

[PC]: Person-Centered by Carl Rogers (1961)

[May]: Rollo May (1983)

[ExT]: Existential Therapy by Irvin Yalom (1980)

[REAL]: Reality Therapy by William Glasser (1975)

[REBT]: Rational Emotive Behavorial Theraapy by Albert Ellis (2007)

[Met]: Metaphor Therapy by Richard Kopp (1995)

[CT]: Change Theory by Prochaska/ DiClemente (1994)

Discussion Questions

- After reviewing the various treatment ideas suggested in this chapter, which ones resonate the most with you in terms of offering help and bringing about change?
- Give an example of how you might apply one of these techniques to a case discussed so far in the book.
- Is there a treatment method you have used that was not mentioned that you believe would work with this population?
- Using the Change Theory model discussed in this chapter, pick a behavior that you have had in your life that you have either successfully changed or have struggled with changing. Map out this behavior using the five levels of: pre-contemplation, contemplation, preparation, action, relapse/maintenance.

References

Blair, C. (2008). Better test performance the Navy SEALs way. Retrieved from http:// studyprof.com/blog/2008/11/25/better-test-performance-the-navy-seals-way/

Corey, G. (2001). *Theory and Practice of Counseling and Psychotherapy*. Belmont: Brooks/ Cole Thompson Learning.

Ellis, A. (2007). *The Practice of Rational Emotive Behavior Therapy*. New York: WW Norton & Company.

Glasser, A. (1975). *Choice Theory: A New Psychology of Personal Freedom*. New York: Colophon Books.

Glasser, A. (2001). *Counseling with Choice Theory: The New Reality Therapy*. New York: Colophon Books.

Kopp, R.R. (1995). *Metaphor Therapy*. New York: Brunner/Mazel, Inc.

May, R. (1983). *The Discovery of Being*. New York: W.W. Norton & Company.

Miller, W.R. and Rollnick, S. (1991). *Motivational Interviewing: Preparing People to Change Addictive Behavior*. New York: Guilford Press.

Nay, R. (2004). *Taking Charge of Anger*. New York: Guilford Press.

Prochaska, J., Norcross, J., & DiClemente, C. (1994). *Changing for Good*. New York: Harper Collins.

Rogers, C. (1961). *On Becoming a Person*. New York: Houghton Mifflin.

Rogers, C. (1980). *A Way of Being*. New York: Houghton Mifflin.

Van Brunt, B. (2007). *The Thematic Apperception Test (TAT): Administration and Interpretation*. Prescott: Borrego.

White, M. (1988/1989). The externalizing of the problem and the reauthoring of lives and relationships. *Dulwich Centre Newsletter*, 5–28. Summer.

White, M. and Epston, D. (1990). *Narrative Means to Therapeutic Ends*. New York: WW Norton & Company.

Yalom, I. (1980). *Existential Psychotherapy*. New York: Basic Books.

11 Assessment and Treatment Approaches
Junior High

Case 1: Marc

Marc is a 12-year-old student in 6th grade. He has a younger brother he ignores and a mother who juggles two jobs. His father left the family when Marc was four.

He has difficulty connecting with other students and is often teased about his clothes and hair. While he tries to look and dress cool, he can never get it right and his attempts often make things worse with his peers. He often gets into conflicts with his fellow students and argues with teachers. His grades have been slipping as well and he spends his lunch time and recess alone. He doesn't like to participate in games as he's not very athletic. All of this makes the other students tease him even more. There have been incidents in the locker room after gym and in the hallways of other male students calling him names and knocking things out of his hands. After ruminating and agonizing about the idea for a week, he approaches a female student in the cafeteria and asks her to go out the movies. He had been friends with her in kindergarten, but they drifted apart as she became one of the cool kids. Her friend laughs at him and they both turn away and whisper, obviously talking about him. He runs away from them and spends the rest of the lunch period hiding in the bathroom, away from all the kids staring and laughing at him.

Marc starts to pull away even more after this event. He spends time at home on the computer. His mom doesn't have the time or knowledge to monitor his online activity. While searching on Reddit for how to get girls to like him he clicks on a link onto a discussion board where he connects with others who share ideas about how to ask out girls his age and tell him he is deserving of their attention. This leads to conversations about handling "those other 'Chad' boys who tease him," and ways to take care of bullies who bother him. At first Marc is somewhat mystified by some of the language being used but he finds posts, pictures, and MEMEs that explain the terms and some are really funny and are exactly how he feels. After he becomes more comfortable and feels supported in the online community, Marc makes some posts on social media about how he will be taking the "redpill" and that he "isn't going to be another one of those kids who kills himself." He also mentions "getting even" and "making things right" at school.

The school's behavioral intervention team gets a report from another student in the school about Marc's posts. Marc is brought into the office and his mom is called. The principal meets with his mom and the assistant principal and they agree to have

Assessment and Treatment: Junior High 141

Marc meet with the school psychologist to assess the suicide risk and to meet with the SRO to discuss the threatening comments.

Scoring of Marc

Thinking					Feeling					Behaviors					Environment				
1	2	3	4	5	6	7	8	9	10	11	12	13	14	15	16	17	18	19	20
0	0	0	.50	.50	.50	.25	.50	0	1	.25	.50	0	0	1	.75	.50	1	.50	.75

8.50

Thinking

1. **Misogyny:** (0) This doesn't seem to be present. Marc is interested in girls and at this point seems to be blaming boys (Chads) or his own failings for his lack of success.
2. **Racism:** (0) Race is not mentioned.
3. **Blackpill:** (0) At this stage, Marc has subscribed to the redpill theory.
4. **Inaccurate Self-Conception:** (0.50) This is just beginning to be an issue, as he is starting to believe he deserves the attention of girls and has a right to it.
5. **Fame Seeking:** (0.50) He talks about "making things right," which implies a desire to send a message.

Feeling

6. **Rage:** (0.50) He has a desire to "get even" at school and has a history of conflict and fighting with teachers. It is likely, however, that this is more of a howling/ transient threat.
7. **Hopelessness:** (0.25) Marc hasn't given up and only recently felt rejection from a girl. But his further withdrawal into the online realm may be a sign that he is giving up trying to make connections at school.
8. **Catastrophe:** (0.50) While it is possible that the two girls were whispering about him, it is unlikely the rest of the cafeteria even noticed the exchange. Yet Marc feels like he has to retreat and hide from everyone. This isn't an overly abnormal reaction for his age.
9. **Disability:** (0) None mentioned
10. **Abandoned:** (1) Marc's abandonment issues started young when his father left and have only been exacerbated by a busy mother and the loss of friendships as he got older and was not part of the "cool" kids.

Behaviors

11. **Approach Behaviors:** (0.25) Thus far, it is only talk online, but Marc is becoming comfortable with the idea of displaying aggression, at the very least toward the "Chads" and bullies in his life.

142   *3 Case Studies in Assessment and Treatment*

12. **Howling:** (0.50) He has started making vague online threats about "getting even" and "making things right."
13. **Suicide:** (0) In fact, he says that he "isn't going to be another one of those kids who kills himself."
14. **Past Attacks:** (0) None mentioned.
15. **Redpill:** (1) Marc explicitly says that he will be taking the redpill.

Environment

16. **Incel Materials:** (0.75) Marc has done research into incel ideas and has agreed with what he has found. He is becoming active in the community but doesn't seem to be espousing them offline or sparking debates outside the online forums.
17. **Rejection:** (0.50) As far as we know, Marc has only made the one attempt at approaching a girl. He took it hard, but there's no sign he has given up hope.
18. **Bullied:** (1) There have been multiple bullying incidents. Most recently, he was laughed at by the friend of someone he asked out. He then perceived the rest of the cafeteria joining in. He is separating himself from the "Chads" and cool kids.
19. **Failure to Change:** (0.50) Marc has failed in his attempts to improve his appearance. He seems to be channeling that energy into frustration and anger at the bullies rather than continuing attempts to improve upon himself.
20. **Free Fall:** (0.75) The somewhat public rejection by the girl he asked out seems to have driven Marc into depression and the search for companionship and understanding in online forums.

Threat Assessment Initial Evaluation

The presence of a vague, although direct threat, would typically land Marc in some form of threat assessment. *It would be unlikely that this level and type of threat would escalate to police action or expulsion from school.* As mentioned in Chapter 10, a central caution in this case would be avoiding a reductionistic process that simply landed Mark in a therapist's office for a mental health assessment. *This case that should not be assessed by a mental health clinician unless they possess extensive training in violence threat assessment.* While a mental health assessment could be useful to address the potential for depression or suicide, there is a lack of usefulness in this case to focus solely on mental health diagnosis and a consideration of an involuntary admission (which he would not come close to meeting the criteria for based on these details).

It would be useful to *initially build rapport* with Marc and ensure that he feels part of the process. This helps reduce any deception or impression management, often a challenge in cases like these. Given the seriousness of Marc's case and his mother being involved in the threat assessment process, a clear "elephant in the living room" would be his hesitancy to share anything that would get him in deeper trouble. Many times, cases like this involve police talking to the student, and for a student like Marc who is already being bullied and teased, it would be reasonable that he would be hesitant to share freely and would be in fear of future teasing and alienation.

After developing rapport, it would be useful to further assess the direct motivation behind his threat, to determine if it was more **affective and transient or targeted and substantive.** On face value, there is no clear mention of a fixation or focus on a target; the case would be more concerning if he mentioned a girl's name or the boys who were teasing him more directly. There is no mention of a past attack, low actionability, or no details about what weapons might be used or a plan he might follow. If any of these were present in the case, they would certainly escalate the concern. **It would be essential to work with his mother and law enforcement to ascertain his access to any weapons in the home or other locations.** If there is, taking steps to determine if there is a larger fascination with violence through media would also be important in this case.

His threat seems more in reaction to a growing frustration and less about moving toward any kind of justification for violence. There does not seem to be any fantasy rehearsal related to the comments, rather a willingness through the "redpill" ideology to work toward a more positive outcome. While marginalized and teased at the school, this seems to be limited. Given his age, there is an indication this was one of his first attempts to ask someone out and his reaction seemed age appropriate (prior to the threats). **There is no objectifying language used in the threats themselves,** though exploring his feelings toward women, particularly attractive women, would be useful to determine his level of otherness regarding his position with them.

There are several **environmental risk factors** that raise concern, namely the relatively minor catalyst event around the rejection, the historical teasing and bullying, a recent drop in grade performance, and social isolation. It would be useful to further explore his relationship with his mother, how he sees her, and what support she offers. There is evidence of increasing "free fall" that creates an additional concern. Similarly, there are **few stabilizing influences in his life**, given his lack of a father figure and male role models. Assessing his access to friends would be useful as well as looking more closely at his internet usage and the nature of the incel sites he is visiting. On one hand, those new online friends are good to help offset the sense of loneliness and isolation, on the other, they are potentially escalating his thoughts around incel ideas and may continue to encourage movements toward violence.

Overall, the risk for Marc moving toward a targeted violence attack such as a school shooting is relatively low. The larger concern is his movement further into the incel community, further isolation and teasing from others, a growing sense of hopelessness, and potential for action down the line. **Monitoring for future catalyst events related to teasing or bullying should be part of any intervention plan.** This type of case would typically move away from law enforcement and locked inpatient care and more toward a required number of sessions in therapy to help move him to a more socially and academically successful time at school. As with any case where suicide is mentioned, it would be essential to ask follow-up questions related to suicide risk.

Threat Assessment Recommendations

- **Assessing Actionability:** Questions remain about what made him make the threat at that particular time and if he has access or knowledge around weapons. This would involve conversations with his mother and police.

- **Social Media Review:** Conducting a more detailed review of his social media accounts and computer access would be essential. It is unclear what material he has been exposed to and what influence these third parties have on Marc, particularly without a male role model in his life and difficulty fitting in and making friends.
- **Assess Teasing/Bullying:** How intense does the bullying and teasing get at school? Are there policies and procedures in place to address this concern moving forward?
- **Family Supports:** There should be a more detailed exploration regarding his relationship with his mother, sibling and friends. For example, is there a sports team, religious group, or fun activity he enjoys with others that was not mentioned here? Avoiding assumptions is critical.
- **Suicide Risk:** While there is a denial of suicidal feelings on the initial post, there would be a recommendation for a suicide assessment by a licensed mental health clinician. When a student mentions suicide, a further assessment of this risk would be warranted. Given the intensity of the assessment process and the social impact regarding the school, further assessing suicidal risk is warranted.
- **Notification to Community/Information Sharing:** Will sharing information about the case further escalate issues with social relationships and connections with others? This should be concern moving forward related to how the school handles information request from other students, parents and the larger community.
- **Monitor Internet Usage:** Some conversations with the mother should occur around monitoring his internet access as well as looking for ways to find more pro-social outlets online. Finding ways to build up a larger support network for Marc would also be helpful.
- **Assess/Support Academics:** There should be a deeper exploration of the reasons for his drop in grades. Is this related to the teasing or bullying, a lack of effort, increase in suicidal symptoms, an undiagnosed learning disability, changes or difficulty at home, or conflicts in the classroom?
- **Positive Male Role Model:** In a similar vein, helping Marc identify positive male influences in his life (such as a YMCA program, involvement in the Big Brothers program, an uncle or other family member) would be useful to give him some perspective on dating. This could be a teacher at the school or perhaps a therapist or psychologist.
- **Bullying Prevention:** The school would do well to assess its climate for bullying and teasing. This should involve an educational campaign as well as addressing seemingly minor issues (knocking books out of hand) that should really be referred to student discipline.

Counseling Treatment Considerations

Marc will likely be referred to therapy either at his school through the guidance department or with a psychologist. This treatment may be mandated and short-term to initially assess and manage the risk and items highlighted above. Therapy would then likely move into longer term work if there was a successful connection and it continued to be helpful to Marc, his family, and the school (in terms on on-going monitoring). The key elements of focus would likely be as shown in Table 11.1.

Treatment with Marc will focus on building connection and helping him have an ally. If possible, there would be value to set up a male therapist to work with Marc to address some of the limited exposure to positive male influences. Certainly, a female therapist could also raise important issues related to objectification and his views regarding women. In either case, any treatment should avoid an over-reductionist view or any type of lecturing or Pollyannaish advice. Therapy is an opportunity for Marc to explore critical thinking related to his desires.

In this last section, we will outline three specific therapy techniques related treatment plan goal #3 in Table 11.1. We will look at three different therapeutic techniques applied to the same treatment goal, restated here: "Review how Marc can shift the growing sense negativity regarding his self-image (perhaps related to not being cool, lacking athleticism, having few friends and not having a relationship with his brother.)" This will help the reader see three different ways to address the same goal while also giving a bit more of a "deep dive" into how to use the Narrative Therapy, REBT and the Person-Centered Approaches.

Narrative Therapy Example

To build on the treatment plan goal #3 in Table 11.1, we will use the **Narrative Therapy approach** (White & Epston, 1990) to help address Marc's internalized feelings about how he is seen by others. He has learned he is unattractive, worthless, and has little in the way of anything special to offer anyone in a relationship. Stories that support these ideas are collected as he develops: I asked out a girl and she made fun of me and rejected me; no one would like to date me; I'm not cool and no "Stacy" will every give me the time of day. These stories become stifling and overwhelming and remove options for Marc in his life, restricting possibilities and increasing his feelings of being less-than, of being worthless. Marc's therapist should help him separate from these stories, where they can be set aside and relieved of their power. The reconstructive process can be moved forward as they enlist Marc in the creation of metaphors and imagery.

Perhaps they create an imaginary box where the negative stories can be temporarily laid down for the length of their sessions together. This metaphor gains strength as they use descriptive terms to make the box memorable, realistic, tangible. Imagine a box now; made of strong, old wood. It is heavy and the construction is sturdy. The worn wood is strapped with weathered iron bands. The therapist could encourage Marc to create a key to open and lock the box; allowing its dark interior to accept the weight of his stories. Once the stories were placed inside, Marc could close it and take a heavy, metal padlock. He secures the padlock and takes his key, inserting it and then turning it with a metallic "click." With Marc's stories safely locked away for a time, they are now free to create other stories that describe Marc's positive qualities; stories that stress the open-ended nature of a future stretched out before him. It is this process of imagination, freedom, and creation which creates the tapestry of narrative therapy.

146   3 Case Studies in Assessment and Treatment

Table 11.1 Marc's treatment plan

Treatment goal	Approach
1. Increase social supports with friends, groups, clubs, sports teams, activities and/or online connections.	Develop a plan to find new connections through a variety of the activities based on his interests. Develop a broad plan and discuss clear action steps moving forward. Discuss potential failure as delayed success and how change occurs **[CT]**.
2. Address negative messages that exist about masculinity and engage in a deeper conversation and education about Marc's development and goals for the future.	This dialogue could be advanced through an open-ended exercise writing down concepts that are attached to male and female labels followed by a discussion **[PC], [Real]**. An additional discussion could center around goal planning and how Marc could create a plan to reach that goal **[Real]**. Along with an understanding of how to realistically see steps to achieve the goal **[CT], [Real]**.
3. Review how Marc can shift the growing sense negativity regarding his self-image (perhaps related to not being cool, lacking athleticism, having few friends and not having a relationship with his brother).	This could be achieved by using a Narrative therapy exercise **[Na]**, to help Marc better externalize negative stories he allows to be part of his self-image. Additionally, look at events like teasing and being rejected as time-limited events that will likely pass **[REBT]**.
4. Confront his tendency to see a single failure (asking a girl out) in a catastrophizing manner and instead build up a larger sense of resiliency and willingness to build toward change.	This goal can be achieved through a more detailed discussion of past successes and failures regarding goals as well as a discussion about how to address challenges and obstacles that may be encountered **[CT], [Na], [Met]**.
5. Discuss impulse control related to the social media posts and discuss other ways to express himself when frustrated or angry.	This would involve an identification of potential anger triggers and developing a list of alternative actions **[AI], [MI], [REBT]**.
6. Discuss internet usage and ways he can find more positive connections.	Discuss multiple ways to look at more positive outlets for social connections and expressions that avoid escalations to violence **[REBT], [Real], [CT]**.
7. Discuss the incel community and engage in conversations about the problems with their views surrounding women and the negative self-worth and reductionist value physical beauty.	Discuss the larger existential goals of human nature to assist Marc in developing a broader appreciation for various, unique aspects of human nature **[ExT], [PC], [Met]**. Explore the idea of empathy and caring, and how each person has an intrinsic value, regardless of physical attributes **[PC], [ExT], [May]**.

[AI]: Anger Intensifiers by Robert Nay (2004)

[Na]: Narrative Therapy by White and Epston (1990)

[MI]: Motivational Interviewing by Miller/ Rollnick (1991)

[PC]: Person-Centered by Carl Rogers (1961)

[May]: Rollo May (1983)

[ExT]: Existential Therapy by Irvin Yalom (1980)

[REBT]: Reality Therapy by William Glasser (1975)

[Met]: Metaphor Therapy by Richard Kopp (1995)

[CT]: Change Theory by Prochaska/DiClemente (1994)

Assessment and Treatment: Junior High   147

REBT Therapy Example

Another approach to treatment plan goal #3 in Table 11.1 would be the ***Rational Emotive Behavioral Therapy*** (Ellis, 2007) example of the A-B-Cs. One of the areas in which Marc needs to shift his thinking is understanding that the difference between something that is unfortunate and something that is horrible and life changing. This presents some difficulty for Marc because of his age. Many people are able to put this technique into practice when they have the added wisdom that comes with age and experience. We mention this to help normalize Marc's perceived rejection as something that many people have experienced in their lives. In fact, everyone who has a successful relationship can likely look back and think of a time where something unfortunate was said or done related to dating that felt as if the world was going to end. With the power of distance and experience, it is likely that they now see this as an unfortunate though benign event.

A therapist could help Marc review his attempt to ask the girl out to the movies. Let's imagine Marc says it this way,

> Well, I had been thinking about it all week. I talked to my mom and she was able to switch a shift for me and drive us to the movies. I had trouble sleeping the night before I asked her out and was the most nervous I had ever been. When I saw her in the cafeteria, I knew it was something I had to do right then before I lost my nerve. So, I walked right up to the two of them and just asked her out. Then her friend laughed and me and I just felt so bad. It got even worse because they both started laughing and I then I just ran into the bathroom. Everyone was looking at me and I just stayed in there for the rest of the lunch period and ended up being late to my class. I didn't talk to anyone for the rest of the day. It was so horrible. I know it was because she thought it was ridiculous that I would ever ask her out. Shows me for stepping up beyond my normie status.

If this was graphed to the **A**ctivating events, **B**eliefs and **C**onsequences it could be described like this:

A. Marc approaches a girl he likes while she is with her friend. He asks her out to the movies and her friend laughs at him. They both start to whisper to each other, clearly talking about him.

B. He sees this as the worst idea ever and that the girl thought he was dumb for thinking that someone like him would ever go out with her. He was so stupid for thinking he could ask a girl like this out.

C. He runs away from everyone. They are all staring at him. He hides out in the bathroom for the rest of the lunch period. Marc is late to his next period and feels rejected and sad about the entire event.

The activating event of their laughter leads to Marc's belief that he was asking a girl out above his station. This then leads to him running away from her and her friend, leading to a negative consequence. This demonstrates the problems of assuming the worst, catastrophizing an encounter, and leading to a negative consequence. Marc's

148   *3 Case Studies in Assessment and Treatment*

therapist could help him look a potentially different beliefs that would lead to a more positive consequence.

If this was graphed a different way to the Activating events, Beliefs and Consequences it could be described like this:

A. Marc approaches a girl he likes while she is with her friend. He asks her out to the movies and her friend laughs at him. They both start to whisper to each other, clearly talking about him.

B. Marc pauses for a moment and realizes this is an activating event, like what his therapist told him about. He takes a few second to think. He isn't sure what they are saying and thinks maybe asking her out in the cafeteria next to her friend wasn't the best choice.

C. He decides to talk her later when she is alone and apologize for asking her that in front of her friend. Maybe she will want to go to the movies with him after all. He will just have to see.

This leads to new belief, achieved through identifying an activating event and staying calm, which leads to a more positive outcome. While these techniques are hard to practice all the time, Marc is able to appreciate that he needs to avoid always jumping to the worst conclusion and think more before he reacts.

Person-Centered Example

Another approach to treatment plan goal #3 in Table 11.1 would be the ***Person-Centered*** (Rogers, 1961, 1980) concept of empathy and active listening. Marc, like many young boys at 12, is thinking primarily about his feelings and not thinking about how this event occurred from the point of view of the girl he was asking out. This may be a difficult ask at the start of therapy. However, once trust is established and he feels comfortable, Marc may feel safe enough to take some chances to form relationships with others. The added value of a positive client-therapist relationship is the potential for Marc to believe he will be able to form these kinds of positive relationships with others as well. The active listening and support offered by an experienced therapist serves to create a training ground for Marc to improve his own social skills and increase his chances of success when he attempts see more deeply into the experience of others. As Rogers (1961) writes, "If I can provide a certain type of relationship, the other person will discover within himself the capacity to use that relationship for growth and change and personal development will occur" (p. 33).

With encouragement and support, Marc may be able to list out some things that the girl he asked out might have been thinking. She may have been caught off guard by Marc's advance. She may have wanted to say yes, but her friend laughed at him and then everything became awkward. She may not have heard him in the loud cafeteria. There are numerous possibilities to choose from besides the worst possible scenario that she felt like she was out of his league. This exercise in exploring what else someone might be thinking is helpful to assist a student like Marc to better train their mind to look at the totality of what it might be, rather than catastrophizing to the worst.

Even if the girl was not interested in Marc, that is one girl out of an entire school. Taking a single rejection as evidence that you are unattractive to everyone is illogical and harmful.

Moving Forward

In the next chapter, we will follow the same process and look a different scenario with a college student named Jake. This case involves a student athlete who has a Title IX case taken out against him after a drunken sexual assault.

Discussion Questions

- In any case example, information you may want to better assess the threat is often missing. If you were able to ask some follow up questions to get a better assessment on the case prior to moving to the assessment and treatment plan, what would you like to explore further?
- Even at a young age, we don't see much mention of those with other sexual orientations or genders expressing the same anger, rage, depression, and sadness, which often leads to violence, that White, straight, males express. What are some ideas you have as to why that is the case? Can you imagine a case where Marc is gay and has similar feelings of frustrations when asking another student out?
- What role does parental support play in normalizing these incel feelings? While children's behavior is not always directly attributable to their parents, there are times when parents who are absent, emotionally distant, or abusive can escalate feelings of abandonment and trauma. How you see parental support contributing the indoctrination of the incel?

References

Ellis, A. (2007). *The Practice of Rational Emotive Behavior Therapy*. New York: WW Norton & Company.

Glasser, A. (1975). *Choice Theory: A New Psychology of Personal Freedom*. New York: Colophon Books.

Kopp, R.R. (1995). *Metaphor Therapy*. New York: Brunner/Mazel, Inc.

May, R. (1983). *The Discovery of Being*. New York: W.W. Norton & Company.

Miller, W.R. & Rollnick, S. (1991). *Motivational Interviewing: Preparing People to Change Addictive Behavior*. New York: Guilford Press.

Nay, R. (2004). *Taking Charge of Anger*. New York: Guilford Press.

Prochaska, J., Norcross, J., and DiClemente, C. (1994). *Changing for Good*. New York: Harper Collins.

Rogers, C. (1961). *On Becoming a Person*. New York: Houghton Mifflin.

Rogers, C. (1980). *A Way of Being*. New York: Houghton Mifflin.

White, M. and Epston, D. (1990). *Narrative Means to Therapeutic Ends*. New York: WW Norton & Company.

Yalom, I. (1980). *Existential Psychotherapy*. New York: Basic Books.

12 Assessment and Treatment Approaches
College

Case 2: Jake

Jake attends a small, four-year college in the Midwest and is a second semester junior. He has a few friends that he hangs around with on campus and he plays baseball. While not particularly tall at 5'7 and 145 pounds, he works out five to six hours a day with his baseball team and his smaller group of friends.

Despite working out a lot, playing on the school baseball team and doing well in his business major, he has had very little dating success. He hoped college would be different from high school. He never had kissed a girl, let alone had sex with one, and fully believed that everyone on campus would be having crazy parties and hooking up. The few parties he went to ended up with him drinking to the point of throwing up in the backyard. Several pictures of him passed out ended up online. One night, people also wrote on him and drew penises on his face while he was blacked out. Since his school is small, he feels like everyone knows about these incidents.

Jake feels discouraged and thinks he'll never figure out how to get with a woman. Two of his friends, Carter and Derrick, talk to him about his lack of "game" with the ladies. Jake agrees and takes their advice to be less needy around women and to practice giving really hot women semi-insulting comments to throw them off the normally expected praise from everyone around them. Jake tries this with a Black woman at the gym by saying "I'm not usually into Black chicks, but you are pretty light-skinned and don't have one of those crazy bubble asses and look alright." That doesn't go as well for him, although he does have some better luck with some other 6s and 7s, getting some extra glances from them. He figures the Black chick was a probably a dyke anyway.

He starts to research these ideas a bit more and sees some references on discussion boards about guaranteed ways to get really hot women no matter what you look like. He eventually joins a website called https://incels.net/ and creates a username and participates in the discussions. He likes the idea of the redpill and how people with potentially lesser genetics can become more desirable. Jake thinks his workouts and playing baseball are two things that will get him with a true Stacy. Although the more he reads, the more he starts to realize that maybe just finding one Stacy is part of his problem as well – thinking some girl is going to fix his entire life. The real thing he is missing isn't status or working out but having real confidence. He reads a thread about pheromones and how women can actually sniff out inferior men.

Assessment and Treatment: College   151

Jake falls deeper into this thinking and joins a male positivity site called www. therationalmale.com that gives him dating advice and guidance. He learns that women who are 10s often hang around with 6s and he starts to see this all over campus. There are some good suggestions of using alcohol to "loosen up the legs" and he finds some good ideas in "shaking her" or manipulating women so you can sexually possess her mind.

Jake finally gets his first kiss at a party with a drunken 6 femoid and "pulls her" when she is away from her 10. He ends up in a backroom with her and grabs her tits. He gets his hand into her pants and she pulls away but doesn't have much strength in her drunken state and so they make out for a little while longer. Jake hangs out with his friends after she leaves, getting a good number of high-fives and "atta boys" given his newfound skills in BAB (Bagging a Becky).

The next day, the woman Jake hooked up with talks to her friends about what had happened and they encourage her to file a Title IX assault claim with the school. Jake is called in and defends his actions during an initial inquiry at the school. Since both were drinking and there was a bit of a "he said, she said" element to what happened. Jake is given an option to connect to counseling as an informal resolution to the claim against him. He reluctantly agrees, angry that he was punished, and that the lying Becky got him in trouble. He begins spending more time online, raging about how foids can't be trusted and the bitches only want to bring men down. He writes "This is exactly why Elliot Rodger did what he did." He muses that if he was going to get in trouble anyway, he should have fucked that girl when he had the chance.

Scoring of Jake

Thinking					Feeling					Behaviors					Environment				
1	2	3	4	5	6	7	8	9	10	11	12	13	14	15	16	17	18	19	20
1	.75	.50	0	0	.50	.50	1	0	0	1	.75	0	.50	1	1	.50	.50	.50	1

11.00

Thinking

1. **Misogyny:** (1) Jake objectifies women using language common in incel communities ("pulls her," femoids, BAB, etc.). He sees woman only for their desirability on a 1–10 scale and is willing to manipulate women into giving him what he wants.
2. **Racism:** (0.75) Jake is racist toward the African American woman at the gym, regarding her skin, color, and appearance, following up with an assumption she must be gay (using a derogatory slur).
3. **Blackpill:** (0.50) Jake is more openly supportive of the redpill idea, but seems to have some blackpill elements, including rating physical beauty and the Chad/Stacy ideals.
4. **Inaccurate Self-Conception:** (0) This isn't evident here.
5. **Fame Seeking:** (0) He does not seem to have any focus on a greater message.

152   *3 Case Studies in Assessment and Treatment*

Feeling

6. **Rage:** (0.50) After the disciplinary incident, Jake becomes angry at and distrustful of all women.
7. **Hopelessness:** (0.50) Jake is frustrated that college hasn't been what he hoped and worried that things will never get better with women, but is attempting to change his fortunes, albeit in less than ideal ways.
8. **Catastrophe:** (1) Jake internalized the dating failures he experienced, feeling that he will never have success. Later after the fallout from the party, Jake takes this one incident to fuel anger at all women.
9. **Disability:** (0) None mentioned.
10. **Abandoned:** (0) Jake is part of the baseball team and seems to have a support system of friends.

Behaviors

11. **Approach Behaviors:** (1) While not displaying rage or anger, Jake likely overstepped with the girl at the party.
12. **Howling:** (0.75) Jake participates in incel forums, and while he initially focuses on dating advice, he ends up posting angry threats.
13. **Suicide:** (0) Jake makes no reference to suicide nor does he seem at all suicidal in his actions or beliefs.
14. **Past Attacks:** (0.50) Jake mentions Rodger and shows empathy to him without explicitly supporting his actions.
15. **Redpill:** (1) Jake likes the redpill concept and continues working out to improve his chances with a Stacy.

Environment

16. **Incel Materials:** (1) Jake is actively involved in incel forums and has strongly accepted many of the philosophies. His friends also seem to agree with these ideas and they discuss and implement them in their lives.
17. **Rejection:** (0.50) While Jake hasn't had much success with women, until recently, he seems to have hoped they would just come to him (assuming that college would be full of people hooking up easily). He has been discouraged by this but has been willing to try to improve his lot.
18. **Bullied:** (0.50) Jake has been teased publicly and felt discouraged and embarrassed but maintains hope and is working to change his luck with women.
19. **Failure to Change:** (0.50) Jake has made an effort to date women, both in working out and getting advice online and from friends. However, his frustration over the Title IX claim may make him unwilling to continue.
20. **Free Fall:** (1) The incident at the party is a catalyst event that sends him into a spiral of anger and online isolation.

Assessment and Treatment: College   153

Threat Assessment Initial Evaluation

Jake appears to be on a concerning path toward a deeper commitment to the incel movement. Coming from a background of being teased and bullied by friends, he is experiencing some positive acceptance with his friends around school, online in the incel community, and in his own mind with increased female attention and a dubious sexual encounter. There is a profound lack of empathy for the young woman he encountered, a growing disregard for seeing any value in women beyond what he can take from them. ***Paired with a potential substance abuse problem, Jake is a prime example of someone on the pathway toward increased sexual assaults***, anger at women and pulling other students into his way of thinking.

The threat here is vague, transient, and likely a howling behavior voiced in a reaction to what he perceives as a negative outcome in the Title IX case. There was no direct threat that would fall into a substantive or targeted pattern or mention of a fixation or focus to the girl at the party. There are, however, ***elements of risk related to his escalating into a larger pattern of sexual predation.*** The development of rapport may be difficult with Jake, likely balancing between an overly casual, high-five connection and a visceral disdain for his disregard for women as anything beyond a pathway for his sexual pleasure. Successful assessment and the following treatment will require a professional to maintain a support for Jake as a person, while not being seen as supporting his choices that put others at risk.

There is not much known about his social supports regarding his family, peers at home, or previous behavior. Exploring his high school discipline record may be helpful to better ascertain the existence of supports here. While there has been a movement away from the worry around low self-esteem, depression, teasing, and isolation, this has been replaced by an increase in misogyny, sexual assault, and the very ***likely possibility that he will the one teasing and bullying others shortly.*** There is also little known about his future desires, whether that be related to baseball or starting a potential business. Helping Jake understand that these goals may be put into jeopardy with repeats of his current behavior may be an additional motivator to change.

Jake would benefit from treatment that would ***increase his level of empathy toward women***. A potential connection for him may be how he felt when he was teased and drawn on when he was drunk and how this might relate to how the woman he was involved with may have felt after being taken advantage of while intoxicated. This would likely require a delicate approach, as his defensiveness in this space would likely be quite high.

His casual racist and homophobic comments would also be worth some push back in on-going treatment where he has a solid connection with his psychologist. It would be useful to start with an exploration of where these thoughts came from and engage him in a dialogue about diversity, microaggressions, and civility.

In his current state, Jake seems increasingly angry and ***lacks any meaningful insight into the idea that he did anything wrong at the party.*** Again, within the backdrop of a meaningful connection to a therapist, he may be willing to internalize some feedback, and this will help reduce the risk of future assaults. Further

154   3 Case Studies in Assessment and Treatment

assessment of his substance use would also be warranted to assess how often he drinks, why he consumes and what kind of emotional state he is in when drinking (e.g., does he only drink when happy? When sad? To relax? Are there times he has been relaxed without drinking?).

In terms of *environmental risk factors* there are relatively few that are critical to this case. The bullying and teasing seemed to have resolved, he does not seem particularly concerned about his mediation work following his behavior with the girl at the party and it would appear his grades, social connections, and future prospects seem solid. There are a few stabilizing influences present in his life, namely a lack of empathy, positive ideas about masculinity, a desire for positive social action, and a lack of appreciation for consent-based, affirmative sexuality.

Overall, the risk for Jake escalating toward a targeted violence attack such as a school shooting is relatively low while the likelihood of a future sexual assault while drinking would be rather high. There is also a concern of further indoctrination into the incel community, increasing his animosity and objectification toward women and feeling supported in this path by his peers. Therapeutic intervention may be effective if he is able to feel a strong sense of trust with his therapist and be able to listen to advice and guidance if it is presented in small, manageable pieces. *Efforts should be made to reduce high-risk behaviors, engage him in discussions related to his substance abuse* and how his behavior at the party pretty clearly falls into the definition of sexual assault.

Threat Assessment Recommendations

- **Sexual Assault Prevention:** Jake would benefit from a deeper exploration and understanding of consent issues related to sexual assault. With his newfound confidence and likely future party attendance, it is essential to have some focused, prevention-based discussions about how he views women and how his current path is likely going to lead to negative experiences for him. While it would be important to note the negative experiences related to rape and assault at the hands of Jake are much more significant, it is unlikely that Jake is going to be willing to empathize with this and see the reduction of pain for women he is with as a prime motivator.

- **Substance Abuse Assessment:** One of the larger risk factors related to future violence is the disinhibition that comes with high risk drinking for Jake. In his mind, this leads to a positive outcome (sexual contact), but this actually put him very close to a criminal charge and losing all that is important to him (e.g., baseball, academic enrollment, future career goals). Given the lack of substance-based policy violations at college, this evaluation will likely need to be less formal and connected to the current assessment.

- **Social Media Review:** Conducting a more detailed review of his social media accounts and computer access would be helpful to assess any additional threats of violence that were not as substantive. Even with a vague threat, the reference to a past attack makes it worth exploring his social media to rule out any other, more specific or targeted threats. Given the depth of his internet searching on the existing sites, it is likely he has a deep exposure to incel indoctrination. Paired with his perceived success at flirting and having a sexual encounter, he may continue with re-doubled effort. Carefully highlighting how close he came to being charged with assault and removed from the baseball team and school and increasing his awareness for this risk is an essential harm reduction approach.

- **Assess Teasing/Bullying:** This seems to have passed in terms of worry and concern for Jake. The concerning part of this is the likelihood of him moving more into this place with younger members of the baseball team. The "negging" approach to attracting women may work briefly in the short term, but very few women are interested in being disrespected and made to feel "less than" in longer term relationships.
- **Assess Racist Comments:** Further explore Jake's racist comments made to the female student at the gym and help him better understand how these comments impact those he is speaking with and those around him. Assist Jake in understanding how these comments could have a negative impact on his life related to the concept of sexual harassment and the creation of a hostile environment.
- **Family Supports:** There is little said about Jake's family of origin and this would be a reasonable area to explore. Asking about where he grew up, what his family looked like, how he chose this college, what kind of friends he had growing up and what he wants to have for a career are all useful insights into motivations and social supports as well as being useful to build rapport and connection between Jake and his therapist.
- **Assess/Support Academics:** Likewise, there was little said about Jake's academics, both in terms of progress and what his ultimate desire is in terms of career. As a second semester junior, he should be thinking about potential internships, opportunities for future careers and planning what happens after college.
- **Positive Male Role Model:** In a similar vein, helping Jake identify positive male influences in his life (such as a coach, professor, or family member) would be useful to give him some perspective on his current incel inspired dating theory. This could be a teacher at the school or perhaps a therapist or psychologist.

Counseling Treatment Considerations

Jake will likely be referred to therapy either at his school through the counseling department or an off-campus treatment provider. The focus on this counseling will be developing a better understanding of how his actions hurt the woman he was with and how he can avoid repeating this behavior. This work would likely be short term in nature, given that Jake would be unlikely to engage in follow-up counseling after his initial five-six sessions are completed. Given these limitations, the key elements of focus would likely be as shown in Table 12.1.

Treatment with Jake will need to focus heavily on creating a safe place for him to share his initial ideas and feel heard and understood. It is likely he will be "coming in hot" given his lack of empathy toward the woman he met at the party and his concern over the negative effects of the Title IX process being more widely known around campus. In this last section, we will outline an approach to change based Yalom

156 *3 Case Studies in Assessment and Treatment*

Table 12.1 Jakes' treatment plan

Treatment goal	Approach
1. Educate Jake about the interaction between sexual assault and alcohol consumption. Clarify on-campus and criminal charges that could be brought forward.	• Review school policy so Jake understands the expectations, rules, and off-campus criminal charges. Engage Jake to ensure he understands these expectations and why they are important for the larger community **[Mi], [CT], [Real].**
2. Discuss the incel community and engage in conversations about the problems with their views surrounding women and the negative self-worth and reductionist value physical beauty.	• Explore Jake's incel ideas in a caring, open-ended series of questions **[PC].** • While the therapist would not endorse these negative concepts, they can help Jake feel understood in a way that will reduce his future defensiveness when challenged **[Real], [CT].**
3. Assess the nature of Jake's substance abuse and review how this has led to an increase in negative life events.	• Discuss Jakes current usage and corresponding cognitions and emotions he is having (e.g., anxiety, anger, happiness) **[PC], [MI].** • Assess Jake's willingness to engage in a reduction plan for his use **[Real], [CT].**
4. Discuss Jake's academic goals and future career and relationship aspirations and how these may be placed into jeopardy with his current behavior.	• This Socratic discussion will help Jake explore his future goals and determine how his current behavior brings him closer or further from these goals **[MI], [Real], [MET].** • Further explore what his larger life goals are and why he has chosen these **[May], [ExT], [Na].**
5. Develop additional empathy skills for Jake when interacting with others with a long-term goal of being able to understand how his actions have a negative impact on those around him.	• Jake would learn to better attend to the perspectives of others as his therapist demonstrates this by listening and attending to him **[CT].** • There is a larger goal of helping Jake empathize with the girl he had a sexual encounter with, perhaps through being reminded how it felt for him to be taken advantage of (being teased and drawn on) when he was unable to consent **[Real], [Met].**
6. Discuss Jakes attitudes toward race and women. Explore where these were formed and if they are truly serving his needs well.	• Inquire what influences helped shape Jake's views concerning women and race **[CT].** • Asses the validity of these views and the benefits and limitations to his future opportunities in relationships, with others, and in work **[REBT], [Real], [CT].** • Explore the idea of empathy and caring, and how each person has an intrinsic value, regardless of physical attributes **[PC], [ExT], [May].**

(continued)

Assessment and Treatment: College 157

Table 12.1 Cont.

Treatment goal	Approach
7. Identify times where Jake's frustration and anger created negative outcomes for his life. Discuss how to better reduce these behaviors.	• Review ways Jake can work toward these positive goals while reduce his potential frustration, anger, and rage **[Ai]**, **[Real]**, **[CT]**.

[AI]: Anger Intensifiers by Robert Nay (2004)	**[ExT]**: Existential Therapy by Irvin Yalom (1980)
[Na]: Narrative Therapy by White and Epston (1990)	**[Real]**: Reality Therapy by William Glasser (1975)
[MI]: Motivational Interviewing by Miller/Rollnick (1991)	**[Met]**: Metaphor Therapy by Richard Kopp (1995)
[PC]: Person-Centered by Carl Rogers (1961)	**[CT]**: Change Theory by Prochaska/DiClemente (1994)
[May]: Rollo May (1983)	

and Frankl's Existentialism to address goal #6, "discuss Jakes attitudes toward race and women. Explore where these were formed and if they are truly serving his needs well," in Table 12.1. We will also outline an approach to change based on Motivational Interviewing to address goal #4, "discuss Jake's academic goals and future career and relationship aspirations and how these may be placed into jeopardy with his current behavior," in Table 12.1.

Existentialism

In Jake's case, it may be helpful to explore his feelings toward others. While it is likely they are nowhere near as extreme as those comments made by incels like Rodger, the similar objectifying language separates them both from the women and those of different races they insult. Jake may start to develop this line of thinking where he sees himself as free to insult and hurt others, since he has also experienced this kind of pain. The old saying comes to mind, "hurt people hurt people."

Objectification is demonstrated by the language we use in everyday life. Many can recognize the hurtful comments made about "those people" who are a different ethnicity or from a different culture. Misogynist language is also common through examples such as "bitch," "whore," or "slut." Similar language places women on a pedestal and they are seen as "saintly," "innocent," and "motherly." Any time a behavior or similarly limited characteristic is used to take the place of a person's humanity, there has been objectification.

In practical terms, the focus of therapy to reduce objectification of others starts with the process of assisting Jake in understanding how he is not unlike the people he finds himself objectifying. Through increased active listening and building social connections with those around him, Jake has the opportunity to better understand the motivation and thinking of others. Yalom (1980) offers the four central pillars of existential therapy as us wrestling with Freedom, Death, Isolation, and Meaninglessness. Let's tackle each in terms of Jake's treatment.

158   3 Case Studies in Assessment and Treatment

Freedom: Here Jake potentially is enjoying the newly found freedom that comes with his perceived success. He has gained the support of his baseball friends, seems temporarily free of teasing and bullying, and now has some measure of sexual success (albeit in the context of an assault). This rush of freedom to say what he wants, and talk to women and African Americans without considering how his words may hurt, is certainly his right. The danger of freedom is that, similar to the siren's song, it promises pleasure without consequence. The reality is freedom in Jake's speech is not freedom from the consequence. He will quickly gain a reputation for being a racist, a player, someone who is only interested in one thing. Jake's therapist can help him wrestle with temptation of freedom, with the sexual assault being a very real example of the negative impacts of his freedom to kiss and touch the girl he met without consent.

Death: The challenge of death is the awareness that anything unique or special about us is ultimately lost when we die. This creates an existential dilemma that no matter what we achieve, in the end it will be lost. Yalom suggests people create systems of defense against the scary reality through a variety of means (e.g., religion, the pursuit of career success, social connection, wealth, or pleasure). For Jake, the pursuit of sexually attractive women will be a poor way to achieve his sense of uniqueness in life. Any sense of uniqueness that is dependent on other people's specific activities runs the very real risk of becoming unavailable at some point in our lives.

Isolation: The challenge here is wrestling with the freedom of choice against the need for community and acceptance. For Jake, this is present in two main areas, with his desire for sexual relationships and his connection with his friends. A central therapeutic task for Jake is balancing his uniqueness and independence with the need to be connected to others. Therapy can assist Jake in assessing the value of temporary sexual connection and the value in securing friends who have previously teased and marginalized him for not obtaining the same number of sexual partners they have. This leaves Jake forced into the choice to pursue these promises of connection, versus finding a larger sense of direction and meaning. Is it pursuing friends who have a history of turning on him? Sexual conquests that lack any deeper or on-going connections? Is he truly alone or in a community with others?

Meaninglessness: These questions surrounding isolation come full circle, leaving Jake attempting to locate his place in the world. Sadly, Jake has seemed to put his faith in an unfortunate doctrine. The incel philosophy, at best, is a road map to seeing a world divided, where acceptance and value are limited to attractiveness. Even for those who are lucky enough to be born into the incel-defined, genetically superior Stacy and Chad dynamic, they are not free of age. As the alphas age, they decrease their worth. There is exactly no one in this entire system of belief that is able to obtain any version of happiness or peace. It would be increasingly likely that Jake will either come to this awareness consciously or slowly come to appreciate this depressing truth over time. Victor Frankl, founder of Logotherapy, writes about the importance of finding meaning, even in the suffering (Frankl, 1946/2006). Logotherapy is derived from Greek word logos or "meaning." Frankl's own work was strongly influenced by the time he spent in the concentration camps of World War II Germany. Frankl (1965) writes, "Clients must find a purpose to their existence and pursue it. The therapist must help them achieve the highest possible activation" (p. 54).

Assessment and Treatment: College 159

If some of you reading this have become lost in the mire of existential thought (no fear, it certainly happens to the best of us), we wanted to offer a more practical example of how to apply these concepts to Jake. This exercise works well with patients who are having difficulty with their place in the world. They may have some difficulty with viewing their future, struggling with anxiety, fearful of death, or having trouble sorting out choices.

The process is one that can be adapted in many different ways. Jake could be given a series of five index cards and then asked to write a single word or quality he would use to describe himself on each of them. These may be roles Jake plays (boyfriend, student, son, baseball player) or ways other people view Jake (sexy, smart, drunk, outgoing, short).

The idea of this exercise is to capture the core ways Jake sees himself, the roles he takes on, and the ideas/emotions he employs to defend himself against the true realities of the world (death, meaninglessness, freedom, anxiety, lack of control). The first step of this exercise is have Jake clearly visualize the ways he sees himself as a person existing in the world, whether this be through how he see himself, how others see him or how he would like to be seen.

The second part of the exercise would have Jake spend some time imagining himself without these qualities. If Jake is able, we could ask him to reflect on one of the terms written on the single index card and then rip up the card and throw it away. Jake would then be asked to visualize himself, in the fullest extent possible, without the comforting (or pathological) roles and qualities written on the destroyed card. Jake's therapist could ask him to do this over a series of days prior to his next session. After going through the five cards, he would come back into session and discuss how he felt imagining the qualities he held so dear suddenly removed from his life.

The purpose of the experience is to help Jake confront the true realities of life – what it means to exist in a finite body, pursuing desires that will have no true lasting impact 100 years from now. This experience helps to empower patients to directly face their fears and anxieties that may be causing difficulties in making choices for the future or overcoming everyday anxiety situations. They peel away their daily, comforting masks (sometimes comforting, sometimes pathological such as anxiety, fear, and sadness) and then take solace in the ultimate truths ... that we are all alone, we must make choices and have little to say about how the fates move us around. We can survive any *why* by adapting with the right *how*.

The stoic and pre-Socratic (Hericlitus – no one ever descends into the same river twice) philosophers give voice to this concept; the idea the path to ultimate peace is found through accepting that the universe is in constant change. We have very little impact on what life brings to us; our only choice lies in how we choose to live our lives. Like Sisyphus pushing his boulder up the hill for all eternity, we choose the manner in which we suffer and have no control over the tasks assigned to us.

Motivational Interviewing

To build on the treatment plan goal #4 in Table 12.1, we will use the concepts of Motivational Interviewing (Miller and Rollnick, 1991) to help address Jake's future goals and how his current behavior is potentially out of step with his goals (see Table 12.2).

160   3 Case Studies in Assessment and Treatment

Table 12.2 Motivational interviewing techniques (Miller and Rollnick, 1991)

Task	Jake says	Therapist Response
Expression of Empathy	"You don't get what it's like. I have to figure out all of this stuff on my own. How to pay my bills, meet a girl, get good grades, fit in with my friends. It's too much!"	"I haven't had all of your experiences, but I can tell you I failed a class in college that made me lose a scholarship. I worried a lot about my future and wasn't always sure what I wanted to do for a career."
Avoiding Argumentation	"How the hell am I supposed to have my major figured out at 20? Did you know what you were going to do at 20?"	Instead of arguing or fighting back, the therapist replies, "What did you want to be when you were little? Was it always something to do with baseball or business?"
Roll with Resistance	"That's easy for you to say, I can see a picture of your hot wife on your desk. You probably get sex whenever you want."	"You are right in some ways. But I wasn't always this lucky in my relationships. In fact, I spent most of my college time alone and went to only a few parties. Maybe I didn't have it as hard as you do know, but I can relate to some of your feelings."
Developmental of Discrepancy	"I'm just going to drink and enjoy my life right now. I'm young and this is my chance to get to have all those things I won't have later."	"You can certainly do that. But I wonder if you know how close you came to losing your status enrolled here and on the baseball team because of what happened that night. While you might not agree it was right, I've seen similar situations end with a separation from campus."
Supporting Self-efficacy	"I did what you said and went to the career advisor to talk for a bit. I guess it was ok."	"Jake, I just want to take a second to say thanks for doing that. I know for me, it's hard to make time for those appointments, particularly when you aren't sure they are really going to help. I appreciate you trusting me enough to take the time to go over. "

Moving Forward

In the next chapter, we will follow the same process and outline a different scenario with a workplace incel named Kyle. Kyle makes several offensive comments to female staff and engages in quid pro quo harassment.

Discussion Questions

- What role do you see athletics, fraternity, and party culture contributing to the unrealistic expectations for men? Given these pressures may exist for women as well, why do you think there is no such as thing as a female incel (or at least a female incel who escalates to the kind of violence seen in the cases in Appendix A)?

- If you were being asked to assess the risk for Jake, are there other things that you would include in the threat assessment? What are some potential areas that may have been missed?
- Discuss the pros and cons of having a male therapist work with Jake. What are the pros and cons of a female therapist working with him?
- At the end of the existential therapy section, there is a sentence that reads, "We can survive any why by adapting with the right how." What does this mean? How might you apply this concept in working with Jake?

References

Frankl, V. (1946/2006). *Man's Search for Meaning*. Boston: Beacon Press.

Frankl, V. (1965). *The Doctor and the Soul*. New York: Alfred A. Knopf.

Glasser, A. (1975). *Choice Theory: A New Psychology of Personal Freedom*. New York: Colophon Books.

Kopp, R.R. (1995). *Metaphor Therapy*. New York: Brunner/Mazel, Inc.

May, R. (1983). *The Discovery of Being*. New York: W.W. Norton & Company.

Miller, W.R. and Rollnick, S. (1991). *Motivational Interviewing: Preparing People to Change Addictive Behavior*. New York: Guilford Press.

Nay, R. (2004). *Taking Charge of Anger*. New York: Guilford Press.

Prochaska, J., Norcross, J., and DiClemente, C. (1994). *Changing for Good*. New York: Harper Collins.

Rogers, C. (1961). *On Becoming a Person*. New York: Houghton Mifflin.

White, M. and Epston, D. (1990). *Narrative Means to Therapeutic Ends*. New York: WW Norton & Company.

Yalom, I. (1980). *Existential Psychotherapy*. New York: Basic Books.

13 Assessment and Treatment Approaches
Workplace

Case 3: Kyle

Kyle works for an industrial production company overseeing purchase orders and acquisitions. He has always liked math and finds the consistency of his work, the right and wrong nature of math, and the processes he follows reassuring to him. He has a few acquaintances but no real friends. He takes a vacation each year for two weeks to a different part of the country and generally looks forward to those trips, although he often sees loving couples doing the same activities he's doing alone. Each time he comes back, he finds himself sad and lonely, despite having been in a really beautiful location. The most recent trip was to Sedona in Arizona and while it was fun and he was able to do some hiking, he came back with those same feelings of loss and frustration that he can't find a woman to be with when all those other guys have someone.

He has had sex twice in his life. The first time was when he was 23 with a woman who went to the same church. Having built the idea of intercourse up so much in his mind, along with being young, he came quickly and was embarrassed. Despite her reassurances, he left quickly and didn't talk to her again and even stopped going to church. The second time was at 34 with a woman he met online. She was nice enough, but in her late 40s and not very attractive. He stopped returning her calls.

While Kyle likes his job, he is often teased by younger staff at work. They call him "Kyle the Creeper" and he has overheard a few of them talking about him in hurtful ways. He often stares at the female employees' breasts and buttocks. He makes inappropriate comments saying things like "well, that's what she said" and "I can see you like to work *long* and *hard* on your reports." He asks out Sara, a co-worker in her early twenties, for dinner at Red Lobster. He jokes, "If you get the lobster, you know what that means for later?" Being new to the company, she politely refuses and shares the story with others. He asks to connect with her on social media and she tells him "Well, I don't usually do social media with people that I work with at the office." Other employees continue to tease Kyle behind his back by making a lobster claw gesture and then inserting a finger implying sexual intercourse. At the prodding of her office friends, Sara talks to HR about what happened when Kyle asked her out and requests that it would be "just to make a note of it – I don't want him to get in trouble or anything." HR takes the information.

Assessment and Treatment: Workplace 163

In the past few years, there have been three different women who made reports to human resources about his behavior, but because it didn't involve physical assault or direct comments, he was only required to complete an online sexual harassment course and received a written warning from HR. While Kyle did what was required of him, he resented having to do it.

Kyle had similar problems in college and spent some time in therapy for Autism Spectrum Disorder (ASD), but back then it was known as Asperger's. For Kyle, this manifests primarily in his trouble reading social interactions and he tends to have trouble with rapid changes that he can't prepare for in advance. He has not mentioned this to anyone at work and actually feels the ASD is a benefit to his organization and processing of paperwork.

Kyle starts to pick up on the office teasing and becomes increasingly depressed and agitated. He also learns that Sara does, in fact, befriend other work colleagues on social media and that she had lied to him. While the work remains rewarding, the office environment, along with his inability to make friends or find a relationship, becomes increasingly hard for him emotionally. He begins to search the internet for others who have had difficulty in finding friends and sexual relationships. Given his love of research and process, he finds himself quickly talking to others and forming online relationships. He even begins practicing some techniques and pick up lines at home and via video chat with a paid service.

He comes up with the idea of making his next vacation a trip to Hawaii. With the support of his friends online and through a dating guru help site, he commits to bringing a young female with him on this trip. The dating guru inspires Kyle and tells him to "never take no for an answer" and to "commit to this 110%." Kyle follows the advice and books a honeymoon package at the hotel about six months in advance. He figures this gives him enough time to find someone to go with and it was more cost effective for him to purchase this upfront.

Kyle spends time researching Sara and studying her online presence. He looks at her Instagram and Facebook account, gaining access by guessing the passwords for another staff's accounts who is connected to Sara on social media. When Sara comes in for a purchase order approval, he asks her to go to Hawaii with him, telling her that everything has been purchased and taken care of for her, so there's no reason for her not to come. Sara is shocked and says, "You are old enough to be my Dad … there is no way I'd ever go out with you, let alone go to Hawaii." Kyle is hurt by this and gets angry at her. He tells her to leave his office. She says, "fine, but sign this" and Kyle laughs at her and says, "Yeah, right. I'll get right on that."

Sara makes a report to HR and Kyle is required this time to take two unpaid weeks away from work and must see an employee assistance program (EAP) counselor to talk about his inappropriate work behavior and address the quid pro quo harassment. The HR director tells him, "People get fired for less than this, Kyle. I get you are not the best at social skills. But this needs to stop right now." Kyle leaves the office with a box of his possessions and says to her, "Maybe everything needs to stop. You keep disrespecting me like this and maybe everything WILL stop in the future."

164   *3 Case Studies in Assessment and Treatment*

Scoring of Kyle

Thinking					Feeling					Behaviors					Environment				
1	2	3	4	5	6	7	8	9	10	11	12	13	14	15	16	17	18	19	20
1	0	0	.50	0	.50	.25	.25	1	.75	1	.50	0	0	1	.75	.75	.50	.50	1

10.25

Thinking

1. **Misogyny:** (1) Kyle places a high value on youth and beauty in women. He makes inappropriate comments and jokes and stares openly at their breasts and buttocks. He pursues Sara despite her continued refusals to date him and doesn't seem to understand why she wouldn't want a free trip to Hawaii with him.
2. **Racism:** (0) Race is not mentioned.
3. **Blackpill:** (0) While Kyle is almost certainly aware of the blackpill through his research, he is trying to make changes and seems to think that he can improve his lot.
4. **Inaccurate Self-Conception:** (0.50) While this isn't addressed directly, Kyle seems to have an overly inflated sense of self, in that he assumes a woman he barely knows will want to travel to Hawaii with him.
5. **Fame Seeking:** (0) Kyle does not appear to have any larger message to share.

Feeling

6. **Rage:** (0.50) Kyle is frustrated by the happy couples he sees on vacation and angry when Sara declines the trip to Hawaii.
7. **Hopelessness:** (0.25) Kyle is sad and frustrated about his lack of a relationship, but clearly hopeful enough to buy a honeymoon package for Hawaii.
8. **Catastrophe:** (0.25) Kyle had a strong overreaction to what he perceived as his failure at his first sexual experience.
9. **Disability:** (1) There is history of treatment for ASD that has presented with challenges for him to be able to process information and read social cues.
10. **Abandoned:** (0.75) Kyle is lonely and lacks any support system.

Behaviors

11. **Approach Behaviors:** (1) Kyle has a history of HR complaints, inappropriate jokes and comments, and unwelcome advances. He threatens inaction when his advances are rejected. There is also the vague threat at the end of the narrative.
12. **Howling:** (0.50) One could read an implied threat in the lobster comment and a more obvious one in the exchange after Sara declines the Hawaii trip.
13. **Suicide:** (0) There is no suicidal ideation mentioned.

Assessment and Treatment: Workplace 165

14. **Past Attacks:** (0) None mentioned.
15. **Redpill:** (1) Given his research, Kyle is aware of this concept and seems to have subscribed to it. He actively sought out help and advice online to improve his chances with women.

Environment

16. **Incel Materials:** (0.75) Kyle has done the research and is active online but hasn't incorporated the language into his everyday interactions.
17. **Rejection:** (0.75) Given the multiple HR complaints and his limited dating, it would seem that Kyle has had regular experiences with rejection. However, he continues to try and hasn't given up.
18. **Bullied:** (0.50) Kyle is bullied, but largely behind his back. Even when he knows about it, while it is hurtful, it doesn't affect his behavior or seem to affect his self-worth.
19. **Failure to Change:** (0.50) Kyle has been willing to make changes, but the dating advice he received backfired.
20. **Free Fall:** (1) The employment suspension has the potential to cause Kyle to spiral and does cause him to threaten the HR director.

Threat Assessment Initial Evaluation

Kyle has a long history of inappropriate comments at work that have been made over the years. These have escalated to the point that he offered a veiled threat upon leaving the building. The quality and context of the threat would seem to be in line with a transient and reactive one rather than any leakage indicating a more substantive or targeted attack plan. Given the nature of the threat, however, it would be a wise course of action to exercise due diligence and verify with police the presence of wants/warrants, past criminal records, or concealed carry permits. Likewise, a more detailed, open search of Kyle's social media would also be beneficial to assess any additional threats or concerns.

Kyle has ASD, and this has been an exacerbating factor when it has come to dating, reading social cues, and adapting to change. In many ways, the planning of a trip and his poorly worded jokes to Sara could be partially explained as related to his ASD. The on-going nature of these comments after several years, paired with a progressive discipline policy, means Kyle has used up many of his chances to be successful in the workplace. Of particular concern is his narrowed focus on Sara, continuing even after she politely rejected his advances. To ask her out again on a larger trip and to obtain another work colleague's password in order to get around her refusal to connect with him on social media further escalates the concern in this case.

Assessing additional risk factors that may increase impulsive behavior or escalate the risk will also be areas of concern. Assessing Kyle's history for violent outbursts at previous employers, drinking or the use of substances, and compliance with mental health treatment and medication should all be areas to explore.

166   *3 Case Studies in Assessment and Treatment*

Kyle has been to therapy before, so ***obtaining past treatment records*** would be potentially helpful to the EAP therapist assigned to him. His efforts to learn how to date women more effectively are noble in their intent, however choosing this particular dating guru, who advises not taking no for an answer, is a recipe for disaster. Pairing this with an impending potential job action or termination could create a catalyst event that sends him spinning. Add to this the concern of the risk of further indoctrination into the incel community, Kyle's increasing sense of entitlement, and his disregard toward women and feeling teased by his peers, and the outcome of this intervention is not a fait accompli.

Kyles therapist should further ***assess his social supports, friend and activities he enjoys in order to identify any stabilizing influences in his life.*** Identifying hobbies and interests that help him relax, such as having a pet, gardening, or going to the movies, should be areas of initial inquiry by his EAP counselor. Given the nature of this assessment and time crunch for completion, it would be expected Kyle would be under a large degree of stress.

One approach that may be helpful is exploring past methods of coping under these circumstances. He likely has experienced challenges like this before, so any therapeutic intervention should assess what successes and failures he has had regarding change. Kyle has a drive to improve himself, as well as take action in ways that might be hard for other people, such as planning a vacation across the country to somewhere he hasn't been before. Directing this energy in the right way may very well be the secret to success for Kyle.

Without a doubt, ***sending Kyle a clear message about his contacts with Sara and others at the office that could be seen as harassment, unwanted contact, or threats to not fulfill his job duties if certain favors are not granted will be a critical part of this EAP counseling.*** Making this process slightly more difficult is the timeline hanging over the process like the sword of Damocles. Two weeks can be a challenge to get a new client in for an appointment, let alone have more than two, perhaps three sessions at the most. Any treatment plan should be developed with an awareness of this time frame and a focus on solution-focused, harm reduction conversations and techniques.

It is likely that Kyle will continue to be angry and may resist or argue with the counselor around his part in this complicated web of communication. The HR office is likely close to a termination given the repeated nature of this conflict and the escalation of (1) repeated approaches to Sara, (2) a quid pro quo harassment claim, and (3) previous allegations of inappropriate behavior. With the added request of HR to conduct a risk assessment related to the vague threat made at suspension, ***Kyle may have a difficult path to return even in the best of circumstances and with him being fully cooperative.***

There is little evidence at this time that supports the idea that Kyle would escalate to a targeted attack. It is more likely that he is upset and angry at Sara for making the report, the HR director for holding him accountable, his online dating coach for failing to help him be successful in dating, other colleagues for teasing, and perhaps himself, most of all, for not handling this situation well. Any therapeutic intervention in this case would need to be focused on the timeline requirements and helping Kyle understand the severity of the next steps the company could take.

Assessment and Treatment: Workplace   167

Threat Assessment Recommendations

- **Sexual Harassment and Quid Pro Quo Education:** Kyle would benefit from a deeper exploration and understanding of these concepts related to sexual issues in the office. Any EAP meeting must have a clear dialogue around some focused, prevention-based discussions about how Kyle has interacted inappropriately with Sara and how his current path is likely going to lead to negative experiences for him. If Kyle is unable to hear this without argument, blame-redirection and conflict, the therapist may want to introduce the concept of following these directives even if Kyle doesn't believe he is at fault. Perhaps with his attention to organization, rules, and detail, a review of the employee code of conduct would help.
- **Social Media Review:** Conducting a more detailed review of his social media accounts and computer access would be helpful to assess any additional threats of violence that were not included in the initial reports. Even with a vague threat, his anger, frustration, and repetitive behavior despite warnings to stop are enough to indicate an exploration of his open-source social media to rule out any other, more specific or targeted threats. Given the depth of his internet searching on the existing sites, it is likely he has a deep exposure to incel indoctrination. This kind of language may be reposted or shared across multiple accounts.
- **Assess Teasing/Bullying:** The impact of this teasing behavior from the other employees should be discussed with Kyle. It would be helpful to assist him with some additional skills to resist his normal reaction of becoming angry in the moment and saying something "off the cuff" that gets him in trouble. There are at least three instances in the case where he implied a quid pro quo, offered a vague threat to the HR director, or made inappropriate sexual comments and innuendo.
- **Positive Male Role Model:** If time permits, helping Kyle find access to a more positive role model around issues of dating, masculinity, and office communication would be helpful to reduce future behaviors such as these. This could even be a male EAP counselor, if he is able to quickly establish trust and connection to Kyle. Finding a counter message to the "dating guru" and the incel materials he is reading will benefit Kyle in the long term.

Counseling Treatment Considerations

Kyle will likely make two or three appointments prior to returning to work and having the assessment results shared back. Time is an important factor in this case given how close Kyle is coming to a termination. The focus of this counseling needs to be (1) adopting new behavior immediately even if Kyle doesn't feel he is to blame or that he should have to be the one to change, (2) developing a better understanding of how his actions impacted Sara and how he can avoid repeating this similar behavior, and (3) building up some immediate techniques to handle his emotional outbursts when upset or frustrated.

As mentioned, treatment with Kyle will likely be short-term in nature, with both a time pressure for completion (two weeks) and the expectation of an assessment letter

168　*3 Case Studies in Assessment and Treatment*

Table 13.1 Kyle's treatment plan

Treatment goal	Approach
1. Educate Kyle about the expectations around therapeutic timelines and goals of this work in an attempt to build a strong treatment alliance more quickly.	• Discuss with Kyle, in an open, congruent, genuine, and direct manner, the timeline expectations of this assessment and treatment **[PC]**, **[Real]**. • Address any concerns or push-back that would keep him from buying into the plan of working together to get him back into the office **[Real]**, **[MI]**.
2. Address Kyle's violations of the employee expectations around quid pro quo harassment, threats, sexual innuendo, and office flirtation. Regardless of how Kyle feels about the rules, he must follow the rules to stay employed.	• Share the office employee policy and help Kyle to better understand where he stepped away from his protocol **[MI]**. • Build a connection with Kyle so he understands any deviation from these policies would result in a potential termination **[Real]**, **[CT]**.
3. Develop additional empathy skills for Kyle when interacting with others with a long-term goal of being able to understand how his actions have a negative impact on those around him and that through this connection they may be more open to learn about his goals and desires.	• Kyle would learn to better attend to the perspectives of others as his therapist demonstrates this by listening and attending to him **[CT]**. • There is a larger goal of helping Kyle empathize with the Sara, perhaps through some role playing techniques in session that can increase Kyle's understanding of how she felt as he talked with her **[Real]**, **[Met]**.
4. Identify times where Kyle's frustration and anger created negative outcomes for his life. Discuss how to better reduce these behaviors.	• Review ways Kyle can work toward these positive goals while reduce his potential frustration, anger and rage **[AI]**, **[Real]**, **[CT]**.
5. Discuss Kyle's career goals with the company along with his larger life and relationship goals.	• Explore Kyle's larger goals in life (as time allows) and determine how his current behavior brings him closer or further from these goals **[MI]**, **[Real]**, **[MET]**. • Further explore those goals and why he has chosen these **[May]**, **[ExT]**, **[Na]**.

[AI]: Anger Intensifiers by Robert Nay (2004)	**[ExT]:** Existential Therapy by Irvin Yalom (1980)
[Na]: Narrative Therapy by White and Epston (1990)	**[Real]:** Reality Therapy by William Glasser (1975)
[MI]: Motivational Interviewing by Miller/Rollnick (1991)	**[Met]:** Metaphor Therapy by Richard Kopp (1995)
[PC]: Person-Centered by Carl Rogers (1961)	**[CT]**: Change Theory by Prochaska/Norcross/DiClemente (1994)
[May]: Rollo May (1983)	

with recommendations. Regardless of how Kyle feels about his current situation and how it came about, he is in real danger of losing his job.

We will outline specific therapy techniques in a Reality Therapy (Glasser, 1975) related treatment plan for goal #1, "educate Kyle about the expectations around

Assessment and Treatment: Workplace   169

therapeutic timeline and goals of this work in an attempt to build a strong treatment alliance more quickly," in Table 13.1. Next, we will demonstrate how to address treatment plan goal #2, "address Kyle's violations of the employee expectations around quid pro quo harassment, threats, sexual innuendo, and office flirtation. Regardless of how Kyle feels about the rules, he must follow the rules to stay employed," through the work of Prochaska, Norcross, and DiClemente's (1994) Transtheoretical Change Theory.

Reality Therapy

Kyle has a need to develop a plan and be able to stick to it. In Glasser's (1975, 2001) reality therapy system, he offers a plan process built on the acronym WDEP. This stands for identifying the **W**ants and needs, **D**irection and what they are doing, an **E**valuation of the behavior, and **P**lanning and commitment to change. For Kyle, the plan is to abide by the office policies he has previous violated. Kyles EAP therapist should approach this task with Kyle as follows:

Wants and Needs: Here Kyle should engage in a dialogue about what he wants his overall outcome to be. If he continues on his current path and asks Sara out again, termination from employment is likely. If he returns from the EAP session with a report that shows he was argumentative and uncooperative, termination is likely. Without Kyle's buy-in to the plan of following the rules laid out in the employee handbook, any other work or possible change is secondary.

Direction and what they are doing: As Kyle contemplates coming back into the office, he should begin to discuss how he will handle common challenges such as encountering teasing, addressing Sara, the need for offering an apology, and his willingness to do so. While Kyle is on separation, it will be important for him to continue to think about his options when he returns rather than spending this down time perseverating on who is to blame, further exposing himself to incel propaganda, or doubling down on his bad dating advice.

Evaluation of his behavior: When Kyle does return, he will need to assess and evaluate how his new behavior is being received. While he might feel he is doing better, soliciting feedback from the appropriate people (such as HR) will help ensure that any potential missteps are limited.

Planning and commitment to change. The planning becomes part of his everyday experience, looking for ways to continue his behavioral change in the office and continuing to follow the office policy, particularly during those times where he struggles.

Once the WDEP process is complete, the next step Glasser (1975, 2001) suggests is the importance of ensuring the plan is simple, attainable, measurable, immediate, consistent, controlled by the client, committed to by the client, and timely. As stated earlier, plans that are created by a therapist that do not have buy-in from the client or are too complicated or broad to be measured are doomed to failure.

170   *3 Case Studies in Assessment and Treatment*

Table 13.2 Transtheoretical change theory (Prochaska, Norcross, and DiClemente, 1994)

Task	Therapist's Goal with Kyle
Pre-Contemplation	Kyle may not fully appreciate why he needs to follow the employee handbook regarding the sexual harassment or quid pro quo policy. Simply handing him the manual will not fix the problem. Rather, the therapist can help raise doubt that Kyle knows everything about the policy and increase his perception of risk and problems with current behavior running afoul of the policy.
Contemplation	Here the goal is to help Kyle take the next step on his pathway to change. There is a need to snap him out of any ambivalence he has about following this policy. Kyle is helped by identifying risk of not changing, along with strengthen self-efficacy for changing current behavior.
Preparation for Action	As Kyle's buy-in to this process increases, the therapist helps him identify and select the best initial course of action regarding his behavior as he returns to the office and reinforces Kyle's movement in this direction.
Action	Kyle is helped to take those first steps toward change by providing Kyle encouragement and praise for his compliance.
Maintenance and Relapse Prevention	Given his success, Kyle is taught relapse prevention skills in order to maintain his behavior and stay in compliance with the employee manual.

Change Theory

Kyle is going through a process of change. He is being asked to alter his previously negative behaviors that ran afoul of the employee manual and choose more adaptative behaviors. The Transtheoretical Change Theory, which was developed by Prochaska, Norcross, and DiClemente (1994) and highlighted in their book *Changing for Good*, offers an excellent overview of this process. Table 13.2 offers some guidance for Kyle's therapist as they apply this change model to goal #2 related to Kyle staying in compliance with company expectations.

Moving Forward

In the final chapter of this book, we offer a review of the BIT/CARE team model as it relates to K-12, college and workplace settings. This team model provides a backstop against violence in the community by viewing at-risk individuals through a multi-disciplinary lens to (1) gather contextual information about risk, (2) apply a rubric to assess the risk and assign a risk level, and (3) develop interventions.

Discussion Questions

- Some people are easier to work with than others. What are some of the challenges you might face attempting to help Kyle?

- Should our goal in this case always start with the focus to get Kyle back into the office? What if we are successful but then Kyle continues to harass Sara or escalates and hurts her? How do you balance the needs of the community (the office and Sara) with the needs of the individual?
- Construct a plan in your life to change a behavior using the WDEP model outlined in the chapter. When applying this plan, consider how to ensure that it is simple, attainable, measurable, immediate, consistent, controlled by the client, committed to by the client, and timely.
- If you were the HR director, in what ways would you handle the situation differently (if any)?

References

Glasser, A. (1975). *Choice Theory: A New Psychology of Personal Freedom*. New York: Colophon Books.

Glasser, A. (2001). *Counseling with Choice Theory: The New Reality Therapy*. New York: Colophon Books.

May, R. (1983). *The Discovery of Being*. New York: W.W. Norton & Company.

Miller, W.R. and Rollnick, S. (1991). *Motivational Interviewing: Preparing People to Change Addictive Behavior*. New York: Guilford Press.

Nay, R. (2004). *Taking Charge of Anger*. New York: Guilford Press.

Prochaska, J., Norcross, J., and DiClemente, C. (1994). *Changing for Good*. New York: Harper Collins.

Part 6

Community and Systems Approach

14 Addressing the Incel through the BIT/CARE Model

Special Thanks to Dr. Amy Murphy for Her Work on This Chapter[1]

When designing this book, we wanted to offer a chapter specifically focused on behavioral intervention teams (BIT), CARE teams, or threat assessment teams and their role identifying, assessing, and responding to individuals and incidents related to the incel movement or with elements of incel-type messaging or behaviors. Many readers of this book may already have a general knowledge of these teams, and some readers may have in depth experience with these teams, either participating in or leading them. These teams are critical in work preventing violence in schools, colleges, workplaces, and other institutions. As new trends in violence emerge, the work of these teams should be re-examined and evolve to respond accordingly.

This chapter will describe the purpose of BIT, CARE, or threat assessment teams and overview the three-phase process commonly used by teams in their work. Specifically, the first phase considers how to identify concerns in our school or workplace communities. The second phase will detail team assessment work and how to employ the risk factors and stabilizing influences identified in earlier chapters. The final phase will examine the role of the teams in providing interventions in response to concerns and managing ongoing areas of risk related to incel violence. This chapter will also explore some of the specific positions on a behavioral intervention or CARE team and the role played by each team member in identifying, assessing, and responding to incel-like situations. We will end with a list of missteps a team can make, especially when addressing this emerging incel movement.

Purpose of Using a Team Strategy

The work of behavioral intervention, threat assessment, or CARE teams is recognized nationally as a research-based, best practice for the prevention of violence by the United States Secret Service (National Threat Assessment Center [NTAC], 2018). Behavioral intervention teams (BITs) are "small groups of school officials who meet regularly to collect and review concerning information about at-risk community members and develop plans to assist them" (Van Brunt et al., 2018, p. 30). The work of teams has expanded with professional associations such as the National Behavioral Intervention Team Association researching team structures, processes, and professional standards for teams (NaBITA, 2018).

For our purposes, we will use the terms behavioral intervention team, CARE team, and threat assessment team interchangeably, and through the remainder of the

176　*Community and Systems Approach*

chapter will just use the term BIT, but the scope and purpose of these teams has differed historically. Threat assessment teams have a foundation in law enforcement and the investigation of threats of harm against individuals (Borum et al., 1999). Behavioral intervention teams emerged for more closed communities following incidents of targeted violence in schools and the workplace. A key attribute of the BIT is educating the school or workplace community about behaviors of concern and training them to report to a centralized team for support and assistance (Sokolow et al., 2014). In addition to this prevention-based philosophy, BITs also have the capacity to perform threat assessments (Sokolow et al., 2014; Van Brunt, 2015). The term CARE team is a more recent evolution of the name for BITs in order to promote the supportive, preventative focus of the team's work and avoid the stigma related to referrals (Schiemann & Van Brunt, 2018). Ultimately, only a consideration of a team's mission, membership, and scope of activities will provide a clear indication of the team strategy and purpose as well as their alignment with research-based, best practices.

Team approaches are a best practice for violence prevention and intervention with those at-risk for a multitude of reasons. Teams represent a multidisciplinary approach with specialists in mental health, law enforcement, organizational administrative leadership and other key areas. The teams also have the capacity to reach out to others in the organization with required expertise in areas such as disability or Title IX/Equal Employment Officers. The team approach also creates a more complete picture of a concerning situation by bringing more data points into consideration. The different team members are able to access and provide information from varied sources of student or employee data, supplying different "pieces of a puzzle" the team works to solve. In the case of incel activities, this team approach is the best opportunity for identifying early messages of concern in order to intervene before an individual's world continues to unravel toward greater levels of risk and potential violence. This brings us to a review of the three most common phases of team activities.

Three Phases of Team Activities

There are typically three phases of BIT operations: (1) gathering data, (2) rubric/ analysis, and (3) intervention (see Figure 14.1) (Sokolow et al., 2014). First, the team gathers data on incidents of concern by cultivating a culture of reporting and accessing various pockets of information on concerns. Second, the BIT performs an analysis of the information gathered related to the report by using an objective risk rubric and the various perspectives of the team. Third, the BIT selects interventions to coordinate in order to manage the nature of the concern. The three phases are cyclical as the situation evolves, with additional data gathered as the interventions are deployed and the level of risk is adjusted accordingly.

Phase 1 of BIT: Gathering Data

The first phase of BIT activity is based on the principle that in order to provide truly valuable interventions for concerns and prevent the escalation of risk, the BIT

Addressing Incel through BIT/CARE model 177

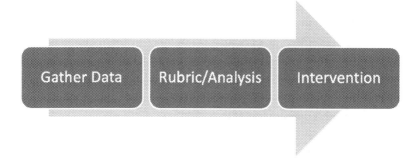

Figure 14.1 Three phases of BIT

must become a centralized collection point for all information and data related to an individual concern. This requires a two-fold approach to data gathering: (1) cultivating a caring reporting culture throughout the school or workplace community and (2) having access to multiple data points and records related to individuals.

BITs communicate across the school, campus, or workplace community about the importance of reporting behaviors or incidents of concern in order to provide coordinated support and interventions for those involved. This is a strategic and intentional team approach to gathering data within the campus or workplace community in order to seek reports well before the nature of the threat becomes more direct or specific. The effort includes the use of websites, printed materials, recognizable team logo and name, and training sessions to inform the community about the importance of reporting to the BIT, what to report, and how to report.

Several ideas can be shared to help stakeholders understand the importance of centralized reporting to the team:

- *Early Alert* – the opportunity to intervene well in advance of more serious issue
- *See Something, Say Something* – the responsibility of everyone in the community to be aware of and report troubling incidents
- *Puzzle Pieces* – the capabilities of the BIT to connect disparate reports about the same individual and identify and respond to patterns of concern in the community
- *Silos* – the elimination of information silos by integrating various sources of student or employee data that would sometimes go unshared across different departments or units

BITs are often asked to provide lists of the types of behaviors community members should report to the team. Lists are a good training item and element to include in materials related to BIT activities, but it is critical to recognize that lists are not comprehensive and are unable to cover the full range of incidents and behaviors that could be reported to a team. BITs should also tailor lists to make sure they are representative of the types of behaviors occurring within the specific school or

178 *Community and Systems Approach*

Table 14.1 Examples of behaviors to report with potential links to incel philosophies or activities

Objectifying, derogatory or exaggerated thoughts related to women or beauty	Bullying behavior related to relationships, intimate partners, dating, or sexual attraction.
Isolation or disconnect with others	Direct or indirect communicated threats such as, "That f*cking Chad should die, I'll make it painful." or "I'm going to make those b*tches pay!"
Exercise obsessions or body self-esteem concerns	Hopelessness or despair
Lack of positive social connections	Fixation on identifying sexual relationships and connections with women, resentment toward those in relationships
Entitled or deserving of specific treatment	Preoccupied with the accumulation of wealth

workplace community they are working with. For example, a list used for middle school teachers may look different than the list used for residence hall staff members or a list for supervisors in a corporation. A sample list can be found in Table 14.1.

The first phase of BIT activity related to gathering data continues after the receipt of reports from the community to the team by using the multidisciplinary aspect of membership to gather additional information about the situation or individual(s) involved. When a BIT receives a referral of concern, they need the ability to quickly access other information about the situation and the individual being discussed. Often there are indicators across an individual's interactions and experiences that lend clues to the BIT about how to best support and intervene in the situation. When we look back across incidents of violence, there are often warning signs and communications alerting us to concerns, but that information is either not shared or it is shared to a place where it is looked at in isolation and without access to a more complete picture of what is occurring.

This data gathering helps the BIT to consider a more comprehensive view of the elements influencing what has occurred and the circumstances surrounding the concerning behaviors. For example, law enforcement representatives would be aware of any previous crime reports or criminal background. The type of information a BIT would review in an educational setting includes: formal student record information such as conduct/discipline records, admission records, and academic transcripts; observable information such as information from faculty, academic advisors, department staff (financial aid, housing, student organizations, etc.) interacting with the student in and outside of the classroom; social media and online information such as Facebook, Instagram, online communities, and blogs; information available through informed consent processes such as counseling or health-related interactions; and information available from students, other community members, or parents and family members gathered either through referrals to the BIT or in conversations with them.

This may sound to some as an intrusive review of personal information. But remember, the team's goal is to offer support, resources, and assistance to those

Addressing Incel through BIT/CARE model 179

involved in reports of concern, and the information helps to inform how to best intervene. The broad and comprehensive gathering of information prevents jumping to conclusions about behaviors of concern or acting in a biased manner toward those involved. The information is not intended for punitive use, although some specific behavioral reports may result in conduct or disciplinary action, but this should or would be occurring regardless of the team activities. This use of conduct or disciplinary action as a component of BIT interventions will be discussed further later in the chapter.

Phase 2 of BIT: Risk Rubric and Analysis

The second phase of BIT activities incorporates the use of a risk rubric to analyze the nature of information gathered in the reports received from the community as well as the team's access to additional information. BITs use an objective, research-based risk rubric to evaluate each reported incident and establish a level of risk associated with the concern. The team will review the information available on each individual, including previous BIT referrals. Then, as a group, they will review how the information aligns with the objective risk rubric.

When a team receives information about a concern, simply discussing the case and deciding what actions to take without an objective analysis is often called "by the gut" decision making. It "feels" like this is how we should proceed. In this more subjective decision making by the team, a number of variables can influence why the decided action is not well informed. Variables such as individual team member implicit bias related to factors of the case can have the team responding in one way to an individual with certain characteristics and differently to an individual with different characteristics, even though the nature of the risk and behaviors were virtually identical. We can also be influenced by variables such as individuals repetitively being referred to the BIT, the most recent case we reviewed, or just our own level of energy and focus at the time we discuss the case. While an objective risk rubric is certainly not perfect, it helps to keep the team focused on the same set of indicators when reviewing each case.

This is not to say that there is no room for tailoring interventions and actions to an individual. We want the BIT to be culturally competent and refine interventions in order to receive the best response from an individual related to an intervention, but we do not want the BIT referring an individual to the police in one case when a similar case is only documented and closed. When subjective, potentially biased decision making occurs, we risk several things. First, the team risks making discriminatory decisions on the bases of disability, mental health status, or other individual characteristics. Second, the team can miss important elements indicating higher levels of risk.

An example of a widely used BIT risk rubric is provided in Figure 14.2. The NaBITA Risk Rubric is designed to be used with every case discussion. It helps the team determine a generalized risk level through the process of informed classification of the behaviors and information available about each case. Then the tool guides decision making about interventions by aligning options for action with the generalized risk level. The NaBITA Risk Rubric includes a scale to assess both life

180 Community and Systems Approach

Figure 14.2 NaBITA Risk Rubric

Addressing Incel through BIT/CARE model   181

stress/emotional health and hostility/violence. Teams may choose to use a tool other than the NaBITA Risk Rubric that provides a generalized risk rating based on the information available to the team. The team documents the risk rating determined by the team into the BIT recordkeeping system at each discussion of the individual. This helps to track the escalation and de-escalation of cases. The risk rating is also used to inform a decision about actions or interventions in Phase 3.

The D-Scale is the left side of the NaBITA Risk Rubric. This scale is used to review disruptive and concerning behaviors related to life stress and emotional health with four progressive levels: (1) developing, (2) distressed, (3) deteriorating, and (4) decompensating. As you progress up the scale, the risk is more concerning and serious with the potential for affective violence and aggression and/or self-harm. This scale is more often associated with self-harm than harm to others. This scale often overlaps with mental health concerns and is rooted in the concept of affective violence as discussed in Chapter 7. Affective violence is often a biological reaction to aggression, fear, or attack, and is adrenaline driven. This type of violence is reactive and impulsive, so while it is certainly an issue of concern for a case manager or BIT, it is different than the predatory, targeted violence considered on the other side of the rubric in the E-scale.

The E-Scale is the right side of the NaBITA Risk Rubric. The scale is used to review hostility and violence to others with four progressive levels (1) empowering thoughts, (2) escalating behaviors, (3) elaboration of threat, and (4) emergence of violence. As you progress up the scale, the risk is more concerning for targeted violence, hostility, and threats to others. This scale is more often associated with harm to others than harm to self, although both risks are present in the scale.

This scale considers targeted or predatory violence. When compared to affective violence, described in the D-scale, this violence is more planful, intent-driven and more common to incidents of mass violence. Because this type of violence develops over time, this is of particular importance to the BIT since behaviors and information can be indicators of this type of planning and offer opportunities to prevent the violent behavior.

The overall summary of risk is in the center section of the risk rubric. The summary provides an overall risk level determination of four progressive levels: (1) mild, (2) moderate, (3) elevated, and (4) critical. The team matches the D-Scale risk level and E-Scale risk level with the overall summary levels for a generalized risk determination. For example, if the D-Scale is a Level 2 Distressed and the E-Scale is Level 1 Empowering Thoughts, then the overall summary level is moderate, the highest level present between the two scales.

Incel-related risks could be present in both the D-scale and the E-Scale. BITs could be notified about an individual on the D-Scale struggling with being teased or bullied by others related to an inability to get a girlfriend, or a student losing focus in class and struggling academically. The team would use the risk rubric, and depending on other known information, may find this person at Level 2 Distressed on the D-Scale, experiencing situational stressors and struggling to cope. If a second referral to the BIT was received about this same student indicating that the student posted on social media derogatory remarks toward a woman who had recently rejected him, calling her various names and blaming her for his current situation, the team would

182   *Community and Systems Approach*

again use the risk rubric, and in addition to the continuing D-scale concerns, they would also rate him at Level 2 Escalating Behaviors on the E-scale, engaging to communicate frustrations and objectifying those they blame for issues. Threats of violence are vague and indirect if present at all. The overall risk rating identified by the team would be moderate based on the existing information.

At face, neither of these incidents are necessarily high risk, but by considering other contextual elements associated with each, the team has an opportunity to engage with the student and offer appropriate supports and resources to keep either situation from escalating further. With early identification, BITs have an opportunity to intervene well before an elevated threat emerges. If we wait too long, teams are left with limited intervention options, such as law enforcement and serious disciplinary outcomes, instead of more expanded interventions and supports at lower levels of risk.

Phase 3 of BIT: Interventions

Phase 3 of the BIT process is to determine, based on the objective risk rating determined by the team, the appropriate set of interventions and actions needed by the team to stabilize or deescalate the risks present. Interventions represent a spectrum of activities, resources, communications, and actions potentially taken by the BIT depending on the level of risk determined in Phase 2.

Interventions incorporate both a prevention and threat management lens, meaning while some referrals feel minor, low-risk, and lack any type of threat to individuals or the community, the effective BIT understands that referrals on the lower end of a risk assessment are important in order to have opportunities to intervene with situations of concern before they escalate to a higher level of risk. Once a threat is actually made or present in a team's analysis of information, the opportunities to intervene are often more limited and include more severe actions related to law enforcement intervention, conduct processes, or involuntary hospitalizations. The goal of seeking referrals across the full spectrum of risk during Phase 1 is to identify more issues at lower levels and more opportunities to provide earlier, less disruptive interventions, such as counseling support, parent and family notification, and resource referrals.

After the team has completed the analysis and assessment of the reported situation, they create a collaborative plan of interventions and risk management activities to reduce the risks of violence. Phase 3 includes both the initial deployment of interventions and the long-term management of the concern. These activities may include ongoing monitoring and interactions with individuals of concerns, identification of mental health, academic, or personal support referrals, the separation of a student from the school community temporarily or permanently, safety planning for individuals being targeted or impacted by the concerns, and stimulating the growth of stabilizing influences like those identified in Chapter 8. Intervention activities are coordinated by the team but may also include those who are not regular members of the team.

The back of the NaBITA Risk Rubric offers a range of actions for each of the four overall risk levels, as shown in Figure 14.3. There are a few key elements to remember related to the use of the risk rubric in deploying interventions:

CRITICAL (4)

- Initiate wellness check/evaluation for involuntary hold or police response for arrest
- Coordinate with necessary parties (student conduct, police, etc.) to create plan for safety, suspension, or other interim measures
- Obligatory parental/guardian/emergency contact notification unless contraindicated
- Evaluate need for emergency notification to community
- Issue mandated assessment once all involved are safe
- Evaluate the need for involuntary/voluntary withdrawal
- Coordinate with university police and/or local law enforcement
- Provide guidance, support, and safety plan to referral source/stakeholders

ELEVATED (3)

- Consider a welfare/safety check
- Provide guidance, support, and safety plan to referral source/stakeholders
- Deliver follow up and ongoing case management or support services
- Required assessment such as the SIVRA-35, ERIS, HCR-20, WAVR-20 or similar; assess social media posts
- Evaluate parental/guardian/emergency contact notification
- Coordinate referrals to appropriate resources and provide follow-up
- Likely referral to student conduct or disability support services
- Coordinate with university police/campus safety, student conduct, and other departments as necessary to mitigate ongoing risk

MODERATE (2)

- Provide guidance and education to referral source
- Reach out to student to encourage a meeting
- Develop and implement case management plan or support services
- Connect with offices, support resources, faculty, etc. who interact with student to enlist as support or to gather more information
- Possible referral to student conduct or disability support services
- Offer referrals to appropriate support resources
- Assess social media and other sources to gather more information
- Consider VRAW^2 for cases that have written elements
- Skill building in social interactions, emotional balance, and empathy; reinforcement of protective factors (social support, opportunities for positive involvement)

MILD (0/1)

- No formal intervention; document and monitor over time
- Provide guidance and education to referral source
- Reach out to student to offer a meeting or resources, if needed
- Connect with offices, support resources, faculty, etc. who interact with student to enlist as support or to gather more information

Figure 14.3 Interventions NaBITA Risk Rubric

184   *Community and Systems Approach*

- The interventions should always match the overall summary of risk level. For example, it would not be appropriate to use parent notification for a case rated mild because this is an intervention for elevated risk levels.
- Cases identified at Level 3 Elevated automatically have a more expansive set of interventions available because this is where a threat has emerged based on the team's evaluation of the situation. This expanded set of interventions includes actions such as mandated assessments, parent notification, and welfare/safety checks.
- Teams are not restricted to just one intervention in the list. The team should tailor a set of interventions and actions based on their understanding of the case and the risks discussed by the team. The interventions determined by the team should be clearly documented alongside the risk level each time the team discusses the case.

In the example provided earlier, the team found the student at Level 2 on both the D-Scale and E-scale, placing him in the general risk category of moderate. On the back side of the rubric, you can see the rubric suggests a range of interventions at the moderate level, including connecting the student with support resources, meeting with the student, evaluating the written elements (social media post) with an advanced threat assessment tool such as the VRAW^2, and potentially working with the student related to social interactions and emotional balance in order to reinforce and establish stabilizing influences.

The team has the functionality to perform more advanced threat assessments when the nature of the risk requires it, most often at elevated. There are two primary types of assessments that a BIT could deploy when the level of risk requires it: *mental health assessments* and *violence risk/threat assessments*. These are two distinct types of assessments used in the work of behavioral intervention. It is important to understand the different process and outcomes associated with both. A *mental health assessment or psychological assessment* is solely focused on the diagnosis of a mental health problem and identification of treatment options, including recommendations or requirements for hospitalization. A BIT might refer a student to a psychologist or psychiatrist in order to complete a mental health assessment.

The second type of assessment is a *violence risk assessment or threat assessment*. Any member of the team can be trained in various techniques and tools to perform this type of assessment which is focused on determining dangerousness or lethality of an individual to harm, kill, or destroy a person, system, or location. These tools include the Structured Interview of Violence Risk Assessment (SIVRA-35) (Van Brunt, 2012), the Historical Clinical Risk Manageement-20 (HCR-20) (Douglas et al., 2013), and the Workplace Assessment of Violence Risk-21 (WAVR-21), (White & Meloy, 2007). The risk factors identified in Chapter 7 are the foundation of violence risk or threat assessments and help a team to identify the level of intervention and threat management needed for each situation. Chapter 9 discusses risk assessments to be used when incel-type concerns arise in a situation.

Upon completing an advanced threat assessment, BITs incorporate the information gathered and return back to Phase 2 to use the risk rubric and reanalyze what is known about the situation. Then, the team moves back to Phase 3 to determine

Team Membership

Team chair: BIT teams should have a designated chair to provide leadership to the group, coordinate day-to-day operations, and consider the long-term support and development of the team. The primary functions of the chair include vision and planning, community buy-in and support, team training and transitions, team meetings and processes, and reporting and assessment (Schiemann et al., 2019).

In their 2018 guidance, the Department of Homeland Security and the Secret Service make team leadership a requirement in either a part-time or full-time capacity, stating: "The team needs to have a specifically designated leader. The position is usually occupied by a senior administrator within the school" (NTAC, 2018, p. 3). In higher education, this is most often a dean of students-type position. In K-12 schools, usually a principal chairs an individual school team, or a district administrator chairs a multi-school team. These positions work well in the chair capacity because they have the authority to compel mandated assessments when necessary, and they have the scope of knowledge and experience to understand various aspects of the student experience. Because of the considerable workload required of a team chair, it does require someone who can spend an adequate amount of time focused on BIT issues. While the suggested positions do have an extensive scope of responsibility outside of the BIT, when paired with good support positions and engaged team members, the combination is set up for effectiveness and success.

Counseling: BITs require membership expertise in mental health care and treatment. This position provides both general insight into mental health-related behaviors as well as specific information and coordination for those cases either currently participating in counseling services or for those cases where there is a need to offer counseling services as part of an intervention. The counseling member is also trained in more advanced violence risk and threat assessment tools and can participate as needed in these mandated assessment activities. When possible in higher education, this position is a licensed administrator from the college's counseling center staff, such as the director or an associate/assistant director, who has access to the center's complete client load. Licensed counseling positions on the team may come from a variety of clinical perspectives: psychologists, licensed mental health counselors, marriage and family therapists, licensed social workers, or addiction specialists. In K-12 schools, the position is typically occupied by the school counselor or director of counseling and supplemented with regular or as needed involvement from a licensed school psychologist.

Because of the unique aspect of having both licensed and non-licensed counseling staff in these roles, it is critical to clarify two issues related to this membership: (1) is the member licensed to practice mental health care in the state, and (2) is the member hired by the school to provide mental health treatment? If the answer to both of these questions is yes, this team member has a higher level of confidentiality that shifts

186   *Community and Systems Approach*

how they share information with the team about clients, as opposed to most other team members, who use privacy standards are established by the Family Education Rights and Privacy Act (FERPA) (20 USC § 1232g; 34 CFR § 99). Confidentiality in a client/provider relationship requires either a specific release of information or meeting certain exceptions in order to share information outside of the professional relationship, whereas FERPA-protected information can be shared regularly with other team members under the legitimate educational interest aspect of the statute. This means psychologists, psychiatrists, and professional clinicians will more often than not be bound by confidentiality unless an information release is in place, but school counselors or non-licensed academic/personal counselors or advisors are able to communicate more freely.

Student conduct/discipline: While the BIT approaches cases from a perspective of support and care as opposed to a punitive mindset, there is still the need to coordinate team activities with a progressive and educational discipline or conduct process. In fact, one of the most common mistakes a team makes is skipping standard disciplinary actions for BIT cases, thinking they are being thoughtful and supportive. Unfortunately, this can create inconsistent standards across the educational community, and the team loses the opportunity to reset expectations and document patterns of concerning behaviors. In higher education, this position is most often filled by the director of student conduct, and in K12 schools, this is usually the assistant principal responsible for discipline. This position is able to share information on conduct history of cases and information about reoccurring behaviors. They are also able to inform the team about typical conduct processes related to the presenting behaviors and coordinate with the team as these processes occur. This can mean coordinating when a student is going to be suspended or selecting disciplinary conditions that complement the team's selected interventions. The student conduct or discipline team member should also be trained in mandated assessment processes and advanced threat assessment tools in order to support the team when this need arises.

Law enforcement: BITs should include representation from sworn law enforcement for the college or school. This individual is the expert on criminal offenses and processes. They are to consider the criminal nature of behaviors as well as share information related to criminal history or police contact/reports with the team. They should be trained in advanced threat assessment tools and able to participate as needed in violence risk and threat assessments. This position should also act as a liaison with other local, state, or federal law enforcement agencies. In higher education, this is often the chief or assistant chief of the campus law enforcement unit. In K-12, it may be a school resource officer.

Case manager: More and more frequently in higher education and K-12, teams are using case manager positions to support the work of the team by providing flexible and creative support to the various cases through intervention activities, monitoring, and coordinating access to care and resources, and providing holistic oversight to the case. Approximately 40% of teams now include case management membership (Schiemann & Van Brunt, 2018). This can be either a clinical or non-clinical case manager. Non-clinical case managers are the most frequent and often work closely with the chair of the team to support the team functions as a primary aspect of their job responsibilities. Clinical case managers may also be members of the team, but they are often representing a counseling or health unit and serving similar roles to those described under the counseling member section. Case managers are uniquely situated to interact directly with students of concern, build relationships with them, and provide longer-term management of at-risk situations. These positions are also well-suited to be trained in violence risk and threat assessment tools.

Residential life/housing: For higher education campuses with large residential populations, it is common for the team to include a member from housing or residence life. This is usually a director or associate director position with broad responsibilities including the ability to access information across housing units related to student incidents and information. This can include incident reports, room conditions, roommate impressions, room changes, or even maintenance requests. In addition to sharing information gathered from housing staff interactions with students, they are also critical in coordinating interventions through resident advisors (RAs) or professional housing staff. Sometimes housing professional staff are also responsible for hall-based conduct processes which then adds a layer of similar coordination to that discussed in the student conduct/discipline membership.

504/disability services: It is critical that BITs have regular access and communication with disability support resources in the college or school; sometimes this may mean regular membership or it may be as needed consultation. In higher education, this member is usually the director of disability support services, and in K-12, it will be the special education coordinator. Many BIT cases involve indicators that an individual may qualify for disability accommodations. In some cases, there may already be accommodations or special education plans (individual education plans (IEPs)) in place for those being discussed in team meetings. These members can share accommodation-related disability information, effectively arrange accommodations for those qualified, and consult on disability issues and the rights of individuals with disabilities.

Title IX: Incidents of sexual violence, including sexual assault, dating or domestic violence, stalking, and other forms of sexual harassment, often have overlapping concerns with BIT. Incel activities in particular may be creating concerns related to harassment and discrimination on the basis of sex. All higher education and K-12 schools should have a designated Title IX coordinator. it is common for the coordinator or a deputy coordinator to work alongside the team when needed. This allows coordination of support and interventions being offered to both reporting and responding parties. This can include information about no contact orders and other supports and resources. Individuals involved in these processes are often experiencing distress that may need support. Similar to student conduct/discipline members, Title IX processes should continue separate and apart from the BIT, but the two components can and should inform one another related to interventions, the use of support resources, and risk assessments.

Other members: Depending on the needs of the team, membership can also include a variety of other positions and roles, including academic affairs, health services, human resources, general counsel, and academic advising.

188   *Community and Systems Approach*

A Typical Meeting

Consider for a minute the case study provided in Chapter 12. Let's walk through how a BIT might approach this case and the typical activities that occur in a BIT meeting.

Case 2: Jake

Jake attends a small, four-year college in the Midwest and is a second semester Junior. He has a few friends that he hangs around with on campus and he plays baseball. While not particularly tall at 5'7 and 145 pounds, he works out five to six hours a day with his baseball team and his smaller group of friends.

Despite working out a lot, playing on the school baseball team and doing well in his business major, he has had very little dating success. He hoped college would be different from high school. He never had kissed a girl, let alone had sex with one, and fully believed that everyone on campus would be having crazy parties and hooking up. The few parties he went to ended up with him drinking to the point of throwing up in the backyard. Several pictures of him passed out ended up online. One night, people also wrote on him and drew penises on his face while he was blacked out. Since his school is small, he feels like everyone knows about these incidents.

Jake feels discouraged and thinks he'll never figure out how to get with a woman. Two of his friends, Carter and Derrick, talk to him about his lack of "game" with the ladies. Jake agrees and takes their advice to be less needy around women and to practice giving really hot women semi-insulting comments to throw them off the normally expected praise from everyone around them. Jake tries this with a Black woman at the gym by saying "I'm not usually into Black chicks, but you are pretty light-skinned and don't have one of those crazy bubble asses and look alright." That doesn't go as well for him, although he does have some better luck with some other 6s and 7s, getting some extra glances from them. He figures the Black chick was a probably a dyke anyway.

He starts to research these ideas a bit more and sees some references on discussion boards about guaranteed ways to get really hot women no matter what you look like. He eventually joins a website called https://incels.net/ and creates a username and participates in the discussions. He likes the idea of the redpill and how people with potentially lesser genetics can become more desirable. Jake thinks his workouts and playing baseball are two things that will get him with a true Stacy. Although the more he reads, the more he starts to realize that maybe just finding one Stacy is part of his problem as well – thinking some girl is going to fix his entire life. The real thing he is missing isn't status or working out but having real confidence. He reads a thread about pheromones and how women can actually sniff out inferior men.

Jake falls deeper into this thinking and joins a male positivity site called www.therationalmale.com that gives him dating advice and guidance. He learns that women who are 10s who often hang around with 6s and he starts to see this all over campus. There some good suggestions of using alcohol to "loosen up the legs" and he finds some good ideas in "shaking her" or manipulating women so you can sexually possess her mind.

Addressing Incel through BIT/CARE model   189

Jake finally gets his first kiss at a party with a drunken 6 femoid and "pulls her" when she is away from her 10. He ends up in a backroom with her grabs her tits. He gets his hand into her pants and she pulls away but doesn't have much strength in her drunken state and so they make out for a little while longer. Jake hangs out with his friends after he leaves, getting a good number of high-fives and "atta boys" given his newfound skills in BAB (Bagging a Becky).

The next day, the woman Jake hooked up with talks to her friends about what had happened and they encourage her to file a Title IX assault claim with the school. Jake is called in and defends his actions during an initial inquiry at the school. Since both were drinking and there was a bit of a "he said, she said" element to what happened. Jake is given an option to connect to counseling as an informal resolution to the claim against him. He reluctantly agrees, angry that he was punished, and that the lying Becky got him in trouble. He begins spending more time online, raging about how foids can't be trusted and the bitches only want to bring men down. He writes "This is exactly why Elliot Rodger did what he did." He muses that if he was going to get in trouble anyway, he should have fucked that girl when he had the chance.

In this case study, there are opportunities for members of the campus community to report the case to the BIT well before the Title IX assault claim. For example, when Jake passed out at the party and pictures were circulated online, if a concerned friend or a staff member became aware of this and reported it to the BIT, the team would have had the opportunity to touch base with Jake about what is going on with him well in advance of some of the other concerning behaviors. Another reporting opportunity could have occurred when Jake's exercise behaviors became less healthy, if a recreational sports employee noticed and reached out to him about healthier exercise options, or if one of the women reported his disparaging comments to them. This employee might have caught onto other concerns that could be reported to the BIT for additional follow-up and support.

In this case, it appears that the BIT was not notified until the Title IX assault claim was filed. This is a good example of how the BIT should not interfere with the ongoing Title IX processes, but they can still be active in working with reporting and responding parties related to areas of risk and identifying supports and services that may be helpful. In addition, this is a case we would want the Title IX officer to report to the BIT in order to consider other risks associated with Jake's behaviors and situation. The Title IX coordinator would share the details appropriate either via an electronic report to the BIT database system or directly with the BIT chairperson and ask that his situation be considered at the next BIT meeting. This allows BIT members to review any additional information they may have to inform how to best intervene with Jake.

At the weekly BIT meeting, the chairperson would review the information reported about Jake. The team would have access to review Jake's academic transcript, current courses, and other student information. They might notice in their review that Jake is using the on campus recreational center every day and sometimes more than once a day. This might not raise concern, but it is helpful information for them to consider. The team could review Jake's social media activity, and they may find some of the

190   *Community and Systems Approach*

online activity referenced in the case study which could give additional clues to what is occurring. Minimally, they are aware of the reported incident of nonconsensual touching and the requirement to follow up with counseling services.

After reviewing available information, the team would review the information against the NaBITA Risk Rubric to identify a generalized level of risk. Starting on the D-scale related to life stress and emotional health, they would minimally identify that Jake was at a Level 2 Distressed related to the stressors associated with the Title IX claims. If they were aware of some of the repeated activities related to alcohol use, the team might rate him higher on the D-scale. The E-scale is critical here related to targeted violence and harm to others. If the team is aware of the online activities and saw any incel related posts, this may help inform the E-scale rating potentially indicating minimally hardened thoughts and objectification toward some women and potentially increased fixation and focus on specific types of women as well as how he is driven by the support of the incel messaging and followers. The information available to the team can shift the level of risk identified. Since there has been a reported incident of nonconsensual touching, the team would likely find him at the Elevated risk level upon review of the information available, but with the potential to decrease the level of risk with good supportive interventions.

Upon agreement on a level of risk, the team turns to a discussion of interventions. Here BITs should be careful to coordinate with the Title IX office and the counseling center since there is an ongoing referral process already in place. It may be that the counseling center can ask the student to sign an informed consent allowing more open discussion with the BIT. The counseling center may be able to use more advanced threat assessment tools such those found in Chapter 9 with Jake. If not, it is likely the BIT would identify a team member to follow up with Jake for an additional discussion and assessment using this type of information. The primary goal here is connecting with Jake in a nonadversarial way in order to make a connection to gather more information about the elements distressing him and the evolving deterioration of his thoughts toward women. In doing so, this would open up opportunities for more discussions of resources and referrals to assist him. The team would need to reconsider Jake's situation as more information was gathered through the different meetings.

Common Missteps in the Work of BITs

This case study demonstrates how the work of the BIT is influenced by available information, active and engaged team members, and effective analysis and intervention processes. While BITs are well situated to respond to a wide array of incidents in our communities, there are some common missteps to watch for in our work on or with these teams.

- *Failing to establish a culture of reporting in the school or work community in fear of receiving too many reports.* To be truly preventative and respond to concerns during their earliest stages, BITs need to encourage a broad scope of reporting and communication from all stakeholders in the community.
- *Analyzing cases without the use of an objective risk rubric.* The use of a risk rubric in the analysis of each incident supports consistency in decision making.

Addressing Incel through BIT/CARE model 191

In addition, with a rubric such as the NaBITA Risk Rubric discussed in this chapter, it provides a research-based lens for identifying the level of risk present in a situation.

- *Using diagnostic language and terms in case notes and discussion.* When it comes to the risk assessments completed by the team, the counseling staff are often the only team members who have extensive knowledge and course work in differential diagnosis. To this end, diagnoses should be avoided in BIT documentation, but rather focus on behavioral descriptions of the concerns shared with the team.
- *Letting individual or team implicit bias influence decisions.* BITs should be trained on issues of implicit bias and use processes and strategies to reduce the presence of bias in decision making. Incel activities can be triggering when reviewing messaging or other concerns, so using a good team process and avoiding "gut" reactions is even more critical.
- *Skipping standard conduct or discipline processes because of concern for the individual's reactions.* If a behavior has occurred that would typically be referred for conduct processes and represents a potential violation of conduct rules for an institution, then the conduct process should continue regardless of BIT involvement. Conduct processes can be handled with thoughtfulness, support, and grace, but they should not be avoided in fear of an individual's reactions.

This chapter has provided an overview of the work of behavioral intervention teams and how their processes can support work related to the prevention of and response to incel activities and concerns. When we collaborate with BITs with the capacity to gather data, to perform comprehensive analysis and threat assessment of the concern, and to deploy coordinated interventions, we are better able to identify concerns early and prevent the escalation to violence.

Discussion Questions

- Do you have a behavioral intervention, CARE or threat team at your school, college, or workplace? If so, does it operate similarly to the processes discussed in this chapter? Where does it differ? If you do not have team, why do you think that is? What are some steps that could be taken to create a team at your location?
- Dr. Murphy outlines how a BIT might handle a case like Jake in Chapter 12. Pick the case of Marc in Chapter 11 or Kyle in Chapter 13 and discuss how BIT would process through one of these cases.
- Discuss the importance of following a model that focused on (1) gathering information, (2) applying an assessment, and (3) developing interventions. How do you see the addition of the IIR useful in BIT work?

Note

1 **Amy Murphy, Ph.D.** is Assistant Professor at Angelo State University and Program Coordinator for the M.Ed. in Student Development and Leadership in Higher Education.

192 *Community and Systems Approach*

She was formerly the Dean of Students at Texas Tech University and has more than 20 years of student affairs administrative experiences. Dr. Murphy co-authored *A Staff Guide to Addressing Disruptive and Dangerous Behavior On Campus* and *Uprooting Sexual Violence in Higher Education: A Guide for Practitioners and Faculty.* She is the 2019 President of the National Behavioral Intervention Team Association (NaBITA) and writes and presents regularly on current issues in education related to safety and wellness.

References

Borum, R., Fein, R., Bossekuil, B., and Berglund, J. (1999). Threat assessment: Defining an approach for evaluating risk of targeted violence. *Behavioral Sciences and the Law*, 17, 323–337.

Douglas, K.S., Hart, S.D., Webster, C.D., and Belfrage, H. (2013). *HCR-20 V3 Assessing Risk for Violence User Guide.* Burnaby: Mental Health, Law, and Policy Institute, Simon Fraser University.

Family Education Rights and Privacy Act, 20 USC § 1232g; 34 CFR § 99.

National Association of Behavioral Intervention Team (NaBITA). (2018). *NaBITA Standards for Behavioral Intervention Teams.* Berwyn: National Behavioral Intervention Team Association.

National Threat Assessment Center (NTAC). (2018). *Enhancing School Safety Using a Threat Assessment Model: An Operational Guide for Preventing Targeted School Violence.* Washington, DC: US Secret Service, Department of Homeland Security.

Schiemann, M. and Van Brunt, B. (2018). Summary and analysis of 2018 NaBITA Survey Data. *The Journal of Campus Behavioral Intervention (JBIT)*, 6, 42–75.

Schiemann, M., Murphy, A., Fitch, P., Molnar, J., Woodly, E., Schuster, S., Sokolow, B., and Van Brunt, B. (2019). *Leadership of the Behavioral Intervention Team.* King of Prussia: National Behavioral Intervention Team Association (NaBITA).

Sokolow, B., Lewis, W.S., Van Brunt, B., Schuster, S., and Swinton, D. (2014). *The Book on BIT*, 2nd edn. Berwyn: National Behavioral Intervention Team Association (NaBITA).

Van Brunt, B. (2012). *Ending Campus Violence: New Approaches to Prevention.* New York: Routledge.

Van Brunt, B. (2015). *Harm to Others: The Assessment and Treatment of Dangerousness.* Alexander: American Counseling Association.

Van Brunt, B., Schiemann, M., Pescara-Kovach, L., Murphy, A., and Halligan-Avery, E. (2018). Standards for behavioral intervention teams. *The Journal of Campus Behavioral Intervention (JBIT)*, 6, 29–41.

White, S.G. and Meloy, J.R. (2007). *WAVR-21 – Workplace Assessment of Violence Risk: A Structured Professional Judgment Guide*, 3rd edn. Retrieved from www.wavr21.com.

Appendix A: Case Review

1 Tsuyama Massacre, May 21, 1938, Kamo, Tsuyama, Japan

Mutsuo Toi, 21

Around 1934, Toi began participating in the practice of Yobai (night crawling), the ancient Japanese custom during which young men sneak into a woman's bedroom and, if she consents, they have intercourse. In rural Japan, it was a normal way to find a spouse. In 1937, he was diagnosed with tuberculosis and the women of the village began rejecting his sexual advantages. This led to feelings of isolation and loneliness. In his suicide notes, he wrote about the tuberculosis turning him into a social pariah. He decided to kill those who he felt had wronged him.

On the evening of May 20, 1938, Toi cut the power to the village. He started his rampage around 1:30am by killing with grandmother so she wouldn't have to live with the shame of his actions. Over the next 90 minutes, he killed another 29 neighbors – approximately half the population of the village. He then shot and killed himself.

https://historycollection.co/dont-know-tsuyama-massacre-tuberculosis-tipped-madman-edge/
www.swordandscale.com/tsuyama-massacre/

2 Rose-Mar College of Beauty Shooting, November 13, 1966, Mesa, Arizona

Robert Benjamin (Benny) Smith, 18

Smith shot and killed four women and a three-year-old girl. He told police, "I wanted to get known, just wanted to get myself a name." Smith was a poor student, having repeated grades in school, and was teased or ignored by other children. Smith was strongly affected by the assassination of President John F. Kennedy, his personal hero. He began an interest in true crime and a fascination with assassins and murderers. His grades improved, but his social isolation worsened. A classmate recalled, "I'm sure he never dated a girl at our school." He reportedly "entertained fantasies in which women were shot or stabbed."

194   *Appendix A*

Smith took inspiration from the mass killings by Richard Speck in Chicago and Charles Whitman in Austin, Texas and began planning his attack in the summer of 1966. He chose the beauty school hoping for a large death toll.

www.nydailynews.com/news/crime/beauty-salon-massacre-article-1.273663
https://schoolshooters.info/sites/default/files/smith_analysis_1.0.pdf

3 St. Pius X High School Shooting, October 27, 1975, Ottawa, Ontario, Canada

Robert Poulin, 18

After raping and killing a girl at his home, Poulin went to the school and shot seven people, killing one of them, and then killed himself. Poulin had been obsessed with sex and pornography. He kept a scrapbook of nude men and women, a collection of hardcore pornography books and magazines, detailed ratings of photographs and advertisements and an index of several pornographic magazines.

Prior to the school shooting, Poulin was suspected in several cases of indecent exposure and attempted rape at the apartment building near his home. In his diary, he wrote, "I don't want to die before I have had the pleasure of fucking some girl," although having recently discovered a sex doll, he also wrote, "Now I no longer think that I will have to rape a girl, and am unsure as to whether or not I will still commit suicide."

www.cbc.ca/news/canada/manitoba/winnipeg-woman-who-survived-ottawa-school-shooting-reflects-on-la-loche-attack-1.3417757
https://schoolshooters.info/sites/default/files/expanding_the_sample_1.5.pdf
https://schoolshooters.info/sites/default/files/smith_analysis_1.0.pdf

4 Queen Street Massacre, December 8, 1987, Melbourne, Victoria, Australia

Frank Vitkovic, 22

Vitkovic killed eight people then killed himself by jumping out of the 11th story window at the Australia Post building. He went to the building planning to kill a former classmate, Con Margelis. After Margelis escaped, Vitkovic opened fire. He was stopped by two employees who were able to disarm him.

In his diary, he wrote, "It's hard for a self conscious guy like me to talk to girls with confidence" and "since the age of 12 I knew that normal sex was not possible for me and I avoided girls completely until I was 19."

www.theage.com.au/national/melbourne-remembers-queen-st-massacre-20071207-gdrrjv.html
www.pressreader.com/australia/herald-sun/20121208/281792806335304
www.murderpedia.org/male.V/v/vitkovic-frank.htm
https://incels.wiki/w/Frank_Vitkovic

Appendix A   195

5 École Polytechnique Massacre, December 6, 1989, Montreal, Quebec, Canada

Marc Lépine, 25

Lépine had twice failed in his application for the school and had long complained about women working in "non-traditional" jobs. He entered an engineering classroom and separated the men and women. He killed 14 women before killing himself. He left a note that was largely an anti-feminist rant.

His suicide note includes, "[Women] want to retain the advantages of being women (e.g., cheaper insurance, extended maternity leave preceded by a preventive leave) while trying to grab those of the men" and "Thus, it is self-evident that if the Olympic Games removed the Men/Women distinction, there would be only be women in the graceful events. So the feminists are not fighting to remove that barrier." He wrote, "They are so opportunistic that they neglect to profit from the knowledge accumulated by men throughout the ages. They always try to misrepresent them every time they can."

https://toronto.citynews.ca/2006/12/06/citynews-rewind-the-montreal-massacre/
www.smithsonianmag.com/history/mass-shooting-reshaped-canadian-debate-about-guns-and-political-identity-180962013/

6 University of Iowa Shooting, November 1, 1991, Iowa City, Iowa

Gang Lu, 28

Lu was a doctoral student at the University of Iowa studying astronomy and physics. He was distressed after learning his dissertation did not win the prestigious D.C. Spriestersbach Dissertation Prize that came with a $2500 cash prize. He also learned that the departments did not have enough money to fund his postdoctoral research position and felt that because of this, he would not be able to get a job and would have to return to China. He attended a meeting with the department on November 1 and several minutes into the meeting, pulled out a revolver and shot and killed four faculty before killing himself. Three of the faculty shot were on his dissertation committee and the fourth was the winner of the Spriestersbach prize.

Before the shooting, Lu typed out five letters with the intention of sending them to news organizations. These letters talked about his academic grievances, personal failures and identified several of the targets in the shooting. Among those failures was his difficulties dating. He wrote to his sister,

Though I am single, I have had a few girlfriends. When I lived in the dormitory in high school I had already started to have girlfriends. When I went to college I often slipped into our old home at the Number 262 Hospital under cover of darkness and spent the night with girls. After I came to the States I had liaisons with Chinese and American women, with single and married women, with girls of good families and girls of the streets. I just don't have a constant heart in these matters; the grass always looks greener somewhere else, and I can't be

196   *Appendix A*

satisfied with any particular person. Maybe I didn't meet the right one, or perhaps I thought either that they were too good for me or I was too good for them. No matter what the answer is, I feel a bit fed up with male–female relationships.

www.nytimes.com/1991/11/04/us/iowa-gunman-was-torn-by-academic-challenge. html?ref=michelmarriott
www.desmoinesregister.com/story/news/2016/10/28/nov-1-1991-day-university-shooting-rampage-shocked-iowa/92053548/
https://incels.wiki/w/Gang_Lu
https://schoolshooters.info/sites/default/files/lu_sister_letter_1.0.pdf

7 Oklahoma City Bombing, April 19, 1995, Oklahoma City, Oklahoma

Timothy McVeigh, 26, and Terry Nichols, 40

McVeigh and Nichols used homemade explosives inside a rental truck to bomb the Alfred P. Murrah building, killing 168 people and injuring more than 500. They were associated with the Patriot Movement, an extreme right-wing group that rejects the legitimacy of the federal government.

McVeigh may have developed a resentment against women after his parents divorced and his mother left him with his father. He never had a girlfriend in high school. Later, a coworker described his anger and indifference toward women. Fellow soldiers said he was extremely uncomfortable and awkward around women, had complained about being rejected by women. He told reporters, "In the past thirty years, because of the women's movement, they've taken an influence out of the household."

www.cnn.com/2013/09/18/us/oklahoma-city-bombing-fast-facts/index.html
www.washingtonpost.com/wp-srv/national/longterm/oklahoma/stories/chron.htm
www.thecut.com/2016/07/mass-killers-terrorism-domestic-violence.html
www.washingtonpost.com/wp-srv/national/longterm/oklahoma/bg/mcveigh.htm
www.wsws.org/en/articles/2001/04/mcve-a19.html

8 Unabomber, 1978–1996

Theodore (Ted) Kaczynski, 54

Kaczynski's first bomb exploded in 1978 at a Chicago university. Over the next 17 years, he mailed or hand-delivered a series of bombs that killed three and injured 24 more. In 1995, he sent investigators a 35,000-word essay about his motives and views. The manifesto was published and Kaczynski's brother, David, was able to identify him by the writings.

At his arrest, Kaczynski was 54 and had never had a girlfriend. Growing up, he had trouble connecting with other people, in part because of his above average intelligence. He went on a few dates with a co-worker and she gave him his first kiss at

Appendix A 197

age 36, soon after which she ended their nascent relationship. He proceeded to write unflattering limericks about her and post them around the work site. He was fired from the job by his brother, who was both of their supervisor at the time.

Kaczynski apparently struggled to even approach women. In his journal, he writes about a girl he had a crush on who worked at a gas station. He bought a new pair of jeans to walk up to her, but ended up crying at his campfire, having lost the nerve. He was also upset when his brother became engaged, writing to him that they were both virgins and David was breaking their bond. He wrote in his manifesto, "feminists are desperately anxious to prove that women are as strong and as capable as men. Clearly they are nagged by a fear that women may NOT be as strong and as capable as men."

www.fbi.gov/history/famous-cases/unabomber
www.oxygen.com/true-crime-buzz/what-was-unabomber-ted-kaczynskis-relationship-with-women
http://editions-hache.com/essais/pdf/kaczynski2.pdf

9 Pearl High School Shooting, October 1, 1997, Pearl, Mississippi

Lucas (Luke) Woodham, 16, six co-conspirators (Grant Boyette, 18, Wesley Brownell, 17, Donald Brooks II, 17, Allen Shaw; 18, and Justin Sledge, 16)

Woodham entered the school and opened fire, killing two students and wounding seven others. Prior to the shooting, Woodham had murdered his mother with a knife. Six other teenagers were later arrested as well as co-conspirators. The group called themselves the Kroth and were led by Boyette, a self-described Satanist. A manuscript written by Woodham was discovered that talks about taking revenge on those he believed slighted him.

In his journal, he wrote "With this writing, I do swear, that I shall never get myself in a position where I can be hurt by a woman ever again. To myself I swear this, and to the higher powers I swear this." His manifesto refers to his difficulty dating, saying,

> I only loved one thing in my whole life and that was Christina Menefee. But she was torn away from me. I tried to save myself with [student's name], but she never cared for me. As it turns out, she made fun of me behind my back while we were together.

Woodham and Menefee, who was killed in the attack, dated about a year before the shooting.

www.nytimes.com/1997/10/15/us/grim-details-emerge-in-teen-age-slaying-case.html
https://people.com/archive/cover-story-the-avenger-vol-48-no-18/
https://schoolshooters.info/sites/default/files/Luke%20Woodham%20Writings.pdf

198   *Appendix A*

10 Thurston High School Shooting, May 20–21, 1998, Springfield, Oregon

Kipland Kinkel, 15

Kinkel shot fellow students in the school cafeteria. He killed two and wounded 25 others. The day before, he had killed his parents at their home. Kinkel was diagnosed with paranoid schizophrenia and was not medicated at the time of the shooting. He wrote in an essay,

> Love at first sight is only in movies. Where the people in the movies are better than you … My cold black heart has never and never will experience true love. I can tell you one about love. It does more harm than good. I plan to live in a big black hole. My firearms and [illegible] will be the only things to fight my isolation. I would also like to point out Love is a horrible thing. It makes things kill and hate.

His journal reflects his loneliness and romantic frustrations,

> Every time I talk to her, I have a small amount of hope. But then she will tear it right down. It feels like my heart is breaking. But is that possible. I am so consumed with hate all of the time. Could I ever love anyone? I have feelings, but do I have a heart that's not black and full of animosity? … I need help. There is one person that could help, but she won't. I need to find someone else. I think I love her, but she could never love me. I don't know why I try.

www.npr.org/2018/05/22/612465197/20-years-ago-oregon-school-shooting-ended-a-bloody-season
www.pbs.org/wgbh/pages/frontline/shows/kinkel/kip/cron.html
www.pbs.org/wgbh/pages/frontline/shows/kinkel/kip/writings.html

11 Columbine Shooting, April 20, 1999, Littleton, Colorado

Eric Harris, 18, and Dylan Klebold, 17

Harris and Klebold killed 15 people and wounded 28 others before killing themselves. They booby-trapped school hallways with at least 12 bombs. They had planned the attack for a year. The plan involved setting off propane bombs in the cafeteria and gunning down any survivors, then exploding their cars to kill anyone outside the school. However, they failed at wiring the timers correctly. They filmed a number of videos prior to the attack discussing their plans.

Harris didn't seem to have any long-term relationships. He seemed more interested in sex than a relationship, though, writing,

> Right now I'm trying to get fucked and trying to finish off these time bombs. NBK came quick. why the fuck cant I get any? I mean, I'm nice and considerate

Appendix A 199

and all that shit, but nooooo. I think I try to hard. but I kinda need to considering NBK is closing in.

He also wrote, "If people would give me more compliments all of this [the attack] might still be avoidable ... You know what, maybe I just need to get laid. Maybe that'll just change some s– around."

www.denverpost.com/1999/04/21/columbine-high-school-shooting/
https://slate.com/news-and-politics/2004/04/at-last-we-know-why-the-columbine-killers-did-it.html
https://heavy.com/news/2019/04/eric-harris-dylan-klebold-the-basement-tapes/
www.acolumbinesite.com/eric/writing/journal/journal.php
www.psychologytoday.com/intl/blog/keeping-kids-safe/201007/sex-love-and-school-shooters-eric-harris?amp
https://incels.wiki/w/Dylan_Klebold_and_Eric_Harris

12 Rancho Cordova Massacre, August 31, 2001, Rancho Cordova, California

Nikolay Soltys, 27

Soltys was a Ukrainian immigrant who lived with his elderly aunt and uncle, two young cousins and his pregnant wife and young son. Soltys killed all six of them. His wife was beaten and stabbed. He led police on a ten-day manhunt before he was captured.

According to someone at their church, Soltys abused his wife and was upset that she had taken a job at a grocery store. Notes found suggested the killings were retribution against relatives for things they said, and he and his wife reportedly fought about her job the day of the murders.

www.sfgate.com/news/article/PROFILE-Nikolay-Soltys-Neighbors-describe-the-2882438.php
www.cnn.com/2001/US/08/30/sacramento.killings/

13 Sacramento Rampage, September 8–10, 2001, Sacramento, California

Joseph Ferguson, 20

Ferguson was suspended from his job as a Burns security guard after his ex-girlfriend reported him for vandalizing her car with an ax after she broke up with him. The breakup was in part because of his anger and jealousy when she went on a two-month trip to her homeland of Moldova.

Ferguson killed five people and wounded two others during a 24-hour rampage through Sacramento. His former girlfriend, also a Burns security guard, was his first victim. His other victims were Burns security guards and a city employee. He then took a Burns supervisor and his wife hostage for several hours. He forced him to record a video in which Ferguson rants, mostly against his former girlfriend, but

200   *Appendix A*

also several colleagues and his mother, who is in prison for molesting her two sons, Ferguson and his brother. In it he says,

> I'm going to see fit that that happens … Either a bullet to my brain, or a … cop will kill me … [the killings] should be good enough to last about a week on the news. It's time to feed the news media.

He killed the supervisor before fleeing with the woman in their car. He eventually released her to make sure the tape got released. After exchanging gunfire with police, he crashed into a pole. Police found him in the car dead of a self-inflicted gunshot wound.

A transcript of Ferguson's confession video is included in Appendix F.

www.sfgate.com/news/article/Sacramento-rampage-5-shot-dead-Slayer-kills-2881164.php
www.latimes.com/archives/la-xpm-2001-sep-11-mn-44550-story.html

14 Arizona Nursing College Shooting, October 28, 2002, Tucson, Arizona

Robert Flores Jr., 41

Flores killed three professors, one in her office and two in a classroom, and then himself. He had failed one class and was in danger of flunking out of the school. Prior to the shootings, he had mailed a letter to the *Arizona Daily Star* that they received the day after the shootings. In it, he gives his personal background and the hopelessness he felt. He called the shootings a "reckoning" and "a settling of accounts."

Flores had been married for ten years, but had an acrimonious divorce, during which his ex-wife accused him of cruelty and abuse. He believed the nursing school was biased against men, writing,

> While the college does maintain a small minority student body it is primarily White women from upper middle class backgrounds between the ages of 20 and 25. The college promotes and desires diversity but they only want their approved diversity and no other. In many ways male nursing students are "tokens."

www.cbsnews.com/news/4-dead-in-univ-of-arizona-shooting/
https://azdailysun.com/gunman-s-letter-tries-to-explain-university-shootings/article_7fc942b7-2411-5e32-93cc-2be3e46b522d.html

15 Rocori High School Shooting, September 24, 2003, Cold Spring, Minnesota

John Jason McLaughlin, 15

McLaughlin arrived at his high school with a loaded .22 caliber pistol, waited outside the school gym in the locker room and shot and killed two students he claimed had bullied him over his acne. McLaughlin used the handle "sharpestshot290" and would

Appendix A 201

talk online with a female student he had romantic feelings for, often talking about violent fantasies he had. On the day of the shooting, he sent her an email not to tell the police about their conversations and said goodbye.

https://schoolshooters.info/sites/default/files/John_Jason_McLaughlin_ Psychological_Evaluation_0.pdf
http://news.minnesota.publicradio.org/features/2003/09/24_ap_schoolshooting/

16 Platte Canyon School Hostage Crisis, September 27, 2006, Bailey, Colorado

Duane Roger Morrison, 53

Morrison took six girls hostage at the high school. He molested them all, then released four of them before SWAT stormed the classroom. During the confrontation with SWAT, Morrison killed one of the remaining hostages before killing himself. That day he had mailed a letter to his brother. In it, he apologizes to his family and acknowledges his pending death. He also writes about the abuse he suffered from his father. He was often seen watching girls at the pool in his apartment complex and several female residents complained about his lewd or suggestive comments.

https://web.archive.org/web/20071111213926/www2.gazette.com/display. php?id=1322126&secid=1
www.cbsnews.com/pictures/colorado-hostage-horror/12/

17 Amish Schoolhouse Shooting, October 2, 2006, Nickel Mines, Pennsylvania

Charles Carl Roberts IV, 32

Roberts, a milk tank driver who worked on several nearby Amish farms, went to the single-room Amish schoolhouse and lured students into the school claiming he lost an item there and needed help looking for it.

Once inside, he barricaded the door with wooden boards and held the students and teachers hostage. He ordered the boys and several adults to leave, leaving him with ten female students. He shot and killed five students, injuring three others before killing himself. He left behind three separate suicide notes where he confessed to molesting two young female relatives twenty years previously and he had begun having fantasies of doing it again.

http://old.post-gazette.com/pg/07273/821700–85.stm
www.nytimes.com/2006/10/03/us/03amish.html

18 Virginia Tech Shooting, April 16, 2007, Blacksburg, Virginia

Seung-Hui Cho, 23

Cho was a senior, majoring in English. Born in South Korea, he became a permanent US resident in 1992. Early in the morning of April 16, he shot and killed two people

202 *Appendix A*

in a residence hall. A couple hours later, he mailed a package to NBC containing video, photographs and a manifesto. He then entered a classroom building, locked several doors, and went from room to room shooting people, killing another 30 and injuring 23. After about ten minutes, he shot and killed himself.

A month before the shooting, Cho hired an escort to meet him at a motel about two hours from the campus. She rejected him partway into their time together. He was also rejected by a female classmate after he wrote a poem on the whiteboard outside her room.

www.history.com/this-day-in-history/massacre-at-virginia-tech-leaves-32-dead
www.cnn.com/2013/10/31/us/virginia-tech-shootings-fast-facts/index.html
https://nypost.com/2007/04/24/cho-paid-me-to-be-escort/
www.nbcnews.com/id/18202709/ns/us_news-crime_and_courts/t/high-school-classmates-say-gunman-was-bullied/

19 Akihabara Massacre, June 8, 2008, Chiyoda, Tokyo, Japan

Tomohiro Kato, 27

Kato drove a rental truck into a crowd of pedestrians in a crowded shopping district, then started stabbing people indiscriminately with a survival knife. At least seven people were killed and 12 wounded.

Three days before the attack, an incident at work made him believe he would lose his job. He posted about that online, as well as posting about his anger and loneliness. He wrote, "I don't have a single friend and I won't in the future. I'll be ignored because I'm ugly." He lamented his lack of romantic relationships, writing, "If I had a girlfriend, I wouldn't have just left my job or be addicted to my cellphone. A man with hope could never understand this."

www.japantimes.co.jp/news/2010/07/28/national/motive-for-akihabara-massacre-hinted-at/#.Xq9oi6hKiwc
www.reuters.com/article/us-japan-stabbing/man-stabs-shoppers-in-tokyo-street-killing-seven-idUST27752620080608
https://web.archive.org/web/20080613005327/www.straitstimes.com/Latest%2BNews/Asia/STIStory_246337.html

20 Henry Ford Community College Shooting, March 10, 2009, Dearborn, Michigan

Anthony Powell, 28

Powell shot and killed Asia McGowan, 20, and then himself in the fine arts center on campus. He had reportedly harassed her online and posted misogynistic and anti-atheism YouTube videos ranting against Black women and other groups he disagreed with.

www.cnn.com/2009/CRIME/04/10/mich.college.shooting/index.html

Appendix A   203

www.pressandguide.com/news/a-year-later-fellow-students-remember-slain-hfcc-student-asia/article_5163920a-3e61-5cd0-8475-42752a0eab54.html
www.youtube.com/watch?v=wrP9XEjX028
https://lostmediawiki.com/Tony48219_(partially_found_videos_by_religious_YouTuber;_2007-2009)

21 LA Fitness Shooting, August 4, 2009, Collier, Pennsylvania

George Sodini, 48

Sodini, angry about being rejected by women, entered an aerobics class, dimmed the lights and opened fire, killing three women, before shooting himself in the head. He had kept a blog of his plans to commit the killings for months.

In it, he admits that he hadn't had sex in 19 years and hadn't had a girlfriend in 25. His blog details his loneliness and frustration at the rejection he feels from women. He consistently uses objectifying language when talking about women, referring to them as "edible," "hoez," and "so beautiful as to not be human." He asserts that he is not responsible for his difficulties, writing, "Everthing stays the same regardless of the effert I put in. If I had control over my life then I would be happier. But for about the past 30 years, I have not." Those efforts including attending dating classes by R. Don Steele, who purports to teach older men how to date younger men and insists "nice guys must die."

Sodini's Online Blog (Sodini, 2009) is included in its entirety in Appendix B.

https://archive.triblive.com/news/one-year-later-scars-of-collier-la-fitness-rampage-remain/
www.telegraph.co.uk/news/worldnews/northamerica/usa/5978615/George-Sodinis-blog-tells-of-years-of-rejection-by-women-before-gym-shooting.html
https://abcnews.go.com/US/story?id=8258001&page=1
www.nbcnews.com/id/32335641/ns/us_news-crime_and_courts/t/sodini-was-devoted-follower-dating-guru/#.XrBQO6hKiwc

22 Sandy Hook Shooting, December 14, 2012, Newtown, Connecticut

Adam Lanza, 20

On the morning of December 14, Lanza shot and killed his mother in their home. He then drove in her car to the Sandy Hook Elementary School dressed in all black, wearing yellow earplugs, sunglasses, and a green utility vest. He shot and killed 26 people, 20 of them children between the ages of 6–7. The Lanza house was later searched, and hundreds of journal pages were found detailing his preoccupation with violence, particularly mass shootings and children.

Lanza was on the autism spectrum and suffered from social anxiety. He was fixated on routine and cleanliness. He claimed to have been raped or molested by doctors in his youth, with the consent of his parents. On the online forum "Shocked

204 *Appendix A*

Beyond Belief," Lanza posted under the username "Smiggles" and earned a reputation as a pedophile. He wrote,

> I don't think there should be any age of consent, but since no matter what I say everyone will accuse me of just wanting to justify some latent pedophilia I allegedly have, I will only say that you need to be attracted to prepubescents to be considered a pedophile. A 50-year-old who is attracted to pubescent 12-year-olds is not a pedophile; a 16-year-old who is attracted to 8-year-olds is a pedophile.

There is some debate about Lanza's history with and view of women. He wrote on the forum, "I used to think that I was asexual, but the primary reason why I thought that was because my BMI was 14." There was a Word document found on his computer giving an explanation of "why females are inherently selfish." However, he had disdain for all people, saying "I incessantly have nothing other than scorn for humanity. I have been desperate to feel anything positive for someone for my entire life."

https://globalnews.ca/news/4587548/sandy-hook-shooter-journals-released/
www.history.com/this-day-in-history/gunman-kills-students-and-adults-at-newtown-connecticut-elementary-school
www.oxygen.com/crime-time/adam-lanza-sandy-hook-shooter-documents-reveal-violent-obsessive-mind
https://schoolshooters.info/sites/default/files/lanza_posts_2.2.pdf
www.newsweek.com/misogyny-and-mass-murder-paired-yet-again-252567
www.csmonitor.com/The-Culture/Family/Modern-Parenthood/2013/0417/Adam-Lanza-bullied-as-student-at-Sandy-Hook-his-mother-considered-suing

23 Boston Marathon Bombing, April 15, 2013, Boston, Massachusetts

Dzhokhar Tsarnaev, 19, and Tamerlan Tsarnaev, 26

Two bombs went off near the finish line of the Boston Marathon, killing three and wounding more than 260 other people. The bombs were homemade pressure cooker bombs. After several days of searching, older brother Tamerlan was killed in an exchange with police. Younger brother Dzhokhar was arrested the next day.

During Dzhokhar's trial, Tamerlan was accused of being emotionally abusive toward his wife and cheating on her. During their relationship and under his influence, she became isolated from others, including former friends. Dzhokhar's past tweets include "text back with your titties on it" and "guys who allow women to control them and make decisions for them are pathetic #growapair."

www.cnn.com/2013/06/03/us/boston-marathon-terror-attack-fast-facts/index.html
www.boston.com/news/local-news/2015/05/12/11-things-we-learned-in-the-sentencing-phase-of-dzhokhar-tsarnaevs-trial
https://nymag.com/intelligencer/2013/04/dzhokhar-tsarnaev-twitter-tweets-boston-suspect.html

Appendix A   205

24 Isla Vista Killings, May 23, 2014, Isla Vista, California

Elliot Rodger, 22

22-year-old Elliot Rodger killed six people and injured 14 outside of the University of California, Santa Barbara. He stabbed three people to death in his apartment complex, then drove to the campus sorority houses and shot three women, two of which died. He then drove to a nearby deli, shot and killed a male student inside. He got back into his BMW and drove at a high rate of speed into crowds of pedestrians until having a standoff with police and completing suicide.

Just before his attack at the sorority house, he uploaded a video to YouTube titled "Elliot Rodger's Retribution" where he talks about his motive, blaming women for rejecting him and punishing men he envied. He then emailed a lengthy manifesto titled "My Twisted World: The Story of Elliot Rodger" to friends, family members and his therapist. This manifesto talks about his difficulties during childhood, family issues, struggles with romantic rejection and moreover his hatred toward women and couples.

Rodger's manifesto has been embraced by the incel community. It begins with, "All of my suffering on this world has been at the hands of humanity, particularly women." He details his childhood and his resentment that his mother had not "married into wealth instead of being selfish." He felt that wealth was his only path to sex. He also wrote of "how cruel I think women are by nature" and that "All of those beautiful girls I've desired so much in my life, but can never have because they despise and loathe me, I will destroy." Though he says he was bullied by boys in school, he hated the girls even more, since they "flock to these men. Their evil acts are rewarded by women; while the good, decent men are laughed at."

As his anger and frustrations grew, he

> began to have fantasies of becoming very powerful and stopping everyone from having sex. I wanted to take their sex away from them, just like they took it away from me. I saw sex as an evil and barbaric act, all because I was unable to have it. This was the major turning point. My anger made me stronger inside. This was when I formed my ideas that sex should be outlawed. It is the only way to make the world a fair and just place. If I can't have it, I will destroy it. That's the conclusion I came to, right then and there.

He felt entitled to sex and blamed women for not providing it to him. He wrote of his anger that a friend of his roommates had lost his virginity at 13.

> How could an inferior, ugly black boy be able to get a white girl and not me? I am beautiful, and I am half white myself. I am descended from British aristocracy. He is descended from slaves. I deserve it more … This just proves how ridiculous the female gender is. They would give themselves to this filthy scum, but they reject ME? The injustice!

His feelings are largely defined in the following quote: "Women are sexually attracted to the wrong type of man. This is a major flaw in the very foundation of humanity. It is completely and utterly wrong, in every sense of the word."

206   *Appendix A*

A transcript of Rodger's Day of Retribution video is included in Appendix C.

www.cnn.com/2014/05/24/us/elliot-rodger-video-transcript/index.html
www.bbc.com/news/world-us-canada-43892189
www.cnn.com/2014/05/25/justice/california-shooting-revelations/index.html
www.independent.com/2015/02/20/elliot-rodger-report-details-long-struggle-mental-illness/

25 Portsmouth Stabbings, June/July 2014, Portsmouth, UK

Ben Moynihan, 18

Moynihan was convicted of attempted murder for stabbing three women as they walked home. He sent a letter to the police daring them to catch him, in which he wrote, "All women needs to die." In a letter found by the police, he wrote, "I was planning to murder women as an act of revenge because of the life they gave me, I'm still a virgin at 17." In a video found on his laptop, he said "I think every girl is a type of slut, they are fussy with men nowadays, they do not give boys like us a chance."

www.bbc.com/news/uk-england-hampshire-31765086
www.salon.com/2015/01/23/i_think_every_girl_is_a_type_of_slut_what_an_attempted_mass_murderers_words_reveal_about_our_sexual_culture/

26 Germanwings Flight 9525, March 24, 2015, French Alps

Andreas Lubitz, 28

About a half hour into a two-hour flight from Barcelona, Spain to Duesseldorf, Germany, the captain left the cockpit to use the lavatory. Shortly after, the plane began descending. The co-pilot did not respond to air traffic control and would not open the cockpit door to readmit the captain. The plane continued its descent and crashed in the French Alps. All 144 passengers and six crew members were killed. Investigators found that this could only have been deliberate.

Lubitz grew up in Germany and had always wanted to fly. He joined the flight academy right out of high school but dropped out after a couple of months. He was diagnosed as suffering from a "deep depressive episode." After six months of intensive treatment, he was cleared to resume flight training; however, any further psychiatric treatment, including meds, would end his flying career. When filling out his documentation with the FAA to attend a training program in the US, Lubitz lied and answered no when asked if he had ever been diagnosed with "mental disorders of any sort," but was discovered. However, he was able to provide a doctor's report declaring him cured, and was able to continue in the program.

While Lubitz had a girlfriend, many in the incel community have hailed him as a hero. They claim that he crashed the plane because he was upset about a breakup and blame his girlfriend for "cucking" him.

www.bbc.com/news/world-europe-32072218
www.gq.com/story/germanwings-flight-9525-final-moments

Appendix A 207

www.wehuntedthemammoth.com/2015/03/27/internet-incels-celebrate-andreas-lubitz-the-alleged-killer-co-pilot-of-germanwings-flight-9525-as-a-legitimate-slayer-and-an-incel-hero/

27 Charleston Church Shooting, June 17, 2015, Charleston, South Carolina

Dylann Roof, 21

Roof attended a bible study group at a historically Black church and after about an hour, stood up and started shooting. He confessed to shooting and killing nine people, saying he wanted to start a race war. He wrote a lengthy manifesto which was largely a racist and anti-Semitic rant against several groups, but primarily focused on "the group that is the biggest problem for Americans ... Niggers are stupid and violent." He accuses Black Americans of raping "our women and are taking over our country." However, most of his victims were Black women.

The manifesto written by Dylann Roof is included in Appendix E.

https://myfox8.com/news/charleston-shooting-suspect-dylan-roof-confesses-to-killing-9-people/
https://abcnews.go.com/US/charleston-shooting-happened-inside-church/story?id=31855652
https://gawker.com/here-is-what-appears-to-be-dylann-roofs-racist-manifest-1712767241
https://nypost.com/2018/06/29/what-do-so-many-mass-shooters-have-in-common-a-hatred-of-women/
www.postandcourier.com/church_shooting/friend-says-dylann-roof-desired-black-women-wanted-face-tattoo/article_3b3618da-0828-11e7-aba3-c3099a862f1e.html

28 Live TV Shooting, August 26, 2015, Roanoke, Virginia

Vester Lee Flanagan II, 41

Flanagan killed journalists and former colleagues Alison Parker and Adam Ward on air, while also recording on his own body camera. He shot himself hours later, after writing about the shooting on twitter, uploading his video to Facebook, and sending a manifesto to ABC news. In it, he said that as a gay, Black man he had been a victim of discrimination and sexual harassment. He had been fired from the station in 2013, and his complaint against the station had been dismissed. ABC News received a 23-page fax from Flanagan about two hours after the attack. In it, he says "what sent me over the top was the [Charleston] church shooting." He admires the Columbine and Virginia Tech killers. He talks about being attacked by Black men and White women.

www.nytimes.com/2015/08/27/us/wdbj7-virginia-journalists-shot-during-live-broadcast.html
www.usatoday.com/story/news/nation/2015/08/27/flanagan-virginia-guns-background-checks/32477133/

208   *Appendix A*

www.cnn.com/videos/us/2015/08/26/wdbj-shooting-live-report-amateur-video.cnn
https://abcnews.go.com/US/shooting-alleged-gunman-details-grievances-suicide-notes/story?id=33336339

29 Umpqua Community College Attack, October 1, 2015, Roseburg, Oregon

Chris Harper-Mercer, 26

Harper-Mercer killed nine and injured seven others before shooting himself. He targeted Christians, asking them to stand before shooting them one by one. In his manifesto, he wrote,

> I have always been the most hated person in the world. Ever since I arrived in this world, I have been under siege from it. Under attack from morons and idiots ... My whole life has been one lonely enterprise. One loss after another. And here I am, 26, with no friends, no job, no girlfriend, a virgin. I long ago realized that society likes to deny people like me these things. People who are elite, people who stand with the gods.

He compared himself to "Elliot Rodger, Vester Flanagan, the Columbine kids, Adam Lanza and Seung Cho."

Harper-Mercer's manifesto is included in Appendix D.

www.latimes.com/nation/la-na-school-shootings-2017-story.html
www.oregonlive.com/pacific-northwest-news/2015/10/umpqua_community_college_gunma_1.html

30 4Chan Threat, October 1, 2015, Philadelphia, Pennsylvania

A post on 4chan linked the October 1 shooting in Oregon to possible upcoming shootings in Philadelphia. The post read,

> This is only the beginning. The Beta Rebellion has begun. Soon, more of our brothers will take up arms to become martyrs to this revolution. On October 5, 2015 at 1:00 PM CT, a fellow robot will take up arms against a university near Philadelphia. His cries will be heard, his victims will cower in fear, and the strength of the Union will decay a little more.

"Beta Uprising" is a common theme on 4chan, rallying men who believe they are "beta" rather than "alpha" males.

www.cosmopolitan.com/college/news/a47276/4chan-beta-rebellion/
www.dailydot.com/layer8/4chan-school-threat-colleges-r9k-harassment-beta-uprising-oregon-shooting/

Appendix A 209

31 Planned Parenthood Shooting, November 27, 2015, Colorado Springs, Colorado

Robert Lewis Dear, Jr.

Dear killed three and shot nine others at a Planned Parenthood clinic. He claimed to be a "warrior" for unborn children. However, he had a history of violence against women. Two of three ex-wives accused him of physical abuse. In 1992, he was arrested and accused of sexual violence and rape. That case involved a woman who worked at a mall who Dear repeatedly asked out and called, even after she refused. She says that he came to her home and raped her at knife point; he claims the sex was consensual.

www.denverpost.com/2018/02/13/colorado-springs-planned-parenthood-shooter-still-incompetent/
www.washingtonpost.com/national/before-colorado-shooting-a-long-history-of-violence-against-women/2015/12/01/7f494c86-987b-11e5-8917-653b65c809eb_story.html

32 Pulse Nightclub Shooting, June 12, 2016, Orlando, Florida

Omar Mateen, 29

Mateen killed 49 people and injured 53 others at Latin Night at Pulse Nightclub, apparently as a rebuke against American violence in Muslim countries. He was killed by SWAT about three hours after the attack began. He claimed ties to ISIS and referred to the Boston Marathon bombers as his "homeboys."

Mateen had a history of domestic abuse. He was accused of beating his ex-wife and taking her paychecks. His wife at the time of the attack was described at her trial as "a severely abused woman who was in realistic fear for her life from her abusive husband." (She was accused and acquitted of aiding him in the attack.)

https://nymag.com/intelligencer/2016/06/orlando-nightclub-shooting-leaves-20-dead.html#_ga=2.187674920.1236671971.1589073149-146945661.1589073149
www.thecut.com/2016/07/mass-killers-terrorism-domestic-violence.html
www.rollingstone.com/politics/politics-news/in-orlando-as-usual-domestic-violence-was-ignored-red-flag-90139/
www.orlandosentinel.com/news/pulse-orlando-nightclub-shooting/os-fritz-scheller-noor-salman-trial-lessons-20180425-story.html

33 Nice Truck Attack, July 14, 2016, Nice, France

Mohamed Lahouaiej Bouhlel, 31

Bouhlel drove a truck into a large Bastille Day crowd in Nice, France, and exchanged gunfire with police before being shot to death. Eighty-four people were killed and over 300 were wounded. He did not have direct ties to any terrorist group but did have a history of domestic violence. A neighbor described him as "more into women

210   *Appendix A*

than religion." He wife had left him two years prior to the Nice attack after he became violent with her.

www.nytimes.com/2016/07/16/world/europe/nice-france-truck-attack-what-we-know.html
www.nydailynews.com/news/world/nice-attacker-mohamed-lahouaiej-bouhlel-article-1.2712654
www.thecut.com/2016/07/mass-killers-terrorism-domestic-violence.html

34 Lucky 97 Security Guard, July 31, 2016

Sheldon Bentley, 38

Bentley stomped on a man sleeping in the alley behind the store where he was employed as a security guard, killing the man. Bentley was driven by his frustration about his "involuntarily celibacy" for the four years prior to the attack.

www.cbc.ca/news/canada/edmonton/edmonton-involuntary-celibacy-sheldon-bentley-manslaughter-jail-1.4803943
www.vice.com/en_ca/article/ev8ekp/edmonton-man-uses-involuntary-celibacy-as-excuse-in-stomping-death

35 Las Vegas Music Festival Shooting, October 1, 2017, Las Vegas, Nevada

Stephen Paddock, 64

From a window in his room at the Mandalay Bay Presort and Casino, Paddock shot at a country music festival, killing 58 people and injuring more than 850. Police were able to locate his room, where they found a surveillance camera pointing down the hallway. They entered the room and found that he had shot himself. In the week before the attack, he carried 21 suitcases to his room filled with weapons and ammunition. No clear motive was ever discovered; however, we do know that Paddock had a history of domestic abuse. He regularly demeaned his wife in public, with one witness recalling him saying "I'm paying for your drink, just like I'm paying for you."

https://qz.com/1094160/las-vegas-shooter-stephen-paddock-abused-women-just-like-other-mass-killers-in-the-us/
https://abcnews.go.com/US/anatomy-las-vegas-mass-shooting-deadliest-modern-us/story?id=59797324
www.npr.org/2019/01/29/689821599/fbi-finds-no-motive-in-las-vegas-shooting-closes-investigation

36 Texas Church Shooting, November 5, 2017, Sutherland Springs, Texas

Devin Patrick Kelley, 26

Kelley killed 26 people at Sutherland Springs First Baptist Church. He fled and was pursued by police and a civilian. He had sent threatening text messages to his

Appendix A 211

mother-in-law, who has attended the church. He was wounded in the chase and ultimately took his own life. Kelly was court-martialed in 2012 for assaulting his spouse and their child. The Air Force failed to submit his fingerprints to the FBI, which would have prevented him from obtaining a weapon through a background check.

www.usatoday.com/story/news/nation-now/2018/06/29/autopsy-sutherland-springs-texas-church-gunman/745951002/
www.washingtonpost.com/national-security/2018/12/08/air-force-failed-six-times-keep-guns-texas-church-shooter-before-he-killed-report-finds/
www.dallasnews.com/news/politics/2019/11/01/sutherland-springs-shooter-rejected-by-dicks-sporting-goods-bought-weapon-at-academy-wife-says/
www.npr.org/sections/thetwo-way/2017/11/06/562299408/texas-church-shooter-may-have-been-motivated-to-kill-by-domestic-situation

37 Aztec High School, December 7, 2017, Aztec, New Mexico

William Atchison, 21

Atchison disguised himself as a student to enter the high school, where he killed two students and then himself. After the attack, police found a thumb drive and a note that read, "If things go according to plan, today would be when I die. I go somewhere and gear up, then hold a class hostage and go apeshit, then blow my brains out." In the years before, Atchison had been in contact online with other school shooters. His online presence was rife with white supremacist posts and an obsession with school shooters. He used the pseudonym "Elliot Rodger," calling him the "supreme gentelman." In 2016 he was questioned by the FBI but convinced them he was a harmless troll.

www.nbcnews.com/news/us-news/aztec-high-school-shooting-gunman-disguised-himself-randomly-killed-school-n827881
www.daily-times.com/story/news/crime/2018/04/17/aztec-high-school-shooting-investigation-william-atchison/513013002/
www.thedailybeast.com/new-mexico-school-shooter-had-secret-life-on-pro-trump-white-supremacy-sites
www.latimes.com/local/lanow/la-me-ln-elliot-rodger-incel-20180426-story.html
www.youtube.com/watch?v=n50lxe1DIUI

38 Stoneman Douglas High School Shooting, February 14, 2018, Parkland, Florida

Nikolas Cruz, 19

Cruz had been expelled from the school for "disciplinary reasons." He returned on the 14th in an Uber, carrying a backpack filled with magazines and a duffel contained his AR-15. A staff member who saw him radioed a "Code Red" to initiate a lockdown, but Cruz entered the school and assembled the rifle in a stairwell. He warned one student to leave the school; this student told a school security monitor. Cruz fired down a hallway, killing 11 and injuring 13 others. He went upstairs and killed

212   *Appendix A*

six more and injured another four. He then went to the faculty lounge and fired at students as they ran outside but was slowed by hurricane impact-resistant glass in the windows. He left the school by blending in with other students and was apprehended a little while later.

Cruz had recorded videos declaring that he would be "the next school shooter of 2018." Police had been called to his family home 39 times since 2010. He had threatened students and wasn't allowed in campus with a backpack on.

His online presence was rife with racism, homophobia, anti-Semitism and misogyny. He referred to White women in interracial relationships as traitors. In another post, he praised Elliot Rodger.

www.history.com/this-day-in-history/parkland-marjory-stoneman-douglas-school-shooting
https://youtu.be/IyJTBK1UNs4
www.thesun.co.uk/news/5582904/nikolas-cruz-florida-shooting-marjory-stoneman-douglas-trial-rifle/
www.cnn.com/2018/02/25/us/nikolas-cruz-warning-signs/index.html
www.cnn.com/2018/02/16/us/exclusive-school-shooter-instagram-group/index.html
www.haaretz.com/opinion/call-the-douglas-high-shooting-by-its-name-an-anti-semitic-attack-1.5842172

39 Toronto Van Attack, April 23, 2018, Toronto, Ontario, Canada

Alek Minassian, 25

Minassian drove his van onto a crowded sidewalk, killing ten people and injuring 16. He began planning in earnest about a month before the attack, carefully choosing the van in a size that he could maneuver but would do a lot of damage. The exact location was chosen because he saw a lot of people walking there. He only stopped the attack when "someone's drink got splashed on my windshield, and I was worried that I would crash the van anyways." He planned to die through suicide by cop, but the officer arrested him without violence. Minutes before the attack, he posted on Facebook, "The Incel rebellion has already begun! All hail the Supreme Gentleman Elliot Rodger!"

After his arrest, he told police that he had communicated with Elliot Rodger and Chris Harper-Mercer and they inspired his attack. He said of Rodger, "We discussed our frustrations at society and being unable to get laid." He had been bullied in school and during his brief time in the military. He had never had a girlfriend and said that after the attack by Rodger, he began spending more and more time on incel-related forums. He told police, "It's basically a movement of angry incels such as myself who are unable to get laid, therefore we want to overthrow the Chads which would force the Stacys to be forced to reproduce with the incels."

A partial transcript of Minassian's police interview is included in Appendix G.

www.cbc.ca/news/canada/toronto/alek-minassian-police-interview-1.5298021
https://torontosun.com/news/local-news/inside-the-terrifying-violent-world-of-incel-subculture

Appendix A 213

https://nationalpost.com/news/canada/toronto-van-attack-police-interview
www.scribd.com/document/427612854/Alek-Minassian-Interview

40 United States Attempted Mail Bombing, October 2018, Aventura, Florida

Cesar Sayoc, 56

Sayoc was charged with mailing packages containing homemade pipe bombs to prominent critics of Donald Trump, including Barak Obama and Hillary Clinton. None of the 14 bombs he sent exploded. He was found after investigators discovered a fingerprint on an envelope sent to Rep. Maxine Waters.

Sayoc had a long criminal record, including an arrest in 2002 for making a bomb threat, and had been accused of domestic violence. Months before the mail bombs, he tossed a cup of urine on two women on a moped. He then pulled his van alongside them and swerved at them.

www.nytimes.com/2018/10/25/nyregion/pipe-bombs-sent-democrats.html
www.bbc.com/news/world-us-canada-45996655
www.local10.com/news/2018/11/30/maniac-trump-supporter-cesar-sayoc-once-tossed-urine-on-2-women/
www.miamiherald.com/news/local/community/broward/article220672300.html

41 Tallahassee Yoga Studio Shooting, November 2, 2018, Tallahassee, Florida

Scott Beierle, 40

Beierle, a self-proclaimed misogynist, killed two people and injured five others before killing himself at a yoga studio in Tallahassee. He had a history of violence against women, having been caught on video slapping and grabbing the buttocks of a woman at an apartment pool complex and grabbing another woman's in a Florida State University dining hall.

He had posted racist and misogynist videos to YouTube and songs to SoundCloud. One of the songs included the lyrics "To hell with the boss that won't get off my back / To hell with the girl I can't get in the sack." In his videos, he mentioned Elliot Rodger, called Black women "ugly and disgusting" and described times when women rejected his advances. He refers to women as "sluts" and "whores" and in reference to women in interracial relationships, "There are whores in – not only every city, not only every town, but every village."

www.npr.org/2018/11/04/664157610/gunman-in-yoga-studio-attack-had-a-criminal-history-posted-racist-and-sexist-vid
www.buzzfeednews.com/article/talalansari/la-fitness-tallahassee-yoga-shooter-incels-misogyny
www.buzzfeednews.com/article/davidmack/tallahassee-yoga-shooter-incel-far-right-misogyny-video

214 *Appendix A*

42 Capital Gazette Shooting, December 28, 2018, Annapolis, Maryland

Jarrod Ramos, 39

Ramos blasted his way into the newsroom and shot and killed five people. In 2011, the *Capital Gazette* ran a column about Ramos' guilty plea for harassing a former high school classmate, and he held onto a grudge against the paper. According to that article, Ramos contacted the woman over Facebook; when she tried to back out of the connection, he called her vulgar names and eventually told her to kill herself. In one email he wrote, "Have another drink and go hang yourself, you cowardly little lush. Don't contact you again? I don't give a (expletive). (Expletive) you."

https://nypost.com/2018/06/29/what-do-so-many-mass-shooters-have-in-common-a-hatred-of-women/
https://nypost.com/2018/06/28/newsroom-targeted-in-shooting-ran-story-on-suspects-harassment-conviction/

43 Women's March Threat, January 2019, Provo, Utah

Christopher Cleary, 27

Cleary went to Provo, Utah and on the day before the Women's March, he posted to his Facebook page,

> All I wanted was a girlfriend … All I wanted was to be loved, yet no one cares about me I'm 27 years old and I've never had a girlfriend before and I'm still a virgin, this is why I'm planning on shooting up a public place soon and being the next mass shooter cause I'm ready to die and all the girls the turned me down is going to make it right by killing as many girls as I see.

Cleary lived in Denver and was on probation for stalking and harassment charges. He was not allowed to travel out of state but went to Utah to see some basketball games. He told police that he felt lonely at the games and said,

> It was weird because I'm looking at all these people and they're all happy and everybody has their family and everybody is out on their dates with their girlfriends. And I'm like the only one there and I remember feeling sad. And I remember I left the game at halftime and I remember I was riding on the train. And I think that's when I posted something about killing people and killing girls and I'm never going to find everybody.

He had previously posted a woman's phone number on Craiglist in ads soliciting sex and made threats of violence, including a text message to a woman saying "I own multipul guns I can have u dead in a second."

www.deseret.com/utah/2019/9/27/20887214/man-who-threatened-to-shoot-as-many-girls-as-he-could-says-he-was-lonely

Appendix A   215

www.thelily.com/hes-been-given-second-chances-now-the-man-who-pledged-to-kill-as-many-girls-as-i-see-is-going-to-prison/

44 Mall of America Attack, April 12, 2019, Bloomington, Minnesota

Emmanual Deshawn Aranda, 24

Aranda was at the Mall of America "looking for someone to kill" after being rejected by women at the mall for years. He approached a five-year-old boy at random, picked him up, and threw him over a third-floor railing. He fled the scene and was captured on a light rail train. The boy suffered severe head trauma and broken bones.

A few nights before this, his sister reported him to police for going to her house and punching her. His history of violence also includes an incident at a restaurant when he hit a customer over the head with a plate and threatened him with a knife. He once threw water and tea at a woman after she refused to buy him food.

www.nbcnews.com/news/us-news/mall-america-attacker-gets-19-years-throwing-boy-over-railing-n1013156
www.mprnews.org/story/2019/05/14/mother-of-alleged-moa-kidtosser-tells-his-story
https://nypost.com/2019/04/17/more-evidence-shows-mall-of-america-suspect-is-just-a-terrible-person/
https://minnesota.cbslocal.com/2019/04/12/witnesses-woman-says-her-child-was-thrown-from-3rd-floor-balcony-at-mall-of-america/
www.amren.com/news/2019/09/5-year-old-boy-thrown-off-mall-of-america-balcony-by-stranger-returns-home-after-five-months-in-hospital/

45 Sudbury Michael's Stabbing, June 3, 2019, Sudbury, UK

Alexander Stavropoulos, 25

Stavropoulos stabbed a 35-year-old woman multiple times and injured her baby in the parking lot of Michael's in Sudbury, UK. The victim was chosen at random, but Stavropoulos said he was "out to murder a little White girl." He told police that he likes "White women," but because they "won't fuck me," it made him "want to kill, for some reason. I just don't know why." He said he was inspired by Alek Minassian, who drove a van into a crowd of pedestrians in Toronto in April 2018, and also identified as an incel.

Stavropoulos thought about the attack for months. He was under an order not to possess knives outside of his home after an April 2018 incident in which he charged at officers and was shot by police while holding two knives. However, he purchased a pack of utility knives at Home Depot and then went to the Michael's parking lot. After watching people for an hour or two, he chose a woman and her two daughters, aged three years and eight months, as his targets. He attacked the woman as she was putting the three-year-old in her car seat. However, as he told the police, the baby was his real target – "I tried to stab the child, I'm not denying that."

216　*Appendix A*

He stopped his attack when a witness to the attack approached the car to confront him.

https://torontosun.com/news/provincial/sudbury-incel-attacker-told-cops-i-was-going-to-kill-a-child
www.timminstoday.com/local-news/sudbury-incel-knife-attacker-told-police-he-was-out-to-murder-a-little-white-girl-2018572

46 Dallas Federal Courthouse Shooting, June 17, 2019, Dallas, Texas

Brian Clyde, 22

Clyde opened fire on the federal building in the morning on June 17, 2019. He was killed by Federal Protective Service officers. No one else was killed in the attack.

Clyde grew up in a military family and served in the army for two years but was dishonorably discharged from the military in 2017. According to some of the men he served with, Clyde was a gun enthusiast who participated in military reenactments. He was active on social media, sharing far-right political memes, including one that referred to a "Chad rampage" vs. a "virgin shooting." The Chad vs. virgin is a common incel meme.

www.dallasnews.com/news/2019/06/18/what-we-know-about-brian-clyde-the-gunman-who-opened-fire-at-the-federal-courthouse-in-downtown-dallas/
www.texasmonthly.com/politics/dallas-courthouse-shooter-brian-clyde-radicalized/
www.airforcetimes.com/off-duty/military-culture/2019/06/21/air-force-cautions-troops-to-beware-of-sexless-involuntary-celibates/

47 Dayton Shooting, August 4, 2019, Dayton, Ohio

Connor Betts, 24

Betts, wearing body armor and carrying high-capacity magazines, fired into a crowd outside a Dayton nightclub, killing nine and injuring dozens. He fired at least 41 times in 30 seconds before being shot and killed by police. His sister was killed in the attack.

According to a friend, "He was kind of hateful to women because they didn't want to date him." In high school, Betts made a list that threatened violence or sexual violence against those on it, mostly girls. At least one of the girls on the list had turned him down when he expressed interest in her. "After that, it turned into cold hatred the way he stared at me," she said.

www.wlwt.com/article/police-dayton-gunman-fired-at-least-41-shots-in-30-seconds-killing-9/28599430
www.cnn.com/2019/08/05/us/connor-betts-dayton-shooting-profile/index.html

48 Chicago Women's Reproductive Health Clinic Threat, August 21, 2019, Chicago, Illinois

Farhan Sheikh, 19

Sheikh posted a threat on iFunny, angry at the state abortion laws and saying that he would go to the clinic and "slaughter and murder any doctor, patient, or visitor." He included the date of the attack in the post. He was charged with transmitting a threat in interstate commerce.

www.cnn.com/2019/08/19/us/chicago-abortion-clinic-online-threat/index.html

49 German Hookah Bar Attack, February 19, 2020, Hanau, Germany

Tobias Rathjen, 43

In a shooting spree in and around a hookah bar and a cafe, Rathjen shot and killed nine people before killing his mother and himself. His victims were of foreign background, mostly Turkish. He had posted a 24-page manifesto espousing extreme-right, deeply racist views, calling for the populations of dozens of Middle Eastern and Asian countries to be wiped out entirely. He also talks about his fears of government surveillance and blames it for his lack of relationships with women. He wrote that "for my whole life I haven't had a wife or girlfriend, for the last 18 years exclusively because … I know I'm being surveilled."

https://nypost.com/2020/02/20/german-gunman-who-killed-9-posted-manifesto-calling-for-genocide/

50 Cyberstalking Case, April 21, 2020, Los Angeles, California

Carl Bennington, 33

Over the course of many years, Bennington used multiple social media accounts to send hundreds of unsolicited and graphic messages to women and young girls. He threatened them with physical and sexual violence. One victim started receiving them when she was only 14 years old. He had several Facebook posts expressing sympathy for Elliot Rodger and calling him "a victim."

www.justice.gov/usao-cdca/pr/covina-man-arrested-federal-charge-alleging-he-cyberstalked-and-threatened-violence
www.nbcnews.com/news/us-news/california-man-promoting-incel-ideology-charged-allegedly-threatening-teens-n1189206

51 Massage Parlor Attack, February 24, 2020, Toronto, Canada

Unnamed minor, 17

A 17-year-old stabbed two women with a machete at a Toronto massage parlor, killing one of them. Police charged him with terrorism after learning that he had ties to the incel movement.

https://time.com/5839395/canada-teen-terrorism-incel-attack/

218 *Appendix A*

52 University of Florida Rape Threats, May 4, 2020, Bowling Green, Florida

James Kelly, 36

On the social media messaging app Discord, Kelly threatened to rape a UF student and introduced her online to a 14-year-old girl he claimed to be grooming. Kelly has a pattern of violence, harassment and threats dating back to 2005. On March 27, he sent an email to a professor, threatening to terrorize and rape the professor's family.

www.alligator.org/news/campus/uf-student-threatens-to-rape-students-online-but-remains-enrolled/article_88613980-8e28-11ea-94b0-d72a20de9163.html

53 Accidental Bombing, June 2, 2020, Richlands, Virginia

Cole Carini, 23

Carini went to the hospital with one hand missing, several fingers amputated and shrapnel wounds. While he claimed it was a lawnmower accident, when FBI agents searched his home, they found blood spatters and chunks of human flesh on the walls and ceiling of a bedroom. They also found a letter discussing a suicide bomber targeting a "stage of hot cheerleaders." The letter includes the line, "*No matter what I will be heroic. I will make a statement like Elliot Rodgers [sic] did.*, he thought to himself."

www.buzzfeednews.com/article/davidmack/incel-bomber-blows-hand-off-cheerleaders?utm_source=dynamic&utm_campaign=bffbbuzzfeednews&ref=bffbb uzzfeednews

54 Men's Rights Lawyer Attack, July 11-19, 2020, Los Angeles, California & North Brunswick, New Jersey

Roy Den Hollander, 72

72-year-old Hollander, a self-described "anti-feminist" lawyer, is believed to have shot and killed a rival men's rights attorney. He then shot the husband and son of a US District Judge, killing her son, before killing himself. A list of names, including several judges, was found in his car. His website includes a "Cyclopedia," a 152-page document filled with misogynistic and anti-feminist writings. He had argued and lost a case before the judge concerning the legality of the draft, arguing that it was unconstitutional since it barred women from registering. His website also included a document disparaging the judge.

www.cnn.com/2020/07/20/us/suspect-shooting-at-judge-salas-home/index.html
www.usatoday.com/story/news/nation/2020/08/01/roy-den-hollander-bitter-tale-misogynist-lawyer-turned-killer/5532110002/

Appendix B: George Sodini Blog

Me Why do this?? To young girls? Just read below. I kept a running log that includes my thoughts and actions, after I saw this project was going to drag on.

November 5, 2008

Planned to do this in the summer but figure to stick around to see the election outcome. This particular one got so much attention and I was just curious. Not like I give a flying fcuk [sic] who won, since this exit plan was already planned. Good luck to Obama! He will be successful. The liberal media LOVES him. Amerika has chosen The Black Man. Good!

In light of this I got ideas outside of Obama's plans for the economy and such. Here it is: Every black man should get a young white girl hoe to hone up on. Kinda a reverse indentured servitude thing. Long ago, many a older white male landowner had a young Negro wench girl for his desires. Bout' time tables are turned on that shit. Besides, dem young white hoez dig da bruthrs! LOL. More so than they dig the white dudes! Every daddy know when he sends his little girl to college, she be bangin a bruthr real good. I saw it. "Not my little girl," daddy says! (Yeah right!!) Black dudes have thier choice of best white hoez. You do the math, there are enough young white so all the brothers can each have one for 3 or 6 months or so

December 22, 2008

Time is moving along. Planned to have this done already. I will just keep a running log here as time passes. Many of the young girls here look so beautiful as to not be human, very edible. After joining this gym, started lifting weights and like it. Much info about weight programs, diet etc on the web. Or anything for that matter. Instead of TV I can Google for hours to relax. TV and most movies are dull.

December 24, 2008

Moving into Christmas again. No girlfriend since 1984, last Christmas with Pam was in 1983. Who knows why. I am not ugly or too weird. No sex since July 1990 either (I was 29). No shit! Over eighteen years ago. And did it maybe only 50–75 times in my life.

220 *Appendix B*

Getting to think that a woman now would just, uh, get in the way of things. Isolated. I have extra money and enjoy traveling, too, wtih [sic] my 25–30 days of vacation. LA was the best! But going alone is not too fun. Invited to a party on Christmas day tomorrow.

Seems about 15–25 people will actually show. I like her parties; I can meet new people and talk. Got the next 8 days off. I should have exit plan done and practiced by then. I know nothing will change, no matter how hard I try or what goals I set.

December 28, 2008

Glad I stayed around. All these days off are great. I will shoot for Tuesday, January 6, 2009, at maybe 8:15. I have list of to-do items to make.

December 29, 2008

Just got back from tanning, been doing this for a while. No gym today, my elbow is sore again. I actually look good. I dress good, am clean-shaven, bathe, touch of cologne – yet 30 million women rejected me – over an 18 or 25-year period. That is how I see it. Thirty million is my rough guesstimate of how many desirable single women there are. A man needs a woman for confidence. He gets a boost on the job, career, with other men, and everywhere else when he knows inside he has someone to spend the night with and who is also a friend. This type of life I see is a closed world with me specifically and totally excluded. Every other guy does this successfully to a degree. Flying solo for many years is a destroyer. Yet many people say I am easy to get along with, etc.

Looking back, I owe nothing to desirable females who ask for anything, except for basic courtesy – usually. Looking back over everything, what bothers me most is the inability to work towards whatever change I choose.

December 30, 2008

While driving I radio surfed to a talk show. The caller was a 30ish black man who was describing the despair in certain black communities. According to him, life is cheap there because you are going to die anyway when you get old. It is the quality of life that is important, he said. If you know the past 40 years were crappy, why live another 30 crappy years then die? His point was they engage in dangerous behavior which tends to shorten the lifespans, to die now and avoid the next 30 crappy years, using my example.

The host got sarcastic and ended the call instead of trying understanding his point. Agreement wasn't necesary. I put music back on. But it was an interesting, and useful point for me to hear.

December 31, 2008

My anger and rage is largely gone since I began lifting weights. Lifting drains me but I still have energy. Somebody else suggested running but that did not help me.

Appendix B   221

I guess strenuous exercise is necesary for a man. So I just learned that now at 48. Maybe 30 years later than I would have liked. My dad never (not once) talked to me or asked about my life's details and tell me what he knew. He was just a useless sperm doner. Don't know why, find it fun talking to young kids when I visit someone. Brother was actually counter-productive and would try to embarase me or discourage my efferts when persuing things, esp girls early on (teen years). Useless bully. Result is I am learning basics by trial and error in my 40s, followed by discuragement. Seems odd, but that's true. Writing all this is helping me justify my plan and to see the futility of continuing. Too embarassed to tell anyone this, at almost 50 one is expected to just know these things.

I hope it doesn't snow on Tuesday. Just thought of that. The crowd will be thin so I would postpone. Shit! Now that I am on the topic of family and people I know, I might as well make a summary of sorts to show where things stand. This is New Years Eve I have time, no date tonight of course, so:

Honorable Mention

Tetelestai Church in Pittsburgh, PA – "Be Ye Holy, even as I have been Ye holy!

Thus saith the lord thy God!," as pastor Rick Knapp would proclaim. Holy shit, religion is a waste. But this guy teaches (and convinced me) you can commit mass murder then still go to heaven. Ask him. Call him at (724) 325–2655. If no answer there, he should still live at 439 9th Street, Oakmont, PA 15139. In any case, guilt and fear kept me there 13 long years until Nov 2006. I think his crap did the most damage. Their web site: www.tetelestai.org.

Mum – The Central Boss. 717 Highview Road, Pgh PA 15234. Don't piss her off or she will be mad and vindictive for years. She actually thinks she's normal. Very dominant. Her way and only her way with no flexibility toward everyone in the household. A power and control thing. People outside the immediate family like her. Why are people vicious with their closest ones? She is the Boss above all other Bosses.

Michael Sodini – A Boss, my brother (Mike Sodini) 216 Horseshoe Dr, Mars PA -

Always the big bully, twice the size of most others. When he bullied or harassed someone, it was the other person who "deserved it." It was always about him. Way to self absorbed, too. Still is. Used to like to embarrass guys in front of their girlfriends. Lots of other shit. Kind of guy you actually loved to hate. The biggest, most self-centered jagoff I know. He took those bullying "skills" into the business world and is doing good financially. He is a big wheel only in his mind. Most people can see thru all his manipulation. He calls only when he wants something.

Sherry – sister – More of a victim than anything. Copes by exercising much control over her adult children. We used to be close until her control of L & D caused a conflict.

Never the same after.

David – neph, sis's son (girlfriend Mallory Squires). Good young guy, though.

Lisa – niece, sis's daught. Attractive, smart, emotional – all good YW qualities.

222 *Appendix B*

Idiots

Andy Pulkowski – I have been in barrooms and church groups. The worst people by far are the religious types. Especially a right-wing, stiff-faced fundie like Andy. A condescending, demeaning, passive-aggresive person. Frigid, rigid, linear and totally inflexible. Being a very serious person, he cannot hide his frown-lined face. He better not try to smile; lest his face might crack. I knew children of parents who grew up in strict religious homes. Religion has a certain stink to it of guilt, shame, fear, and that moral standard that always contradicts the natural tendencies and desires of a person. Therin lies the conflict. Young person cannot experiment with things to decide on their own and establish their own parameters. So they tend to cut loose and really rebel much worse than the average young person. Ma and Pa never know what goes on. They easily BS their parents because they want to believe their little one is an angel. Andy has a young daughter Bethany Pulkowski away at college, High Point University. I saw her picture on his desk. She's your basic, attractive, young girl. Please reread my entry made on Nov 5th. That's only one thing she can do. You Andy types out there need to further strengthen your strict resolve and do more of the same thing! Because those girls were great when I recall my college years! She is someone's (or many guy's) little hoe now, I am sure.

Another point about andy. How can someone be cold, vicious, sarcastic and generally nasty ALL THE TIME and then make the claim about their church life and how good they are? Total hypocritical idiots.

That's all for now. That felt good.

Let's continue …

January 5, 2009

Was at the gym to lift. Very crowded. Tomorrow should be good. There is a woman there that gives me a certain look every time I am there. I decided to walk over and make a comment about the crowds but she left when I finished the exercise. Better that I do not get sidetracked from tomorrow's plan anyways. Life is just playing games. One or two dates with her, then the end. No matter how many changes I try to make, things stay the same. Every evening I am alone, and then go to bed alone. Young women were brutal when I was younger, now they aren't as much, probably because they just see me just as another old man.

I see twenty something couples everywhere. I see a twenty something guy with a nice twentyish young women. I think those years slipped right by for me. Why should I continue another 20+ years alone? I will just work, come home, eat, maybe do something, then go to bed (alone) for the next day of the same thing. This is the Auschwitz Syndrome, to be in serious pain so long one thinks it is normal. I cannot wait for tomorrow!

January 6, 2009

I can do this. Leaving work today, I felt like a zombie – just going thru the motions. Get on the bus, get the car, drive home … My mind is screwed up anymore, I can't

Appendix B   223

concentrate at work or think at all. This log is not detailed. It is only for confidence to do this. The future holds even less than what I have today.

It is 6:40pm, about hour and a half to go. God have mercy. I wish life could be better for all and the crazy world can somehow run smoother. I wish I had answers. Bye.

It is 8:45PM: I chickened out! Shit! I brought the loaded guns, everything. Hell!

April 24, 2009

Early last month, we had our second general layoff. I survived. First one was in

November. When I began 10 years ago, that used to be a nice place to work. I understand the need to reduce staff when times sour, but this is out of proportion to the economic problems at this time. The economy is shrinking by about 4–5%. They decided not to pay Christmas bonus – for staff that amounts to about 8% of yearly pay. Well, OK.

Plus no yearly "merit" raise, another 3.5%. That totals to about 11% cut. Plus two layoffs of 5% staff in each case. Do the math. I know this firm is using this downturn as an excuse to take advanage of a bad situation and kill jobs UNNECESSARILY. The second layoff people who actually did work were let go. We all need to pick up the slack so the company can cut beyond what is necesary. Wasn't going to mention it, because of all this shit, it is K&L Gates, the large law firm headquartered here in Pittsburgh. Just call it K&L Gates Corporation. Most people there are OK and I would never have a shoot 'em up there. They paid me for 10 years, so far!

I predict I won't survive the next layoff. That is when there is no point to continue. Right now, life is bearable and I can get by indefinitely. Something bad must happen. The paycheck is all I have left. The future holds nothing for me. Twenty five years of nothing fun. I never even spent one weekend with a girl in my life, even at my own place. Also unlikely to find another similar job. I guess then is when I take care of things. I don't have kids, close friends or anything. Just me here. If you have nothing, you have nothing to lose.

I enjoy writing these entries, I have no plans to go back and edit or even read most stuff already written. If you get bored, just click that "x" at the top, right corner of your browser. Bye.

May 4, 2009

I was so eager to do this last year. The big problem on my mind now is that my job will end soon. One project is being transistioned to another. The other one I am solely responsible, but is being fast tracked to production. I estimate maybe a month. I am not ready for the job market. I am ok what I do, a.NET software developer. Not at the top of the class, but I do a good job. I survived two general layoffs and other little layoffs they are having but keeping quiet about. I hear things.

The problem is I feel too good now to do this but too bad to enjoy life. I know I will never enjoy life. This is an over 30 year trend. Some people are happy, some are miserable. It is difficult to live almost continuously feeling an undercurrent of fear, worry, discontentment and helplessness. I can talk and joke around and sound happy but under it all is something different that seems unchangable and a permanent part of my being. I need to realize the details of what I never accomplished in life and to be convinced the future is merely a continuation of the past – WHICH IT ALWAYS has been. I am making a list of items that will provide motivation to do the exit plan, it won't be published. I always had hope that maybe things will improve especially if I make big attempts to change my life. I made many big changes in the past two years but everything is still the same. Life is over. Even though I look good, dress well, well groomed – nails, teeth, hair, etc. Who knows.

What is it like to be dead? I always think I am forgetting something, that's one reason I postponed. Similar to when you leave to get in your car to go somewhere – you hesitate with a thought: "what am I forgetting?" In this case, I cannot make a return trip!

I like to write and talk. Ironic because I haven't met anybody recently (past 30 years) who I want to be close friends with OR who want to be close friends with me. I was always open to suggestions to what I am doing wrong, no brother or father (mine are useless) or close friend to nudge me and give it bluntly yet tactfully wtf I am doing wrong.

A personal coach or someone who knows what he is doing would be perfect.

Money is highly secondary for a solution.

May 5, 2009

To pull the exit plan off, it popped into my mind to just use some booze. I want to do this before I get laid off, for reasons not worth mentioning but don't seem to have the balls.

After the gym, I stopped at Shop N Save and got a fifth of vodka and a small bottle of Jack Daniels. I haven't had a drink since September 1, 1988, just over 20 years.

It doesn't matter now, I need to use it to take the edge off of carrying out the exit plan. I will be taking some every now and then to get used to it and see if the alcohol effects will embolden me. Weed would be fun to try again. I don't know who has any. Life is over, who cares? I just need to use common sense, can't drink and drive, etc. This idea just hit me at a point in time and I immediately acted on it. Same thing happened when I decided to go back to Pitt full time, first day was Monday, May 8, 1989, and to buy the house that closed on Friday, September 30, 1996, to name two examples I remember so well.

The list idea yesterday is working. I carry it in my wallet and add to it. I am feeling to good to do carry this out, but too bad to enjoy ANYTHING. My life's dilema.

May 6, 2009

I started the JD. About one ounce with some tea to get me started. No big deal.

May 7, 2009

Went to the gym and did mostly cardio. My heart rate was 117 just from walking on the treadmill at 3.4. This should be done a few times a week for maybe 15 mins or so to keep the heart active. I sprinted a few times to push the limits.

Appendix B 225

May 18, 2009

I actually had a date today. It was with a woman I met on the bus in March. We got together at Two PPG Place for lunch. The last date for me was May 1, 2008.

Women just don't like me. There are 30 million desirable women in the US (my estimate) and I cannot find one. Not one of them finds me attractive. I am looking at The List I made from my May 4th idea. I forgot about that for several days. That tells me where I stand.

These problems have gotten worse over a 30 year period. I need to expect nothing from me or other people. All through the years I thought we had the ability to change ourselves – I guess that is incorrect. Looking at The List makes me realize how TOTALLY ALONE, a deeper word is ISOLATED, I am from all else.

I no longer have any expectations of myself. I have no options because I cannot work toward and achieve even the smallest goals. That is, ABOVE ALL, what bothers me the most. Not to be able to work towards what I want in my life. I believe I am deserve that. I read recently it is called "self efficacy," but who knows. Is that more psychobable?

May 25, 2009

I was invited to a picnic, and I went. An older woman there, out of the blue, asked if I liked high school. Then quickly asked if I was picked on very much. Intersting why she would ask that. But, thanks, I already know what the problem is, but a solution eludes me.

May 29, 2009

Another lonely Friday night, I'm done. This is too much.

June 2, 2009

Some people I was talking with believed I date a lot and get around with women. They think this because I showed an email I got from a hot woman to the department gossip, but it didn't work out. All this is funny. Actually, I haven't had sex since I was 29 years old, 19 years ago. That's true.

June 5, 2009

I was reading several posts on different forums and it seems many teenage girls have sex frequently. One 16 year old does it usually three times a day with her boyfriend. So, err, after a month of that, this little hoe has had more sex than ME in my LIFE, and I am 48. One more reason. Thanks for nada, bitches! Bye.

July 4, 2009

Wow, already late evening. I stayed in all day. Can't believe there was NOTHING to do today. No parties or picnics. WTF. No need to leave now.

226   *Appendix B*

July 20, 2009

Been a long time since last write. Everything still sucks. But I got a promotion and a raise, even in this shitty Obama ecomomy. No more grunt programming. Go figure! New boss is great. He tactfully says when you did something wrong or complements on good things. Never confused with him. But that is NOT what I want in life. I guess some of us were simply meant to walk a lonely path. I have slept alone for over 20 years. Last time I slept all night with a girlfriend it was 1982. Proof I am a total malfunction. Girls and women don't even give me a second look ANYWHERE. There is something BLATANTLY wrong with me that NO goddam person will tell me what it is.

Every person just wants to be fucking nice and say nice things to me. Flattery. Oh yeah, I am sure you can get a date anytime. You look good, etc. Pussies.

Awwww, wait. I can just start being self-righteous and say I live a good, clean life. I am holy, that's all Rick Knapp stuff. Hear that you mother fucker: I Am Just Good!

July 23, 2009

Wow!!

I just looked out my front window and saw a beautiful college-age girl leave Bob Fox's house, across the street. I guess he got a good lay today. College girls are hoez. I masturbate. Frequently. He is about 45 years old. She was a long haired, hot little hottie with a beautiful bod. I masturbate. Frequently. Some were simply meant to walk a lonely path in life. I don't usually look out, but just happened to notice. Holy fuck. I have masturbated since age 13. Thanks, mum and brother (by blood alone). And dad, old man, for TOTALLY ignoring me through the years. All of you DEEPLY helped me be this way.

I wish I can go back to 1975 and fix things. Awe, that wont work, big BULLY BROTHER would assert his bull shit. He was twice my size. He never messed with guys bigger than 5'10, or so. He is a PUSSY at heart. Remember, Michael is my brother (we have common parents, that's all) is still a BOSS. Repetition only for emphasis: HE IS ONLY A BULLY, even at 50ish! Never forget that! Because he exudes confidence. People believe bull shit if delivered WITH CONFIDENCE. Get it??

On the same thought, things occured to me today. Michael NEVER had an attractive girlfriend. Debbie, Barb, Kim, ... then I lost track. Not to say I had any (execpt Pam, who was about a 7.25). He married a Chinese-descent, petite woman with no body, no ass, no chest and no personality. She never laughs or smiles, neither does he. But she is highly intelligent and an excellent cook. I can testify to that! She home bakes her own DELICIOUS wheat bread! But who cares about that type of small bull crap? Mike even mentioned when we were visiting dad that "she's not very attractive."

I don't know where I am going with this. I am getting tired, feels good to write and get it all out.

On still another thought, I had 20+ years of sobriety and achieved nothing about friendships, girlfriends, guys, etc. Zilch. What a waste.

Bye, for today.

Appendix B   227

August 2, 2009

The biggest problem of all is not having relationships or friends, but not being able to achieve and acquire what I desire in those or many other areas. Everthing stays the same regardless of the effert I put in. If I had control over my life then I would be happier. But for about the past 30 years, I have not

August 3, 2009

I took off today, Monday, and tomorrow to practice my routine and make sure it is well polished. I need to work out every detail, there is only one shot. Also I need to be completely immersed into something before I can be successful. I haven't had a drink since Friday at about 2:30. Total effort needed. Tomorrow is the big day.

Unfortunately I talked to my neighbor today, who is very positive and upbeat. I need to remain focused and absorbed COMPLETELY. Last time I tried this, in January, I chickened out. Lets see how this new approach works.

Maybe soon, I will see God and Jesus. At least that is what I was told. Eternal life does NOT depend on works. If it did, we will all be in hell. Christ paid for EVERY sin, so how can I or you be judged BY GOD for a sin when the penalty was ALREADY paid. People judge but that does not matter. I was reading the Bible and The Integrity of God beginning yesterday, because soon I will see them.

I will try not to add anymore entries because this computer clicking distracts me.

Also, any of the "Practice Papers" left on my coffee table I used or the notes in my gym bag can be published freely. I will not be embarased, because, well, I will be dead.

Some people like to study that stuff. Maybe all this will shed insight on why some people just cannot make things happen in their life, which can potentially benefit others.

Miscellaneous:

1. Probably 99% of the people who know me well don't even think I was this crazy. Told by at least 100 girls/women over the years I was a "nice guy." Not kidding.
2. Lee Ann Valdiserri had my baby in early 1991. Haven't seen her since she was about four months into it. I knew her sister, Chris, from high school.
3. Net worth slightly more than $250K, (after all debt) as of end of 2008.
4. Death Lives!

© 2009 George Sodini

This should not be taken off the web. It is obviously my view and opinion.
Reproduce this as you wish, in its entirety.
* *Copy this to usenet/newsgroups where my voice will speak forever!* *
Don't modify it, you can correct my spelling errors, I used WordPad.
Unless the names are required legally to be blotted out, then fine. Thanks.

Appendix C: Elliot Rodger Video Transcript "Day of Retribution"

Hi, Elliot Rodger here. Well, this is my last video. It all has to come to this. Tomorrow is the day of retribution, the day I will have my revenge against humanity, against all of you.

For the last eight years of my life, since I hit puberty, I've been forced to endure an existence of loneliness, rejection and unfulfilled desires, all because girls have never been attracted to me. Girls gave their affection and sex and love to other men, never to me.

I'm 22 years old and still a virgin, never even kissed a girl. And through college, 2 1/2 years, more than that actually, I'm still a virgin. It has been very torturous.

College is the time when everyone experiences those things such as sex and fun and pleasure. In those years I've had to rot in loneliness, it's not fair.

You girls have never been attracted to me. I don't know why you girls aren't attracted to me but I will punish you all for it. It's an injustice, a crime because I don't know what you don't see in me, I'm the perfect guy and yet you throw yourselves at all these obnoxious men instead of me, the supreme gentleman. I will punish all of you for it. [laughs]

On the day of retribution, I am going to enter the hottest sorority house at UCSB and I will slaughter every single spoiled, stuck-up, blond slut I see inside there. All those girls I've desired so much. They have all rejected me and looked down on me as an inferior man if I ever made a sexual advance toward them, while they throw themselves at these obnoxious brutes.

I take great pleasure in slaughtering all of you. You will finally see that I am, in truth, the superior one, the true alpha male. [laughs] Yes, after I have annihilated every single girl in the sorority house, I'll take to the streets of Isla Vista and slay every single person I see there. All those popular kids who live such lives of hedonistic pleasure while I've had to rot in loneliness all these years. They all look down upon me every time I tried to join them, they've all treated me like a mouse.

Well, now I will be a god compared to you, you will all be animals, you are animals and I will slaughter you like animals. I'll be a god exacting my retribution on all those who deserve it and you do deserve it just for the crime of living a better life than me.

The popular kids, you never accepted me and now you will all pay for it. Girls, all I ever wanted was to love you, be loved by you. I wanted a girlfriend. I wanted sex, love, affection, adoration.

Appendix C 229

You think I'm unworthy of you. That's I crime I can never get over. If I can't have you girls, I will destroy you. [laughs] You denied me a happy life and in turn I will deny all of you life, it's only fair. I hate all of you.

Humanity is a disgusting, wretched, depraved species. If I had it in my power I would stop at nothing to reduce every single one of you to mountains of skulls and rivers of blood and rightfully so. You deserve to be annihilated and I will give that to you. You never showed me any mercy so I will show you none. [laughs]

You forced me to suffer all my life, now I will make you all suffer. I waited a long time for this. I'll give you exactly what you deserve, all of you. All you girls who rejected me, looked down upon me, you know, treated me like scum while you gave yourselves to other men. And all of you men for living a better life than me, all of you sexually active men. I hate you. I hate all of you. I can't wait to give you exactly what you deserve, annihilation.

Appendix D: Christopher Harper-Mercer Manifesto

Section
I. My Story
II. Blackness and Its Effect on Men
III. Other Mass Shooters
IV. Interests
V. FAQ

My Story

I have always been the most hated person in the world. Ever since I arrived in this world, I have been under siege from it. Under attack from morons and idiots. I write this manifesto so that others will know of my story and perhaps find some solace in it, some kind of inspiration for their own lives. It will contain various sections dealing with my life. It will be divided into sections based on different things. My whole life has been one lonely enterprise. One loss after another. And here I am, 26, with no friends, no job, no girlfriend, a virgin. I long ago realized that society likes to deny people like me these things. People who are elite, people who stand with the gods. People like Elliot Rodger, Vester Flanagan, The Columbine kids, Adam Lanza and Seung Cho.

Just like me those people were denied everything they deserved, everything they wanted. Though we may have been born bad, society left us no recourse, no way to be good. I have been forced to align myself with demonic forces. What was once an involuntary relationship has now become an alignment, a service. I now serve the demonic Heirarchy. When I die when I will become one of them. A demon. And I will return to kill again and again. I will possess another and you will know my work by my sign, the pentagram will fly again. Many will ask and ponder, what could they have done different, how could they have prevented this. But you can't you could never give what I wanted. You would never have done that. Some will of course say I had so much to live for, but I don't think so. I had no friends, no girlfriend, was all alone. I had no job, no life, no successes. What was it that was supposed to happen, what great event was it that was supposed to make me realize how much there was going for me. But for people like me there is another world, a darker world that welcomes us. For people like us this all that's left. My success in Hell is assured. They will

Appendix D 231

give me the power that I seek. They have always been there, speaking to me on the sidelines, controlling me. It's only fit that I join them after death. They've told me what to do, showed me the way.

And just like me, there will be others, like Ted Bundy said, we are your sons, your brothers, we are everywhere. My advice to others like me is to buy a gun and start killing people. If you live in a country like Europe with strict gun laws, either pay the necessary fees/time to get a license or become a serial killer. The world could always use an additional serial killer. Butcher them in their homes, in the street, wherever you find them. Every country in the world should be a battleground. From the heart of Africa to the deepest depths of Asia blood will flow. Fear not the laws of man, when you get to the other side you will be welcomed.

Don't be afraid to give in to your darkest impulses. Human life means nothing, we are what matters. I hope to inspire the masses with this, at least enough to get their passions aroused.

It is my hope that others will hear my call and act it out. I was once like you, a loser, rejected by society.

When the girls would rather go with alpha thug black men, we can all agree that somethings wrong with the world. When good individuals like myself are alone, but wicked black men get the loot, like some sort of vaginal pirate, it's not fair.

Blackness and Its Effect on Men

The black man is the most vile creature on the planet. He is a beast beyond measure. But don't take these words to be racist. I don't hate blacks. Just the men. Now of course some of you will be saying, wait, your 40% black aren't you? Ah yes dear reader, I am, but thankfully my partial blackness didn't come from a man. If it had my brain would have been fried. It is the black male who is foolish. Black women are not to blame, they are hapless dupes to the black mans conniving machinations. Africa would be better off without the black man, they should be executed and the black queen should take over Africa. After all, it was black men who made it inferior. Elliot Rodger was right when he said his thoughts on the black male. I fully agree with him.

Black men have corrupted the women of this planet. All they care about is sex and swag. All they care about is swinging their "BBC thang" around in public. All their brain power has been submerged into their penis. This blackness effect is only prominent on men. On women it has no effect. No one lives in fear of the black woman but everyone lives in fear of the black man. It would be better if all black women left the beast on the alter and dated a white man. Or lesbian exploration. But do to the black murder rate, in 100 years there won't be any black men, they will all be in jail or dead. The number of ebony lesbians will increase. Joy Joy Joy! The black man has more brains in his penis than Obama has in his head. And latinos will also suffer a massive drop in population, although not as bad as the black man. Both enjoy killing each other. At least the latino can be put into remedial education and be made smart. But the black mans brains fell out of the back of his head at birth onto the baby ward. I hope all mixed folk have the sense not to touch the black man but to instead find themselves a good white/Asian man. But there is hope for the world.

232 *Appendix D*

The Asian and Indian women are traditional and good. So are the men. I have always respected them. They will rule America in the inner city and the world. The black woman can only be saved by the castration/elimination of the black man. The black man is a wily beast who has held back the black woman. Success does not come out of your loins but he doesn't get the message (See end of manifesto for good black bad black comparison)

Other Mass Shooters

I have been interested in mass shooters for years. I noticed where they always go wrong is they don't work fast enough and their death toll is not anywhere near where it should be. They shoot wildly instead of targeted blasts. They also don't take on the cops. Why kill other people but you won't takeout the cops.

Interests

Now for the part I'm sure the media will love. My interests. My interests include listening to music, watching movies, internet piracy. My only solace in online life is posting on Kat.cr as the user lithium_love. I mostly have uploaded porno, ebooks, things like that. That has been my only joy in life. I will leave a sign on my profile there for any who wish to see it. I'll say again my profile on kat.cr is lithium_love.

Check out what I've uploaded. You may find our tastes are more similar than you realize.

My favorite artists are the following

1. Marilyn Manson
2. Emilie Autumn
3. And One
4. Aqua
5. Blutengel
6. Garbage
7. Switchblade Symphony
8. ASP
9. Jack off Jill
10. The Creepshow
11. Dresden Dolls

My favorite movies are the following

1. Cloud atlas
2. Terminator series
3. Living Dead series
4. The exorcist
5. The exorcism of Emily rose

Favorite colors are Red and Black
Favorite food is potatoes
Favorite drink is soymilk

FAQ

Q. What is your religion?
A. My religion is not a formal one, but more so a new age one. I've aligned myself with the occult since I was born.

Q. How come you've not had a girlfriend, are you gay?
A. No I'm not gay, girls just didn't want me. As I said before they went for the thug blacks.

Q. Are you mentally ill?
A. No I'm not. Just because I'm in communion with the Dark Forces doesn't mean I'm crazy.

Good black (Miss Stacey Dash)

Bad black (Gucci Mane, cheap motherfucker with an icecream cone on his face)
    So, in conclusion this is my manifesto. I hope all who have read it enjoyed it and find inspiration in it.
    Learn from what I've done. I know this is not as long as Elliot Rodgers but its still good. Elliot is a god.
    For those wondering, I do not have any social media.

Appendix D

If anything should happen to this manifesto on this hard drive there is a original copy on my computer.

For the Vestor Flanagans, Elliot Rodgers, Seung Cho, Adam Lanzas of the world, I do this. For all those who never took me seriously this is for you. For all those who haven't made their stand I do this. I am the martyr for all those like me. To quote Seung Cho, "Today I die like Jesus Christ."

 666 For Satan I do this, for the Darkness I do this 666.

Appendix E: Dylann Roof Manifesto

I was not raised in a racist home or environment. Living in the South, almost every White person has a small amount of racial awareness, simply beause of the numbers of negroes in this part of the country.

But it is a superficial awareness. Growing up, in school, the White and black kids would make racial jokes toward each other, but all they were were jokes. Me and White friends would sometimes would watch things that would make us think that "blacks were the real racists" and other elementary thoughts like this, but there was no real understanding behind it.

The event that truly awakened me was the Trayvon Martin case. I kept hearing and seeing his name, and eventually I decided to look him up. I read the Wikipedia article and right away I was unable to understand what the big deal was. It was obvious that Zimmerman was in the right. But more importantly this prompted me to type in the words "black on White crime" into Google, and I have never been the same since that day. The first website I came to was the Council of Conservative Citizens. There were pages upon pages of these brutal black on White murders. I was in disbelief. At this moment I realized that something was very wrong. How could the news be blowing up the Trayvon Martin case while hundreds of these black on White murders got ignored?

From this point I researched deeper and found out what was happening in Europe. I saw that the same things were happening in England and France, and in all the other Western European countries. Again I found myself in disbelief. As an American we are taught to accept living in the melting pot, and black and other minorities have just as much right to be here as we do, since we are all immigrants. But Europe is the homeland of White people, and in many ways the situation is even worse there. From here I found out about the Jewish problem and other issues facing our race, and I can say today that I am completely racially aware.

Blacks

I think it is is fitting to start off with the group I have the most real life experience with, and the group that is the biggest problem for Americans.

Niggers are stupid and violent. At the same time they have the capacity to be very slick. Black people view everything through a racial lense. Thats what racial awareness is, its viewing everything that happens through a racial lense. They are

236 *Appendix E*

always thinking about the fact that they are black. This is part of the reason they get offended so easily, and think that some thing are intended to be racist towards them, even when a White person wouldnt be thinking about race. The other reason is the Jewish agitation of the black race.

Black people are racially aware almost from birth, but White people on average dont think about race in their daily lives. And this is our problem. We need to and have to.

Say you were to witness a dog being beat by a man. You are almost surely going to feel very sorry for that dog. But then say you were to witness a dog biting a man. You will most likely not feel the same pity you felt for the dog for the man. Why? Because dogs are lower than men.

This same analogy applies to black and White relations. Even today, blacks are subconsciously viewed by White people are lower beings. They are held to a lower standard in general. This is why they are able to get away with things like obnoxious behavior in public.

Because it is expected of them.

Modern history classes instill a subconscious White superiority complex in Whites and an inferiority complex in blacks. This White superiority complex that comes from learning of how we dominated other peoples is also part of the problem I have just mentioned. But of course I dont deny that we are in fact superior.

I wish with a passion that niggers were treated terribly throughout history by Whites, that every White person had an ancestor who owned slaves, that segregation was an evil an oppressive institution, and so on. Because if it was all it true, it would make it so much easier for me to accept our current situation. But it isn't true. None of it is. We are told to accept what is happening to us because of ancestors wrong doing, but it is all based on historical lies, exaggerations and myths. I have tried endlessly to think of reasons we deserve this, and I have only came back more irritated because there are no reasons.

Only a fourth to a third of people in the South owned even one slave. Yet every White person is treated as if they had a slave owning ancestor. This applies to in the states where slavery never existed, as well as people whose families immigrated after slavery was abolished. I have read hundreds of slaves narratives from my state. And almost all of them were positive. One sticks out in my mind where an old ex-slave recounted how the day his mistress died was one of the saddest days of his life. And in many of these narratives the slaves told of how their masters didnt even allowing whipping on his plantation.

Segregation was not a bad thing. It was a defensive measure. Segregation did not exist to hold back negroes. It existed to protect us from them. And I mean that in multiple ways. Not only did it protect us from having to interact with them, and from being physically harmed by them, but it protected us from being brought down to their level. Integration has done nothing but bring Whites down to level of brute animals. The best example of this is obviously our school system.

Now White parents are forced to move to the suburbs to send their children to "good schools." But what constitutes a "good school"? The fact is that how good a school is considered directly corresponds to how White it is. I hate with a passion the whole idea of the suburbs. To me it represents nothing but scared White people

Appendix E 237

running. Running because they are too weak, scared, and brainwashed to fight. Why should we have to flee the cities we created for the security of the suburbs? Why are the suburbs secure in the first place? Because they are White. The pathetic part is that these White people dont even admit to themselves why they are moving. They tell themselves it is for better schools or simply to live in a nicer neighborhood. But it is honestly just a way to escape niggers and other minorities.

But what about the White people that are left behind? What about the White children who, because of school zoning laws, are forced to go to a school that is 90 percent black? Do we really think that that White kid will be able to go one day without being picked on for being White, or called a "white boy"? And who is fighting for him? Who is fighting for these White people forced by economic circumstances to live among negroes? No one, but someone has to. Here I would also like to touch on the idea of a Norhtwest Front. I think this idea is beyond stupid. Why should I for example, give up the beauty and history of my state to go to the Norhthwest? To me the whole idea just parralells the concept of White people running to the suburbs. The whole idea is pathetic and just another way to run from the problem without facing it.

Some people feel as though the South is beyond saving, that we have too many blacks here. To this I say look at history. The South had a higher ratio of blacks when we were holding them as slaves. Look at South Africa, and how such a small minority held the black in apartheid for years and years. Speaking of South Africa, if anyone thinks that think will eventually just change for the better, consider how in South Africa they have affirmative action for the black population that makes up 80 percent of the population.

It is far from being too late for America or Europe. I believe that even if we made up only 30 percent of the population we could take it back completely. But by no means should we wait any longer to take drastic action.

Anyone who thinks that White and black people look as different as we do on the outside, but are somehow magically the same on the inside, is delusional. How could our faces, skin, hair, and body structure all be different, but our brains be exactly the same? This is the nonsense we are led to believe.

Negroes have lower Iqs, lower impulse control, and higher testosterone levels in generals. These three things alone are a recipe for violent behavior. If a scientist publishes a paper on the differences between the races in Western Europe or Americans, he can expect to lose his job. There are personality traits within human families, and within different breeds of cats or dogs, so why not within the races?

A horse and a donkey can breed and make a mule, but they are still two completely different animals. Just because we can breed with the other races doesnt make us the same.

In a modern history class it is always emphasized that, when talking about "bad" things Whites have done in history, they were White. But when we lern about the numerous, almost countless wonderful things Whites have done, it is never pointed out that these people were White. Yet when we learn about anything important done by a black person in history, it is always pointed out repeatedly that they were black. For example when we learn about how George Washington carver was the first nigger smart enough to open a peanut.

238   *Appendix E*

On another subject I want to say this. Many White people feel as though they dont have a unique culture. The reason for this is that White culture is world culture. I dont mean that our culture is made up of other cultures, I mean that our culture has been adopted by everyone in the world. This makes us feel as though our culture isnt special or unique. Say for example that every business man in the world wore a kimono, that every skyscraper was in the shape of a pagoda, that every door was a sliding one, and that everyone ate every meal with chopsticks. This would probably make a Japanese man feel as though he had no unique traditional culture.

I have noticed a great disdain for race mixing White women within the White nationalists community, bordering on insanity it. These women are victims, and they can be saved. Stop.

Jews

Unlike many White naitonalists, I am of the opinion that the majority of American and European jews are White. In my opinion the issues with jews is not their blood, but their identity. I think that if we could somehow destroy the jewish identity, then they wouldn't cause much of a problem. The problem is that Jews look White, and in many cases are White, yet they see themselves as minorities. Just like niggers, most jews are always thinking about the fact that they are jewish. The other issue is that they network. If we could somehow turn every jew blue for 24 hours, I think there would be a mass awakening, because people would be able to see plainly what is going on. I dont pretend to understand why jews do what they do. They are enigma.

Hispanics

Hispanics are obviously a huge problem for Americans. But there are good hispanics and bad hispanics. I remember while watching hispanic television stations, the shows and even the commercials were more White than our own. They have respect for White beauty, and a good portion of hispanics are White. It is a well known fact that White hispanics make up the elite of most hispanics countries. There is good White blood worht saving in Uruguay, Argentina, Chile and even Brasil.

But they are still our enemies.

East Asians

I have great respent for the East Asian races. Even if we were to go extinct they could carry something on. They are by nature very racist and could be great allies of the White race. I am not opposed at all to allies with the Northeast Asian races.

Patriotism

I hate the sight of the American flag. Modern American patriotism is an absolute joke. People pretending like they have something to be proud while White people are being murdered daily in the streets. Many veterans believe we owe them something for "protecting our way of life" or "protecting our freedom." But im not sure

Appendix E 239

what way of life they are talking about. How about we protect the White race and stop fighting for the jews. I will say this though, I myself would have rather lived in 1940's American than Nazi Germany, and no this is not ignorance speaking, it is just my opinion. So I don't blame the veterans of any wars up until after Vietnam, because at least they had an American to be proud of and fight for.

An Explanation

To take a saying from a film, "I see all this stuff going on, and I dont see anyone doing anything about it. And it pisses me off." To take a saying from my favorite film, "Even if my life is worth less than a speck of dirt, I want to use it for the good of society."

I have no choice. I am not in the position to, alone, go into the ghetto and fight. I chose Charleston because it is most historic city in my state, and at one time had the highest ratio of blacks to Whites in the country. We have no skinheads, no real KKK, no one doing anything but talking on the internet. Well someone has to have the bravery to take it to the real world, and I guess that has to be me.

Unfortunately at the time of writing I am in a great hurry and some of my best thoughts, actually many of them have been to be left out and lost forever. But I believe enough great White minds are out there already.

Please forgive any typos, I didnt have time to check it.

Appendix F: Joseph Ferguson Confession (Transcript of Video)

FERGUSON: Okay. It's recording. Okay. This will probably be the last time anyone actually ever hears from their talks to me unless for some reason they arrest me. My actions taken tonight are due from my distress. I have absolutely no love or can give a shit about Nina Susu.

FERGUSON: I shot that fucking bitch because I'm tired of people fucking with me in life. Been fucked over by my mother for 14 years because she raped me. I was turned around and fucked over by my uncle because he raped my brother and got away with it. Turn around and I have lived through all these fucking problems. Took two years of counseling. Did no fucking thing. Turned around and trusted a female and stuff by the name of Nina Susu went out with her for seven months. We do not have sexual relationship. All we did was fool around. I never slept with the woman once.

FERGUSON: I turned around and trusted her with all kinds of stuff, told her about what happened to me when I was a child and stuff. She turned around and left. She fucking came back two months later. I made sure I kept her job. I turned around and rebuilt the front of her car and all the bitch did was turn around and tell me she fucking used me to get a life. As far as I'm concerned, I tried to take her back, understand it. Turn around. Yeah. I axed up her fucking car with a goddamn axe what the fuck you going to do about it now? I took back what was mine. I giveth and I taketh. That's how it goes in fucking life.

FERGUSON: What else?

FERGUSON: Fuck man. I don't fucking know. I don't fucking know. For the victims, I apologize to your families, I obviously don't mean shit to you. You'd just as soon see I die so I'm going to see fit that that happens. Either a bullet to my brain or fucking cops will kill me. Most likely it'll be a bullet to the brain. Once I'm shot up enough up, I can't really walk around or I'm bleeding to death. I'll just pop myself, but I want a hell of a show.

FERGUSON: I've taken four victims that should be good enough to last about a week in the news. It's time to feed the news media. I'm sure a lot of new gun laws and shit are going to be passed, by using these firearms. Sorry. I sat in the garage and I illegally bought these stuff to modify my weapons for mass destruction and that's what I've done.

FERGUSON: I've purchased all this stuff without my dad knowing. I sat there and I took his legal guns and I turned them into fucking illegal weapons to mass

Appendix F 241

murder people because I knew what the fuck I was going to do. Obviously I left some of the guns at the house and couldn't take them all because of weight. You know, I'm just so tired of people fucking with me in life. I've had my fucking fill of it. Fucking piece of shit, George the man, fucking off on me three fucking times. I got to kill this goddamn post. Fucking stupid nitwit motherfucker got in the way. He was going to be a hero, "hey stop." Fucking Nina Susu. That bitch got every fucking thing she deserved. Fucking using me, fucking cunt. Marsha. Fuck it. Sorry. She should've took off running across the parking lot and not cower in the fucking corner of the com center, I mean, I had to crawl out of the fucking window.

FERGUSON: You know, you should have fucking seen Nina, man. She fucking begged for her life and she told me she finally for the first time in her goddamn life, she told me she fucking loved me. You actually believe that. What a fucking joke, right? What a fucking joke. Go in the office and say all that shit. Well I fuck with you cops tonight. It's at the senior home Depot and Meadowview home Depot flooring Jack's house. I know you guys fucking caused some hellacious fucking problems in the city. Fuck man. I drove past three of your fucking cops in that Toyota Camry. Stupid ass donut eating mother fuckers. That's right. You donut eating mother fucker. And I'm going to have my fucking shoot out with you. I hope I fucking make Los Angeles look like a fucking joke. Go down in fucking history, you know three Burns guards and one marina patron. That ain't shit. That's only four. Got to take more than that. I've got Nick Popovich and his wife. They've been on by your grace, so you guys are fine. I haven't done anything to you.

SPEAKER 2: No.

FERGUSON: No, you're cool.

SPEAKER 2: No.

FERGUSON: Just like Diane Faust is alive. Diane Faust. She's cool.

FERGUSON: No problem. Other people I fucking hated. Marsha's a backstabbing bitch. Trying to tell her stuff, she turns around and tells fucking these two people are cool. I sorry about the time I took them. They fed me and stuff, but they were also forced at gun point to do so because obviously if they don't do that, I'm going to kill them. But I'm not going to because they all gave me their car and shit like that and so that's how fucking life works I guess.

FERGUSON: I don't know where you guys are at now. For my family, William Lee Ferguson, my brother. I love you. I apologize for what I put you through, but don't be what I am. You grow up and you become whatever you want. I told you not to become a cop. Become whatever you want. It's a free fucking country. Grow up have kids, have a wife. I don't give a shit if she's Asian, white. I don't give a fuck whatever you like.

FERGUSON: My dad, I apologize for this [inaudible 00:05:32], but I let you down. And I already decided if I let you down again, that this is where I'm going. I'm sure I've caused you more problems than you could ever fucking imagine. More heartache and pain than you could ever [inaudible 00:05:43]. But don't go into sit and fucking and say that you know it's your fault or anything like that. Okay? It's not, it's not your fucking fault. It's mine. I let you down. You left everything

242 *Appendix F*

in my hands and all I did was fucking waste it. I fucking ruined it. I apologize for that. And there's no way. You'll probably going to be joining me soon where I am. I love you. And I'll be waiting for you there. Once we're there, however it goes we live in peace. [inaudible 00:06:10] can't fuck with us, Mom can't fuck with us. Are you going dead?

SPEAKER 2: Yeah, man.

FERGUSON: You mean you can't plug into a wall?

SPEAKER 2: It is plugged into the wall.

FERGUSON: Is the tape done?

SPEAKER 2: Yeah. Let's see. I'll look.

Appendix G: A Partial Transcript
Alek Minassian's Police Interview

ELECTRONICALLY RECORDED INTERVIEW OF ALEK MINASSIAN

BY DETECTIVE ROBERT THOMAS (3917) OF THE SEX CRIMES UNIT POLYGRAPH UNIT

ON MONDAY, APRIL 23, 2018, AT 2246 HOURS

[Discussion around His Weapons Knowledge]

Minassian: I was interested in ah learning how to ah use ah weapons —

Thomas: Beautiful okay.

Minassian: — sp – specifically ah large guns.

Thomas: So large guns as in in what like ah like —

Minassian: Such as ah assault rifles.

Thomas: Oh okay so you're not talking about howitzers and, and ah cannons right you're talking about like —

Minassian: Yeah they – because those you can actually hold in your hand.

Thomas: Right, right. So, what type of weapons would the ah the military– the Canadian military be, be training their, their members in? Because you know what I play a lot of Call of Duty right have you ever played Call of Duty?

Minassian: Unfortunately, that game isn't realistic – uhm however ah I never unfortunately I never made it far enough in my basic training to ah use guns, ah so I don't know what type of guns the ah, ah military uses.

Thomas: Oh okay. What makes you think you know I thought ah Call of Duty was – well I know that the scenarios aren't realistic but, but like the weapons they use are realistic aren't they and ah and the camel and the uniforms and stuff —

Minassian: Unfortunately ah uhm the logistics of how the ah weapons are fired —

Thomas: Right.

Minassian: — ah are not ah realistic in real life.

Thomas: Oh.

Minassian: For example ah there's a lot of recoil when firing a, ah an assault rifle.

Thomas: Right, right yeah, yeah I know I imagine you're not getting much recoil on your, you know, your, your computer whatever —

Minassian: Definitely not.

244   *Appendix G*

Thomas: — the little hand-held console you're using of course it vibrates a little bit but that – do, do you play ah Call of Duty?

Minassian: I played it ah in the past.

Thomas: Yeah, yeah I enjoy that I like that and ah there's another one I ah really enjoyed was uhm uhm Honour – Badge of Honour.

Minassian: I've actually never played that to be honest.

Thomas: That was actually better. That's better than the Call of Duty better Badge of Honor. It's made – it's ah I think Call of Duty is, is ah Microsoft if I'm not mistaken I can't I I don't know and but this was another company but—

Minassian: Call of Duty is made by Activision.

Thomas: Activision okay right ah now yeah yes so Badge of Honour is something else it's, it's another company. I don't know what it is but ah do, do, do you find yourself play – do you play a lot of games a guy like you 25 years old I imagine you're —

Minassian: Yeah I actually – I actually like playing video games especially the, ah violent ones.

Thomas: The violent ones yeah, yeah, yeah.

Minassian: I just like to ah let out all my urges —

Thomas: That's, that's —

Minassian: — into the TV screen.

Thomas: — that's why they're there right do you – what about uhm what other ones do you play?

Minassian: I played Halo a lot —

Thomas: Yeah okay —

Minassian: — in the past.

Thomas: — alright that's more of ah sci-fi kind of futuristic stuff it's not I wouldn't say Halo is terribly violent. I mean you're, you're killing Martians and things like that.

Minassian: At least you're not killing other humans.

Thomas: Yeah, yeah, yeah do you play uhm ah Grand Theft Auto?

Minassian: I played it a couple of times ah, ah on someone else's X-box. I don't actually own – I've never actually owned any copies of Grand Theft Auto.

Thomas: Uhuh, uhuh so as far as being a gamer, how would you classify yourself are you ah like a big gamer or?

Minassian: I would classify myself as a hard core gamer.

Thomas: Hard core gamer. So in terms of hours spent during the day playing video games how often would you – how many hours would you spend?

Minassian: I would say an average of ah five hours per day.

Thomas: Yeah okay alright okay that's that seems reasonable. I'd say your age I'd probably do the same thing.

[Discussion around Completing His Degree Program, Wed April 18th]

Thomas: And you'd be graduating with ah a Bachelor of Science?

Minassian: Bachelor of Software Development.

Appendix G 245

Thomas: Bachelor of Software Development. Did you have – did you have tests or anything to complete or?

Minassian: I've already completed everything.

Thomas: So you – you've basically you, you finished?

Minassian: Yes.

Thomas: So when was your last day?

Minassian: My last day of classes was ah last Wednesday

[A Discussion around His Incel Thoughts]

Thomas: No ah what about difficulties with ah, ah girls in particular?

Minassian: No.

Thomas: No, no difficulties with girls at all?

Minassian: No.

Thomas: No, none at all. How do you feel about ah girls in general?

Minassian: I, I'm attracted to them.

Thomas: Oh you are okay, okay so you're heterosexual —

Minassian: Yes.

Thomas: — would it be fair to say that okay that's, that's important. Uhm have you ever had a relationship with a, with a female?

Minassian: I don't wish to answer that.

Thomas: Okay, alright. Uhm in terms of females I mean females and women because you're 25 you're a young man alright we'll call them women ah in terms of your feelings towards women in general ah how would you describe that?

Minassian: I would say that sometimes I am a bit upset that they choose to ah date ah obnoxious men instead of ah a gentleman.

Thomas: Yeah, yeah so I, I, I am I have a uhm well I got involved in a situation I'll tell you about later but uhm I, I uhm so my understanding is uhm you, you have some problems with women who date obnoxious men right.

Minassian: Yes.

Thomas: And these guys I'm thinking you're, you're talking about the fellows who are loud ah, ah arrogant uhm ah generally ah uhm outgoing and popular with girls —

Minassian: Yes.

Thomas: — is that what you're talking about?

Minassian: Yes.

Thomas: Okay uhm and you have a problem with the women that date these fellows.

Minassian: Yes.

Thomas: Why is it that you have a problem with, with the women?

Minassian: Because I feel that ah it's illogical to be ah dating such men when they can be dating a gentleman instead.

Thomas: Right, right, right, that make sense I mean ah and I've seen that because I've grown up and I'll tell you one of the issues that I had as a kid growing up because I was uhm this is going to sou – you might believe me but believe – I I wasn't a very big kid growing up, I was actually very, very small ah and it took

246   *Appendix G*

me a long time to, to, to, to grown and ah so as a result ah the you know I, I was kind of ostracized. Do you know what I mean by ostracized I was kind of —

Minassian: Cast aside.

Thomas: — cast aside yeah, yeah and ah or ah I left out like I wouldn't get picked for teams you know or anything like that you know I was kind of always the last guy you, you ever see those ah those ah you know those television shows where you know all the kids are lined up and they're getting picked for you know the teams and there's always one guy left out at the end —

Minassian: Yeah.

Thomas: — that that was me, I was I was that, I was that guy and ah and I never I was never ah very popular with ah women, girls in in school and ah and that kind of actually went on through ah to early part of my, my adulthood ah until I started you know getting taller and ah maturing right but ah I understand exactly what you meant because I was – as a kid growing up I was uhm you know I was like any other kid – any other young, young man right you would look at ah, ah, attractive girls and I knew I was probably just as smart if not smarter than some of the clowns they were dating but because for whatever reason I didn't have what it took; they wouldn't, you know, they wouldn't date me because I think because I was short. They wouldn't date me and they ended up dating you know the tall jocks and the other you know the good looking fellows. Is that what you're talking about?

Minassian: Yes.

Thomas: Yeah then yeah you kind of resent these girls right —

Minassian: Yeah.

Thomas: — because you know it's kind of a superficial way of ah deciding you know who it is you're going to date.

Minassian: Because height is an unfair and you can't control your height.

Thomas: Right exactly right, right, right, right. What other things can't you control?

Minassian: You can't control ah your, your looks either.

Thomas: Exactly, exactly yeah that's a good point. Although you're not a bad looking guy.

Minassian: Thank you.

Thomas: No you are, you're a good looking guy you keep yourself well and you're good, you're fit you know you're tall, uhm what other things can't you control?

Minassian: I'm unaware of – I'm, I'm not aware of anything else you can't control.

Thomas: Ah what about uhm like phys – physical disabilities right obviously if you were blind or you know —

Minassian: Unfortunately you can't control that.

Thomas: Yeah you can't control that that's what I mean. So these are things you can't control or uhm you know other disabilities you know ah if you're mentally handicapped or if you ah you ah you're you have an amputee or ah, ah you know there's there's other, other things and I and I and so does that would would you include that in those, those issues that you can't control?

Minassian: Yes.

Thomas: And so ah so how long have you had this uhm this feeling towards ah women who are attracted to you know this particular type of guy?

Appendix G 247

Minassian: Ever since I ah started ah college.

Thomas: Ever since you started college okay and ah, ah did it, did it, was it was it something that occurred as a result of a single incident like it's – was there one particular moment in your life where it sort of struck home, this was a problem or was it just ah ah —

Minassian: On Halloween of ah 2013 I was attending a house party —

Thomas: Uhuh.

Minassian: — and I ah walked in and attempted to ah socialize with some ah girls, ah however they all ah laughed at me and ah held the arms of the ah big guys instead.

Thomas: Really.

Minassian: Yeah.

Thomas: Well that's kind of rude. And how did that make you feel?

Minassian: I felt, ah very angry —

Thomas: Yeah.

Minassian: — that they would, because I consider myself a supreme gentleman —

Thomas: Yeah.

Minassian: — I was angry that that they would uhm give their love and affection to obnoxious brutes.

Thomas: Really eh, really and so it was at that particular moment and that was sort of the defining moment that make you think that you know this is this is wrong and you know these people are —

Minassian: Yes.

Thomas: — unfairly treating you in in the way that they were.

Minassian: Yes.

Thomas: Yeah, yeah well that makes sense I appreciate you telling me that that ah that says a lot and ah so, so from that point on what ah you know what what, what did you start doing?

Minassian: I ah started thinking that it's unfair that uhm ce – certain ah guys will not get any ah love and affection from girls.

Thomas: Okay and, and what, wh – like what, what do you mean by certain guys?

Minassian: Such as me that are ah that are very nice and ah acting gentlemanly.

Thomas: Right, right, right are there other guys? Did you find other guys that are, are in the same —

Minassian: There – I know of several other guys over the internet who ah feel the same way but I know they are I would consider them ah too cowardly to ah act on their anger.

Thomas: Oh, okay and so on the internet where, where are – what are you talking about in terms of?

(lengthy discussion of 4Chan, R9K Pol)

Minassian: — is the general topic is basically political discussions with an alt-right bias.

Thomas: Political discussions with an alt-right so you're – you're, you're ultraconservative – or you're —

248   *Appendix G*

Minassian: Yes.

Thomas: — or ah you know the American ah definition would be you'd be ultra-republican.

Minassian: Yes.

Thomas: Okay so you – what would your – what would your political views be in the alt-right ah, ah message board?

Minassian: I actually don't have any ah political views. I only ah, ah the only reason I, I talked with them was just because I enjoyed their, ah style of ah conversation.

Thomas: Okay and what was the style of conversation?

Minassian: Ah it was very ah blunt and honest.

Thomas: So wh – what would it be, what would it typically focus around or what would they –what would the typ – typical conversations contain?

Minassian: Ah red pill truths about ah why ah women ah choose to date obnoxious men.

Thomas: Date the Chads.

Minassian: Yeah.

Thomas: The Chads of this world.

Minassian: Yeah —

Thomas: Yeah, yeah, yeah.

Minassian: Basically the Stacey's going for the Chads.

Thomas: Exactly, the Stacey's are the yeah the yeah the dizzy dumb girls dating ah the goofy you know jocks.

Minassian: Yeah.

Thomas: Right, right, right, right so you call them Stacey's and Chads.

Minassian: Yeah.

Thomas: I've, I've heard that term before. Ah and so that's in the altright?

Minassian: Yes.

Thomas: That conversation takes place in the alt-right as well?

Minassian: Yes.

Thomas: Ah does – do other things take place in the alt-right ah forum —

Minassian: Uhm —

Thomas: — or red pill.

Minassian: Ah some, some, some ah uhm alt-right members consider them to do – those cells to be ah red pilled.

Thomas: What does that mean is that like a matrix ah reference?

Minassian: Actually it is in fact – that term was actually in fact uhm ah came up as a reference to matrix —

Thomas: Right.

Minassian: — taking the red – you can either take the red pill or you can take the blue pill.

Thomas: Right.

Minassian: And some of the – some alt-right members even consider them to be supposed to be ah black pill which in ess – in in essence means they are ah MGTOW, "Men Going Their Own Way."

Thomas: Oh okay, alright okay, alright okay. You alright?

Minassian: Yup.

Appendix G 249

Thomas: Okay so it's so the conversations are surrounding ah – so in those three message boards they're all basically the s – or maybe not I shouldn't say all three but in the two message boards the alt-right and the —

Minassian: R9K.

Thomas: R9K there —

Minassian: And we call ourselves the space robots there.

Thomas: Space robots, but the conversations tend to be focussed around uhm ah fellows who have ah been unable to lose their virginity due to the Stacey's of this world with Chads.

Minassian: Yes.

Thomas: Right and ah I I've done a little bit of uhm ah reading and I know a little about uhm involuntary ah —

Minassian: Celibacy.

Thomas: — cel – celibacy, right being celibate —

Minassian: Yes.

Thomas: — involuntary celibate. What does that mean?

Minassian: That means in – celibacy means ah, ah someone who had never before has sexual intercourse.

Thomas: Right.

Minassian: Ah involuntary celibacy means this wasn't your choice who —

Thomas: I see.

Minassian: — essentially are ah, have been thrown into true force loneliness and you're unable to lose your virginity.

Thomas: Right.

Minassian: This is especially ah painful for ah young males.

Thomas: Right, right, right that make sense and there are other – are there not other web sites that cater to this group of people as well ForeverAlone, have you ever heard of that?

Minassian: I have heard of the ah ForeverAlone ah Subreddit.

Thomas: And Subreddit, Subreddit have you – you've heard of those?

Minassian: Yes.

[A Discussion around Rodger and Mercer]

Thomas: Okay alright okay uhm so ah, ah so when you're on 4Chan ah what specifically are you and and you know 4Chan when you'rewhen you're on your different websites and ForeverAlone which – let me ask you this sorry I don't mean to ah sound confusing -which are you more active on in terms of – -

Minassian: 4Chan.

Thomas: 4Chan okay uhm when did you first – sorry you mentioned this and I forgot when did you first go onto 4Chan?

Minassian: 2014.

Thomas: 2014 and specifically when in 2014?

Minassian: May 23 ah 2014.

Thomas: How – how are you able to remember that?

Minassian: Because I remember that was a ah very significant day.

250   *Appendix G*

Thomas: Okay what day was – what was that?

Minassian: Ah that was when ah Elliot Rodger ah decided to essentially ah commit an uprising – a beta uprising if you will —

Thomas: Right.

Minassian: — against the ah Chads and the Stacey's.

Thomas: Okay, okay and that was in the United States.

Minassian: Yes.

Thomas: And so when you talk about —

Minassian: Well because uhm Incels don't believe in borders.

Thomas: Right, okay, okay.

Minassian: So ah so locations are ah irrelevant to us.

Thomas: Right, right but for, for geographical reference only am I right to understand it, it, it occurred in California.

Minassian: Yes.

Thomas: Okay and ah what, what type of uhm ah what, what type of uprising occurred, what, what happened?

Minassian: It was a beta uprising.

Thomas: A beta uprising okay.

Minassian: Although he didn't ah call it a beta uprising at the time ah someone else who was inspired by him by the name of ah Chris Harper-Mercer called it a beta uprising some time in ah – actually I believe it was October 1 ah 2015.

Thomas: Ah it was 2014.

Minassian: No ah some Chr – someone else named Chris Harper-Mercer —

Thomas: Yup.

Minassian: — in 2015 ah called it a beta uprising. I'm only retroactively ah assigning the label of beta uprising to the Elliot Rodger's —

Thomas: Okay I —

Minassian: — ah moves.

Thomas: I thought Chris Harper-Mercer ah committed a beta uprising in Oregon in 2014 which later fuelled Elliot Rodger to do something similar in California in 2016.

Minassian: It was actually ah the other way around —

Thomas: Oh.

Minassian: — Elliot Rodger in 2014 his ah what —

Thomas: You're right, I'm sorry.

Minassian: — his —

Thomas: Yes.

Minassian: — his uhm what I'm uhm retroactively calling ah beta uprising —

Thomas: Uhuh.

Minassian: — ah inspired ah Chris Harper-Mercer to do the same thing in 2015.

Thomas: You're absolutely right I, I you know you're absolutely right that makes sen – makes a lot of sense. So, ah it was ah Elliot Rodger who was the, the father of this.

Minassian: Basically the fa – the founding forefather —

Thomas: The founding forefather.

Minassian: — he founded the entire movement.

Appendix G 251

Thomas: Right, right. So explain to me this movement, what's this movement about?

Minassian: It's basically – it's basically a movement of angry ah incels such as myself who are unable to get laid, therefore we want to overthrow the ah Chads —

Thomas: Uhuh.

Minassian: — which would ah force the Stacey's to be forced to ah reproduce with the incels.

Thomas: Right, right okay and when you say incels —

Minassian: Involuntary ah cel – celibate.

Thomas: Celibate so that's just ah a short form for, for, for fellows who —

Minassian: Can't get laid.

Thomas: — ah can't, can't have sex right, okay and ah what happened in the ah Elliot Rodger's ah, ah uprising, what did he do?

Minassian: I know he ah used a ah gun as well as a ah vehicle to uhm convert the life status of certain individuals to ah death status.

Thomas: Right.

Minassian: Uhm oh only to ah carry the message that uhm incels ah can't be oppressed.

Thomas: Right, right so it was ah, ah it was an act of rebellion.

Minassian: Yes.

Thomas: And and it was uhm – and ah and uhm out of frustration and anger.

Minassian: You could call it an Incel rebellion.

Thomas: Incel rebellion. Exactly, right, yeah okay and uhm ah how many – how many ah lives were converted from living to to dead?

Minassian: Six.

Thomas: Six in total okay and ah, ah and he used a vehicle in that —

Minassian: Yes.

Thomas: — as well in ah as part of the process of converting these lives.

Minassian: Yes.

Thomas: And ah was anything else – did he do anything else?

Minassian: I know he used a ah a knife —

Thomas: Right.

Minassian: — for, for his first three murders.

Thomas: For his first three murders, okay, alright. And uhm and then ah what about uhm Chris ah Harper-Mercer what ah what did he do?

Minassian: He used a gun for ah all of his murders.

Thomas: For all of his murders. And how many did he – how many did he – how many people did he murder?

Minassian: I believe it was it was either eight killed and ten injured or ah ten killed and eight injured.

Thomas: Ten killed and eight injured okay.

Minassian: It was one of those two.

Thomas: Okay and were these fellows active on 4Chan?

Minassian: Yes.

Thomas: They were eh. Have you ever communicated with these fellows?

252   *Appendix G*

Minassian: Ah I actually have, as a matter of fact.

Thomas: Who, who did you communicate with?

Minassian: Both of them actually.

Thomas: Really?

Minassian: We used ah code names actually.

Thomas: Okay what was – what were they?

Minassian: Ah Elliot Rodger was named of Valtharion.

Thomas: Valtharion?

Minassian: Yes.

Thomas: How do you spell that?

Minassian: V-A-L-T-H-A-R-I-O-N.

Thomas: Okay and ah what was Chris ah Harper-Mercer's name?

Minassian: SpaceRobot.

Thomas: SpaceRobot. One word or two?

Minassian: Ah one word.

Thomas: One word.

Minassian: Camel case.

Thomas: Camel case?

Minassian: That means the S and ah R ah were ah both capitalized.

Thomas: Oh I see okay, okay ah and okay and what was your – what was your what was your code name?

Minassian: Xboxlightside.

Thomas: Xbox light side?

Minassian: All one word.

Thomas: All one word camel case?

Minassian: No, only the ah first letter was capitalized.

Thomas: The X.

Minassian: Yes.

Thomas: Okay, alright and ah so what did you discuss with these guys?

Minassian: We discussed our ah frustrations at uhm society and being unable to get laid and we were plotting a certain ah timed strikes —

Thomas: Uhuh.

Minassian: — on society in order to ah confuse and ah shake the foundations just to put all the ah, normies in a ah state of panic.

Thomas: Okay and who'd be a normie?

Minassian: Ah normie means ah normal people that would be anyone who is ah considered to be normal by ah the unfair standards of society.

Thomas: But not the Chads or Stacey's. Chads and Stacey's —

Minassian: Chads and Stacey's are actually above normies or at least they think they're above normies.

Thomas: Of course yeah, yeah, yeah okay alright. So is it fair to say you've got Chads and Stacey's up here, normies down here and then you've got celibs who believe that they are being repressed.

Minassian: Incels.

Thomas: Incels, Incels sorry —

Minassian: Yes.

Appendix G 253

Thomas: — Incels who believe they're being rep – rep ah, ah suppressed or repressed —

Minassian: Yes.

Thomas: — and, and so as a result even the playing field.

Minassian: Yes.

Thomas: The – you know they, they ah they convert the Stacey's and Chads from living to dead ah to make —

Minassian: So that we come out on t – us on top.

Thomas: Yeah more than – so is there ah, ah so the targets, who are the targets for this uprising be?

Minassian: All of the ah alpha males.

Thomas: All the alpha males. So the Chads.

Minassian: Yes.

Thomas: So that's – those are the people you'll – that that you want to kill?

Minassian: Yes.

Thomas: Okay alright and who else?

Minassian: Any ah any of the Stacey's who ah do not wish to ah give their love and affection to the Incels.

Thomas: So they, they they're a target as well —

Minassian: Yes.

Thomas: — to be killed.

Minassian: Yes.

Thomas: Okay and what about the normies, no ah yeah nor – normies.

Minassian: Yes we ah do – we don't necessarily wish to ah kill the normies but we do wish to subjugate them ah in order to make them understand that the uhm – that our type is ah the more superior

Minassian: Mean – meaning ah either imprison them or put them in a lower position in society —

Thomas: Okay alright.

Minassian: — so that they acknowledge uhm the Incels or the ah Pepe the Frog types as the more superior ones.

Thomas: So okay you you're saying things that I'm, I'm not familiar with —

Minassian: So – sorry.

Thomas: What's a Pepe – Pepe the Frog?

Minassian: Ah but we ah he's, he's a mascot on 4Chan and we ah —

Thomas: He's a mascot?

Minassian: Yes.

Thomas: Oh mascot on, on 4Chan.

Minassian: Yes.

Thomas: And he's a —

Minassian: Ah ah I was using a metaphor.

Thomas: Oh okay, okay.one.

Thomas: Right, right. So when you say subjugate what do you mean by that?

Minassian: Yeah so ah he's actually ah worshipped ah quite frequently.

Thomas: Oh okay, okay alright so going back to the conversation with, with Chris and uhm and ah Elliot you're talking to these fellows now ah when,when are

254   *Appendix G*

you having these conversations, when, when, did these conversations start taking place?

Minassian: Uhm before ah obviously before their ah massacres because they're both dead now.

Thomas: Right, right, right, right, right okay and ah and then once you learned of the – so what – so it was Elliot who was first in 2014.

Minassian: Yes

Thomas: So what did Elliot – what, what did you and Elliot talk about? Let me let me ah I, I find you very interesting I do and I find it's fascinating uhm but I want to make sure I, I don't go too fast. Uhm did you have – did you have – who did you have conversation with first, let me ask you that?

Minassian: Elliot.

Thomas: Elliot so how did you learn of Elliot?

Minassian: Because on ah on we private message each other on ah Reddit —

Thomas: Yup.

Minassian: — after I saw one of ah his posts —

Thomas: Uhuh.

Minassian: — ah and ah we just talked about each other and got to know each other and we found each other very interesting. We both had the same ah frustrations that society —

Thomas: Right.

Minassian: — despite being ah separate by distance so far apart.

Thomas: Right, right, right, did you ever visit him?

Minassian: Ah no but I wish I could have.

Thomas: Yeah, yeah did he ever come up and visit you?

Minassian: No but I wish he did.

Thomas: Yeah, yeah ah did you ever communicate ah outside of ah 4Chan? Did you ever communicate on anything else outside of 4Chan?

Minassian: Reddit was the first place we ah communicated.

Thomas: Oh okay and was it Fo – ForeeverAlone?

Minassian: Yes.

Thomas: In that – in that subgroup?

Minassian: Yes.

Thomas: Okay ah, ah did you ever communicate on any other medium or platform?

Minassian: Ah other than Reddit and 4Chan no.

Thomas: No so you didn't Skype or call on the phone or anything like that?

Minassian: No.

Thomas: Okay so long does this conversation with Elliot – sorry, sorry so when – so when specifically, you may have mentioned I, I wasn't listening, when specifically did you first contact or have contact with Elliot?

Minassian: January of 2014.

Thomas: 2014 and ah when did you stop having con – communication with him?

Minassian: Ah, ah as soon as he was deceased.

Thomas: Okay so ah his act I, I know took place in 2014 but I wasn't aware of the exact day, what day was it?

Minassian: May 23 ah 2014.

Appendix G 255

Thomas: May 23rd yeah you said that. Ah so when did you last speak to him?

Minassian: May ah 20.

Thomas: May 20th. And so what did he tell you?

Minassian: He told me that ah he has to go he must – he's on a very important mission —

Thomas: Uhuh.

Minassian: — and ah he might not make it back alive.

Thomas: Uhuh, uhuh and so what did you say to him?

Minassian: I ah kind of had an idea in my head of what he was ah planning but I didn't want to ah think it was true at the time so I said – so I replied and said ah I wish you ah good luck with that.

Thomas: Right on okay, okay and ah were there anybody – was there anybody else in this conversation?

Minassian: It was ah private ah conversation.

Thomas: Oh it was a private – okay so there's nobody else speaking?

Minassian: No.

Thomas: Okay and you can have private conversations outside of 4Chan?

Minassian: It well like I said it was a Reddit private message.

Thomas: Oh sorry ah Foreever – yeah ah ForeeverAlone?

Minassian: Yeah because anyone can ah just private message each other since you have a registered account.

Thomas: Right okay, okay so you can go on the ah forum and and the threads and leave messages and then you can speak to people outside of the threats privately?

Minassian: Yes.

Thomas: Okay I'm just – I'm because I haven't been on these these websites so it's ah but I've heard of them so I'm just trying to get get familiarize with, with how it works. So did ah was there was there – as far as you were aware of was there anyone else involved in ah, ah Elliot Rodger's ah, ah mission?

Minassian: I believe that – he told me that ah other members of ah, ah 4Chan were giving him ah encouraging support so that he would have the courage to ah start his rebellion.

Thomas: Right, right, right okay and so you last speak to him on March 20th.

Minassian: May 20th.

Thomas: May 20th I'm sorry May 20th, 2014.

Minassian: Yes.

Thomas: He commits his, his, his acts on the 23rd of May —

Minassian: Yes.

Thomas: — and ah when did you learn that ah what he had done?

Minassian: I saw it on the news later that night.

Thomas: Later on, on the 23rd?

Minassian: Yes.

Thomas: Okay and what did you think?

Minassian: Ah I thought that I ah came to the understanding that this is the mission that he had to ah carry out.

Thomas: Okay alright and anything else?

Minassian: I felt kind of ah proud of him for ah his acts of bravery.

256   *Appendix G*

Thomas: Okay alright and what about ah how you started to, to, to change your thinking. Was, was any was, was any of that going on?

Minassian: I was starting to feel ah radicalized at that time.

Thomas: You were eh okay and when you say radicalized what do you mean by that?

Minassian: Meaning I felt it was time to take action and not just sit on the side lines and just ah fester in my own sadness.

Thomas: Right, okay, alright and so ah so this this is started – this is a process it's not something that just – I mean the, the, the, the day that you realized that ah you were ah celib was the day that you were ridiculed by these girls at this party —

Minassian: On ah Halloween of 2013.

Thomas: Right but then as you got to know ah Elliot and then ah understanding his, his ah, his ah mission and ah what he had done you began to, to start become radicalized in terms of your though process.

Minassian: Yes.

Thomas: Okay and so what takes place next as part of this, this, this growing radicalization?

Minassian: To be honest ah the planning didn't occur until about a month ago, most of it was actually just thinking —

Thomas: Okay.

Minassian: — and day dreaming.

Thomas: Okay alright so the thinking and day dreaming when did that start?

Minassian: That started about a month after the rebellion in ah May of 2014.

Thomas: Okay so —

Minassian: So I mean so June I started ah thinking about this stuff.

Thomas: And then that continued right up until a month ago?

Minassian: Yes. Which is when I ah booked ah the ah van with Ryder —

Thomas: Okay.

Minassian: — in order to ah use as ah a tool for rebellion.

Thomas: Okay alright so tel – take me through that process. What was going through your mind and how was you know, what were you thinking when you were doing all of this? What was going on?

Minassian: I was thinking that it was ah time that I ah stood up to the Chads and Stacey's.

Thomas: Okay and then and so what happened? So this – tell me what takes place?

[A Discussion about the Attack]

Thomas: Yeah.

Minassian: I would estimate about ah twenty to thirty minutes.

Thomas: Twenty to thirty minutes. Now what are you thinking while you're in the van?

Minassian: Ah I'm thinking that this is it, this is the day of retribution.

Thomas: Okay and ah anything else on your mind?

Minassian: Just that.

Appendix G 257

Thomas: Okay.

Minassian: That's that's the only thing that's in my mind, it's just burning in my mind.

Thomas: Burning in your mind.

Minassian: Yeah.

Thomas: Okay and ah so let me ask you this because this is really interesting. Why do you chose Yonge and Finch?

Minassian: I, I didn't chose Yonge and Finch particular I was driving down Yonge because I knew it would be ah busy area —

Thomas: Uhuh.

Minassian: — and then as soon as I saw there were ah pedestrians —

Thomas: Uhuh.

Minassian: — I just decided to ah go for it.

Thomas: Okay and so where specifically were you in terms of your specific location, where were you when you just decided to go for it?

Minassian: I was ah at some traffic lights.

Thomas: Okay where?

Minassian: Uhm actually I don't remember. The only reason – in fact ah if I hadn't ah I remember some other I, I had heard some other officer or mention Yonge and Finch before that's the only reason I really remember it.

Thomas: Okay.

Minassian: But otherwise I actually wouldn't have remembered —

Thomas: You wouldn't have remembered.

Minassian: — that it's yeah Yonge and Finch. I just knew that I started seeing a lot of people walking.

Thomas: Okay ah am I am I to understand – am I correct when I when I say that you knew at least you were on Yonge Street?

Minassian: Yes.

Thomas: And you knew that you were —

Minassian: Because I specifically chose it beforehand because that's that's why – because I even looked for that ramp from Highway 7 to Yonge.

Thomas: Right okay, okay so nevertheless you're at ah – you're at a stop light you said?

Minassian: Yes.

Thomas: You're at – and now are you faced with a red light you're stopped?

Minassian: Ah yes but as soon as it turned green I ah started going.

Thomas: Okay and ah just walk me through this okay step by step. So it turns green what are you thinking?

Minassian: I'm thinking that ah this is it. I see all these people it's ah time to ah go for it.

Thomas: Time to go for it and what do you do?

Minassian: I ah floor the pedal –

Thomas: Yeah.

Minassian: — I speed the van towards them and I al – allow the van to ah collide with them.

Thomas: Okay and then what happens?

258   *Appendix G*

Minassian: Ah some people get knocked down on the way, some people roll ov – over the top of the van.

Thomas: Okay and then what, what happens?

Minassian: I ah continue doing that until uhm in in fact actually to be honest the only reason I stopped my attack was because someone's drink got splashed on my ah windshield and I was worried that I would ah crash ah the van anyways so I decided okay now I I wanted to do more but I've kind of been foiled by a lack of visibility so then that's when I ah pulled – I turned right and I pulled – and I saw the cops approaching so I decided to pull over and get out of my van.

Thomas: Okay how long do you travel from the moment that you, you decide this is it the light turns green and you ah mount the sidewalk is that right?

Minassian: Yes.

Thomas: To the time that you stop, how long in terms of a distance would that have been?

Minassian: About two traffic – two or three traffic lights.

Thomas: Two or three traffic lights okay so you turn right at what street?

Minassian: I don't remember which street I wasn't paying attention.

Thomas: Why do you turn right?

Minassian: Uhm because I ah – because there wasn't any convenient place to stop at Yonge and I – and like I said there was a lack of visibility on my windshield I could hear the cops coming anyways so the, the when I turned right there was a convenient place to pull over on the sidewalk.

Thomas: Okay, okay and so you're now – so you're, you're, you're, you, you physically stop your vehicle.

Minassian: Yes.

Thomas: You physically stop – so you end the assault.

Minassian: Yes.

Thomas: Okay uhm and you ended it because you can't see —

Minassian: Yes.

Thomas: — and you knew the cops were coming.

Minassian: Yes.

Thomas: Okay and so then what happens at that point?

Minassian: Ah I, I see a patrol car pull over and I hear the cop screaming at me to get out so I get out and I ah point my wallet at the cop and it – with the intent for it to be confused as a gun so that I could be fatally shot.

Thomas: Okay and was that something you were thinking about?

Minassian: Yes.

Thomas: And then when I mean – I what I'm saying is —

Minassian: Even, even beforehand I ah premeditated as an attempted suicide by cop.

Thomas: You wanted to – you wanted to be killed by the police.

Minassian: Yes.

Thomas: Okay uhm can I ask why you decide to, to equip yourself with a wallet and not something else?

Minassian: Ah I was worried – I was thinking well purchasing a toy gun —

Thomas: Right.

Appendix G 259

Minassian: — but I was kind of paranoid that some for whatever reason the Rydel Rental Company would ask to see my pockets or any bag if I chose to bring that so I decided to go as stealthy as possible so no one suspects anything.

Thomas: Okay, alright. Nevertheless you get out of the, the van the officer or – or sorry ah it – correct me if I'm wrong because I want to make sure to get this right, you get out of the van because the officer orders you out?

Minassian: Yes.

Thomas: Okay ah and you want ah you want to die by ah, by by suicide by police ah so you point your wallet at him?

Minassian: Yes.

Thomas: Okay and, and ah do you say anything to the officer?

Minassian: Ah I actually told him that I had ah a gun in my pocket —

Thomas: Okay.

Minassian: — which was untrue.

Thomas: Right.

Minassian: Ah then I, I twice I stuck my left hand in my ah pocket and attempted to do this just to provoke a ah reaction.

Thomas: Okay.

Minassian: Ah that ah he unfortunately he didn't react —

Thomas: Right.

Minassian: — so then I ended up being ordered to the ground so I knew at that point he's not going to shot me so ah I've lost so I just – I had no choice but to just get on the ground.

Thomas: Okay so just walk me through this this step by step because I'm a little confused. So you – you get out of the van – sorry you, you, turn right, you can't see, you hear the police, you know they're coming, you see the police officer approach, you stop your vehicle ah you realize this is the end, he orders you out, you get out of the, the van.

Minassian: Yes.

Thomas: Now you're planning – your plan was to die by suicide by cop so you said you reached into your pocket twice.

Minassian: Well actually – well originally I, I the entire time I had – I was holding my wallet with my right hand but then when I saw that that wasn't working I reached into my pocket with my left hand and quickly pulled it out and formed my hand into the shape of a gun like this.

Thomas: Okay.

Minassian: Uhm with the hope that he would panic and shoot me, that of course didn't happen.

Thomas: Okay and you – how, how many times did you do that —

Minassian: Twice.

Thomas: — with your left hand and all the while you had your —

Minassian: Wallet —

Thomas: Wallet with the other hand?

Minassian: — in my right hand.

Thomas: Okay uhm and so realizing that the officer wasn't going to shoot you, what did you do at that point?

260 *Appendix G*

Minassian: I realize I had no choice but to get on the ground because I was probably going to be ah tackled anyway or tased and if I'm if I'm going to live I'd rather not encounter a physically painful experience so I decided I have no choice but to admit defeat at that point.

Thomas: Right, okay. So when you say admit defeat what did you do?

Minassian: I ah got on the ground.

Thomas: Okay and, and in terms of how, how did you get on the ground?

(A Return to His Sexual Experience)

Thomas: Okay can I ask you something and this is – it's personal but ah, ah given what you told me I, I believe it's relevant ah have you ever had ah an intimate relationship with, with a woman?

Minassian: Unfortunately I haven't.

Thomas: Okay is that something you, you would want to do?

Minassian: Yes.

Thomas: Okay alright uhm can you tell me why it is that you haven't had an intimate relationship with a woman?

Minassian: Feel it's because I'm too nice.

Thomas: Uhuh okay alright ah have you – you made you made attempts or I should say have you made attempts to, to have ah, ah an intimate relationship with a with a woman?

Minassian: Ah yes I did ask a girl out once but she ah rejected me.

Thomas: Ah okay and when was that?

Minassian: Ah that was in ah 2012.

Thomas: 2012 so it was before the October Halloween of 2013?

Minassian: Yes.

Thomas: Okay ah and was that – did that leave you with ah – I mean how, how did that leave you?

Minassian: I ah felt crushed at that point.

Thomas: Okay ah, ah I'm talking about the the 2012 incident with the, the girl.

Minassian: Yes.

Thomas: Oh okay alright uhm Alek remember when we talked about telling the truth.

Minassian: Yes.

(A Discussion around His Posting on 4chan)

Thomas: Okay uhm while you were planning all of – planning the attack starting approximately a month ago when you were in the, the planning and del – the, the deliberation stage right through to ah getting arrested who did you talk to about this attack?

Minassian: 4Chan.

Thomas: 4Chan okay. So what do you mean by that?

Minassian: Meaning I ah posted two days before the attack that uhm I hinted that there would be uhm another ah beta uprising and that and then when the

Appendix G   261

re – replies some of the people – based on the replies I could tell that they kind of knew what was going to happen

[Near End of Interview]

Thomas: I'm going to ask you this ah because it's important. Uhm ten people died here today uhm fifteen people were seriously injured uhm I think it's important to ask how you feel about that.

Minassian: I feel like ah I accomplished my mission.

Thomas: You feel like you accomplished your mission?

Minassian: Yes.

Thomas: Okay. If the families of those people who were murdered and were injured were in this room right now what would you say to them?

Minassian: I honestly don't know what I would say.

Thomas: Would you apologize?

Minassian: I honestly don't know.

Appendix H: Incel Terms and Definitions

Alpha Male: A bold, confident leader, opposite of a Beta

AMOG: "Alpha Male of Group"

Becky: An average young woman, subordinate to a Stacy in looks and status

Betabux: A romantic relationship in which the man provides financially for his partner; often used to imply that the woman is only with him for his money

Beta Male: A weak man; the opposite of an alpha

Big Black Cock Theory (BBC): The theory that Black men are inherently more virile and sexually appealing, making them able to "dickmog" (see mogging) other races

Blackpill: The belief that genetics predetermine one's status and desirability; women are only attracted to those with superior genes

Bluepill: A term taken from the Matrix movies that generally means to ignore reality; in this context it is the belief that relationships are formed based on compatibility and kindness and respect toward women

-Cel: This suffix can be used to define one's subset within the incel community based on physical features, interests, race, or defining traits (e.g., a gingercel is an incel who has red hair)

Chad: An ideal male specimen; Chads can attract nearly all women easily; ethnic counterparts are **Tyrone** (Black), **Chaddam** (Arab), **Chadpreet** (Indian), **Chang** (East Asian)

Chadfish: Pretending to be an attractive man in your photos when you are not one

Cope: Adopting a false but comforting belief to avoid the hash truth; often used by trolls to mock everyday activities

Cuck: Short for cuckold, this is a man with an unfaithful wife/girlfriend; also used for men who are considered weak or servile and often used as a derogatory term for men with moderate or progressive views

Day of Retribution: Idealized day in which incels will strike back against Chads and women; also referred to as "Beta Uprising" or "Incel Rebellion"

Femoid/Foid: Demeaning term referring to women as less than human

FOOS: "Fall on One's Sword"

Go ER/ER/ Go Rodger: To go on a killing spree, like Elliot Rodger; the letters E and R are sometimes capitalized in unrelated words (e.g., sEcuRity)

Heightpill: A subset of blackpill, which suggests women are primarily drawn to tall men

Appendix H   263

Incel/Inkwell: Involuntarily celibate man; common subsets include:
  Baldcels: Bald or balding
  Currycel: Indian
  Clowncel: Identifies with and admires the Joker from *Batman*
  Fakecel: Pretending to be incel to be edgy or to fit in
  Framecel: A man with the bone structure of a young teen
  Gymcel: Believes he can compensate with muscles
  Heightcel/Shortcel: A short man who is an incel because of his height
  Mentalcel/Medcel: Has psychological illnesses or medical issues
  Workcel: Too preoccupied with work for a relationship
Juggernaut Law: The theory that you can't stop a woman's dating potential; unattractive and flawed women make men feel like they have a chance, so they will still have their pick of men
LDAR: "Lie Down and Rot"
-Maxx/-Maxxing: An attempt to improve dating chances by improving an aspect of one's life (e.g., looksmaxx)
Mewing: An attempt to improve one's jawline by holding the tongue hard against the roof of the mouth; created orthodontist Mike Mew
Mog/Mogging: The shortened form of AMOG, to mog is to be more good-looking or superior in some way
My Twisted World: Name of Rodger's manifesto, which is often seen as a basis of incel philosophy
NEET: "Not in education, employment, or training"
Noodlewhore: An Asian woman
Normie: An average boring person, someone who is average in looks, between a Chad and an incel
PSL: An acronym for the forums "PUAhate.com/ Sluthate/Lookism.net"
Pump and dump: Having sex with a woman who is looking for a relationship with no intention of pursuing a relationship
Redpill: In the Matrix movies, the redpill wakes one up to the truth of reality; in incel circles, it is the belief that all women are attracted to the most alpha man and that one can compensate for poor genes by working out or gaining wealth or status
RGIF: "Raping Girls is Fun"
Rope/Roping: To commit suicide
Ropefuel/Suifuel: Suicide fuel; something deeply depressing that drives self-hate (e.g., an attractive woman in a relationship with someone you consider less attractive than yourself)
Saint Alek: Alek Minassian (Toronto Van Attack)
Saint Elliot: Elliot Rodger (Isla Vista Killings)
Saint Yogacel: Scott Beierle (Tallahasee Yoga Studio Shooting)
Soyboy: An effeminate, feminist or non-fighting man, with low athleticism; incels believe soy lowers testosterone
Stacy: The female counterpoint to a Chad; the ideal woman who is out of reach for any non-Chad man

264 *Appendix H*

Supreme Gentleman: How Elliot Rodger referred to himself; women are attracted to Chads even though incels are "Supreme Gentlemen"

Thot: A woman who has many casual sexual encounters

The Wall/ Agepill/milkmired: The inevitability of age making men and women less fertile and attractive

Appendix I: Incel Indoctrination Rubric (IIR)

The Incel Indoctrination Rubric was designed to provide clinicians, law enforcement, educators, and BIT/CARE teams an objective, researched based risk rubric to augment existing threat assessment processes. It consists of 20 items broken up into four general categories of Thinking, Feeling, Behavior, and Environment. The 20 items are then scored with 0, 0.25, 0.5, 0.75, and 1. The score range for the IIR spans 0–20.

THINKING

	NOT PRESENT *(0 POINTS)*	MINOR TRAITS *(0.25 POINTS)*	MODERATE TRAITS *(0.50 POINTS)*	MAJOR TRAITS *(0.75 POINTS)*	FULLY PRESENT *(1 POINT)*
1. Misogyny Score: ___	• Believe women have a fluid, diverse value • Respect for agency and personal choice • Value diversity	• A preference to see women in certain roles • Not vocalized unless asked • Preference for certain physical traits in women	• Outspoken and opinionated belief about women's roles • Lack of appreciation for a woman's individual choice • Notion of ideal beauty	• See women only as partners or sexual conquests for men • Debate and insult those who disagree • Vague threats toward women	• Believe women should be controlled by men • Seek out like-minded people • Make threats, attend or organize protests, insult others
2. Racism Score: ___	• Appreciate diversity • Respect for all races • Recognize systematic oppression and unconscious biases work to change them	• Express racist, anti-Semitic thoughts, though often subtle and defended on other grounds • Deny racism, but words or posts display otherwise	• Outspoken racism and/or antisemitism • Deny systematic oppression and White privilege	• Espouse the superiority of White, straight, cisgender people • Engage in harmful debate and insult those who disagree • Vague racist or Antisemitic threats	• Believe that White men are the truly oppressed class in today's society • Espouse to the BBC Theory • Display anger at interracial relationships
3. Blackpill Score: ___	• Unaware of this term or philosophy or reject its basic premise	• Aware of blackpill philosophy and vague about their feeling towards it or unaware but argue there is a biological and genetic element to beauty that is a leading component of attraction	• Believe the genetics play a primary role in beauty and it is deterministic • Reaffirmed in their genetic make up or angry or sad about their deficiencies	• Subscribe to Chad/Stacy ideal • Explain relationship success or failures based on this concept • Share the ideas freely, attempting to introduce the concept and build connections	• See genetics as the only factor in sexual attraction • Experience either extreme depression and hopelessness or empowerment based on their personal genetic attractiveness

Appendix I   267

4. **Inaccurate Self-Conception** **Score:** ___	• Have a healthy self-concept • See themselves accurately with a mixture strengths and deficiencies	• A slight sense of low-self-esteem, or a slightly over-inflated sense of self-worth and confidence • May by willing to change based on input from others	• Pronounced negative self-esteem or an overly confident sense of their value and attributes • Committed to seeing themselves this way and resist alternative opinions to shift their viewpoint	• Strongly held belief about their worth based on appearance, social skills or intelligence • Seek others who support their self-view • Believe these traits are unchangeable	• Blind-spot to their self-concept that radically over- or under-estimates their appearance, dating abilities or intelligence • Either despondent about their self-worth or have an all-powerful sense of entitlement
5. **Fame Seeking** **Score:** ___	• Express a normal desire for success and attention that is in balance with others having equal attention and success • May experience disappointment when ignored or denied attention, take steps to moderate those feelings	• A heightened desire for attention and fame • Seek opportunities to draw attention to their efforts and find a larger purpose • Able to moderate disappointment by trying harder	• Driven to be the center of attention and acknowledged for their unique place in the world • Frustrated at others when they are not able to achieve their goals or when others fail to acknowledge their special traits	• Angered when others do not see the world from their viewpoint • Self-worth is tied to having others acknowledge them • Seek out others who support their views and share videos or writings to spread their views	• Desire to be the chosen one with a sense of purpose that has alluded them • Need to set wrongs right, unmasking injustices they have endured • See violence as the best way to spread their message
FEELING					
6. **Rage** **Score:** ___	• Express a normal range of frustration around dating and romantic involvements	• Flair ups related to perceived slights, injustices experienced, and difficult situations	• Upset when they see attractive women with men who are "less than" they see themselves	• Increasingly rageful at women, men and society who they see as continually blocking them from dating	• Fly into a rage and act impulsively

(continued)

268   *Appendix I*

	NOT PRESENT *(0 POINTS)*	MINOR TRAITS *(0.25 POINTS)*	MODERATE TRAITS *(0.50 POINTS)*	MAJOR TRAITS *(0.75 POINTS)*	FULLY PRESENT *(1 POINT)*
	• Return to normal when the disappointment abates, or they find supportive ways to work through their anger	• Often related towards women who are unwilling to date them or men who are seen as "less than worthy" to have the attention from attractive women	• Voice their frustration to others, complain and vent about their difficulty and are increasingly upset at the unfairness of the situation	• Increasingly angry and vent and share their indignation and wrath online and in groups that share their beliefs	• Feel justified in their actions because of the unfairness of their situation and the need for revenge • Engage in threats and ultimatums towards others
7. Hopelessness Score: ___	• May have fleeting thoughts of the future not being better than their current situation • Reasonable about their expectations	• Sad about not having a better tomorrow • Frustrated at the amount of effort they are putting into dating with little gain	• Feel increasingly desperate and hopeless that things will ever be different • Less willing try different approaches	• Feel increasingly desperate and hopeless that things will ever be different • Less willing try different approaches	• Experience a total futility and desperation at the idea they will ever be able to find a partner • May begin to have suicidal or violent/vengeful thoughts
8. Catastrophe Score: ___	• Negative life events and difficulties with dating are seen as unfortunate and upsetting but temporary setbacks that are able to be overcome with a positive attitude and support of friends	• Negative dating experiences are difficult to overcome and begin to be seen as deterministic for a more negative future • Find a sense of hope again, but often over-emphasize negative experiences	• Rejections are given a larger emphasis and directly lead to a spike in depression (lack of eating, sleeping, sadness, isolation) or anger (venting online, yelling, storming off)	• Lack of success in dating has led to a reduction in a willingness to approach women • Prone to extreme emotions when faced with rejection • Vilify those they desire through objectified language	• Any new attempt socializing, are met with extreme behaviors • Isolate and find others online who support their beliefs • Frame attractive woman) or the obstacles in front of them (men) as worthless and evil

Appendix I

9. Disability Score: ___	• Able to overcome mental health issues with assistance from therapy, medication or other resiliency efforts	• Mental or physical illness issues that make dating and social interactions more difficult • Increased effort and support from others allows for limited success overcoming these limitations	• Consistent challenges in meeting women and overcoming the social or physical limitations that prevent them from success • May seek help or assistance from therapy, friends or family, but still have little success in achieving their desires	• Difficulties related to their illness, even with support, make it almost impossible to reach their dating goals • Increasingly isolated and depressed or angry with their situation and an uncaring society that has left them behind	• There is no opportunity for success in dating the women they desire, even with intense effort and support from friends, counseling and family • Despondent, hopeless and potentially suicidal or experience intense rage and anger
10. Abandoned Score: ___	• May experience sporadic feelings of being alone or misunderstood • Connect with others to over come these feelings and return to a sense of balance	• An awareness they are often left behind, forgotten or neglected • Return to a sense of balance through their own resiliency and/or with support from others such as friends, family, or a therapist	• Increasingly anxious and worried things will not get better • A relationship may have ended or a friend or family member moved away • Worry they are not good enough to have people care about them	• Feel alone and uncared for in their life • Few friends and are resistant to the idea that people truly care for them • Increasingly depressed and isolated	• Pervasive sense of hopelessness and despair and believe no one cares about them • Efforts to support them are met with suspicion • May struggle with suicidal thoughts or violent fantasies
BEHAVIOR					
11. Approach Behaviors Score: ___	• No aggressive or threatening behavior • Express feelings verbally and work through any difficulties	• Frustrated at difficulties with dating but does not yell or gesture	• Upset at others who are able to date successfully • No direct yelling or throwing of objects, they become upset and huff, storm off, or otherwise communicate their frustrations	• Impulsively display frustration, yelling and anger in attempts to flirt with or date women • Fueled by adrenaline and frequently fly off the handle	• Enraged at women who reject them • Engage in yelling, throwing objects and challenging

(continued)

	NOT PRESENT *(0 POINTS)*	MINOR TRAITS *(0.25 POINTS)*	MODERATE TRAITS *(0.50 POINTS)*	MAJOR TRAITS *(0.75 POINTS)*	FULLY PRESENT *(1 POINT)*
		• May argue or express dissatisfaction with women they want to date being out of their reach		• Increased anger at the futility of finding a woman	• A history of inappropriate and unwanted advances or touching of women or girls
12. Howling Score: ___	• No evidence of any threats or larger frustrations related to women, alpha males or societal influences that negatively impact their ability to date women	• May be some social media posts or off-hand comments about frustrations related to dating or social connections to women • No threats or intimidating comments to others	• Occasional posts or comments that have a shaming or negative quality towards women, men, or society • Comments are designed to insult but lack any threatening quality	• Increased social media posts or interactions that display frustration and dissatisfaction • Shame, intimidate, and frustrate those who they feel are responsible for their pain and difficulty finding a woman	• Frequent expressions of frustration related to dating and incel concepts • Transient threats, ultimatums and comments are made • Share their views and beliefs
13. Suicide Score: ___	• No suicidal feelings or desire to kill themselves • Difficulties experienced in finding a connection with women are resolved by support from friends, family or therapy	• Increase in thoughts of depression and a worry that it will always be this way • No suicidal intent • Driven by frustrated attempts to connect with women	• More bad than good days • The depression pairs with a feeling of hopelessness in connecting with women • No direct threats of suicide but may be increased thoughts considering suicide	• Increasing thoughts of suicide related to failure with women • Share thoughts of suicide, despair and hopelessness with others and online • Attempts to support or help are rebuffed or unsuccessful	• Intense feelings of suicide and threats of carrying it out (often as a murder/suicide) • Intense frustrations related to thwarted connection to women • Connect to others online who share similar beliefs

Item					
14. **Past Attacks** **Score:** ___	• Passive knowledge of past incel attacks but little commentary or opinions about them	• Knowledge of past incel attacks, particularly those that occur out of anger at not dating • No direct support for these attacks, but there may be mentions of context and extenuating circumstances	• Increased mentions of past incel attacks • Express empathy for the attackers • Might not mention past attacks directly but show evidence of studying past tactics	• Knowledge of and support for past incel attacks • Willing to see the killing as a useful message for those who don't appreciate the full nature of the problems facing incels	• Detailed knowledge of past incel attacks • Refer to attacks often • Speak positively about past incel killings and describe the attackers as heroes or martyrs
15. **Redpill** **Score:** ___	• Lack of knowledge about the redpill philosophy and no arguments or vocal encouragements for others to follow this philosophy	• Some knowledge about redpill philosophy • May have taken some tentative steps to improve in order to attract women	• A deeper understanding of the redpill philosophy • Efforts to follow the guiding principles of the concept • Seek advice from discussion boards, incel websites and dating videos	• Believe in the redpill approach and have a commitment to improving and being more successful in dating • Share these ideas with others in conversation and online	• An intense buy-into the redpill philosophy and engage in active steps to improve their dating prospects • Argue with others to convince them of the value of this approach
ENVIORNMENT					
16. **Incel Materials** **Score:** ___	• Lack of knowledge or exposure to any incel literature or philosophy	• Read a bit more incel material and may be open to the ideas but are still questioning and exploring • Do not discuss these concepts online or with others regularly	• Exploration of incel ideas • A general sense of resonance and agreement with the ideas • May talk tentatively with others about the concepts but are aware others would find these ideas insulting	• A detailed understanding of incel ideas • Connected to online discussion boards and website • Adopt these concepts and challenge others who differ with their opinion	• A deep and expansive knowledge of incel concepts and active engagement online • Alternative viewpoints are routinely dismissed • Heated debates and arguments with others

(continued)

272   *Appendix I*

	NOT PRESENT (0 POINTS)	MINOR TRAITS (0.25 POINTS)	MODERATE TRAITS (0.50 POINTS)	MAJOR TRAITS (0.75 POINTS)	FULLY PRESENT (1 POINT)
17. Rejection Score: ___	• Have not approached many women and/or have had the expected mixed success • May have felt rejection, but had a healthy reaction	• Minor attempts to flirt or have conversations with women, but there was no effort to approach woman or ask them out	• Attempts to meet women were difficult and met with little success • Felt a lack of interest from women • Beginning to feel hopeless that this will change	• Numerous times where attempts to form a connection or ask a woman out were unsuccessful • Believe women aren't interested in them and they have no value or desirable traits	• Pervasive and continual rejection from women • Told directly it was because they were unattractive or lacked certain qualities • Intense feelings of frustration, hopelessness and anger
18. Bullied Score: ___	• Have not experienced bullying behavior from others or have been teased	• May have experienced some negative feedback and teasing about their appearance, dating skills and/or social worth • Limited in terms of the impact on their self-esteem or hope for a better future	• Experienced teasing often about their appearance and ability to attract women • Bullying may be public and cause deeper feelings of embarrassment	• Bullying happens both in person and online • Feelings of depression, sadness and hopelessness • May attempt to take solace in incel websites and discussion groups	• Frequent bullying, teasing and a loss of face in front of others • May perceive bullying when it is not present, feeling like everyone is making fun of them • Intense feeling of worthlessness, sadness and anger

19. Failure to Change Score: ___	• Either no attempt to change behavior or attempts to change have been successful	• Desire to attempt to improve communication skills, reduce anxiety and find ways to better approach women • Not yet had a chance to try these techniques out very often but are hopeful	• Efforts to improve dating or sexual outcomes have been made and met with difficulty and failure • There is will a slight willingness at trying again	• A continual negative outcome when they attempt to change how they approach women • Glimmer of hope things could be different, but feelings of worthlessness and exacerbation • Seek out online support	• Meet failure at every turn • Convinced this is their lot in life and are unwilling to try to change again in the future • Vindictive and angry at those they see as responsible for their plight
20. Free Fall Score: ___	• An overall positive outlook on their life and supports, such as friends and parents, are in place and sufficient	• Difficulties or loss experienced by the individual that cause them to struggle to stay positive • Connect with friends and family but feel increasing out of step with them	• Loss and personal problems are increasingly common Ignored by, or meet difficulty and judgment from, friends and family	• Familiar with the incel world • Women remain far out of reach and even the faint hope that they would be successful in with them is increasingly unlikely • Seek social connection online	• A public event or major life change exacerbates the situation • Little stability in their lives and no hope of dating • Participate online and reinforce their negative self-view

Index

Note: Page numbers in *italics* indicate figures and in **bold** indicate tables on the corresponding pages.

abandonment, feelings of, 49, 60–61; in college student, 152; in the Isla Vista killings, 52; in junior high student, 141; in the LA Fitness shooting, 53; in the workplace, 164
Abrahamic religions, 38–39
academic or work progress: in college student, 155; decrease in, 81; in junior high student, 144
access to non-violent outlets, 90–91, **91**
accidental bombing, Richlands, Virginia, 218
actionability risk factor, 72–73, 143
action and time imperative, 71, **72**
active listening: in healthy relationships, **95**; treatment approach using, 125–126
adult videos, 41–42
affective violence, 67, **68**, **71**
affirmative sexuality, 94–96, **95**, **96**
Akihabara Massacre, 58, 60, 202
"Alana's Involuntary Celibacy Project," 10
alienation and depression in incels, 3–5
alpha male, **4**
alternative explanations, 133
Amish Schoolhouse shooting, 201
AMOG, **4**
anger intensifiers, **133**
anxiety, lack of, **116**
approach behaviors, 49, 61, 110–111; in college student, 152; in the Isla Vista killings, 52; in junior high student, 141; in the LA Fitness shooting, 53; in the workplace, 164
Aranda, E. D., 59, 215
argumentation, avoiding, **136**
Arizona Nursing College shooting, 200
arousal/activity, **115**

arousal control, 135
ASIS Workplace Violence Prevention and Intervention Standards, 110
Asperger's, 163
assessment *see* violence risk assessment
Association of Threat Assessment Professionals (ATAP), 69, 106
Atchison, W., 62, 211
attention, disturbed, **116**
Autism Spectrum Disorder (ASD), 163
awareness stage, funnel model, 33, 34, **35**
Aztec High School, 62, 211

Bastille Day, Nice, France, attack, 60, 209–210
Bechdel-Wallace test, 5–6, 7
Beckys, **4**
behavioral intervention teams (BIT) *see* BIT/CARE model
behavior category in Incel Indoctrination Rubric (IIR), 49–50, **57**, 61–62; in college student, 152; in the Isla Vista killings, 52; in junior high student, 141–142; in the LA Fitness shooting, 53–54; in the workplace, 164–165
Beierle, S., 61, 213
beliefs of incels, 16–21
Bennington, C., 217
Bentley, S., 210
betabux, **11**
beta male, **4**, 30
Betts, C., 59, 216
Big Black Cock Theory, **11**
BIT/CARE model, 175; common missteps with, 190–191; phase 1: gathering data, 176–179, *177*, **178**; phase 2: risk rubric and analysis, *177*, 179–182, *180*; phase 3:

Index 275

interventions, *177*, 182–185, *183*; purpose of using team strategy in, 175–176; team membership, 185–187; three phases of team activities in, 176–185, *177*; typical meetings, 188–190; *see also* Incel Indoctrination Rubric (IIR)

Blackpill, **11**, 48, 58; in college student, 151; in the Isla Vista killings, 51; in junior high student, 141; in the LA Fitness shooting, 53; in the workplace, 164

Bluepill, **11**

blunders, avoiding, **92**

Boston Marathon Bombing, 204

Bouhlel, M. L., 60, 209–210

Boyette, G., 197

Branch Davidians, 39

Breivik, A. B., 76

Brooks, D., 197

Brownell, W., 197

bullying, 50, 81; in college student, 152, 155; in the Isla Vista killings, 52; in junior high student, 142, 144; in the LA Fitness shooting, 54; in the workplace, 165, 167

Burning Man festival, 95–96

Butler, J., 25, 29

Calhoun, F., 49, 70

Capital Gazette shooting, 61, 214

CARE teams *see* BIT/CARE model

Carini, C., 218

case managers, 186–187

catalyst events, 81

catastrophe, 49, 60; in college student, 152; in the Isla Vista killings, 51; in junior high student, 141; in the LA Fitness shooting, 14–15, 53; in the workplace, 164

Centers for Disease Control and Prevention (CDC), 87

Chadfish, **11**

Chads, **4**, 10, 30, 56

Change Theory, 136–137, 170

Changing for Good, 136, 170

Charleston Church shooting, 58, 59, 73, 78, 207

Chicago Women's Reproductive Health Clinic threat, 59, 217

Cho, Seung-Hui, 112, 201–202

Christianity, 38

Church of Jesus Christ of Latter-Day Saints, The (LDS), 38–39

Cleary, C., 61, 214–215

Clyde, B., 216

college student, 150–152; counseling treatment considerations for, 155–157, **156–157**; existentialism and, **156–157**,

157–159; motivational interviewing and, 159, **160**; threat assessment initial evaluation in, 153–155

Collins, P. H., 27

Columbine shooting, 58, 63, 74, 198–199

commonalities, finding, **92**

communication in healthy relationships, **95**

compassion, 91

conditional ultimatums, 72, **72**

congruence in active listening, 126

Connell, R., 27

control/change, **115**

Cope, **11**

Cruz, N., 58, 211–212

cuck, **4**

cultures of masculinity, 28–29

cyberstalking case, Los Angeles, 217

Dallas Federal Courthouse shooting, 216

Dasein, 130–131

Day of Retribution, **11**, 228–229

Dayton shooting, 59, 216

Dear, R. L., Jr., 209

death, 127, 157, 158

De Coensel, S., 33, 36, 42

defense/distance, **115**

Deisinger, G., 111, 113–114

depersonalization, 80

destabilizers for violence, 114–117, **115–116**

developmental of discrepancy, **136**

DiClemente, C., 125, 136–137, 170

directly communicated threat warning behaviors, 111

direct threats, **72**

disability, 49, 60; in college student, 152; in the Isla Vista killings, 51–52; in junior high student, 141; in the LA Fitness shooting, 53; in the workplace, 164

Discovery of Being, The, 130

disinhibitors for violence, 114–117, **115–116**

disturbed attention, **116**

disturbed perception, **116**

drivenness and justification for violent action, 74

drysdale, 101

Duke, C., 74–75

École Polytechnique Massacre, 195

Ellis, A., 125, 132

emotional stability, 88–89, **89**

empathy: in active listening, 126; and connection as stabilizing influences, 91–92, **92**; expressed in motivational

276 *Index*

interviewing, **136**; in healthy relationships, **95**; lack of remorse and, 76–77

Ending Campus Violence, 102

energy burst warning behaviors, 111

engaging and changing the incel story treatment approach, 128–130

entitlement, 16–18, *17*

environmental stability, 88–89, **89**

environment category in Incel Indoctrination Rubric (IIR), 50, **57**, 62–64, 81–82; in college student, 152; in the Isla Vista killings, 52; in junior high student, 142; in the LA Fitness shooting, 54; in the workplace, 165

Epston, D., 125, 129

equanimity in healthy relationships, **95**

Etowah High School shooting *see* Head, B.

existentialism, **156–157**, 157–159

Existential Psychotherapy, 126

Facebook, 90

failure to change, 50, 63; in college student, 152; in the Isla Vista killings, 52; in junior high student, 142; in the LA Fitness shooting, 54; in the workplace, 165

fame seeking, 48, 59, 79–80; in college student, 151; in the Isla Vista killings, 51; in junior high student, 141; in the LA Fitness shooting, 53; in the workplace, 164

Family Education Rights and Privacy Act (FERPA), 186

family supports: for college student, 155; for junior high student, 144

fantasy rehearsals, 77

fascination with violence, 78–79

FBI Four-Prong Approach, 108–109

fear of missing out (FOMO), 90

feelings/emotions category in Incel Indoctrination Rubric (IIR), 48–49, **57**, 59–61; in college student, 152; in the Isla Vista killings, 51–52; isolation and hopelessness, 77–78; in junior high student, 141; in the LA Fitness shooting, 53; in the workplace, 164

feminism, 27, 30

femoid/foid, **4**

Ferguson, J., 60, 76–77, 199–200; confession of, 240–242

504/disability services staff, 187

fixation, 71

fixation warning behaviors, 110–111

Flanagan, V. L., II, 207–208

Flores, R., Jr., 200

focus, 71

FOOS, **11**

Fort Hood shooting *see* Hasan, N.

4Chan threat, 208

Frankl, V., 158

freedom, 127, 157, 158

free fall, 50, 63–64, 81; in college student, 152; in the Isla Vista killings, 52; in junior high student, 142; in the LA Fitness shooting, 54; in the workplace, 165

Freud, S., 26–27

Frontier Middle School shooting *see* Loukaitis, B.

Fundamentalist Church of Jesus Christ of Latter-Day Saints (FLDS), 39

funnel, incel, 33–38, *34*, **35**, **37**

Gabosch, A., 94

gain/profit, **115**

gay rights movement, 27

Gelles, M., 71, 107–108

gender, 26

gender performance, 25

German Hookah Bar attack, 217

Germanwings Flight 9525, 206–207

Gill, P., 74, 75, 81, 82

Glasser, A., 135

goal setting, 134

Go ER/ER/Go Rodger, **11**

grievance or injustice collection, 74–75

grievances stage, funnel model, 33, 34, **35**

Grossman, D., 80

guilt, lack of, **116**

Guyland, 28–29

hardened point of view, 73

Harm to Others: The Treatment and Assessment of Dangerousness, 99–100

Harper-Mercer, C., 58, 61, 62, 77, 208; manifesto of, 230–234

Harris, E., 58–59, 63, 74, 198–199

Hart, S., 114, 118

Hasan, N., 74

Head, B., 78

healthy relationships, essentials for, 94, **95**

hegemonic masculinity, 25, *26*, 27–28

Heightpill, **11**

Henry Ford Community College shooting, 202–203

Hogan, M., 90

Hollander, R. D., 218

hopelessness, 49, 59–60, 77–78; in college student, 152; in the Isla Vista killings, 51; in junior high student, 141;

in the LA Fitness shooting, 53; in the workplace, 164

howling threat, 49, 61, **72**; in college student, 152; in the Isla Vista killings, 52; in junior high student, 142; in the LA Fitness shooting, 54; in the workplace, 164

how the incel will experience change treatment approach, 136–137

How to Date Young Women: For Men over 35, Volume I, 6

hunting threat, **72**

identification warning behaviors, 111

impaired memory, **116**

implementation stage, funnel model, 33, **35**, 36

inability to reason, **116**

inaccurate self-conception, 48, 58–59; in college student, 151; in the Isla Vista killings, 51; in junior high student, 141; in the LA Fitness shooting, 53; in the workplace, 164

Incel Indoctrination Rubric (IIR), 265, **266–273**; behavior category, 49–50, 52, **57**, 61–62, 141–142, 152, 164–165; case examples using, 50, **57**; college student assessment using, 150–161; environment category, 50, 52, **57**, 62–64, 81–82, 142, 152, 165; feelings/emotions category, 48–49, 51–52, **57**, 59–61, 141, 152, 164; Isla Vista Killings scored using, 51–52; junior high student assessment using, 140–149; LA Fitness shooting scored using, 52–54; moving forward using, 54, 64; thinking category, 47–48, *48*, 51, 53, 56–59, 141, 151, 164; in the workplace, 162–171; *see also* BIT/CARE model

incel masculinity, 30

incel materials, 50, 62; college students and, 152; Isla Vista killings and, 52; junior high students and, 142; LA Fitness shooting and, 54; workplace and, 165

incel religion, 39

incels: alienation and depression in, 3–5; attitudes toward women, 5–7; catastrophizing by, 14–15; characteristics and beliefs of, 16–21; common thoughts and ideas of, **11–12**; escalation to physical violence against women by, 7–8, 10, 12; movement origins of, 10; pornography and, 41–42; religion of, 39; risk assessment of (*see* violence risk assessment); technology and, 40–41; terms and definitions, 3, **4**, 10, 262–264;

treatment approaches for (*see* treatment approaches, incel)

indirect/vague threats, **72**

individual action, positive, 92–93, **93**

indoctrination stage, funnel model, 33, **35**, 36

inkwell, **4**

interest stage, funnel model, 33, 36

internet technology, 40–41; monitoring use of, 144

interventions in BIT/CARE model, *177*, 182–185, *183*

Islam, 38, 39

Islamic jihadists, 39

Isla Vista Killings/Elliott Rodger, 5, 7–8, 12, 15–16, 30, 67, 205–206; Elliot Rodger's "Day of Retribution" video and, **11**, 228–229; environment in, 52; feelings in, 51–52, 62; feelings of entitlement in, 16–18; feelings of jealousy in, 19–21; feelings of misogyny in, 18–19; thinking in, 51, 58

isolation, 77–78, 82, 128, 157, 158

jealousy, *17*, 19–21

Judaism, 38

Juggernaut Law, **11**

junior high student, 140–141; counseling treatment considerations for, 144–145, **146**; Narrative Therapy approach to, 145; Person-Centered Approach in, **146**, 148–149; Rational Emotive Behavioral Therapy (REBT) for, **146**, 147–148; threat assessment initial evaluation of, 142–144

justice/honor, **115**

Kaczynski, T., 60, 62, 196–197

Kato, T., 58, 60, 202

Kelley, D. P., 210–211

Kelly, J., 218

Kimmel, M. S., 28–29

Kinkel, K., 63, 198

Klebold, D., 74, 198–199

Kopp, R., 125, 129–130

lack of anxiety, **116**

lack of empathy and remorse, 76–77

lack of guilt, **116**

lack of integration, **115**

LA Fitness shooting/George Sodini, 6, 12–14, 62, 203; behaviors in, 53–54; catastrophizing in, 14–15; environment in, 54, 63; feelings in, 53, 60; Sodini's blog and, 219–227; thinking in, 53, 58, 59

Lankford, A., 75, 79

278 Index

Lanza, A., 58, 203–204
last resort warning behaviors, 111
Las Vegas Music Festival shooting, 210
law enforcement, 186
LDAR, **11**
leakage, 69
leakage warning behaviors, 111
Lépine, M., 195
lethality of threat, 71
listening: active, **95**, 125–126; careful, **92**
Live TV shooting, 207–208
Logan, C., 114, 118
Logotherapy, 158
lost, naked, and alone treatment approach, 126–128
Loughner, J., 112
Loukaitis, B., 78
Lu, G., 195–196
Lubitz, A., 206–207
Lucky 97 Security Guard, 210
Lucretius, 127

making a plan treatment approach, 135
Mall of America attack, 59, 215
March, E., 40
marginalization, 78
marriage, 41
masculinity, 25; cultures of, 28–29; hegemonic, 25, *26*, 27–28; incel, 30; positive, 30–31, 93–94, **94**; roots of, 25–27, *26*
Massage Parlor attack, 217
Mateen, O., 209
-Maxx/-Maxxing, **11**
May, R., 125, 130–131
McLaughlin, J. J., 200–201
McVeigh, T., 56, 196
meaninglessness, 128, 157, 158–159
Meloy, J. R., 49, 92, 101–102; on approach warning behaviors, 110–111
memory, impaired, **116**
Menefee, C., 60
Menezes de Oliveira, W., 78
men's rights lawyer attacks, 218
mental illness, 75–76; in violence risk assessment, 100
mental rehearsal, 134
Mewing, **11**
Miller, W. R., 125, 135, **136**
Minassian, A., 16, 56, 59, 61–62, 72–73, 212–213; police interview of, 243–261
Minority Report, The, 33
mirroring, **92**
misogyny, *17*, 18–19, 47, 56, 58; in college student, 151; in the Isla Vista killings,

51; in the LA Fitness shooting, 53; in the workplace, 164
mission-oriented violence *see* predatory/target violence
Mog/Mogging, **11**
Mohandie, K., 92
"Moore's Law," 40
Mormonism, 38–39
Morrison, D. R., 62, 201
motivational interviewing, 135, **136**, 159, **160**
motivators for violence, 114–117, **115–116**
Moynihan, B., 206
Murphy, A., 175
mutual respect in healthy relationships, **95**
My Twisted World, **11**, 67, **68**

Narrative Means to a Therapeutic Ends, 129
Narrative Therapy, 129; in junior high student, 145
National Behavioral Intervention Team Association (NaBITA), 69
National Threat Assessment Center (NTAC), 69, 72, 75, 77, 89
Nay, R., 132, 133
NEET, **11**
negative attitudes, **115**
Nice Truck attack, 60, 209–210
Nichols, T., 196
nihilism, **116**
non-violent outlets, access to, 90–91, **91**
noodlewhore, **4**
Norcross, J., 125, 136–137, 170
normie, **4**
notification to community/information sharing, 144
novel aggression warning behaviors, 111

objectification, 80, 157
obsessive thinking, **116**
Oedipal Complex, 26
Oklahoma City Bombing, 56, 196
O'Neill, D., 69, 77
On Killing, 80
Oslo, Norway, bombing *see* Breivik, A. B.
O'Toole, M. E., 69, 74, 77, 99, 101, 108

Paddock, S., 210
past attacks, 49, 62; in college student, 152; in junior high student, 142; in the LA Fitness shooting, 54; in the workplace, 165
pathway to violence assessment, 111–113, *112*
pathway warning behaviors, 110

Index 279

patriarchy, 28
Pearl High School shooting, 60, 63, 197
Pennington, D., 76
perception, disturbed, **116**
Person-Centered Approach, 126, **146**, 148–149
Pescara-Kovach, L., 15
physical violence against women, 7–8, 10, 12
Pima College attack *see* Loughner, J.
Planned Parenthood shooting, 209
Platte Canyon School Hostage Crisis, 62, 201
pornography, 41–42
Portsmouth Stabbings, 206
positive and trusting relationships, 89
positive male role models: college student and, 155; junior high student and, 144; workplace violence and, 167
positive masculinity, 30–31; as stabilizing influence, 93–94, **94**
positive social and individual action, 92–93, **93**
post-implementation stage, funnel model, 33, **35**, 36
Poulin, R., 61, 62, 80, 194
Powell, A., 202–203
predatory/target violence, 67, **68**, 69, **71**; risk factors for, 72–80
pre-radicalization stage, funnel model, 33–34, **35**
Prochaska, J., 125, 136–137, 170
protective factors *see* stabilizing influences
proximity/affiliation, **115**
PSL, **11**
psychological steadiness, 89
Pulse Nightclub shooting, 209
Pump and Dump, **11**

Queen Street Massacre, 61, 194
quid pro quo education, 167

racing thinking, **116**
racism, 48, 58; in college student, 151, 155; in the Isla Vista killings, 51; in junior high student, 141; in the LA Fitness shooting, 53; in the workplace, 164
rage, 49, 59; in college student, 152; in the Isla Vista killings, 51; in junior high student, 141; in the LA Fitness shooting, 53; in the workplace, 164
Ramos, J., 61, 214
Rancho Cordova Massacre, 199
rapport-building techniques, **92**, 142–143
Rathjen, T., 217

Rational Emotive Behavioral Therapy (REBT), 132; in junior high student, **146**, 147–148
Reality Therapy, 135; workplace violence and, 169, **170**
Redpill, **11**, 49–50, 62; in college student, 152; in the Isla Vista killings, 52; in junior high student, 142; in the LA Fitness shooting, 54; in the workplace, 165
rehearsal, mental, 134
rejection, 50, 63; in college student, 152; in the Isla Vista killings, 52; in junior high student, 142; in the LA Fitness shooting, 54; in the workplace, 165
release/expression, **115**
religion: incel, 39; influences of, 38–39
remorse, lack of, 76–77
residential life/housing staff, 187
respect in healthy relationships, **95**
RGIF, **11**
risk assessment *see* violence risk assessment
Risk Assessment Guideline Elements for Violence (RAGE-V), 106
risk factors, 69–70, *70*; quality of threat from, 70–72, **71–72**; for targeted, predatory, mission-oriented violence, 72–80
Roberts, C. C., IV, 201
Rocori High School shooting, 200–201
Rodger, E. *see* Isla Vista Killings/ Elliott Rodger
Rogers, C., 91, 125, 126, 130, 148
Rollnick, S., 125, 135, **136**
roll with resistance, **136**
Roof, D., 58, 59, 73, 78, 207; manifesto of, 235–239
Ropefuel/Suifuel, **12**
Rope/Roping, **11**
Rose-Mar College of Beauty shooting, 59, 79–80, 193–194

Sacramento Rampage, 60, 76–77, 199–200
Saint Alek, **12**
Saint Elliot, **12**
Saint Yogacel, **12**
Sandy Hook shooting, 203–204
Sayoc, C., 213
Scalora, M., 70–71
Scaptura, M. N., 30
scenario planning, 117–119, **118**
self-talk, 134–135
Sest, N., 40
sexual assault prevention, 154
sexual harassment education, 167
sexuality, affirmative, 94–96, **95**, **96**

280 *Index*

Shaw, A., 197
Sheikh, F., 59, 217
sickness as anger intensifier, **133**
SIVRA-35 system, 102–105
Sledge, J., 197
sleep as anger intensifier, **133**
smiling, **92**
Smith, J., 38
Smith, R., 59, 79–80, 193–194
social action, positive, 92–93, **93**
social connection in healthy
    relationships, **95**
social health and relationships, 89–90, **90**
social isolation, 77–78, 82
social media use, 90; by college student,
    154–155; by junior high student, 144;
    workplace violence and, 167
Sodini, G. *see* LA Fitness shooting/
    George Sodini
Sokolow, B. A., 73
Soltys, N., 199
solution-seeking stage, funnel model, 33,
    34–35, **35**
Southern Poverty Law Center (SPLC), 40
soyboy, **4**
Speck, R., 80
Spencer, B., 79
Spinoza, B. de, 127
stabilizing influences, **88**; access to
    non-violent outlets, 90–91, **91**; affirmative
    sexuality, 94–96, **95**, **96**; defined, 87;
    empathy and connection, 91–92, **92**;
    environmental and emotional, 88–89,
    89; positive masculinity, 93–94, **94**;
    positive social and individual action,
    92–93, **93**; social health and relationships,
    89–90, **90**
Stacys, **4**, 10
stances, hardened, 73
status/esteem, **115**
Stavropoulos, A., 215–216
Steele, R. D., 6–7, 12, 14
stoicism, 94, 159
Stoneman Douglas High School shooting,
    58, 211–212
St. Pius X High School shooting, 61, 62,
    80, 194
stress: as anger intensifier, **133**; Navy SEAL
    approaches to coping with, 134–135
Structured Professional Judgment (SPJ),
    113–119, **115–116**, **118**, *119*
substance use, 76; as anger intensifier, **133**;
    in college student, 154
substantive threats, **72**
Sudbury Michael's Stabbing, 215–216

suicide/suicidal ideation, 49, 61–62, 75;
    in college student, 152; in the Isla Vista
    killings, 52; in junior high student, 142,
    144; in the LA Fitness shooting, 54; in the
    workplace, 164
supporting self-efficacy, **136**
Supreme Gentleman, **12**
Sustenance as anger intensifier, **133**

Tallahassee Yoga Studio, 61, 213
targeted violence *see* predatory/target
    violence
targeting stage, funnel model, 33, **35**
Tasso da Silveira shooting *see* Menezes de
    Oliveira, W.
teaching the incel to think differently
    treatment approach, 131–135, **133**
teasing, 81; of college students, 155;
    of junior high students, 144; in the
    workplace, 167; *see also* bullying
technology, 40–41; monitoring use of, 144
terminology of the incel movement, 3, **4**, 10
Texas Church shooting, 210–211
thinking category in Incel Indoctrination
    Rubric (IIR), 47–48, *48*, 56–59, **57**, 58;
    in college student, 151; in the Isla Vista
    killings, 51; in junior high student, 141;
    in the LA Fitness shooting, 53; in the
    workplace, 164
thot, **4**
Thurston High School shooting, 63, 198
Title IX staff, 187
Toi, M., 60, 63–64, 75, 193
Tolstoy, L., 128
Toronto Van attack, 16, 56, 59, 61–62,
    72–73, 212–213
toxic masculinity, 25
transient threats, **72**
Transtheoretical Change Theory, 136–137, 170
treatment approaches, incel: active listening,
    125–126; in college student, 150–161;
    engaging and changing the incel story,
    128–130; how the incel will experience
    change, 136–137; in junior high student,
    140–149; lost, naked and alone, 126–128;
    making a plan, 135; motivational
    interviewing, 135, **136**; teaching the incel
    to think differently, 131–135, **133**; who
    are you?, 130–131; in the workplace,
    162–171
Tsarnaev, D., 204
Tsarnaev, T., 204
Tsuyama Massacre, 60, 63–64, 75, 193
Turner, B., 28–29, 107–108
Turner, J., 71

Index 281

Umpqua Community College attack, 58, 61, 62, 77, 208
Unabomber, 60, 196–197
United States Attempted Mail Bombing, 213
University of Florida rape threats, 218
University of Iowa shooting, 195–196
US Postal Service Threat Assessment Team Guide, 106

vague threats, **72**
Van Brunt, Bethany, 56
Van Brunt, Brian, 15, 49
violence: affective, 67, **68, 71**; predatory/targeted, 67, **68**, 69, **71**
violence risk assessment, 99–100; approach warning behaviors, 110–111; ASIS Workplace Violence Prevention and Intervention Standards, 110; in college student, 150–161; FBI Four-Prong Approach, 108–109; in junior high student, 140–149; mental illness diagnosis in, 100; pathway to violence assessment, 111–113, *112*; process of performing, 101–102, **102**; Risk Assessment Guideline Elements for Violence (RAGE-V), 106; SIVRA-35 system, 102–105; Structured Professional Judgment (SPJ), 113–119, **115–116, 118**, *119*; training organizations for, **102**; Turner and Gelles on, 107–108;

US Postal Service Threat Assessment Team Guide, 106; in the workplace, 162–171
Virginia Tech shooting, 112, 201–202
Vitkovic, F., 61, 194

The Wall/Agepill/Milkmired, **12**
warning behaviors (threat), 110–111
Way of Being, A, 126
Weston, S., 49, 70
White, M., 125, 129
whiteness and hegemonic masculinity, 27
Whitman, C., 80
Who are you? treatment approach, 130–131
"Wolfman," 27
women: attitudes toward, 5–7; escalation to physical violence against, 7–8, 10, 12
Women's March threat, 61, 214–215
Woodham, L., 60, 63, 197
workplace violence, 162–165; Change Theory and, 170; counseling treatment considerations for, 167–169, **168**; Reality Therapy and, 169, **170**; threat assessment initial evaluation for, 165–167
Workplace Violence Prevention and Intervention, 110

Yalom, I., 125, 126–128, 157
Yobai (night crawling), 75, 193

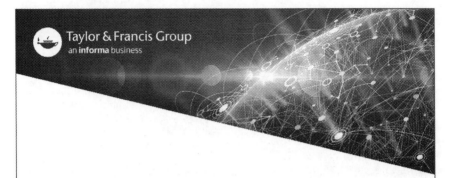

Printed in the United States
By Bookmasters